ACCORDING TO HOOLE

ACCORDING TO HOOLE

*The Collected Essays and Tales
of a Scholar–Librarian
and Literary Maverick*

W. STANLEY HOOLE

Preface by

Lawrence S. Thompson

THE UNIVERSITY OF ALABAMA PRESS

University, Alabama

To My Wife
Addie Shirley Hoole
whose lovingkindness truly makes
my life worth living

PREFACE

Some colleagues have referred to Dr. W. Stanley Hoole—his friends know him as "Bill"—as an "old-fashioned librarian." If he is old-fashioned in the tradition of William F. Poole, John Cotton Dana, J. Christian Bay, or William Warner Bishop—all scholars and capable, adaptable administrators as well—then the old-fashioned way is the one we want. Poole *et al.* would have adjusted themselves readily to the latter twentieth-century tradition which Bill Hoole represents in terms of scholarship, vision in educational policy, and basic librarianship.

The record speaks for itself. The full bibliography of his writings is one of which any scholar might be proud. The "mostly autobiographical" introduction to this book (which will probably be reprinted in many an anthology of Southern literature) should be expanded into a work somewhere in bulk between those of Benjamin Franklin and Josephus Daniels. Bill Hoole does not need a Boswell, although it would be a major privilege to play this role.

I have all sorts of personal reminiscences about Bill—scholarly, social, and just plain friendly. These constitute another book. It is vastly more important to consider Bill Hoole's role as a leader of the Newest South.

He has not been a governor, senator, or federal judge (rejected or accepted!) from the South; but he has examined thoughtfully and meaningfully (for the future of the South and the nation) the most important aspects of our traditions. He has used source material for primary studies, then expanded them in broad general terms, well founded on solid scholarship.

A noteworthy example of his translation of scholarly experience into broad theory is his essay "Of the Librarian's Education," which was first published two decades ago in *The American Scholar*. Some of the truly rut-bound librarians, those who count typewriter spaces on the margin of every catalog card, were a bit taken aback by his forthright analysis of the profession. But in more recent years this "Hoole Doctrine" has taken root in our major research libraries: at long last successful librarianship is becoming less dependent on the librarian's knowledge of the outside of the book and the inside of the library than on the outside of the library and the inside of the book.

Many of our antiquarians have studied the Old South and New South purely from the standpoint of headhunting, a *niveau* of scholarship as remote from Bill Hoole's studies as a minié ball hunt on a Civil War battlefield. In these terms we can readily see that the essays in this volume, while substantively important, are even more significant as seminal research, points of departure for other students who will continue to reveal the proper backgrounds of the Newest South and its supermarket-drugstores.

It is impossible to disregard the milieu in which Bill Hoole grew up and was educated. His fascination for the natural beauty of the South, obvious from his poetic interpretations as well as from his polyphonic prose, tells a story not obliterated even by the luxury motels which probably infest Cape Romain today. The sterner discipline of an older educational system in the public schools and colleges has surely had its effect on Bill Hoole's dedication to scholarship. Even more important, however, was the kindly interest of a scholar of major stature, Jay B. Hubbell, who was effective in bringing out the best in the young man. Neither Hubbell nor Hoole "perished"; but, in addition to their substantial records of publication, they taught, tutored, advised, and established friendships with students.

As a librarian, Bill Hoole's ability is universally recognized. Twenty-three libraries would not have invited him as a surveyor were his reputation not firmly established. Those of us who know him well are generally cognizant of flattering offers he has had from other research libraries throughout the country, and from library schools, but we will never know how many or the sources of all, for Bill Hoole, unlike many of his colleagues, never mentions such matters. The greatest tribute he has received comes from talk behind his back: everyone who has ever discussed him with any of his staff members has the absolute evidence that he is a prime representative of the humane tradition of librarianship. His staff members have long described him as a firm and just man who plays the game by the professional rules, but is an administrator who can make the exceptions when necessary, particularly when an employee's personal welfare is involved.

There is a bit of nepotism in this introduction: Bill Hoole's wife, Addie, is a cousin of a cousin of mine. The happy union suggests that most Southerners can find some sort of kinship. His intellectual kinship was obvious long before we met, and it came from reading his books and essays. The reader of this book will find the same sort of kinship and will recognize here the same modest colossus that Seneca (*Ep.* 76) described: *Parvus pumilio, licet in monte constiterit; colossus magnitudinem suam servabit, etiam si steterit in puteo.*

University of Kentucky   LAWRENCE S. THOMPSON

CONTENTS

ACCORDING TO HOOLE

William Stanley Hoole
(From a portrait by M. W. Edwards, 1972)

INTRODUCTION:
MOSTLY AUTOBIOGRAPHICAL

When Morgan Walters told me that he and the other members of the University of Alabama Press Committee were interested in publishing a selection of my miscellaneous essays in a book, my mind flashed back to the opening paragraph of one of my all-time favorite books, *Treasure Island.* I'm sure you will recall that Jim Hawkins begins his marvelous story by announcing that he had taken up his pen only because "Squire Trelawney, Dr. Livesey, and the rest of these gentlemen" had asked him to do so, "to write down the whole particulars" of his adventure, "keeping nothing back but the bearings of the island," and that only because there was still unlifted treasure. Jim then goes on to say that he remembers "as if it were yesterday" the moment the tarry-haired Old Sea Dog with the dirty, livid sabre cut across his cheek came plodding up to the Admiral Benbow Inn, pulling his battered sea-chest in a hand-barrow behind him and singing "Fifteen men on a dead man's chest—/Yo-ho-ho, and a bottle of rum!"

Well, the day Morgan Walters asked me, I felt pretty much as Jim Hawkins must have felt in his "year of grace 17—." I was proud and pleased—proud because I knew that in the twenty-seven-year history of the University of Alabama Press no member of the faculty or administrative staff had ever been so honored, and pleased because I knew the joy that would be mine in recalling the "whole particulars" of my literary adventures, keeping nothing back, although I feared that most of them, perhaps all, were scarcely worth telling in the first place, let alone the second!

If Morgan and the rest of these gentlemen are willing to take the risk, I reasoned, why shouldn't I? "But, why am I being singled out," I asked him, "when there are others about us much more ...?"

"Because you're different," he broke in, shocking me. "That's right, you are different! You're a literary maverick. Who else writes for *The American Scholar* one day and *Sir!* the next? Who else would describe the tragic death of his own Grandfather in *Vizetelly Covers the Confederacy,* then poke sarcastic fun at his own Great Uncle as a loud-mouthed, cowardly Rebel in *Esquire?* Who else?"

Walking away, I tried to recall whether I had ever thought of myself as different—fun-loving, perhaps satirical, but not "different." True, I had written or edited forty-odd books and two scholarly journals and published about a hundred articles in as many different magazines—the *Saturday Review* and *Progressive Farmer*, *Studies in Philology* and *Holland's Magazine*, *Library Quarterly* and *Facts*, *Field and Stream* and *American Literature*, to contrast but a few—but it was because I thought and lived that way, nothing more. As Pistol put it to Falstaff, the world has been my oyster. Ever since I can remember, my yen for expression has been demanding, as I suppose is the case with all who are born with a creative bent; and, as the years went by, my interest in reading and writing continuously widened. As I remember, it didn't make a great deal of difference what I read or wrote about, just so long as I had a book or a tablet in my lap and a pencil in my hand.

To begin with, at the age of four I started my own "library" with a little book, a sexagesimo-quarto, only 2" x 3", called *Daily Food*, a beloved birthday gift from family friends, now long gone, who inscribed it, "To dear little William with love and good wishes, May 16, 1907." I remember how my Mother, a quick-tempered, aristocratic little lady, half Irish, half French, read the short verses, mostly biblical, to me over and over again, my favorite being, quite naturally, the one dated May 16, although I then had only the vaguest idea of its meaning (and after all the years still wonder about the last line):

> O let me then at length be taught,
> What I am still so slow to learn,
> That God is love, and changed not,
> Nor knows the shadow of a turn.

Then there were the *Mother Goose* rhymes (for some reason the one about three maids in a tub, hey, rub-a-dub-dub still keeps me awake nights, and I often wonder whether Bobby Shaftoe really ever came back to marry the seaport girl or was she, like generations of others, shaftoed again) and *Andersen's Fairy Tales* and Dickens' *Christmas Carol*. As time passed and I began to make out my own words, Horatio Alger's many heroes (remember Ragged Dick and Tattered Tom?) came into my life, along with *Black Beauty, David Copperfield, Oliver Twist, Julius Caesar,* and *The Lady of the Lake,* who, as you will recall, stepped so lightly and so true that "e'en the slight harebell raised its head, elastic from her airy tread." And, of course, *Treasure Island* and Thomas Dixon's *The Clansman,* which was required reading for every Southern boy, even after the showing of "The Birth of a Nation" in 1915.

Many's the time my Mother and I cried together over Black Beauty's broken knees or Oliver's plea for more porridge, but the three books that really tinctured my thinking for all time and sent me off into rapturous spells of adventure came into my little world, oddly enough, in the same year (1911), the year I reached the wondrous age of eight, goin' on nine.

The first of these, as I have said, was *Treasure Island*, the 1911 edition, so gorgeously illustrated by N.C. Wyeth. In all my life, I sincerely believe, I have never enjoyed a single book more than that one. To me it has everything. Even now, in my umpteenth reading of it, I am wafted away into the wonderful world of make-believe, just as I was in the long ago. Jim's frightful experience in the apple barrel and the bodies of Israel Hand and O'Brien lying side-by-side on the sandy bottom of North Inlet, wavering with the tremulous movement of the water, as quick fishes steered to and fro above them—"Backward, turn backward, O Time, in your flight, make me a child again just for tonight!"

The second was Francis T. Miller's *Photographic History of the Civil War* (the next-to-the-last word in that title was a no-no in our South Carolina town, never used even in *im*polite society), but I shall hurriedly pass over it here, because that story follows along later in this book.

The third was *Aesop's Fables*, given me as a Christmas present by Mr. Johnny *Reb* Drake (he always underlined *Reb* which, so help me, was his real name), a friend of my Father and by all odds one of Darlington's most notorious citizens. You see, my Father was a pharmacist, an old-fashioned, plain-spoken, cigar-chewing druggist who owned and operated a real *drug* store—not one of your modern powderpuff places that reeks of frying grease and hamburgers with onions. In all his years of pill-rolling and patent medicine retailing Father never once, not once, stocked a camera, ladies' beauty aids, or a wrist watch (until World War I wrist watches were sissy pieces, anyway, worn only by men who also had lace on their b.v.d.'s). He did go so far as to sell crutches, false teeth, bedpans, and rupture trusses, however, for they were at least "medicinal," and tobacco and lamp chimneys. Otherwise, nothing but drugs, drugs, drugs from 7 a.m. to 10 p.m. every day in the year, including Christmas, New Year's, Fourth of July, and even Confederate Memorial Day, which somehow did not always set too well with the populace. Rows of castor oil, paregoric, and turpentine bottles lined his shelves, along with Mother's Friend, Dr. King's New Discovery, Wine of Cardui, and Thedford's Black Draught. Fletcher's Castoria soothed babies, 666 cured malaria fever, and Carter's Little Liver Pills were good for whatever ailed you. Foul-smelling gummed asafoetida was a popular drug: when rolled into a ball, sacked and tied around one's neck, it warded off both diseases and people. With every purchase Father gave the customer a copy of *The Ladies Birthday Almanac* which predicted the weather a year in advance, solved mathematical problems, instructed

[5]

the reader on planting, harvesting, and childbirth, and guided every man, woman, and child to health and happiness day by day and generation after generation—and still does in 1973.

Father, himself, was quite a character. Tall, thin, stoop-shouldered, and tubercular, he was as smart as a whip, a sort of town oracle. If you needed to know the number of square miles in Texas, for example, or the date of the Charleston earthquake, or why there is never frost on a cloudy morning, or how to foal a mule, you'd ask Doc Hoole (we had no public library in those days). During World War I he hung a huge map of Europe, some six by ten feet, on a wall in his store and, with white-headed pins for the Allies and red for the Germans, posted the day-by-day movements of the armies on the Western Front. Early every afternoon, when the Seaboard train brought in the Columbia *Record* from the state capital, eighty miles away (we had no radios in those days, either) our Negro delivery boy would be at the station on his bicycle to rush a copy back to Father. Meanwhile, the usual crowd had gathered at the store, often spilling out onto the awning-covered sidewalk. Then, standing on a step-ladder, Father would read the news aloud and shuffle the white and red pins back and forth on the map, amidst the excitement of his onlookers. It was a great thrill to me, as a boy of twelve or thirteen, to be a part of all that was then going on in our little world and fifty-odd years later I can still see those pins along the Somme and the Marne and the Meuse and get all goosebumpy recalling the time Father announced that the Hindenburg Line had been broken—the attack spear-headed by the boys of the 30th Infantry Division, which included our own Darlington Guards.

But Father had his sulphuric side, too. I recall the day he told me that, if I could collect a long-overdue account from a "damned old skinflint" named Pollock, I could keep the money! At the tender age of eleven I knew none but the direct approach, so when I met the culprit, I faced up to him with, "Father says you're a 'damned old skinflint' . . ." and, believe me, before I could finish the sentence, Old Man Pollock handed me a wadded $10.00 bill and walked away, grinning like a Cheshire cat. On another occasion I watched Father, his patience exhausted, catch an overbearing Yankee drummer by the nape of his neck and the seat of his pants and hasten him out of the store and into the gutter. It turned out that the salesman, an overdressed dude, had made a cheap joke about the "bars" in the Stars and Bars, without knowing that Father's Father had forfeited his life for the Confederacy at the Battle of Chickamauga. (Like his son after him, Father was also a writer, but for an account of his book you'll have to turn to page 247.)

Now, back to Johnny *Reb* Drake and *Aesop's Fables*. He gave me the book on Christmas, 1911. It was about the prettiest thing I'd ever laid eyes on, bound in red buckram with a hunting boy on the spine and colored pictures of a football player and a baseball player on the front cover, in full uniforms, separated by a gold spread-winged eagle atop the United States flag. In my scrawling eight-year-old handwriting I penned my name on the fly leaf, adding (and this could well have been my creative first), "If by chance I loose (*sic*) this book remember William is my name and Hoole comes after it." Well, as they say, one is what one writes.

I have said Johnny *Reb* was a friend of Father's, but that only partially explains why he gave me a Christmas present, year after year. There was another reason, crass and commercial though it may be—and I would be derelict of my duty to posterity, if I were to withhold it. You see, Johnny *Reb*, a stumpy, red-faced, roly-poly, long-haired man who swung a huge gold watchchain from vest-pocket to vest-pocket across his bulging belly and spit tobacco juice between his teeth, was by profession a patent medicine drummer, the like of which roamed the South for many years after Reconstruction, peddling cure-all tonics and health restorers (usually laden with alcohol) to unsuspecting but, after a swig or two, very happy customers. Row on row of "bitters" of every variety—I remember Hostetter's, Plantation, Kookman's, and one called Electric Bitters—stood in every drugstore, and I assure you the doses were not measured by the teaspoon. "Tonics" were best-sellers, too, the higher the alcoholic content the better the curative powers for indigestion, kidney trouble, loss of appetite, impotence, lumbago, chills and fever, dizziness, foul breath, ingrowing toenails, running sores, and tired feeling. Until about 1911, when Congress passed the Harrison Narcotic Act, countless patent medicines containing opium derivatives were also sold by traveling peddlers as well as by respectable local druggists. Laudunum "drinkers" were fairly commonplace. Paregoric was given to babies with colic, and pure powdered morphine was purchasable over the counter at less than $6.00 an ounce. Several "soothing" remedies for children contained morphine. Popular among them were "toothing powders" which a mother would sprinkle on her breasts before nursing her baby to sleep. No one knows the number of drug addicts who got hooked in this fashion, but it is a well-known fact, proved by countless old Southern drugstore ledgers, that in those days morphine, laudunum, and paregoric were among the most repeatedly purchased items, second only to the "bitters" and turpentine, calomel, and castor oil.

But Johnny *Reb's* product was not a narcotic. It was "Drake's Marvelous Snake-Oil Liniment," a mixture of powdered mustard, chloroform, camphor, cayenne pepper, oil of eucalyptus, and other skin-blistering ingredients, all dissolved in alcohol and turpentine and colored rosy-pink. To smell it was to singe the hairs in your nostrils and to rub

[7]

it on an aching muscle must have been pure agony, for the stuff was as hot as the hinges of hell, even to the hand.

I know all this for a fact, because Father had a contract with Johnny *Reb* to mix the liniment for him in our drugstore in ten gallon batches, pour it into thin little two-ounce vials, cork, label, and package them in orange cartons lettered in red, and deliver them to him for about 10¢ per bottle. Johnny *Reb* would then load up his two-horse wagon and circle the Pee Dee River Basin with a one-eyed Negro fiddler named Moe (short for Mozart), mesmerizing his hearers with music and tall tales and sacrificing his product to the rheumatic, the arthritic, and the muscle-aching for only 50¢ a vial (step up, folks, while the supply lasts!). His modest profit, I reckon, must have been about $200 per ten-gallon batch and a batch would last about a week. Meantime, believe it or not, folks would write to Father's drugstore for additional bottles of the healing concoction, fully believing it as marvelous as Johnny *Reb* told them it was, whether or not their skin puffed and peeled like paint on a sun-baked concrete wall.

As a small boy, my part in all this was to help Moe cork, label, and package the marvelous remedy, on Saturdays mostly when there was no school, for that was Johnny *Reb's* big day: in the South everybody, white and black, for miles around, came to town on Sat'day to mill around the Public Square and do their trading and visiting. It was then that "Drake's Marvelous Snake-Oil Liniment" sold like hot cakes (no pun intended). And for my labors good old Johnny *Reb* Drake, Father's bosom friend, sent me a book on December 25, year after year. He didn't know it at the time, nor did I, but his generosity, backhanded though it may have been, gave me a good push along the path of reading and writing—and to him and his "Marvelous Snake-Oil Liniment" I shall ever be grateful.

(Let me add, albeit parenthetically, that I still own the 1911 editions of *Pictorial History* ... and *Treasure Island,* as well as Johnny *Reb's* gift copy of *Aesop's Fables,* and *Daily Food.* Today they occupy conspicuous spaces in my study and, besides being thumbed from time to time, they often make first-rate conversation pieces with curious visitors.)

Father died in 1919 (I'm glad he lived long enough to fold up his map of the Western Front). Meanwhile, I had reached high school, learned to play shinny (a crude first cousin to hockey, played on any vacant field with homemade clubs made of bent hickory sticks, and a small rubber ball), punt a football in spiral, swim and dive in Black Creek, catch fish by hand in narrow streams by muddying the water and thus forcing them to the surface, and go with girls. Now, just a minute—in our town at that time a boy never "dated" a girl—he would "go" with her. And before you get any notions, let me say that going with a girl didn't mean what you think it did: it meant simply that he was "keeping company" with her and that included "carrying" her to "conversation parties" on Friday nights and, if he really meant business, holding her hand in church. Of course, we had one or two of the *other* kind of girls around and about, but they were mostly "Saturday night" prospects, when the Public Square was filled with shoppers, and nobody much was looking after the hay-filled wagons hitched in the back lots behind the crowded stores.

I remember one particularly top-heavy little "Saturday nighter," Pearlie Mae by name, who was a favorite among all the tenth-grade boys, as well as the eighth, ninth, and eleventh. A stringy-haired blonde she was, every bit of fourteen, structured somewhat on the order of our town water-tank—spindle-legged up to *there*, then suddenly ballooning out above-waist to unbelievable dimensions, bold, bouncy and perfectly cantilevered. She was the secret envy of every girl and the drooling desire of every boy in high school. Every Saturday about dusk Pearlie Mae would appear out of nowhere and waddle duck-like around the Public Square on high-heeled shoes, over-dressed in girlish pink or yellow frills. Soon she'd be circled by two or three giggling admirers who would treat her to a sack of peanuts and a soda-pop or two and then before long they would all disappear in the shadows behind the stores.

The Saturday night I recall most vividly was in early May, just after my fifteenth birthday. During the late afternoon a sudden spring shower had begun to fall, wetting the hay in the wagons. The boys hanging around Father's drugstore were mighty depressed: no one believed Pearlie Mae would dare come out on a rainy night like that. But just then an automobile, a six-cylindered Chalmers, black, shiny, with its isinglass side-curtains flapping and glaring under the street lamp, pulled up to the curb, and "Hook" Patton, one of our classmates, stuck his head out and yelled at us. He had somehow hornswoggled his Old Man into letting him drive the family car to town. And on the front seat beside him sat Pearlie Mae in all her bulbous beauty, soaking wet, but smiling as if she had just been elected the Queen of May.

All at once everything except the sky began to brighten. The boys rushed out and one by one began piling into the Chalmers. Momentarily bewildered, Pearlie Mae uttered only one word—"*Six?*" At least, that's all I heard before Father ran out in the rain, yanked me by my belt, and hustled me back into the drugstore. All he ever said—and this was his true measure as a man—was, "Son, I think 'Hook's' too young to be driving a car at night, don't you?" But a week later I found a brand new copy of *What Every Young Boy Ought to Know* in my bedroom. Parents can surely be subtle when they want to be.

I never found out what happened that rainy Saturday night behind the isinglass curtains in that black, shiny Chalmers (you know how

[9]

it is with boys, they brag a lot), but I've done a lot of guessing. Like the soldier-boy in Wilfred Gibson's poem who went off to war wondering whether the sick old cow died, I guess I'll go till Doomsday not knowing the truth about Pearlie Mae and "Hook" and the others behind the isinglass curtains in that black, shiny Chalmers that rainy Saturday night just after my fifteenth birthday.

It was about this time, my last two years in high school, that I began to widen my horizon in a number of ways. Weighing in at 130 pounds, I played end on the football team and did the punting and drop-kicking, which were my "specialties," held down second on the baseball team, and ran the 100-yard dash in 11 seconds. In my senior year I was elected a class officer and some kind of assistant editor of the *Bulletin* (everybody in our class of thirty was an assistant editor of something). For the newspaper I wrote an occasional sketch or two, long since fortunately forgotten. Scholastically, I managed somehow to hold my own. I made the honor roll, graduating in 1920 near the top of my class, but not *the* top, thanks to Latin and physics. Up to this day I shudder to think of Archimedes' Principle or agricola, agricolae, agricolum. On Saturdays I jerked sodas in Father's drugstore, swatted millions of flies in the display windows, and delivered packages on my bike—all for 50¢ a day. Whenever business was slack or I wasn't snooping around listening to the dirty jokes and small-town gossip of our perennial loafers, I'd pull a book out from under the counter and read, sometimes sneaking it back to the toilet, when the action got exciting. By now I had graduated to popular novels. Between the ages of fourteen and eighteen I must literally have read hundreds, mostly American. I couldn't possibly remember them all, but among those that made everlasting impressions on me were *The Call of the Wild, The Trail of the Lonesome Pine, To Have and to Hold, The Virginian, The Battle-Ground, My Antonia, Alice of Old Vincennes, Miss Lulu Bett, Graustark, When Knighthood Was in Flower*—the list could go on and on. Fixed in my deepest memory, however, are *The Red Badge of Courage, Cease Firing,* and *The Clansman.* Of these, *The Red Badge of Courage,* Stephen Crane's Civil War cameo, stands out as one of the most compelling narratives ever written. Granted, it is episodic, granted, it is perhaps better in detail than in panorama, which is to say that the author was more of a miniaturist than a landscapist, but at the same time grant that few American writers have equalled his unique capacity to dazzle his reader with brief but brilliant bursts of imagistic beauty. His gallant genius shines with prismatic lustre sentence after sentence, as he sees the Battle of Chancellorsville through the eyes of Henry Fleming, a bewildered young Yankee soldier. "The red sun was pasted in the sky like a wafer.... The moon had been lighted and hung in a treetop.... and Tents sprang up like strange plants. . . ."—these alone reveal Crane's camera-like ability to capture a scene with but a single snap, quickly. To Private Fleming cannons "belched and howled like brass devils guarding a gate," soldiers stood as "men tied to stakes," and in a charge his wounded comrades dropped about him like "grunting bundles of blue." Surely, such rapier thrusts of realism, such complete disdain for the conventional, and such sheer stinginess of words proved Crane a prophet for many novelists and poets yet to come, among them Theodore Drieser, Edgar Lee Masters, Erskine Caldwell, Ernest Hemingway, William Faulkner, Carl Sandburg, Sherwood Anderson and more, including Erich Remarque whose *All Quiet on the Western Front* may be called a World War I version of *The Red Badge of Courage:* First Ypres is Chancellorsville, separated by three thousand miles and two generations. The killing and wounding and the agony of dying and the grinning corpse rats are one and the same.

And as for me, at fifteen or sixteen, Stephen Crane opened a wide new door behind which, for the first time, I felt the wonder of a single word, the strength of a single phrase, the power of a single paragraph and came to know that, after all is said and done, writing is largely a matter of mood and that the style is the writer and that he need weigh no opinion but his own, if he would be natural—and free. As they say, character is fate. From that moment I vowed that I, too, would strive to paint my pictures with simple strokes: each word had now become for me a little world all its own.

Largely because he was a druggist, Father had hoped that I would go to Wofford, a small Methodist college in Spartanburg, South Carolina and there prepare myself for the state medical school in Charleston. The first hope I fulfilled, even to the extent of enrolling in the pre-requisite courses, but the second I simply couldn't stomach. And for two good reasons. *First,* I had worked around a drugstore too long, listening to the hypocritical shop-talk of local doctors, ever to take the medical profession too seriously: Dr. Arkwright's jokes about an old lady whom he had hooked on morphine in relieving her migraine headaches, old Dr. Berriman's sarcasms about a hypochondriac he was treating twice a week with a mixture of acetylsalicylic acid (aspirin to you) dissoved in pure ethyl alcohol and colored pink, Dr. Sillcox's tall tales about the old man who had such long "pendulum piles" that he had to swing them back and forth before he could sit down in comfort, and all the other physicians who griped about making house calls, bragged about the number of patients they had and the money they were making, and wise-cracked about being "too busy" when called by an ill person who was "slow pay" or "behind in his account." *Second,* I had by now become too interested in books and reading and writing and their normal counterpart, teaching, to give them up for the "practice" of the kind of "medicine" I had lived with up until September, 1920, when I left home to enter college.

Frankly, my first year at Wofford was almost my undoing. Like thousands of small-town kids, I had never before been away from home. The transition was tremendous, far more so than I had dreamed. For the first time I was without parental protection, on my own to come and go and do as I pleased. I had moved into an entirely new world; a world of rot-gut and running boards, an octopus which grasped me and all but took me out with the tide. Its tentacles were fraternities, football, baseball, poker, bull-sessions, dancing, and girls, girls, girls. During the year, while being "rushed" by a half-dozen fraternities, I made the football and baseball teams, learned that the odds are great against filling an inside straight, and spent roughly half my time running after girls, mostly those at Converse College across town, about a mile from our campus. I also became proficient at dancing the "Charleston" and avoiding being called on in classes by answering the roll with the standard "Unprepared today, Professor," a gimmick permissible in my day.

And that prompts me to say a few cautious words, the fewer the better, about my scholastic record during my freshman year. To be telegraphic about it, it stunk. By mid-term I was on the D or F list in all my subjects, had over-cut most of my classes and received more professor's pink slips, I reckon, than any other student in the history of the college. During the daytime this didn't really bother me. After all, I had my choice of fraternity bids, I could punt a football farther than any man on the squad, and for the first time in my life I had fallen head-over-heels, madly, eternally in love—with Nancy, the only girl in the world. (I didn't know it at the time, but before being graduated in 1924 I was also destined to be madly and eternally in love with Margaret, Ellen, Lucile, Catherine, Agnes, Maybelle, and Becky.) But during the nighttime, when the poker games were over and the dormitory lights were dimmed, I would lie awake, ashamed, thinking mostly of Father and the high hopes he had had for his only son, of Mother who was even now sacrificing for me, and cursing myself for failing to make the most of the best opportunity I had ever had in my life. (No one knows the thousands upon thousands of college students who have suffered similar spasms of agony, but I believe that through my own ordeal of failure I learned a lesson of compassion which has served me long and well.)

If it had not been for a feisty little professor with the Huguenot name of A. Gaillard Rembert (we called him "Knotty" for short), I would have been shipped out of Wofford College at the end of the first semester, star punter or not. A little wisp of a man, "Knotty" weighed only 110 pounds, wore a high stiff collar, sported a handle-bar moustache, and moved about as capriciously as a housefly. In his psychology class he strutted back and forth, back and forth, his hands in pockets, his eyes on the ceiling, mesmerizing his students with his wit and wisdom. Now and again he would wheel suddenly about, point his bony finger at an open-mouthed face, and ask a question. He seldom got an answer. To his students he was Fear in person. (But we learned to love him so much that our class dedicated our yearbook to him "as a token of friendship and affection.")

One day "Knotty" turned on me, brutally, viciously. Struck dumb, I stared—nothing more. Screaming "Ex nihil nihilo fit," he ordered me to see him in his office after class. Unless you have been drawn and quartered, you could never appreciate the agony, the pain, the fiendish torment the human mind can endure under such duress. The torture rack would have brought relief. The chained seconds dragged themselves around the clock, slowly, one after the other, ever slower, until at long last the class bell in the college tower tolled the semifinal of my doom.

I entered the anteroom of "Knotty's" office. There, on a straight-backed chair, the only piece of furniture, I sat gingerly, waiting. I waited. Through the crack under the inner door crawled the grayish smoke of a stale cigar. I waited. For hours, or so it seemed, there was no sound beyond the beating of my heart. And I waited. Then, all of a sudden, Fear stood before me in person, half-hidden in the haze of smoke that had stalked him from his desk. I sprang to attention.

"Hoole," he said in his squeaky voice and shaking his finger, "when you entered Wofford, I hoped you'd amount to something." He paused, thumbed his moustache as if in deep thought, and added, "but I've given up—I don't believe you've got it in you. Good day."

For days those words seared my very soul. I grew madder and madder. The fact that he had "given me up" was more than I could take. By God, I finally determined, I'll show the old geezer how wrong he is. I'll show him, I'll show him. . . .

Now, I do not pretend to know psychology, but surely "Knotty" did. For him it worked. From that day forward my attitude changed, my grades improved, and when the Class of 1924 was graduated, I stood near the top with an overall scholastic record of "distinction" (so stated the commencement program), sufficient later to earn me honorary membership in Phi Beta Kappa.

Aside from my routine class studies at Wofford, football and books (an unholy alliance, I agree) consumed most of my time. I nailed down the varsity quarterback spot my sophomore year and held it through my senior year, at which time my teammates elected me Captain. Weighing 140 pounds (on a team which averaged 190), I called the plays, passed, and did the place- and drop-kicking and punting. Under strict orders from our coaches, I seldom if ever carried the ball: they said I was too valuable as a kicker to risk crushing my little body in contact—so I just called signals, handled the ball, and skipped back, clean out of the action. At kicking, I must admit, I *was* pretty good. Sports writers dubbed me "The Educated Toe." I could spiral a punt 60 to 65 yards with regularity, causing the ball to curve slowly to the receiver's left as it arched, an "art" I had picked up in high school. (Even now, today, when I hear a tv commentator announce that a 290-pound big-time university or professional punter averaged 40-odd yards in a game, my thoughts race back to the 1922 Wofford-Furman game which was reported in the Spartanburg *Herald,* November 19, in these words: "Hoole, Wofford's 140 pound quarterback, was the outstanding star of the game. He punted the ball ten times for an average of 45 yards with his mighty hoof...." *Sic transit gloria mundi.*

As I have said, my other interest was reading. In my literature classes I made many new friendships: from across the sea Chaucer, Wordsworth, Byron, Sidney, Browning, Thackeray, Tasso, Baudelaire, Cervantes, Goethe, Boccaccio, and more; in America, Poe, Whitman, Melville, Simms, Irving, Masters, Lewis, Dreiser, Cabell (whose *Jurgen* I never understood), Garland, Howells, and many more. The college library was my scholastic gridiron. There no boundary lines hemmed me in, no whistles blew, and the time clock ran on and on, far into the night. From this chapter in my career I remember most vividly *Black Oxen, Main Street, An American Tragedy, Winesburg, Ohio,* and *Spoon River Anthology.* The first, based on sex rejuvenation by surgery, was in its day considered very risque; the tongue-in-cheek confusion of sermons and seduction made the second a shocking tragicomedy; and the third was, for me, a sad, sad tale of loneliness, despair, and madness, leavened with bitter protests against the society of my day. (Thinking back on *An American Tragedy* now, in 1971, I am reminded of our own hippie generation whose "beef," if I understand it, is the same as Clyde Griffith's—an overt challenge to those over thirty who would polarize the free-flowing currents of natural life.) The other books, *Winesburg* and *Spoon River,* both Freudian-based, are strangely alike, one prose, the other poetry, both reflecting the emotional agonies and ecstasies of small-town men and women caught up in a pseudo-respectable, but unrelenting and often rancid world over which they have no control. In these books Anderson and Masters are at their original best. Nowhere in our literary heritage, in my humble judgment, are there more powerful microcosms of life or more sympathetic portrayals of man's poignant inability to cope with the realities of existence. There is a sexy Belle Carpenter, a dreaming Joe Welling, a love-hungry Kate Swift, and a pathetic George Willard in thousands of Winesburgs all over America. And in every Spoon

River there is a jealous Amelia Garrick, a demented Frank Drummer, a brokenhearted Emily Sparks, a drunken Benjamin Painter and his dog, and a forgotten, bitter, lonely Hortense Robbins. (Indeed, long before Anderson and Masters they dwelt about us in one form or another—in biblical vignettes, such as the Prodigal Son's rebellion or the David-Bathsheba affair, or in *The Decameron* or *Arabian Nights* or *The Canterbury Tales*.) We who know them weep for them year in, year out, as they move about us, seeking in vain to conceal their true selves behind a transparent facade of societal hostility. Surely, there is no more misery for man than to want to be wanted and not to be wanted. As William James wrote somewhere, when you speak and no one answers, or when you wave and no one turns, or when you smile and no one responds, you have no choice but hatred and, if that fails, you turn your hatred inward to prove yourself to yourself, or into violence to prove yourself to others.

I repeat, few books made such a profound impression on me, a college student, as did *Spoon River* and *Winesburg* and their stream-of-consciousness counterparts which in the 1920's dominated American literature in both style and subject matter, through Ernest Hemingway, Thomas Wolfe, Gertrude Stein, William Faulkner, Erskine Caldwell (even to William March's *Company K*, one of my favorites). For me the romantic moon of sweetness and light had now turned its alluring dark side: I vowed I would read about only the perverted, the erotic, the soul-twisted, the lost and the damned and I would write only in short, terse bullet-bursts, precise, straight-on-target without a single wasted word, like a cablegram. And to prove it, in my junior and senior years I contributed to the college literary journal (I recall one essay, composed shortly after President Wilson's death, which had for an opener this stoccado paragraph: *Woodrow Wilson is dead!*) and wrote sports for the Spartanburg *Sun*, a short-lived competitor of the old *Herald*. In all frankness I must add that these extra curricula activities were not entirely labors of love. Several years after my Father's death my Mother had been bilked into investing most of her inheritance in a new company which in Rock Hill, South Carolina, a few miles away, manufactured Anderson automobiles. As a result, I had to paddle my own canoe my last two college years. Whoever heard of an Anderson?

Be that as it may, the *Bohemian* of 1924 shows me as a grinning boy with a long list of honors, including a block W with three stars and a crescent (for Captain), scholarship honors in my sophomore, junior, and senior years, and many student offices. And beneath, Dogberry's famous line from *Much Ado About Nothing*: "To be a well-favored man is a gift of Fortune." But to this day, looking at that boy dressed in his sweater and plus-fours, with his cap on his head

[15]

like a misplaced bottle top (the "way-out" fashion of the Roaring Twenties), and with a cigarette in his mouth, I shudder and say: "Ex nihil nihilo fit."

Upon graduation I accepted a $100 a month job as a teacher and football coach at Spartanburg High School (our team reached the semifinals for the state championship), but at the end of one year I was lured into the business world by Montgomery-Crawford Company, a local cottonmill supply house, on the promise of higher pay and quick promotion. After a breaking-in period I took to the road in my $400 Ford Roadster, selling nuts and bolts, galvanized pipe, sheepskins and pickers to cottonmill superintendents throughout the Carolinas and North Georgia ($150 a month). Now, if you've ever really seen a round peg in a square hole, you saw me in those dreary days: never was a man more misfitted for his work than I. Selling was not a question of product, however superior, I learned, but of persuading, and persuading was synonymous with bowing-and-scraping, with cowing, with paying homage in a hundred ways from a simple favor to a box of cigars or a fifth of whiskey or, in my particular case, to a pair of tickets on the fifty-yard line. For as long as I dared I tried to bridge the gap between the "super's" world and my own, but in the end I failed—what has a man to do with the stale-sweet smell of aniline dyes and the roar of spinning-mill machinery, when "Beauty is truth, truth beauty,—that is all / Ye know on earth, and all ye need to know" keeps ringing in his ears?

Thus glutted with round-headed stove bolts and switch boxes and dust-down sweeping compound, I quit Montgomery-Crawford in the winter of 1926 and signed up with the Southeastern branch of the Badyear Tire and Rubber Company. Now, you'd think I would have had better sense than to step out of the frying pan into the fire, but the truth is that I had little choice. Badyear dangled a larger pay check in my face and conned me into dreaming that I would soon be transferred (all expenses paid) to their Singapore or Paris or Manila or London office—and I went for that romantic bait like a hungry trout. When it came to the truth, however, I found myself in a blue-collar stockroom job, week after week rolling six, eight, or ten automobile tires, side by side at once, from a huge warehouse to waiting pickup trucks, and shipping inner tubes, puncture patches, and rubber belting to filling stations or manufacturing plants throughout the region. In a conference with our Yankee boss (his last name was Milton and, while I don't remember, his initials must have been S.B.) I asked about Singapore and Paris and he promptly transferred me to a white-collar office job in accounting. There, I had the weighty responsibility of totalling invoices on an adding machine eight hours a day, six days a week (salary $160 monthly), much to the disgust of my fellow workers who looked down their envious noses at me,

[16]

largely because I had something they didn't have (a college degree). Well, in due time they set out to get me. They snubbed me. They maneuvered mistakes to my desk. They whispered about me to Manager Milton who, like a pot-bellied, reared-back character out of Dickens, paraded around the office, peeping over my shoulder. Then, one day in the spring of 1927 the axe fell: Milton harumphed that I was "tempermentally" unsuited for Badyear and that I could pick up my pay check on the way out. I did exactly that—but not before reminding him of his canine ancestry and waving his two-faced hirelings farewell with my thumb on my nose. Since 1927 I have never thought of them without nausea and, needless to say, I'd walk a million miles before putting one of those damned tires on my automobile.

During the two years I was sweating it out at Montgomery-Crawford and Badyear I never ceased wishing one way or another to get out of the weary world of business and back into the wonderful world of books. Old S.B., who wouldn't have knowingly given me the time of day, had suddenly given me that opportunity. I promptly wrote to Professor J. C. Daniel, superintendent of Darlington's St. John's High School, for advice. Receipt of his reply made that day one of the most memorable of my life: he needed an English teacher ($1200 annually) and football coach ($200 a season extra), beginning in the fall of 1927, he telegraphed—would I be interested in the position? A drowning man couldn't have grasped a life preserver quicker than I accepted his offer. To be back in my home town, to work in my own high school, and to live in my own home again—"Oh, Wilderness were Paradise enow."

And there were good reasons. Even then, in 1927 (forty-five years ago!) my roots in South Carolina were nearly two-hundred-thirty years deep and in Darlington County itself about one-hundred-fifteen—and for those of my ilk who believe that no one knows where he's going unless he knows where he's been, few matters are more meaningful. (I know *they* say you can't grow daisies on grandpa's grave, but *they* also say you can't make a silk purse out of a sow's ear!)

Well, anyway, my family in America (all branches: English, French, Irish, etc.) were (are) proud South Carolina Sandlappers and proud Darlingtonians to the very heart. The first Hooles in these parts, Edward and Joseph, came via the Barbadoes from the Lancashire-Cheshire area of England (our crest bears the red Lancastrian rose). Edward was living in Charleston before 1699 and Joseph, a British seaman and wine merchant, was in 1710 not only trading in Carolina, but was also serving on His Majesty's Council in the Barbadoes. His son, Joseph II, was granted 100 acres of land in Amelia Parish, South Carolina, on June 20, 1754 (I own a copy of this grant, signed by "His Excellency James Glen, Esqr. Captain-General, Governor and Commander-in-Chief of the Said Province" in the name of His Majesty

[17]

King George II). Joseph II soon moved on to Prince Frederick Parish where he died in 1768, and his son, Joseph III, aged 28, married Elizabeth Commander of Georgetown in 1787 and built a home in St. James's Santee Parish where their son James was born in 1788. As a young man, James himself moved inland up the Santee-Pee Dee river basin, settling in Darlington County. In 1812 he bought 450 acres of land along Swift Creek and the "Belly Ache [Belle Acres] Branch waters of Black Creek." There in 1818 he met and married Elizabeth, daughter of Sandys ("Sands") Stanley who with his brother John had earlier migrated to Darlington from New Kent County, Virginia and settled on adjoining land grants of 560 acres each "on the South side of Black Creek on the drains of Swift Creek" (I own copies of these 1787 grants, signed by Governor Thomas Pinckney). Meanwhile, the Brunson (Brownson) family had moved to St. James's Santee Parish in 1721 from Chelmsford, England via Massachusetts and Connecticut, and the Bacot (de Vaco of Tours) and DuBose (DuBosc of Dieppe) families had settled in Goose Creek Parish and Prince Frederick Parish in 1685 and 1689, respectively, having escaped France through Holland and England following the Edict of Nantes.

When all these folks got together in the Carolina Santee-Pee Dee region, they began merging with others—the Pennsylvania Dutch Kolbs, the Irish Powerses and the English Allstons, Brockingtons, and Bentons, all of whom became South Carolinians. And now, many long years later, we are proud to say that our families helped tame this wild and beautiful frontier: we fought the Indians, the Spanish, the French, the British (twice), the Mexicans, the Yankees (yep, even them) and out of it all produced, thank God, a happy, happy breed of *Americans*!

So you see, returning to my home town in 1927 to teach (in the same St. John's in which my Grandfather had taught and my father had been schooled) was something very special in my life. Seldom have I been happier than I was in that first school year, 1927–1928. I was a fish in water again. Far removed from the antiseptic stench of dust-down and automobile tires stacked column-high, row after row on warehouse floors, I now had leisure to read and write. To my bosom I closer drew Dreiser, Hemingway, Anderson, Lewis, and Masters and beside them I put Thornton Wilder, Thomas Wolfe (oh, how thrilled I was, reading aloud the roaring, rolling polyphonic passages from *Look Homeward, Angel* and *Of Time and the River*—and even now I cherish a long letter Wolfe wrote me years later when I published some nice things about his *The Story of a Novel*), Joseph Hergesheimer, Willa Cather, Roark Bradford, T. S. Stribling, Edith Wharton, Frank Norris, and John Dos Passos. I devoured fifteen volumes of Stoddard's *Lectures*, all of Shakespeare's plays (except the comedies which I still do not relish), many of Dickens' novels, and read and reread *The Bridge of San Luis Rey, Ethan Frome, Miss Lula Bett,* and *If Winter Comes.* Criticism, biography, and history I read also: I remember particularly Hervey Allen's *Israfel: The Life and Times of Edgar Allan Poe,* Ulrich Phillips' *Life and Labor in the Old South,* Lucy L. Hazard's *The Frontier in American Literature,* and Norman Foerster's *The Reinterpretation of American Literature.* As time passed, I became more and more enamored of antebellum Southern history, fiction (flavored as it was by Sir Walter Scott, that Shakespeare of novelists), poetry, drama, and humor. Into my orbit came William Gilmore Simms, Henry Timrod, Thomas Holley Chivers, Beverly Tucker, Paul Hamilton Hayne, Edgar Allan Poe, John Pendleton Kennedy, John Esten Cooke, Sidney Lanier, Caroline Lee Hentz, and Augusta Evans Wilson. Especially do I remember Augustus Baldwin Longstreet *(Georgia Scence),* Johnson Jones Hooper ("Captain Simon Suggs"), Joseph G. Baldwin *(Flush Times of Alabama and Mississippi),* and George W. Harris *(Sut Lovingood's Yarns).* The list could be lengthened. Actually, everything bound between covers was grist for my literary mill.

Beside my old favorites, *The Red Badge, Winesburg,* and *Spoon River,* I now placed *Look Homeward, Angel, All Quiet on the Western Front* (the last paragraph of which still brings tears to my eyes), and the never-to-be-forgotten poems and short stories of Poe. Even yet, after a thousand times, I thrill to read "If I could dwell / Where Israfel / Hath dwelt, and he where I, / He might not sing so wildly well / A mortal melody, / While bolder note than this might swell / From my lyre within the sky." Someone has written that the single line—"Roll on, thou deep and dark blue Ocean roll!" —would alone have brought Byron lasting fame: if that be so, I suggest that the one-sentence verse from "Israfel" would likewise have immortalized Poe.

It follows naturally, I believe, that one who reads will one day want to write. So it was with me. During my first teaching year in Darlington I wrote a "book" about Poe (which I later used as my master's thesis) and tried my hand at a prose *Spoon River,* modeled after *Winesburg, Ohio,* which by shuffling the first three letters of Darlington I named "Radlington, S.C." Like all small towns, mine had its fair share of off-beat characters. To them I turned for subjects. In my manuscript appeared "Catfish John," a dirty old Greek who wore layer upon layer of hand-me-down clothes, even in summer, and shuffled about town, playing a 6-foot harp and living out of garbage cans (once a bunch of the boys, weary of smelling him, threw him into Black Creek—and while he struggled to shore they found several hundred dollars hidden in the lining of his innermost coat); stone-deaf "Uncle Dub" who held a thin, fan-shaped sheet of metal between his teeth, the better to hear; "Old Pete" Nettleton, a blind ballad singer who moseyed about the streets, fingering a worn-out zither and shrieking such mournful tunes as "Six Feet of Earth Makes Us All of One Kind" and "Please, Mr. Conductor, Don't Put Me Off'n This Train"; "Judge" Charley Bargain who walked the Public Square in second-hand, untied shoes, reciting Hamlet's soliloquy and Mark Anthony's funeral oration and never washed except during summer showers, when he stuck his bare feet out of the window; "Old Man" Williams, a miser who replaced the broken windshield of his Model T with a sheet of plywood, narrowly slotted for vision; K. K. (for Ku Klux) Irving, a well-to-do farmer who owned hundreds of acres of rich land and drove the largest motorcar in town (an Appleton with push-button gear-shift), and swiped 5¢ cigars from the tobacco counter in Father's drugstore; Annielou, the hair-lipped old maid who played piano at our Bijou Theatre and between shows paid tribute to the owner on the projection room floor; and bloody-aproned Herr Sertz, a German butcher who locked and barred the doors and windows of his house to keep the neighbors from listening while he nightly communed with his long-dead wife. There were others, too, but of course "Radlington, S.C." was never printed. Several of these "master-pieces" did find their way into an old scrapbook, however, and because they are buoys which marked the channel of my growth, I have agreed to include a sample in this collection: "Magdalene Christian" (see pages 79–80). (As you note its heavy overtones of Edgar Lee Masters and Sherwood Anderson—remember, I had just turned twenty-four).

Once, in the 1928 spring, with my friend Don Michie, now long departed, I drove the 100-odd miles from Darlington to swim and fish off Cape Romain in Bull Bay, midway between Charleston and Georgetown. There the mystic beauty of the Carolina seacoast held me spellbound: the scrapey rustle of palmetto leaves, the long-limbed oaks hoary with moss, the shrill sad cry of the seagulls, the curling, pounding surf, the slanting sunlight of a pine-forest cathedral (never have I walked nearer to God than there), all, all reached my very heart. Driven, as it were, to create, I expressed myself in a poem which was printed in the Charleston *News and Courier* and later reprinted in our high school newspaper. Good or bad, it proves one point: that I was even then carried away by the sound of words. Perhaps it is worth recording here:

Dawn on Cape Romain

Silver-tipp'd wings curve their solitary way
Between the marshes and the sky,
Like spectral comet on its virgin path
Across a star-lit heaven.

Full-born, the burnished ball,
The blushing debutante of morn,

Divides the silent vastness
And scatters splintering streaks of gold
Amidst the infant waves—
Waves that reach their tiny hands
And sing a simple song.

The drowsy marsh awakes . . .
   Stretches itself four ways in one,
Then softly dances in the sun,
   That heightens ere the dance is done.

Life moves to feel the sudden warmth,
To breathe the tranquil air,
Or furrow out with curved-back fins
A myriad momentary silver slits,
In tribute to the unleashed day . . .

Things big, things small,
Each—all
Do break their nightly vigil and feel free.
The day has come. . . .

I have stated that this, my first teaching year in Darlington, was one of my happiest. But, alas, not the second, third, or fourth—and therein lies a story which deserves a separate telling.

When Father died in 1919, Mother, a hapless widow with two children (my sister Ada was five years my junior), was forced by a take-it-or-leave-it offer to sell a half interest, no less, in our family drugstore to Father's pharmacist, a eunuch-voiced Uriah Heep named Fulcrum. Each year thereafter, for reasons which need no clarification, Mother's share of the profits grew gradually smaller as Fulcrum himself grew increasingly affluent in the community. Toward Mother he was coldly arrogant, even insulting. To protect her interest Mother unwittingly hired an attorney named Phellem but, again alas, it turned out that Phellem was no less skilled than Fulcrum in the game of Heads-I-Win-Tails-You-Lose, and so things got worse instead of better. By the time I returned home to teach, actually before, Mother had begun to take in "roomers" (she spoke of them as "remunerative guests") in order to make ends meet. What with the Anderson Motor Company misadventure and the declining economy following the war, the poor, frustrated little aristocrat had little choice.

After I'd been in town a few days, I went to the drugstore (where as a boy I had spent so many happy hours) and purposely walked up and down behind the counters, determined to draw Fulcrum's fire. I did, and quickly. He ordered me to get out. I refused, adding that as Mother's agent I had as much right to be there as he. With that he grabbed me by the arm and, before I realized it, we were awkwardly slugging away at each other in the narrow aisle amidst a downpour of patent medicines. I managed somehow to pin Fulcrum down, face up on the floor. I straddled him and with clenched fists pounded into his bleeding head a long overdue lesson in fair play. Had it not been for Dr. Berriman, who stopped the fight as a crowd gathered, I might have lived to rue that day. As it was, I gloated over my fisticuff success and afterwards, for as long as Fulcrum remained Mother's partner, I had free run of the drugstore—but financially the trend was downward ever downward.

While all seemed well on the surface, below level Fulcrum was stealthily plotting his course. After all, he held the trump cards. He allowed the drugstore stock to dwindle, delayed payments to wholesalers, messed up accounts collectable, and otherwise extended his own personal welfare far beyond the normal realm of a business "partnership." Meantime, if I recall correctly, he bought acreage in the county, constructed an artificial lake, and built himself a log-cabin, weekend retreat. There, he basked in all his opulent glory.

Seeing no other way out, Mother (against all advice and my pleading) bought back Fulcrum's share, a play which fit precisely into his game pattern. So, one day in the fall of 1928, as I began my second year of teaching and coaching, I suddenly found myself the untrained, unhappy manager of my Father's old drugstore which my frenetic, stubborn, hot-headed mother had bought with money raised, without my knowledge, by mortgaging our family home!

Not until I took stock and checked the ledgers did I discover that the true financial situation of the firm had been skillfully hidden. In brief, Mother had bought the bottom half of an almost empty bottle.

There is no need, I suppose, to describe the maelstrom into which I had been·so suddenly sucked, nor the impact it had upon my life during the next three miserable years. My typical day consisted of arising at six, opening the store at seven, sweeping, cleaning, and stocking until half-past eight, teaching from then until three, coaching football until six, and returning to the store for bookkeeping and clerking until ten. On Saturdays and Sundays it was seven-to-ten, straight-away, no break, with meals in a sack. My teaching and coaching worsened, my mind was a muddle, and because I lay awake night after night trying to figure a way out of my dilemma, my health suffered and my temper shortened. For me life had become a treadmill on which I worked wearily, getting nowhere, gaining nothing, losing all.

From the beginning I knew (though Mother dared not believe me) that reviving the business was hopeless. Month after month the demands of our creditors grew louder while our hypocritical, church-going customers found a thousand reasons for not paying their honest accounts (I never had the heart to refuse credit to any man who needed medicine for his sick wife or baby). Month after month I simply endorsed my personal check from the high school and forwarded it on to the wholesale drug firm which was "carrying" us. In January, 1930 our local bank closed, following the Black October stock market crash, and the store's, Mother's, and my personal deposits were swept away overnight. Now, as the walls of the Great Depression closed in on me, inexorably, I found myself in the most forlorn period of my life.

For three long years I stove off bankruptcy. Meanwhile, by correspondence and short term courses I plowed slowly ahead toward my master's degree. I knew it would at last be my salvation. In the summer of 1930, while attending Columbia University (my sister, now twenty-two, and our new pharmacist kept the store), I met Dr. Jay B. Hubbell, a visiting professor from Duke University. He told me that, if I ever wanted to try for a doctor's degree, he would help me. I returned home, his words ringing in my ears—and a year later, as the sheriff padlocked the bankrupt drugstore and subpoenaed me into court, I wrote him. Within a week I was the unbelievably proud holder of a $750 teaching fellowship in American literature at Duke. (Dr. Hubbell, now eighty-seven, has remained my friend to this day.)

It would be unfair to leave you with the idea that all was rotten in Darlington during these years. Actually, I enjoyed my teaching. My students were the most endearing young boys and girls in the world, and I shall always remember the joy they brought me. Too, I remember my friends, the three "courting couples" who, with me and mine, made up the "Eager Eightsome." We swam, fished, picnicked, hiked, and hunted together: Gladys and J.C., "Check" and Mack, Sybil and Bill, and Martha Sanders and me. Together we tramped the Pee Dee piney-woods in the autumn, shot doves near Flynn's Crossroads, spent weekends at Myrtle Beach, attended chitlin' struts, hunted Indian arrowheads in freshly plowed fields, and barbecued on the banks of beautiful Black Creek. (Legend has it that, if ever you wade in its water, you will never be happy anywhere in the world but Darlington!)

But in September, 1931 I put my old life behind me. Martha, who had come to Darlington to teach mathematics, and I married and moved to Duke. By borrowing on my insurance policy, doing without everything except the barest necessities and skipping a meal now and then (I lost twenty pounds at Duke), we managed somehow to survive. Now and then she supplemented our meager income by clerking part time in a department store (even if a teaching job had been available, the pay-off would have been in discountable "depression script"). I moonlighted by helping football players write weekly themes and by selling the university library a cache of Revolutionary War manuscripts I had unearthed near Darlington. For my dissertation I wrote a 410-page tome entitled "The Literary and Cultural Background of

Charleston, 1830–1860," two chapters of which (on the theatre and periodicals) were later expanded and issued as books.

At Duke, or so I was told, I set some sort of record for publishing several articles and stories while still a student—in *The North Carolina Historical Review, American Literature, Studies in Philology, Kansas Historical Quarterly,* and a few other places, counting a scattering of book reviews. Let me add that this accomplishment was not the result of scholastic superiority—I was just hungry.

By now, I am sure, you realize the satisfaction I reaped in being able, once again, to return to the academic arena. Twice had I been removed from the action, unhappily to sit on the sidelines, but now I was back in the game again, to the end, win or lose. Five years of my thirty-one, I thought, had been wasted in my cottonmill, rubber tire, and drugstore misadventures. Five years behind schedule I was, with a lot of catching up to do from 1934 on.

But as the months passed I began to wonder whether the time I had spent in business had really been wasted, after all. True, I had banked my scholastic furnace, but meanwhile I had learned much I could never have learned elsewhere: it's a long, long way from the silence of a college library carrel to the outcry of a sheriff's deputy. Thus, to the uncouth cottonmill "supers," the double-dealing office managers, the sniveling, fawning Uriah Heeps, and the psalm-singing debt-dodgers (including old Dr. Berriman who refused to pay his $500 account when he learned that our drugstore was failing)—to them, one and all, who have wandered in and out of my life, I owe far more than I can tell. They opened doors for me that would have remained forever closed. Along with Johnny *Reb* and Pearlie Mae and "Hook" and his Chalmers and "Knotty" and "Catfish John" and the rest, they became a part of me. Without them I would surely have viewed life from atop a cheerless ivory tower, alone and through a scholar's eyes, dully—but with them I have stood toe-to-toe on ground level, seeing their faces brighten in satirical horse-laughter and listening to their precious mother wit, rough-and-ready, sounding in my ears. And if I have somehow managed, however poorly, to blend the professional with the popular, the good with the gross, I am glad. I think that is what Morgan Walters had in mind when he called me a "literary maverick." If he had not thought so, this book would not be in your hand.

In the first draft of this preface I cut out with the above paragraph, believing that another would be anticlimactical. I had climbed the slope with you, gentle reader (as they say in the old romances), to a certain plateau and now I needed only to point the way. However, when I began gathering up the miscellaneous essays that follow, I concluded that in all fairness I should tag along a little farther (further?) or else you might wander astray. So . . .

In April, 1934 I went directly from Duke to Jacksonville State College (Alabama) to teach English in summer school, and in the fall I moved on to Birmingham-Southern College as assistant professor—at $150 and $200 a month, respectively. There, in Birmingham, I had the great good fortune of working for President Guy E. Snavely (who, now ninety-one years old, has remained my friend to this day). Indeed, it was he who influenced me, after but one year of college teaching, to make the most crucial decision of my professional career.

English teachers during the Great Depression were a dime a dozen, Dr. Snavely reminded me, but *male* librarians with good academic backgrounds were the scarcest commodity in the educational world. If I would agree, he continued, to attend the University of Chicago Graduate Library School during the summers, he would pay my expenses, appoint me librarian of the college, and double my salary to $300 a month!

To say that I lost sleep over this offer would be shearing the truth. I had sweated through years of preparation for teaching: at first the thought of forfeiting it all on a sudden seemed ridiculous, even impossible. But in the end I accepted and in the summer of 1935 I launched myself on an entirely new stream of endeavor. (Let me add that I have never regretted the decision. A good librarian is a good teacher and good teaching affects eternity—and that's pretty much the whole idea in a nutshell, isn't it? In any case, I have found librarianship a most rewarding career.)

In the fall of 1937, following Dr. Snavely's resignation, my wife and I and our two-year old Martha (see pages 160–163) moved to Baylor University (which I heartily disliked), then, two years later, to North Texas State University (which I dearly liked) and then, five years later, to the University of Alabama where, in August, 1944, I became director of libraries under President Raymond R. Paty.

Meantime, my yen for writing never slackened. If anything, it became more compelling as time passed and my bibliography lengthened. In addition to articles and books, I conducted weekly book review programs over WBRC (Birmingham) and WACO (Waco), wrote literary columns for the Birmingham *News* and the Waco *Tribune-Herald,* served as book review editor of *Alabama: News Magazine of the Deep South,* and was a special literary correspondent of the Dallas *Morning News.* Despite these several activities, far fewer of my efforts were published than were filed in wastebaskets from Alabama to Texas and back to Alabama again (when I think of this I also think a macabre thought: since Earth began many more people now lie beneath than ever trod her surface.) But, all together, in these times I was not unfortunate. Taking as my subjects anything that interested me—I repeat, *anything*—I published wherever I could and for whatever the pay-off. To emphasize my catholicity (please forgive

[25]

me), I feel obliged to mention such articles as those about ponies in *Progressive Farmer*, colleges in war-time in *Holland's Magazine*, house-building in *American Home*, voluptuous Texas females and Edgar Allan Poe in *Sir!* (pages 184–189, 121–123), geriatrics in *Facts* (pages 270–272), four-edge paintings in *Field and Stream*, "Father Was an Author" and "Uncle Stin Was a Hero" in *Esquire* (pages 247–250, 297–302), and "Non-Smokers Have Some Rights . . . Too!" in the *Birmingham News Monthly Magazine* (pages 325–327). By contrast, I was simultaneously being published in *The American Scholar* (pages 238–247), *Saturday Review of Literature* (pages 201–203), and in numerous educational and professional journals, such as *Library Quarterly, Journal of Higher Education, School and Society, Shakespeare Association Bulletin, Journal of Southern History, Childhood Education, Southwest Review, Library Journal*, and *Journal of Liberal Religion*.

In 1936 my first full-length monograph, *Charleston Periodicals . . .* (with a foreword by Jay B. Hubbell) appeared, followed by *Sam Slick in Texas . . .* (with a foreword by J. Frank Dobic) in 1945, *The Ante-Bellum Charleston Theatre* (1946), *Alias Simon Suggs . . .* (1952) which was dedicated to our younger daughter, six-year-old Elizabeth, "without whose constant collaboration this biography could have been completed in less than half the time", *The James Boys Rode South* (1955), *Vizetelly Covers the Confederacy* (1957), *Alabama Tories . . .* (1960), and *Lawley Covers the Confederacy* and *Four Years in the Confederate Navy* (both in 1964).

By now—if you're still with me—you're probably cursing me for cataloguing my own accomplishments in this fashion. I don't fault you, for there is no reading duller than a librarian's catalogue. But the truth is, I am lost in my own literary labyrinth! Trapped in my own machination! I need help! I see no way out for *myself*, except to keep plugging away title by title, paragraph after paragraph, trying first this escape and then that, probing here and there, hoping that sooner or later I will plunge into open field, free and loose. As for *you*, you have a choice: you can slam the book shut and cowardly sneak away like a thief in the night, unhonored and unsung, forever to be hounded by a quitter's remorse, *or* you can skip over the next three paragraphs, *or* you can come along with me, head high, proud, gallant to the end, and . . . oh! thank you—I knew you would!

Well, during these fruitful years, when I was so busily occupied as author and editor, I was also carrying on as chief librarian of three campuses of the University of Alabama (Tuscaloosa, Birmingham, and Huntsville) and four off-campus centers (Mobile, Montgomery, Dothan, and Gadsden). Some idea of the responsibility involved in the operation of this state-wide spread may be suggested by the extreme distances alone: it is 160 miles from Tuscaloosa to Huntsville, 220 miles to Mobile, and 275 to Dothan. Frequent trips by car to all seven stations, especially to the three campuses, were mandatory and monotonous, growing more so as the several libraries grew even larger, and staff, service, and support responsibilities increased proportionately. (For the record: when I came to Alabama in 1944 the total book collection numbered 234,834 volumes; the staff 26; and the total budget, $107,700. In 1968–1969, the final year of operation under the single administrative umbrella, the respective totals were 1,402,777; 137; and $1,497,539).

Despite my mounting managerial duties, I somehow found time in this interlude to serve as editor of *The Alabama Review*, official journal of the state historical association, for its first twenty volumes (1948–1967), of *The Southeastern Librarian* (1952), of the Confederate Centennial Studies (twenty-seven monographs, 1956–1965), and as co-editor of the South Atlantic Modern Language Association *Bulletin* (1947–1952) and *Good Reading*, an organ of the National Council of Teachers of English (1945–1955). Other editorial assignments during this period included *The North Texas Union List of Serials* (1943), two editions of *A Classified List of Books and Periodicals for College Libraries* for the Southern Association of Colleges (1947, 1955), three volumes of *The Annals of Northwest Alabama* (1958, 1959, 1965) for Congressman Carl Elliott, and *Foreign Newspapers in Southeastern Libraries* for the Association of Southeastern Research Libraries (1963). Between 1958 and 1968 I also edited for publication four volumes on the Confederate War and one on World War II: Justus Scheibert's *Seven Years in the Rebel States* ... (1958), John L. Hunnicutt's *Reconstruction in West Alabama* ... (1959), Charles Girard's *A Visit to the Confederate States in 1863* (1962), Paul Pecquet du Bellet's *Diplomacy of the Confederate Cabinet* ... (1963), and *And Still We Conquer: The Diary of a Nazi Unteroffizier in the German Africa Corps* (1968).

In my spare time, as it were, I also contributed sixteen articles and seventy-nine book reviews to *The Alabama Review*, wrote reports on survey studies made of twenty-three college, university, and public libraries in Texas, Louisiana, Mississippi, Florida, North Carolina, and Alabama, co-authored a study of the use of automation in Alabama libraries, wrote a confidential (yet unpublished) history of the National Defense Education Act of 1958 for the U.S. Office of Education, spent almost six months in England, Scotland, Ireland, and Wales, studying libraries under a Fulbright Research Grant, and between 1957 and 1968 served as writer-consultant to the U.S. House of Representatives Committee on Education, the U.S. Office of Education, the President's National Advisory Commission on Libraries (see pages 327ff), and the U.S. Department of Commerce for which, in 1968, I wrote and published a document called *New Technology and the American Economy*.

[27]

Somewhere, during one of his thoughtful but long-winded addresses, I think it was "Of Kings' Treasuries," John Ruskin stepped beside the lectern to ask his listeners for a show of hands as to whether they were with him or against him. At this juncture I feel like doing the same, for I have many times gamboled afar in this prefatory memoir and even now am having difficulty in bringing it to a dead halt. One thing I have learned for sure: it is easier to write about recollections of the long ago than it is to describe events of the here and now. Perhaps my solution then, is simply to stop writing and start talking, for strictly speaking a book is little more than permanent conversation or, if you prefer, crystalized communication. If one has something he believes worth saying (actually, it may be useful or useless), something different, perhaps, but something that he and he alone can say, then the best way to say it is to *talk* it, candidly and straightaway.

Well, in the late fifties, when things were pretty much going my way, my wife went down with carcinoma and the spring of 1960 left me as both father and mother to our fifteen-year-old Elizabeth, still in junior high school (our older daughter had earned a bachelor's and master's degree and moved to Atlanta). Suddenly my little, little world turned topsy-turvy. I had never shopped for groceries, shared in a carpool, done the laundry, or combed and plaited a teenager's hair—but you'd be surprised how quickly you can learn to do these and a thousand other housewifely chores when the chips are down.

And, you'd also be surprised at how suddenly an eligible widower who owns his own home, holds a locally prestigious position, and carries a check-book can become an object of purient compassion among unattached females in his province. Out of nowhere they came, one after the other, all shapes and sizes, bearing baked chickens, cakes, nicknacks, and hot covered dishes (I wouldn't touch that pun with a ten-foot pole), each willing and eager to sew on shirt buttons, wash dishes, vacuum a rug, or *make* a bed.

One particularly buxom, high-spirited grass widow, driver of a cream-colored Cadillac with crimson upholstery, pulled up in my parkway one hot August afternoon while I was mowing the lawn. Whisperingly, she said she just happened to be *passing by* and wondered if there was anything she could do to make me comfy! Now, that, I told myself, was mighty considerate of her—so, I invited her to come in out of the heat. After coffee and cookies, I soon learned that her first tale about making me comfy was all A.O.K. But, frankly, I never have quite understood her second tale, because my home is at the far turn-around of a dead-end street and there's no way on God's green earth she could have just been "passing by," even allowing for her magnanimous contribution to my personal comfort. A few days later another such caller, lugging a large casserole filled to the gunwales with hot shrimp creole, knocked on my back door early one

[28]

morning. To the best of my recollection I had never seen her before, but to this day I admire her brazen approach. After a few preliminaries, mostly small talk, of course, she threw her shoulders back and drew a deep breath (which immediately produced certain bodily mutations) and said frankly in one-two-three order, obviously rehearsed, that she wanted the worst in the world to remarry and supposed I did also, and that she had come around to lay her, well, her *case* before me, without restrictions. In short, like Barcus, she was willing. I was too taken aback to register details, but I think she added something about owning her own home and a small annuity—but, generally speaking, the remainder of the "interview" is still somewhat foggy, despite her disarming devices.

Now, I know that the way to a man's heart is via his stomach, and all that, but it seems to me that when a man is in the market for a mate, especially a second mate, he should be unfettered and absolutely free to determine his own destiny. That reminds me to say that, when I was a boy growing up, my Father repeatedly cautioned me to look out for myself. Every tub must stand on its own bottom, he said—admittedly an old saw, but to me, his adoring young son, a proverb spoken by the wisest man on earth. I have tried hard to live by that maxim, even to the extent of refusing for years to participate in Social Security. Father had taught me to save, to be ready for a rainy day, to be prepared always to take care of myself and my own (nobody else would do it, he added wryly), and the thought that I would ever wind up as a ward of "the Government" was nauseating beyond expression. But, as is often the case with would-be iconoclasts, in the end I surrendered to the pressures of current society and queued up with all the other robots, no longer a name but a statistic: *Claim Number* 419–48–8595 ("Keep this card. Carry it with you. Property of the United States Government!"). All these things I did mechanically—trends of the times, you know—but when it came to choosing a woman to share the rest of my life with me, Father's old adage was ever in my mind, no matter how comfy the Cadillac, how tasty the shrimp creole.

Weighty matters such as this have an uncanny way of working themselves out, even for widowers, if one is just calm and patient. (My Mother's way of saying that was "Everything happens for the best.") For me patience paid off happily in the person of a long-time friend and favorite—Addie Shirley Coleman with whom I had actually been in love long before I had the gumption to admit it. A gracious, generous and lovable lady, she had been a helpmeet and confidante of my ailing wife, a godsend to my motherless young daughter during her most trying years of adolescence, and she had nursed me back from a miocardial infarction. Now, as you well know, the truly genteel have a way of ingratiating themselves into your heart, without flourish

[29]

or design, slowly, ever slowly, until they at last become a part of your very life and all of a sudden your winter of discontent turns into a perfectly delightful springtime of peaceful lovingkindness (*lovingkindness:* the most beautiful word in the English language). So it was with me. And on the last day of May, 1970 Addie and I were married at home, with only our families and dearest friends present, and immediately flew away for a three months' work-holiday in Europe.

I say *work*-holiday advisedly, because I had been awarded a sabbatical leave with grant-in-aid from the University of Alabama to study the activities of the Confederate Ordnance Department in the British Isles, Belgium, France, Spain, and Portugal—and the trip was thus a combination honeymoon and research assignment, share and share alike. Our happiness was boundless.

And, now, at long last, I believe it fitting and proper to end this discourse by reminding you again of the sobriquet Morgan Walters laid on me in the beginning. If anything, I am as much a literary maverick today, in late 1972, as ever I was. If not, how could I ever explain that now, having resigned my post as dean of the University of Alabama Libraries (after twenty-seven years' service), I am dividing my time among teaching in our new Graduate School of Library Service, and researching, editing, and writing. I have recently published John Low's *Logs of the C.S.S. Alabama and the C.S.S. Tuscaloosa, 1862–1863*, written a book (*Florida Territory in 1844*) and four articles (one for *The American Neptune*, three for *The Alabama Review*), and begun another book (*The Confederate Career of Colonel Edward C. Anderson*), all under the auspices of the University of Alabama Research Grants Committee. In addition, I have put the final editorial touches on *A Catalogue of the Yucatán Imprints on Microfilm in the University of Alabama Libraries* and appraised a few manuscripts for the University of Alabama Press. Somehow, in my "off" hours, I take time to do a spot of ghost-writing, inventory my personal library, research for a popular-type biography of Rube Burrow, "King of Alabama Train Robbers," and withal steal a few moments to putter about in my rose garden. For the life of me I couldn't tell you which gives me the greatest pleasure!

But, alas, there is so very, very much left to be done—and for me so very, very little time in which to do it. . . .

University of Alabama   W. Stanley Hoole

WE WHO TEACH*

Library Journal, April 1, 1947 and *Southern Association Quarterly* May, 1947.

One of the most significant problems involved in the improvement of instruction centers about our failure as professional educators to teach man to live intelligently with good books.

Teaching is one of the world's oldest professions. Yet during the countless centuries we have devoted to the art, we have somehow ingloriously fallen short of knighting our students with the zeal for self-mastery through reading. Otherwise, perhaps, we have successfully guarded our realm. Certainly, we have faithfully devised many new methods and mechanics to defend it. Meanwhile, in our efforts we have turned our fickled attention from one new system to another, glossing each over in its own time with apt and nice terminology. From all our assembled philosophies there doubtless arises a certain professional grandeur. But the fact remains, we will admit, that in all our esoteric experiments we have not up to this hour fulfilled our major responsibility to society of inspiring students to want to live understandingly with the best that has been said and thought in the world.

Our secondary school colleagues tell us that an uncommonly high percentage of their pupils laboriously decipher one by one the words of a printed page, trying in vain to piece the puzzle together into a rational whole. College classrooms are likewise filled with memorizers and readers by rote, their tragedy being greater merely because it is of longer duration. All of them, as the saying goes, are still learning to read, not reading to learn. The living spark of the true reader, the genius of critical thought, is missing. They who have never sent a ship out wait at the dock for their ship to come in.

As in writing books with a pen of fire, there is also a way of reading books creatively. No one doubts the joy of surprise that is the reader's as he comes upon a thought out of the past that is his own thought, lying in wait to be said. Nor would we deny the way his heart leaps

---

*An address delivered before a joint meeting of the Commissions on Institutions of Higher Education, Secondary Schools, and Curricular Problems and Research of the Southern Association of Colleges and Secondary Schools, December 10, 1946.

[31]

up when he falls suddenly upon a new-found idea which, with foresight, he stores aside against a rainy day. This we would call flush-reading, hunting, as it were, without a dog. The true reader is better equipped. He brings to the printed page an inventive mind, remembering that the book before him yields dividends only in proportion to his deposits and that the thoughts he reads become alive and luminous only in so far as he conveys to these thoughts the matching genius of his own creativeness.

We who teach are sometimes wont to run around in circles, packing the good but dull earth of our humanities, of our liberal or general learning. We often disagree on principles. Even our definitions are vague, nebulous, often meaningless. Surely the day must come when we who stand on the record as advocating the book will be forced to abandon our platitudes and get down to an analysis of exactly what we have to offer man in his search for truth. And that, unless we are sadly mistaken, will be man's self-reliance upon the originality of his own mind. Nothing we do can change the past, but the future lies before us to shape as we will. Today we read but the "first verse of the first chapter of a book whose pages are infinite."

We who teach, we are told, live in a backward-looking world. The moonglow of the past falls bewitchingly upon it and our eyes are blinded by the sun of the present. Everywhere about us, from waking to sleeping, is the book, the testimony of man's achievement up to our time. This acheivement we honor, for it is the foundation upon which we build. But honoring is not enough. To this great heritage, the legacies of yesterday, we must apply generation after generation the beneficience of our own thought, interpreting yesterday's attainment in the light of today's newer truth. Our responsibility, as teachers, therefore, in the spirit of inquest is to get; but it is our larger responsibility in the spirit of conquest to give. For we want the future to be better than the present, just as we believe, perhaps naively, the present to be better than the past.

The responsibility of directing students to an intelligent use of good books rests squarely upon the shoulders of all of us, the executive, the librarian, and the teacher. Each in his own way has an important role to play. However, it is primarily the teacher who holds the power to unleash and energize the thoughts that well spontaneously from the open and eager minds of those for whom we labor.

Successful teaching is not a matter of methodology. Nor is it merely a matter of erudition. The talent for good teaching consists, also, of an enthusiastic desire for communicating to others those ideas we believe to be ennobling, and of wanting those ideas eternally challenged by the living spark of creative thought. So long as we drain from truth yet another measure just so long will our end-product be pure and imperishable. The moment we cease to teach our students to read thoughtfully and critically, encouraging them to fall wholly back upon the book, at that moment the book becomes a dogmatic tyrant to stifle and dwarf us and at last to render us impotent. There are more errors to be found in print than anywhere else on earth. The enlightened reader is he who refuses to believe anything simply because he saw it in a book. And the teacher to beware is the teacher with one text.

The stimulation of students to self-education through intelligent reading is a primary duty of every teacher. It is also the crowning glory of our profession, for we who teach must realize that we are at best but envoys of truth, not truth itself.

Unless we proclaim, therefore, unreservedly the virtue and strength of good books in the improvement of instruction, resolving always to bring them and our students closer and closer together, we fail to fulfill a major obligation to the society which sanctions our continuance.

OF THE AUTHOR-LIBRARIAN

Printed in *Stechert-Hafner Book News*, New York City,
May, 1952 (reprinted in *ALA Bulletin*, April, 1953
and in *Books*, *Libraries*, and *Librarians*, Hamden, Conn.: Shoe String Press, 1955).

Before attempting to discuss what the librarian should publish, it may be wise for us first to consider a few of the principal reasons why he should publish at all. In so doing we may bring into focus the kind of matter most desirable of publication. For what one publishes and why one publishes are virtually indistinguishable, as inseparable as man and his style of writing. To attempt to divorce them would be foolish: the style is the man and the man is his idea. Thus, if we would determine whether a man is justified in impinging his ideas upon other men through the medium of print, we must first examine the motives which prompt him to wish to be so altruistic or so audacious or so naïve.

The one most powerful force that impels a librarian to put his ideas into print, we think, is the same that drives any other writer—a sincere ardor to communicate to others what he himself has found to be interesting, informational, or ennobling. Considered thus, there is little or no difference, except in kind, between the motive that prompts the writer to publish, the teacher to teach, the singer to sing, or the actor to act, for in each the talent for telling consists not only of erudition but also of enthusiasm for sharing his discoveries, beliefs, or practices with others with whom he enjoys, or thinks he enjoys, an intellectual kinship. About his efforts, then, there is a definitely genuine missionary spirit. Sharing one's ideas with others by publishing them is a joyous and exciting experience equalled in the educative process only by the desire to acquire new ideas for further sharing. The sincere writing man with an idea may thus be likened unto the child with a new toy. Half the fun comes with exhibiting it proudly to the kid next door.

But that is not bad. In writing, as in other creative activities, little is to be gained by hiding one's light under a bushel. (History proves that even the diarist who professed to divulge his innermost thoughts to himself alone cynically trusted that one day his manuscript would be "discovered" or decoded for the benefit of a startled but needy world.) Only by boldly, proudly sending forth his ideas to be scrutinized and criticized can the writer ever test their validity. If they meet with approval, a challenge has been won. If they fail, the challenge yet remains. In either case the author is victorious. For, as the mere act of seeing his meditations reach permanency in print afforded him his first satisfying experience, so did he earn a second success, if the ideas he sponsored were found acceptable. Even if he received only scorn for his efforts, his anguish may be somewhat assuaged by the fact that he fairly delineated his beliefs and, as a sincere writing man, he will not fail to continue his crusade or to profit by his honest mistakes. Moreover, the writing man, whether or not he is a librarian, but particularly if he is, is more often than not an orderly, systematic individual and to him the very mustering and organization of ideas is in itself a pleasurable exercise. Organization is a form of creativeness. It is not difficult, indeed, to believe that an author frequently undergoes genuine enjoyment simply by plotting his thoughts, even if he never touches his pen. And as his ideas gradually emerge from a first dark vagueness into the bright light of clarity, he tingles to a warmth of self-satisfaction. Thus may we say that, win, lose, or draw, publication is the only means at a writer's disposal for whetting his ideas against the flint of public opinion.

If the author is connected with an institution of learning, as most librarians are, his pride of publication pushes on beyond the boundaries of self, of course, to include the entire community of scholars of which he is a member. No longer merely personal, then, his joy becomes communal, for by his own labors has he played a part in enhancing the prestige of his fellows as well as of himself. Beyond even that there yet lies his pride of profession—and he is triply content to have proved his worth to all, at home and abroad, by perpetuating and increasing, if but by an iota, their common fund of knowledge. And that, as everyone knows, is an important element of scholarship.

Among the reasons why a librarian should write for publication there are several, as you may fancy, which must be frankly recognized as neither generous, glamorous, nor noble. They are down-to-earth and they are crass, but they are decent and they are important. However strong may be the librarian's pride or his desire to pass along or test his ideas, he must confess that seldom does he pursue the profession of librarianship solely because he is enamoured of it. Lurking in the shadow of his altruistic devotion to duty is the cold-blooded yearning to become as affluent as possible in his job. Whatever he can do, therefore, within the bounds of professional ethics to enhance the value of his services, he will do, and rightly. There are few librarians who would doubt that, pure though their intentions as the driven snow, the motive which often propels them to put pen to paper is the prestige of promotion, whether by that is meant a better position or a better salary, or both.

Authorship is a wily and seductive maid, however, and the writer must be on constant guard against her trickeries. The urge to share one's ideas with others, as we have observed, is a fascinating experience. It may also be an intoxicant, a powerful, habit-forming narcotic which drugs the author and goads him on beyond reason. Under these conditions, publishing one's writings, like teaching one's ideas or singing one's songs, may be looked upon as an almost wholly selfish endeavor, a balm for the ego, a stimulus to that consciousness which would distinguish the individual from other selves, setting him apart as the one to be admired and desired by the mass. In the extreme the enjoyment received from having others pay obeisance to one's thoughts, whether oral or written, may actually approach the libidinal. Indeed, it is not inconceivable to suppose that in this strange process the writer or teacher may emerge as one whose self-assertion is but a guise to hide a struggle for self-preservation. Communicable ardor, the motivating force which so honestly prompted the writing man in the first place, may then in certain climates deteriorate him to the lowest level of intellectual vainglory and personal conceit.

Therefore, it behooves the writer to be eternally vigilant. He must be wary of the underlying motives which spur him to publication and he must be sure that his immediate eagerness to rush into print is not premised on some flimsy, inconsequential idea which will turn out to be but dull drivel, sophomoric, unimportant, and a discredit to his name and his profession.

This observation seems particularly applicable here, as we examine the profession of librarianship. Too often do librarians with half-baked thoughts and raw skill burn with a passion to publish—and although we might with equal truth level that charge against our kinsmen in other learned professions, the fact that they too are guilty does not render our sins less scarlet. For years now we have filled our journals with professional pap, the quality of which often makes the conscientious among us blush for shame. Except in certain noteworthy instances, the welter of books and articles which have appeared under the banner of librarianship since the founding of our national associa-

[35]

tion in 1876, have been mostly petty and largely of the trade-journal, house-organ level. Indeed, one could almost count on his fingers and toes those of great and lasting value which have stood the test of time and are yet considered profound and indispensable. As an unhappy result, in seventy-five years and more of faith in librarianship we have failed to create a substantial fund of important professional literature, a basic, solid professional literature rich in intellectual content. If ever we wish honestly to know precisely why librarianship does not everywhere enjoy that high degree of academic respectability we so much desire for it, let us search our writings for the only quality by which any profession may claim that respectability—intellectual content in its own right. Then will we know. To confess this today is bitter for us all, but think of the bitterness of tomorrow's librarians, if we continue to fail for another seventy-five years to give learned substance to our publications.

In writing it is far easier to stoop to mediocrity than to rise to goodness and the librarian who either has nothing to say or who lacks the skill to say something well should bravely and unselfishly ignore the call of authorship. But there are among us many who are blessed with both art and wit and to them, the author-librarians, there are open at least four major fields of literary endeavor. None of the fields is new and each has already attracted the attention of men of merit, as we well know. Yet, in each there remain rich, undeveloped areas, waiting to be mined.

The first is of course the strictly professional field of pure and applied librarianship. Here the names of such stalwarts as Melvil Dewey, Charles A. Cutter, Arthur E. Bostwick, Margaret Mann come first to mind, but the list could readily be extended. Their publications have laid a solid foundation upon which the future structure must be built, if librarianship is to endure and prosper. And no one could possibly underestimate the need for sound scholarship in this important, under-girding area of our work. Is it wholly unreasonable to suppose that the scholar-librarian of the future may produce an entirely different approach to the classification of knowledge? Some day, will the genius of scientific discovery aid him in yet undreamed-of interpretations of the printed word?

Closely allied to these library "scientists" are these men and women who have singled out bibliography as their forte: giants like William F. Poole, William I. Fletcher, Henry B. van Hoesen, Isadore Mudge, Earl G. Swem, Anne M. Boyd, and more recently, Clarence S. Brigham, Winifred Gregory, Constance Winchell, A. Frederick Kuhlman, Robert B. Downs, Jessee H. Shera and Frederic J. Mosher. It would be very difficult to find a richer field of literary endeavor for the practicing librarian than bibliography: literally hundreds of subject, descriptive, and annotated bibliographies, to say nothing of national, regional, state, and local manuals, checklists, union lists, finding lists, and guides to collections are urgently needed everywhere in our profession. The surface has scarcely been scratched. In all kinds of libraries, large and small, scholarship of this type fairly cries out for attention. It is perhaps the one most natural outlet for the normal talents of librarianship.

But many librarians, those with uncommon talent, discontent to confine their publishing efforts to the somewhat limited fields of applied librarianship or bibliography, have turned to other disciplines, to the broader reaches of subject matters in the humanities and the several sciences. Here do we find the historian-librarian, the economist-librarian, the sociologist-librarian, the scientist-librarian, the litterateur-librarian, those who have reflected great glory on librarianship through their mastery of other subject specialties. More frequently than not, however, they merge their subjects with librarianship or manage most skillfully to turn back and forth from the nonlibrary to the library discipline with apparent ease and great success. In these broad, varied and extremely fruitful areas the list of librarians extraordinary is long and distinguished: Reuben G. Thwaites, William W. Bishop, Harry M. Lydenberg, Justin Winsor, Josephus N. Larned, and more recently, Louis Round Wilson, Luther Evans, Lawrence C. Powell, Julian Boyd, and Stanley Pargellis, to name but a handful. Surely, for the scholar-librarian the world is his oyster. And one very small world, indeed, if we may dare particularize, is that of local history. However many histories of the 3,069 counties in the nation have been adequately and expertly written we do not know; but we believe that the large definitive history of the United States may never be completed until these smaller single studies are competently done. And who should be better equipped in many counties to pen them than the local librarian?

The fourth major field of literary endeavor which beckons the librarian is the creative, that of the fictionist, the essayist, the biographer, and the poet. Admittedly, one might wish this list of names in this class much longer, but librarians may claim as theirs Frances Newman, the distinguished Georgia novelist who died in her prime, and Carolyn Wells, who somewhat proudly devoted several pages of her autobiography, *The Rest of My Life*, to her career as librarian of the Rahway (N.J.) Public Library. J. Christian Bay is famous as a folklorist, and James K. Hosmer, Lawrence C. Wroth, Reuben A. Guild, Josephus N. Larned, Oscar G. T. Sonneck, and Bernard C. Steiner have won renown as biographers. All are librarians to be proud of as are Siddie Jo Johnson, Anne Carroll Moore, Janet Gray, Eleanor Estes, and Charlie May Simon, who have made their marks in the world of creative

[37]

literature for children. And certainly we must not forget Archibald MacLeish, and Arthur M. Sampley who in 1950 was named by the state legislature Poet Laureate of Texas.

Obviously, librarians who write and publish cannot be so neatly packaged as we have attempted here. For at once the same names keep appearing on more than one list and any single name might well have been placed in another category. Moreover, we have not paid proper tribute to those author-librarians whose efforts have led them into other important areas of endeavor, such as editing, translating, surveying, cartography, printing, anthology, or even floriculture and entomology and other widely divergent fields.

Whatever his avenue of interest, the writing librarian, like the missionary, as we have already insinuated, needs first of all to be filled with zeal to serve his fellow man. For him, though, as for the missionary, zeal alone is not enough. Each must have an appreciation of approaches, as it were, a workable understanding of the rudiments and the ways and means which distinguish his vocation from all others. So must the missionary be grounded in theology, the librarian in the special sciences of his profession. But neither theology nor techniques is the *summum bonum*, as the missionary or the librarian would be quick to acknowledge. Both are often but window-dressings or trade secrets, the means to the desired ends, and seldom if ever the ends in themselves. The real thing for each is breadth and depth of scholarship, a solid bedrock of learning that reaches down beneath the sand of professional trivia. And that, buttressed with talent, endurance, and stubbornness will produce the kind of author-librarian we all desire.

SHAKESPEARE ON THE ANTE-BELLUM CHARLESTON STAGE

The Shakespeare Quarterly,
New York City, January, 1946.

Charleston's early theatrical history, considered by students of the drama to be as noteworthy as that of any other American city, is said to have begun *circa* 1703 when Anthony Aston, a playwright, arrived in the southern seaport "full of Lice, Shame, Poverty, Nakedness, and Hunger— . . . turned *Player* and *Poet* and wrote one Play on the Subject of the Country." Not for thirty years, however, was the walled city to have a formal theatre—the well-known Dock Street Theatre, America's third playhouse. But between its opening, February 12, 1736, and the Civil War at least six additional theatres were erected, the last two (in 1793 and 1837, respectively) with seating capacities of 1200 each, yet the total white population of the city in 1800 was but 9000 and in 1860 had reached only 23,000.

In the eighteenth century Shakespeare's plays received some little attention at the hands of Charleston's theatrical producers. On April 12 and May 10, 1763, *Romeo and Juliet* and *King Lear* were presented by the David Douglass American Company; and in the 1773–1774 season twelve of Shakespeare's plays were acted sixteen times, including (April 20, 1774) the first American production of *Julius Caesar*.

It was not until the turn of the century, however, when the "star" system, or players on special engagement, was introduced, that Shakespeare received fullest attention on the Charleston stage.

Between 1800 and 1860 the theatre (or theatres) of the city were annually opened for "Fall and Winter Seasons" which usually began in October or November and lasted until May or June. A regular stock company, consisting of from ten to thirty members, performed almost nightly throughout the season, themselves taking all roles or, during the engagement of a special player, acting as supporting cast.

That Shakespeare's plays were popular with ante-bellum Charleston audiences is putting it conservatively. Twenty-three of his dramas were produced for a total of 646 times between 1800–1860. Among them was the first American presentation of *A Winter's Tale*, April 1, 1811. Although the works of scores of other leading British and American dramatists were acted in the city, not one of these authors was able to keep pace with the Poet in either the frequency of presentation of any one play or the total number of performances of all plays. Dunlap's (or Smith's) *Pizarro* was presented 88 times, 1800–1858; Bulwer-Lytton's *The Lady of Lyons* 84 times, 1838–1860; Sheridan's *The School for Scandal* 74 times, 1801–1857; and John Tobin's *The Honeymoon* 71 times, 1805–1857. Other oft-performed plays include Dunlap's *The Stranger* (70), Kenney's *Raising the Wind* (61), Coleman's *The Review* and Bickerstaff's *The Spoil'd Child* (each 56), O'Keeffe's *The Poor Soldier* (49), Knowles' *The Hunchback* (48), and Kemble's *The Day after the Wedding* (45).

The following table gives the title and number of performances of each of Shakespeare's plays presented on the Charleston stage between 1800–1860.

PLAYS	1800-1819	1820-1839	1840-1860	Total
Anthony and Cleopatra	0	0	4	4
As You Like It	4	4	13	21
The Comedy of Errors	0	7	6	13
Coriolanus	3	6	1	10
Cymbeline	2	0	0	2
Hamlet	20	19	41	80
Henry IV	8	5	7	20
Henry VIII	3	2	2	7

Julius Caesar	2	8	1	11
King John	1	3	0	4
King Lear	5	10	11	26
Love's Labor Lost	0	0	1	1
Macbeth	24	17	34	75
The Merchant of Venice	7	18	22	47
The Merry Wives of Windsor	7	6	6	13
Much Ado About Nothing	8	14	14	36
Othello	15	21	27	63
Richard III	18	32	40	90
Romeo and Juliet	15	19	29	63
The Taming of the Shrew	19	12	19	50
The Tempest	3	2	0	5
Twelfth Night	0	0	3	3
The Winter's Tale	2	0	0	2
	141	193	267	646

In addition to the above legitimate productions there were many alterations and adaptations of Shakspeare's plays. Not the least important were *Shakespeare's Jubilee*, a "grand olio" in which acts or scenes from several of the plays were performed, and *Man and Wife*, or *Shakespeare's Jubilee* (Coleman). *Chaos Is Come Again*, based on *Othello* (III, 3, 92), was presented twice in one month, and there were frequent presentations of such farces, travesties and interludes as *All the World's a Stage* (Jackman), *To Be or Not To Be, Richard Number III* (Durivage), *Richard III on Horseback, Hamlet Travestie* (Poole), *Othello Travestie*, and *The Merchant of Smyrna*, an afterpiece perhaps based on *The Merchant of Venice*.

It may be supposed that the repetition of Shakespeare on the antebellum Charleston stage reflects in some measure the dramatic tastes of the cultured seaport, yet it must be remembered that some of these dramas may have been presented, not necessarily because of the demands of a discriminating audience, but because they included the favorite roles of the nationally or internationally famous visiting players. In such cases it was doubtless the star and not the vehicle that attracted patrons.

From April 14, 1805, when Thomas Apthorpe Cooper's *Hamlet* inaugurated the visiting star system, and April 2, 1860, when Edwin Booth and Julia Dean joined to play *Romeo and Juliet*, the Charleston theatres were continually visited by such outstanding actors and actresses of the English-speaking stage as Junius Brutus Booth, Edwin Forrest, Edmund Kean, James Hackett, James and Henry Wallack, Charles William Macready, Edward L. Davenport, Charles Dibden

Pitt, James E. Murdoch, George Vandenhoff, John Drew, John H. Dwyer, Clare Fisher, Fanny Fitzwilliams, Fanny Davenport, Anna Cora Mowatt, Annette Ince, and Eliza Logan. Each of course had one or more of Shakespeare's plays in his repertoire. And between special engagements the regular stock, which from year to year included one or more widely known players, also performed Shakespeare to a seemingly never tiring clientele.

Although stage histories of other southern cities are lamentably incomplete, a comparison of Shakespeare's plays presented in Charleston with those acted during one decade in Nashville and two decades in Richmond suggests that the dramatist was extremely popular throughout the entire ante-bellum South. Indeed, famous stars "on tour" usually played the same roles from city to city. The frequency with which *Richard III, Hamlet, Macbeth, Othello, Romeo and Juliet* and other choice "starring roles" were offered reemphasizes the supposition that the player and not always the play was "the thing."

ALABAMA:
DRAMA OF RECONCILIATION

The Alabama Review, Alabama Historical Association, University of Alabama and Auburn University, April, 1966.

Manager A. M. Palmer of the Madison Square Theatre, New York City, having suffered a financial loss on several English plays during the fall of 1891, courageously decided to offer the public an all-American drama. He chose *Alabama* which had been written only three months before by one of his utility players, Augustus Thomas, a native of St. Louis, Missouri. Much to the amazement of the author, the producer, and virtually everyone else connected with its presentation, the four-act "Tale of the Sunny South" proved an immediate success. It recuperated Palmer's losses, established Thomas as a leading native playwright, and through its direct appeal for mutual understanding and respect between the North and the South did much to re-unite the nation which only thirty years before had been torn apart by war and reconstruction.

The locale of *Alabama* is an old plantation home near the thriving little town of Talladega, Alabama. The time is May, 1880. The story is simple, sentimental, satisfying, and appealingly told in natural, witty, easy dialogue. Mrs. Page, a widow, and her son Lathrop are threatened by a relative, Raymond Page, who claims their property on which a railroad is to be built, alleging that her marriage was disputable. Harry Preston, a railroad executive and son of unreconstructed old Colonel Preston and now much changed and unrecognized and known as Captain Davenport, suddenly returns home after a long absence in the North. In love with Mrs. Page, he alone holds the proof that will clear her fair name. Meanwhile, Harry's own daughter, Carey, whom he has never seen, falls in love with Ned Armstrong, Harry's assistant. Colonel Moberly takes up Colonel Preston's quarrel and challenges Raymond Page to a duel which is averted by Harry Preston. Page is subsequently proved the villain and, as Harry reveals his true identity, he and Mrs. Page, Carey and Armstrong, and Lathrop and Colonel Moberly's daughter Atlanta are triply betrothed, the railroad land sale benefits the true owners, and Southerners and Northerners alike rejoice.

In his autobiography, *The Print of My Remembrance* (1922), Augustus Thomas declared that the original idea for *Alabama* was suggested to him by Palmer who once spent a night in Talladega and was impressed with the rustic beauty of the town. Later, in 1885, when Thomas was a member of a traveling theatrical company playing his own *Editha's Burglar*, he too visited Talladega (en route to the "busy little city of Birmingham, Alabama") where he saw a ruined, fallen gateway which had proudly stood at the entrance to an old ante-bellum mansion. And six years afterwards, in January, 1891, as he tossed sleeplessly in his bed at the Lamb's Club in New York City, the symbolic scene reappeared in his mind's eye:

> At the piano downstairs E. M. Holland was playing a melody, then popular, called 'Down on the Farm'.... I could see before me more plainly than many a stage set shown in theatrical light two posts of a ruined gateway, one standing, the other fallen, crumbled. I recognized the picture as of a gateway I had seen in Talladega some years before, but had not consciously thought of since. As I looked at it with some amusement an old man walked through it, stood a moment, and was joined by a young girl who took him by the arm and led him obliquely out of the picture. Two or three times this little action was repeated so definitely that it was impossible for me in any way to connect it with imagination, although the association between Holland's tune, with its rural, sentimental color, and this picture is fairly evident.

Next morning Thomas, pen in hand, drifted along with the dream. The result was a one-act play which he called "Talladega." Producer Palmer and Eugene Presbrey, his stage manager, were enthusiastic over the sketch, adding that Thomas had the "nucleus of a fine big story," but that he would need to expand it and write in character parts for J. H. Stoddard, Maurice Barrymore, Ned Bell, Charles Harris, Henry Woodruff, Agnes Miller, E. M. Holland, and other starring members of Palmer's company. And because "Talladega" was "too exclusive for the theme," they recommended that Thomas change the name to *Alabama*.

Thomas followed every suggestion. When the play was finished, Palmer called together his entire company, Thomas read it aloud,

the delighted players applauded vigorously, and Palmer immediately
assigned the parts, as follows:

Colonel Preston—J. H. Stoddard

Colonel Moberly—E. M. Holland

Squire Tucker—Charles L. Harris

Captain Davenport—Maurice
  Barrymore

Lathrop Page—Henry Woodruff

Raymond Page—Walden Ramsay

Mrs. Stockton—Anne Gregory

Atlanta Moberly—Nannie Crad-
  dock

Mr. Armstrong—Edward Bell

Decatur—Reuben Fox

Mrs. Page—May Brookyn

Carey Preston—Agnes Miller

Delighted with their respective roles, each player entered rehearsals
with unusual enthusiasm. Much to the bewilderment of the other
members of the Lamb's Club, they amusingly affected the Southern
dialect and manner both on and off stage. However, in due time they
too were carried along by the spirit of the little game and the club
became "an organization of two hundred Southern colonels all shooting off cuffs and stroking phantom but magnificent mustaches."

As rehearsals continued, however, Palmer fell into a slough of
despondency. He suddenly saw only failure for *Alabama*. Accustomed
to European plays, he was convinced that no native American play,
particularly one about the recently defeated South, could succeed.
He predicted bankruptcy. One dark day, in deep depression, he told
Thomas that his contract, which ended within two months, would
not be renewed. Thomas, newly married, protested loudly, but to
no avail—and waited patiently.

Everything possible was done to bring the Old South to Broadway
on the opening night of *Alabama* at the Madison Square, April 1.
The scenes, the dialect, the costumes, the characters, even the odor
in the theatre reeked with Southernness: before the performance began
the entire auditorium was sprayed with magnolia blossom perfume.
This theatrical innovation, aided by the orchestra's renditions of
"Down on the Farm," "Carry Me Back to Ole Virginia" and Negro
spirituals, proved quite successful.

But despite the enthusiasm and confidence in *Alabama* exhibited
by everyone else, Manager Palmer remained in an almost panic condition. He disappeared shortly before the first curtain and was finally
found by Thomas hiding behind a post in a dark corner of the gallery.
From this shadowy position the two men, the playwright and the
producer, nervously watched the premiere performance, more afraid
than brave men going into battle. When Act I ended "with mingled
laughter and applause" and the cast was recalled for an unprecedented
five curtain calls, Thomas and Palmer ventured down to the balcony
for Act II. At the end of Act III the audience shouted for the author
and Thomas took their plaudits from the stage. At the close of the
play Thomas and Palmer, now all smiles, were standing on the main

[43]

floor amidst hundreds of well-wishers who eagerly shouted their congratulations. *Alabama* had surpassed everybody's fondest hopes and expectations.

Even the critics were overwhelmed by the "enormous success" of the drama. The New York *World*, April 5, patriotically declared it *"a true American play*, a charming tale of the Sunny South, full of lovely scenic pictures, bright humor and pure sentiment." The *Sun* of the same day described it as "a triumph which will easily last to the end of the season."

> Everybody who has sat under the gentle spell of *Alabama*, [added the *Sun*, April 12] declares that there has been no worthier play at the Madison Square. The success is gratifying to all those who have maintained faith in American drama, and it is essentially pleasing to the friends of Augustus Thomas, who assert that there is no surprise along with their exultation, for they have from the first firmly believed that Thomas, notwithstanding his many failures, would awake some morning to find himself celebrated.

Only J. H. Stoddard as Colonel Preston was adversely criticized. "Among those in *Alabama* supposed to be native and to the manner born, he is never within a thousand miles of Alabama," the *Sun* reviewer stated. "He doesn't so much as weakly attempt the Southern accent . . . and, if he were a stranger to the audiences, they would decline to accept him as a competent actor of the part intrusted to him."

The New York *Times*, April 2, saw in *Alabama* a "successful American play, treating an American subject" and predicted that it would "run profitably just as long as Mr. Palmer cares to keep it before the public, and it is to be hoped that he may be able to prolong his season, because everybody ought to have a chance to see the play."

> 'Alabama's' characters, its atmosphere, its humor are all peculiarly American. Not a line failed to effect last evening, not a single trait of character developed in the action was unappreciated. The best English play of these times could not so surely touch the sympathy of American playgoers. 'Alabama' is a play that will last. It will be as popular in the South as in the North, and the Western people will like it, too.

Nor did Augustus Thomas fail to receive his share of praise. Everyone who had been awaiting a really "good play" from his pen now had it, the *Times* declared. "Thomas is more nearly the ideal American playwright than any other man now writing for our stage. . . . His new play contains the requisites of popular success . . . , variety of characterization, abundant humor, easily appreciated sentiment, and it admits of a fine pictorial display."

After synopsizing the play the *Times* paid tribute, one by one to the performers: Harris as Squire Tucker was "deliciously amusing,"

Stoddard as Colonel Preston was "delightful," and Holland as Colonel Moberly was "exquisitely droll." Maurice Barrymore's performance as Captain Davenport had "dignity, tenderness, and fervor...." All in all, the *Times* found "not a false note in the entire performance, and there is not a dull moment in it."

Three days later the *Times* devoted yet another column to *Alabama*, calling it the best by far of the four new plays then on Broadway ("better even than the beautiful revival of Shakespeare's 'Love's Labors Lost'" at Daly's Theatre, starring John Drew), and hoping that it would "be kept on stage all through next summer." The acting was described as "wholly efficient in every part" and Thomas was again praised, not only for *Alabama* but also for "the promise it brings ... to encourage other American dramatists to persevere in a labor which sometimes seems hopeless."

The New York *Herald*, April 2, joined in the paean of praise for *Alabama*. Describing it as "a charmingly natural play of Southern life," the critic bluntly stated that "he would not have missed the performance for a great deal."

> Looking back to the American productions of the past three years or more I can recall no effort which so nearly satisfies me. What other playwrights have achieved in the rough the author of 'Alabama' has accomplished with delicacy. He has made a play, based on the real life of his own country, which is neither a farce nor a burlesque of that life. And he has made it interesting.
>
> Without betraying truth he has respected form. His dialogue is neat, humorous, and polished; it sparkles with bright speeches and it is plausible.
>
> The construction of the play is far from faultless, though to my mind it is eminently better than that of any earlier work of Mr. Thomas, or, for that matter, of much more popular dramatists. This, however, is almost the only fault I see in 'Alabama' the success of which will, I hope, console both the author and the manager for some recent failures.

Three nights later the *Herald's* theatrical critic returned to see *Alabama* the second time. He was again deeply impressed, so much so that he devoted half a page to the play, including artist's drawings of two scenes.

> Some days ago [he wrote], for the first time in my career I had the pleasing duty put upon me of proclaiming the success of a play by an American author which owed absolutely nothing to a foreign source, which was not frivolous or false or overdrawn and which had literary and (though in a less degree) dramatic merit with fancy human and true pathos, to commend it.
>
> This play is called 'Alabama.' The playwright is Augustus Thomas. Both names should be remembered. We may connect them some day with a reform of our stage methods. And even if this not be so, even should the public verdict be less favorable than I hope it will be, the play will have deserved to live and the author will have much to clear

the guild of playwrights in this country from the suspicion of vulgarity and impotence.... The play is exquisitely staged and finely acted.

Amidst this unprecedented success Manager Palmer startled the theatrical world by announcing that *Alabama* would be withdrawn from the boards on Saturday, May 2—after only one month's run. Everyone concerned, including Charles Frohman and Al Hayman, who had supported Palmer financially, urged him to change his mind and "continue in the lap of this so needed prosperity." But Palmer was a businessman whose word was his bond. Before staging *Alabama*, in his days of depression, he had sublet the Madison Square to another company for a production of Martha Morton's *The Merchant* and he intended to keep the bargain. Pleas from his associates to obtain another house for the new play so that *Alabama* could continue proved futile and, as the *Sun* put it on April 30, "the one signal hit of the season at the Madison Square cannot continue here, more's the pity. It would fill the theatre all summer long."

Meantime, Palmer had contracted with Hooley's Theatre in Chicago for a showing of *Alabama*. There, on May 18, the original New York cast opened amidst much favorable publicity. The Chicago *Tribune*, May 13, quoting the Philadelphia *Ledger*, proclaimed that Thomas' masterpiece "should live and be seen by every one who loves his country." The Chicago *Daily News*, commenting on the unusual advanced sale of seats, likewise stated the next day that to miss *Alabama* would be downright unpatriotic. On the fourteenth the *Tribune* repeated its enthusiasm by advertising that a "trained negro quartet" had been employed to "sing plantation songs" at Hooley's during the production of *Alabama*, both matinee and night performances, thus enhancing the enjoyment of the patrons.

> Chicago will welcome A. M. Palmer's single success of the season in New York [the *Tribune* declared, May 17]. Written by Augustus Thomas, a young American writer, it has been highly commended. Many flattering things have been said of it, and it will be a pleasure to add to them if a seeing justifies anticipation. The action takes place in Alabama at the present time, the background in the distance being the events of the war. The author is said to have given the play the peaceful and restful atmosphere which novelists and playwrights dealing with the conflict have always tried to attain. The company needs no introduction, being the one so long directed by Mr. Palmer.

On May 19, the day following the opening performance, the *Tribune's* reviewer generously synopsized the play act by act, and added,

> 'Alabama' justifies all reports that preceded it, and the audience which filled Hooley's welcomed it to Chicago with a kindness that assured its prosperity. One could hardly convey its charm by relating the plot, which is simple, and not too ingeniously constructed, but it is happy

chiefly in the sentiment which deals generally and generously with the late war, and in the characterization, which is truly and thoroughly Southern. Mr. Augustus Thomas, the author, evidently knows the South and appreciates the best qualities: and without flattery he offers to it an olive branch which is, in its way, as gracious as a wreath of laurel. Others have written of the war, generally in the tragical vein; but other dramas have had a sting of memory which was unwelcome. Mr. Thomas puts his personages at a distance from the conflict, and covers old scars with the amenities of comedy, even as the flowers hide the abandoned cannon at Col. Preston's ruined gates.

As for the actors, the *Tribune* considered Stoddard's portrayal of Colonel Preston as "absolutely life-like," Holland's Colonel Moberly as "a thorough Southerner, and thoroughly the gentleman," Agnes Miller as Carey Preston as "sweet and winning," adding that it was Charles L. Harris, however, who won all hearts by "monopolizing honors in the low comedy role of Squire Tucker."

As *Alabama* attracted crowds night after night, the *Tribune's* critic returned for another look. " 'Alabama' began its second week at Hooley's last night to an overflowing house," he wrote on May 26, "standing room only being the rule." Actually, in order to make space for additional seats, the manager of Hooley's had converted the orchestra pit into seats, forcing the musicians to move under the stage, entirely out of sight of the audience.

Alabama closed at Hooley's on June 7 after a run of three weeks. It was, as the *Tribune* stated, "the largest season the Madison Square Company ever had in this city."

Before returning *Alabama* to New York City for the 1891 fall season, Manager Palmer sent his traveling troupe (as distinguished from his New York troupe), under the direction of Al Hayman, on a tour through the South, beginning at Macauley's Theatre, Louisville, Kentucky on October 8. Welcoming the "new American play," the Louisville *Courier-Journal* on the fourth described it as "not a great play in the sense of thrilling scenes, melodramatic situations, and declamatory lines; but one that moved along quietly, is true to life, wholesome, refreshing, and permeated with the atmosphere of nature."

Augustus Thomas, the author of *Alabama*, journeyed from New York to Louisville to attend the premiere performance. Making the most of the publicity the occasion afforded, Palmer telegraphed Henry Watterson, distinguished author and editor of the *Courier-Journal*, that Thomas was on his way. Watterson promptly printed the message in the issue of October 8, adding that Louisville theatre-goers should not fail "the opportunity of seeing 'Alabama,' one of the greatest successes of modern times." The cast, as published the next day, was as follows:

Colonel Preston—Frank Bangs   *Colonel Moberly*—Burr McIntosh

[47]

Squire Tucker—Odell Williams	*Decatur*—George Bunny
Captain Davenport—Clement Bainbridge	*Mrs. Page*—Jennie Eustace
	Mrs. Stockton—Francis Kinharvie
Mr. Armstrong—Fred G. Ross	*Carey Preston*—Stella Teuton
Lathrop Page—Frederick Conger	*Atlanta Moberly*—Zenaide Vislaire
Raymond Page—J. G. Saville	

On the opening night Thomas, as guest of honor, shared a box with Watterson who in the next day's paper fairly outdid himself in a 1,200-word review of *Alabama's* "first presentation to a Southern audience."

> The result was a triumph for both the talented author and for the excellent company [he wrote]. As act after act increased the demonstrations of satisfaction on the part of the audience, the smile of gratification on the good-natured face of the author broadened into a grin, and when the curtain fell on the last act and the audience stood up and called for the author, he marched upon the stage doubtless full of the satisfaction he strove to express. The reception accorded the play flattering and sincere.

As for the players, Watterson stated that there was not a weak member in the cast. Each gave "an admirable, conscientious and faithful piece of character work." But most pleasant to Augustus Thomas, who had come to Louisville primarily for "the purpose of seeing how his conception of the Southern character would strike a Southern audience," must have been Watterson's conclusion:

> 'Alabama' will doubtless find favor in the South. It is nearer portraiture than anything we have yet in this line, and if it should not succeed its failure to do so could be due only to that exceedingly sensitiveness which already suspects arrogance and ridicule. Its initial performance before a Southern audience certainly justifies the prediction that the South will like it. The audience was large and enthusiastic.

After the performance Henry Watterson entertained Thomas, Hayman, and the male performers at one of the city's most exclusive clubs. As Thomas later wrote in his autobiography:

> Henry Watterson saw to it that our first night was a gala occasion, and the men of the company were invited to a midnight reception at the Pendennis Club. Marse Henry was in his element, ably aided by those Kentuckians who have the Southern instinct amounting to genius for hospitality and entertainment.

Watterson, fully cognizant of Thomas' contribution to American drama and, particularly, the healing influence *Alabama* was exerting on North-South relations, took the floor publicly to proclaim his regard for him. As Thomas stated,

> At an effective moment in the evening he got the attention of the party—close to a hundred men—and with his arm through mine in the centre of the floor explained the circumstances under which our acquaintance had been made, and claimed to be proud that I was a product of a newspaper office.

[48]

Then, shifting his arm over my shoulder . . . and reverting to the play, the subject of which was the reconciliation of two great political sections of the country, he said, 'This boy has done in one night in the theatre what I have endeavored to do in twenty years of editorial writing.'

From Louisville the Hayman company moved to Nashville, Tennessee, opening a three-day season at the Vendome Theatre, Monday, October 11. The *Banner*, October 9, expressed the opinion that *Alabama* was "not a powerful piece of dramatic writing," but that it was a play noted for its "Americanism . . . [and] conspicuous for action and emotion." Following the first performance, the paper stated that a "large and fashionable audience" applauded loud and long.

> From the name and character of the play many expected to experience the usual humiliation of seeing the Northern characters triumph over their Southern brothers, [it added]. In this they were disappointed, as nothing obnoxious or offensive to the most ardent or prejudiced Southron is apparent in the four acts. . . . The play is purely Southern and deals with Southern life in its true light. It is perhaps the fairest representation of the Southland yet seen on the stage. Humor and pathos are blended in happy union, and it is a pretty tale well told.

The cast was described as "good" by the Nashville critic. Frank Bangs, he wrote, sustained the character of Colonel Preston with dignity; Burr McIntosh's Colonel Moberly was "acted splendidly"; Odell Williams as Squire Tucker "gave a clever interpretation of the backwoods magistrate"; Miss Teuton was a "very pretty and pleasing picture of a Southern girl"; and George Bunny's Decatur was "one of the truest and most life-like presentations of the loyal old ante-bellum slave ever seen here."

After its highly successful Nashville season the Hayman troupe moved to the Lyceum Theatre in Memphis. There the *Appeal-Avalanche* heralded its arrival by quoting a long dialogue in the play, praising the stage settings and the cast and noting oddly that "a peculiarity of 'Alabama' is that all its events transpire out of doors." The next day's issue, October 16, devoted almost an entire column to the production, half of which praised the actors and actresses who were described "as clever people as ever appeared on a Memphis stage."

> 'Alabama' deserves the praise it has received [the critic continued]. There are sunbeams for the heart and tears for the eyes in every act. Phases of Southern life and character are portrayed, not caricatured. The idiosyncracies of types of men and women peculiarly Southern are depicted in a strikingly life-like manner. The sentiment of true Southern chivalry is in every line, and although a Southern girl gives her heart to a Northern man, she does not forfeit the esteem of the audience. . . . There is no politics in the play. . . .
>
> The fame of 'Alabama' had preceded it and there were only a few vacant seats in the two back rows of the orchestra circle. The orchestra was filled and there was an unusually large crowd in the gallery. It was an appreciative gathering, and when the orchestra played 'Dixie' before the curtain rose on the first act there was a burst of applause.

[49]

In New Orleans, the next stop on the company's Southern tour, the *Daily Picayune*, October 19–24, devoted four reviews to the play, describing it as a sectional "balm of Gilead that came at the right time and the people have hailed it as an American play worthy to live on the stage." The night after the first performance the *Picayune* told its readers that *Alabama* was "as pastoral as 'As You Like It.' " Following a long synopsis, the writer urged everyone in New Orleans to hurry to the ticket window. "People were turned away at the last two performances," he concluded, and standing room was at a premium.

> 'Alabama' [he wrote, October 20] is a Southern play, and there is no line or sentiment in it a Southerner cannot endorse. The villain of the play is a Southern man, but such a man as would be called a villain in any section of the country. . . . The story all the way is sweetly told. Its reference to the late war is only incidental. It is only a cause for a family estrangement. It breathes peace and reconciliation. 'Alabama' is an eloquent picture of the work of time and nature in healing the wounds of war, and many tears dropped last night from many eyes that saw touches of nature in the beautiful play Mr. Thomas has given the stage. He has done his work admirably and the actors were perfect in their parts.

Two days after closing at New Orleans the Palmer company presented *Alabama* at the Mobile Theatre, the first showing in the State of Alabama.

> There was a large attendance in the theatre last night [the Mobile *Register*, October 27, stated] a large and fashionable attendance. . . . The performance of the play and the play itself leave little to be desired. There is not enough lightness of heart among the young lovers and the comedy element is not quite strong enough to balance the pathos . . . , but otherwise the composition is remarkably clever, the sentiment good and the situations quietly but truly dramatic.

Nevertheless, the *Register* found fault with the poor attempts of the actors to portray Southern characteristics of speech, claiming that they were more Virginian than Alabamian.

> The drawl is not characteristic of Southern people anywhere, and yet the actors in this play drawl and the women draw out their words or rather separate words, until the dialogue threatens at times to drag. Southern women talk as rapidly as any other women in the world, though they have a habit of pausing upon, that is to say, emphasizing the sense of their sentences. They also raise and lower their voice more than do people of the North. This peculiarity does not seem to have yet been noticed by those who desire to represent Southern character. Samples of Virginianisms are the use of 'Ah' for 'I' and 'Sah' for 'Sir.' Old Colonel Preston says: 'We sh'll be pleased to see ye agin, sah.' An Alabamian would put it: 'We shall be pleased to see you agen, sir.'

But the critic concluded, "It will be a long time before so well mounted,

[50]

well arranged, interesting and well cast and acted a play will be seen in Mobile again."

The people of Talladega, the locale of *Alabama*, were not pleased with the portrayal of their town in the play as "an isolated community called Talladega." On October 25 the editor of the Talladega *Reporter*, his heart on his sleeve, opined:

Talladega is of the battle-ground made famous by Jackson in a fight second only to that of New Orleans. It's enlightened precincts since then have produced a great mind every decade, furnishing the nation with ministers to foreign lands, the state with governors, the bench with profound legal talent, the pulpit with world renowned ability and the bar and forum with magnificent minds. It takes but a casual review of history to lift Talladega from advertised obscurity to the very van of intellect-producing cities. We therefore insist that if Talledega is to furnish the imaginary foreground to a wholly imaginary play she will hereafter be credited with six thousand people, the railroads, furnaces and factories, the water and gas works, the ten schools and all the conveniences of a modern city which she has. If her splendid record is to be used as a simple advertisement of the play, we want at least the facts presented.

From Mobile the *Alabama* players went to Charleston, South Carolina where on November 3–4 they presented a matinee and two evening performances in the Academy of Music. "Mr. Thomas' play has unquestionably placed him in the front ranks of the dramatists of the country," the *News and Courier* editorialized on the second. "It is by an American and about Americans" and as such "has created a sensation, both from the literary and dramatic standpoint." Nearly all of the members of the traveling troupe, the paper added, "are actors of established and national reputations, and most of them are favorites in this city." In short, *Alabama* was "a genuine triumph!" On November 5, following the last performances of the afternoon and night before, the *News and Courier* described "the large audiences" and stated that the paper "repeats and emphasizes all that has been said both in commendation of Mr. Thomas' pretty and picturesque drama and of the excellent artist into whose hands its interpretation to Southern audiences has been entrusted."

After the Charleston performances, the Hayman Company opened at the Academy of Music in Washington, D.C. on November 16. Advanced publicity in the *Post*, November 12, advised theatre-goers to buy their tickets early, for this was "an American play written by American about Americans . . . , a most undisputed and emphatic success." On the seventeenth the *Post* added,

The history of the American stage scarcely furnishes another example of a production which has received such unanimous commendation from the press of the country. . . 'Alabama' is typically American, redolent with the atmosphere of purity and patriotism, and telling an uncommonly pretty love story that may go far toward healing the sores of sectional feeling. It is quiet, artistic, fraught with sentiment, poetry, and indigenous humor. The scenery is remarkably beautiful, typical of the soil wherein the scenes are laid. Indeed, last night it was literally so, for the languide perfume of the magnolia floated through the auditorium during the second and later acts.

Meanwhile, as Hayman's traveling troupe was completing its Southern tour, Manager A. M. Palmer was personally preparing his "original cast" or "Home Company" of *Alabama* for its second (1891–1892) New York fall-winter season. Except that Agnes Miller (instead of May Brookyn) now played Mrs. Page; E. S. Abeles (instead of Henry Woodruff), Lathrop Page; and Emily Seward (instead of Anne Gregory), Mrs. Stockton, it was the same as it had been the previous April. Before opening, however, Palmer decided on a two-weeks preliminary or warm-up season at the Chestnut Street Theatre in Philadelphia. There, on October 19, *Alabama* was introduced to a "crowded house which witnessed it with delight."

'Alabama' has truly a Southern atmosphere [the *Ledger* stated, October 19]. It is a succession of charming pictures, without a jarring feature. The situations live before one. Interest is maintained, unflagged, throughout; the developments are natural and untheatric; the lines have generally a homely significance that appeal alike to one's reason and heart, although there is at times a poetic fashioning of the words that disclose literary merit of high order. All that is noblest and truest in the Sunny South is suggested when it is not expressed, and the framed picture of dreamy, idyllic, as rhythmical as a day in June.

After praising Messrs. Stoddard, Holland, Harris, and Barrymore and Misses Booth, Miller, and Seward for their sincere and histrionic charms, the *Ledger* critic concluded, " 'Alabama' is a genuine contribution to dramatic literature."

In New York City the Madison Square Theatre was no longer the home of *Alabama*. Palmer, his eye ever on the box office, had now leased a much larger and older house, formerly Wallack's Theatre but now called Palmer's Theatre, on the corner of Broadway and Thirtieth Street. The new place had twice the seating capacity and was in other ways superior to the old Madison Square. The scenery, "all new and expressly painted for this production," was the work of Homer F. Emens and Richard Marston, names well-known along Broadway. Palmer, of course, expected to fill his new establishment nightly with his new-found hit.

Before the first curtain rose on the night of November 2 at Palmer's Theatre, the Crescent City Quartet sang Negro melodies, setting the tone and spirit of the occasion. In the Manager's Box as a special and honored guest sat the celebrated Sara Bernhardt. And although the audience was as usual large and enthusiastic, according to George C. D. Odell's *Annals of the New York Stage* (1949), the play lacked

[52]

the "intimacy" it had enjoyed in the smaller Madison Square and, hence, lost some of its charm. But the critic of the *Times* was once more carried away.

'Alabama' does not grow old [he wrote, November 3], but adjectives do, unfortunately, and after a while it is well to take approval for granted.... 'Alabama' is a poem of the South—lyric not epic, and its melody has gained not lost, by the change from the Madison Square to Palmer's Theatre.

Continuing, he described *Alabama* as "the most charming of all American plays," praised the performers one by one, and expressed general delight over "the new order" of theatrical things which "began in earnest at Palmer's last evening."

Immediately following the play an event "quite without a parallel in the annals of the stage" took place, as a one-man delegation from Talladega, Alabama stepped out into the glare of the footlights:

At the close of the fourth act the curtain rose again disclosing the players grouped about a handsome piece of floral architecture bearing the words *Alabama* and *Here We Rest*. Then a slender young man, Mr. W. H. Skaggs, ex-mayor of Talladega, stepped forward and made a speech. He said the people of his town had sent him here to express their admiration of the play; to say they accepted it as a picture of the New South and to present these flowers gathered by Colonel Preston's granddaughter on the old Preston place. Mr. Palmer spoke a few words of thanks on behalf of his company and Mr. Thomas, the author of 'Alabama,' said that he had nothing to say except that he was very happy and everyone else was happy.

Mme. Bernhardt, who watched it all from one of the lower boxes, may not have quite understood what she saw, but she applauded as if she did and the other people in the house screamed with enthusiasm.

On January 6, 1892 the one hundredth performance of *Alabama* was presented. The next night Agnes Booth sprained her ankle during the show. "The pain was so great," T. Allison Brown wrote in his *History of the New York Stage* (1903), "that she had to continue the act sitting on a little settee." Emily Seward, her understudy, played the part of Mrs. Page for the next two weeks. On January 11 the cast moved over to Lee Avenue Academy, presented six evening performances and returned to Palmer's to close out the season there on the nineteenth.

Having enjoyed remarkable success earlier in the 1891–1892 season at the Chestnut Street Theatre in Philadelphia, Palmer decided to play that city again. Consequently, from February 9 to 13 *Alabama* drew large crowds at the Broad Street Theatre:

There is no need to dwell upon the pretty story, or skein of stories which are so delightfully woven in 'Alabama' [stated the Philadelphia *Ledger*, February 9].... It was very efficiently told last night by a company of actors who proved themselves to be in hearty sympathy with

[53]

the piece ... and the result was one of those harmonious stage pictures which are rare enough to command attention.

After eulogizing the performances of the players, the critic concluded, "Of the scenery and accessories it is only necessary to say that they were pretty and appropriate, and lent a value without detracting from the action of the play."

Upon the company's return to New York, *Alabama* was presented nightly with matinees at the Columbia Theatre in Brooklyn, March 7–10.

Then, recalling the good fortune *Alabama* had brought him in Chicago in 1891, Manager Palmer next sent his New York company directly to Hooley's Theatre for a second season. Charles Frohman, who had meanwhile along with Al Hayman bought an interest in the play, bet Augustus Thomas $100 that *Alabama* would do a bigger business in Chicago than it had done the first year.

> As it was to be in the same house and we had played to capacity the first time[Thomas later wrote in *The Print of My Remembrance*], I didn't see how that could be, and said so. He wanted to bet, nevertheless, and rejecting cigars and hats as stakes he fixed upon a suit of clothes. I demurred, feeling that it was unsportsmanlike to bet on a sure thing. He generously gave me the advantage, however. The business on the second trip was nearly double, because of the fact, of which C. F. was aware, and I not when he made the bet, that the play had been chosen for the local police benefit and all patrolmen in Chicago were selling tickets. The increased royalties reconciled me to the loss of the bet. The bill for the suit of clothes came in with C. F.'s endorsement. The price, one hundred dollars, amused him greatly....

The Chicago *Tribune*, May 3, 1892, gave advanced notice to *Alabama* as "a brilliant success ... the freshest and sweetest of American plays" and, following the first night's performance, added:

> 'Alabama' has united North and South in its tender pathos and gentle humor; and while other dramas dealing with the Civil War have existed by flattering partisan prejudices, this one by appealing to the highest sentiments of universal humanity has succeeded in making "the whole world kin.' 'Alabama' was written with the ease of one of Burns' poems, and like them it is assured of a graceful immortality. More elaborate pieces have been written on American subjects, but not one so flower-like as this in its growth and fragrance.

Alabama played to full houses at Hooley's for two weeks, May 3–14, winning continuing praise from the *Tribune*. It was, as the paper concluded, presented by "probably the strongest theatrical company in America at the present time."

As the 1892–1893 season began, *Alabama's* popularity had noticeably begun to decline. Palmer's players, now called Palmer's Home Stock Company but still under Al Hayman's management, opened, as it had the year before, in mid-October in Louisville, Kentucky in the Louisville Auditorium, not Macauley's Theatre. The players were billed as the "original New York cast," not last year's "traveling company." Actually, the *dramatis personae* was a mixed group, composed of several members of both casts, as follows:

Colonel Preston—J. H. Stoddard	*Raymond Page*—J. G. Saville
Colonel Moberly—E. M. Holland	*Decatur*—W. Shafer
Squire Tucker—Odell Williams	*Mrs. Page*—Jennie Eustace
Captain Davenport—Francis Carlyle	*Carey Preston*—Leila Wolstan
	Atlanta Moberly—Zenaide Vislaire
Mr. Armstrong—Walden Ramsey	
Lathrop Page—Edward S. Abeles	*Mrs. Stockton*—Emily Seward

Although the play did not receive the stimulating welcome it had received in 1891 (Augustus Thomas was not present and Henry Watterson gave no reception honoring the cast), *Alabama* was sincerely hailed in the *Courier-Journal*, October 9, as "the only drama based upon the Civil War that brings out the true and loyal ways of the Southern people." In not a single city, the paper continued, had *Alabama* received adverse criticism. And on the eighteenth the reviewer wrote the following appraisal of the opening night's performance of "a perfect play, by a perfect company":

> There are few plays before the public today that get nearer the heart than 'Alabama.' The sweet, tender story it tells touches a responsive chord in the heart of the young Northerner and the old Southerner. For the former, there is a taste of romance, love, sentiment, idealistic but unknown in reality away from the land where the air is laden with the odor of magnolias, where the moonlight has a warmth of color not seen elsewhere. For the latter, there are chivalry, manliness, memories of long ago, that it is well to stir up now and then....
>
> The play was staged with the care usually bestowed by the Auditorium management. No detail was overlooked.... The audience was large, and it showed its appreciation of actors and scenes by vociferous applause.

After the Louisville performances the Palmer House Stock Company went directly to Memphis, for some unexplained reason by-passing Nashville where *Alabama* had been so well received in 1891. The Memphis *Appeal-Avalanche,* October 21, reminded its readers that the play had "created a sensation" in the city the year before, and added that this year's performance was every bit as good.

> 'Alabama' is recognized as a Southern play, in which the picturesque features of Southern life and Southern types are produced and not caricatured, in which the war is an incident of the past; and in which there are unions of representatives of each section without the sacrifice of patriotic sentiment on either side.... It is not strange therefore that the Lyceum Theatre last evening was crowded almost to its full capacity. Every box was full, and there were only half dozen or so seats in the rear of the house unoccupied.

The play itself, the reviewer continued, "is of great intrinsic strength. . . . There is a bouyancy about it remindful of the best works of the modern dramatists." The players he described as "artists equal to any on the stage." And, after paying tribute to them singly, he concluded by complimenting John Mahoney, manager of the Lyceum, for his "happy stroke in decorating the theatre with palms and potted plants, all in keeping with the beautiful stage setting remindful of the semitropical climate of Southern Alabama."

After three night performances and a matinee, October 20–22, the troupe moved on to the New Orleans Academy of Music for a similar run there, beginning October 24. Anticipating the arrival of the players, the *Daily Picayune* on the twenty-third emphasized the excellence of the cast, stating that several members, erroneously including the author of "beautiful 'Alabama,' the greatest success of years," were "all of the South." After the first performance the paper added, October 25:

> 'Alabama,' the Southern after-the-war play by Augustus Thomas which made such a decided hit here last season . . . was delightfully presented last night. Small critics have found small faults with this play, saying there are no frogs in Talladega and no bayous in that vicinity. . . . Little lapses of that kind can be found in Shakespeare. 'Alabama' can be taken to heart by the people of the South for its kindly spirit, its good intentions, and its sweetness. It comes soothingly, taking action after the ending of the cruel [war], and Talladega is only a representative town, as it was before the New South gave it new life.

As the season neared its end, the *Picayune* declared (October 26) that *Alabama* was "full of quaint characters, lovely scenes, and charming sentiments. . . . The company is a great one." The audience, it concluded, was composed of the "best people in New Orleans," all of whom will "visit Alabama before the week is over."

The second appearance of *Alabama* in Mobile, October 31, 1892—a one-night stand—fell far short of the success it had won the year before. Although billed as the "engagement extraordinary of the original New York production," it drew only a few patrons, as the critic of the *Register* noted, November 1:

> 'Alabama' which attracted a large audience last season proved but moderately successful at the Mobile Theatre last night, but half a house of people being present. The play was given with all the attention to detail which characterized the performance, and with several of the actors who made so fine an impression here last season. Where changes were made in the cast, original N. Y. impersonators of the roles were chosen. Mr. J. H. Stoddard sustained the part of 'Colonel Preston,' and is to be preferred to Mr. Frank Bangs, who never got over the fact that he had been a star, so was unable to subordinate himself to the requirements of the part. Mr. Stoddard is pleasing in pathetic as well as the vigorous phases of the role, and received a due share of the applause given last night.

[56]

Odell Williams, as Squire Tucker, was "as amusing as ever," E. M. Holland, as Colonel Moberly, "kept the audience in good humor," and all the others "deserve a compliment for their excellent acting," the brief review ended.

In Montgomery, Alabama, where Palmer's Home Stock Company played a one-night stand on November 2, the *Journal* announced it as "the original New York production—the greatest success in years." And the *Daily Advertiser*, November 3, after chiding the troupe for having given Montgomery the "go-by" in 1891, added that the Opera House was filled with ladies and gentlemen who "evidenced their appreciation by frequent and continuous applause." Following a synopsis of *Alabama*, the writer added:

> The name of the play attracts play-lovers in this locality, and its presentation is deserving of the support it is receiving in its second tour of the South. The plot is one of real, every-day life, truly and genuinely American and the company playing it is a very strong one. There was some sentiment, a great deal of love and love-making, charming plantation melodies by negro singers and upon the whole a most excellent play.

The Birmingham presentation of *Alabama*, November 3, 1892 at O'Brien's Opera House, was made noteworthy by the attendance of a large number of citizens from Talladega, headed by the Mayor, who had rented a special train for the occasion. They sat together and "applauded loudly from beginning to end, especially when anything referring directly to their little spot was said. . . ." All together, according to the *Age-Herald*, November 3–4, *Alabama* was witnessed by a "full house." "Never was a more appreciative or more enthusiastic audience assembled" in O'Brien's. Stoddard as Colonel Preston was "the best acting seen on the Birmingham stage in many seasons." Miss Eustace as Mrs. Page displayed talent of the highest class," although her "exaggerated Southern dialect" at times approached the "ludicrous." Guido Marbury as the Negro servant was "good . . . but his pleasing countenance gave him away—he's no villain." And as for the atmosphere of *Alabama*, it was superb:

> A colored quartet, concealed from view by a moon-shadowed ruined gate and hedge, are heard singing their own plantation melodies. The stars blink and the moon sheds her light on the players, and it is one of the attractive pictures in a drama which does not stir up the spirit, but leaves an effect on the minds of the audience like that of a pleasant dream.

The next stop for the traveling troupe was Washington's New National Theatre. There, on November 28, *Alabama* "found many old friends" (who had witnessed the play at the old Academy of Music in November, 1891). "The play is one of which we can well be proud," wrote the critic of the *Post*, November 27, 29, 1892, adding,

[57]

'Alabama' is not a great work in the commonly accepted sense, but, rather, a quiet, half-tone portrait of some of the most characteristic phases of American life and character, which charms by its simplicity and truth.

The *Post's* reporter also found the 1892 cast of *Alabama*, which included J. H. Stoddard, E. M. Holland, J. G. Saville, Jennie Eustace, and Zenaide Vislaire, quite superior to the "second-class company which presented 'Alabama' in Washington last season." All together, *Alabama*, that "lovable Southern play," won the hearts of its patrons as "the most enjoyable of recent plays."

It is very likely that the cast which presented *Alabama* in Washington was composed of members from Palmer's "original New York" company and Hayman's traveling unit. This combined group had earlier (November 2) opened at Palmer's Theatre in New York but, finding business poor, had started moving about from theatre to theatre, on one-, two-, and three-night stands. In any case, it was becoming obvious that Augustus Thomas' *Alabama*, after enjoying more than two years' great popularity, was now about to run its course. As George C. D. Odell, the eminent historian of the New York stage, has stated, Manager Palmer's descent from his exalted position in the theatre was caused by his unfortunate inability to change with the times. If he had been content to remain in the small Madison Theatre, spending winters there, and sending his stock companies to Washington, Philadelphia, Chicago and other large centers in the summer, he might have survived. But the traveling stock company system to which he adhered, already doomed, was finally eliminated as powerful theatrical magnates gained control of the leading actors and plays. The old order changed to new—and Palmer could somehow not change with it.

On December 19–24, 1892 Palmer's players were producing *Alabama* at the Harlem Opera House. In 1893, the incomplete, scattered records reveal, they were at the Columbia Theatre, Brooklyn, September 21–23, and in 1894 at the Grand Opera House, New York City, April 30–May 5—still billed as the "best company of the year." And, as of old, the principal players were still Stoddard, Holland, Ramsay, and May Brookyn.

One cannot know how many times *Alabama* was produced on widely separated stages in various parts of the nation (it was presented for a brief season at the Baldwin Theatre in San Francisco, California in 1891), nor can one predict with certainty the date of its last presentation. Suffice it to say that, if Thomas' masterpiece was mentioned in theatrical literature after 1894, the reference was most likely to have been historical, not contemporary.

For four theatrical seasons between April 1, 1891 and May 5, 1894 *Alabama* was one of the most popular plays on the American stage. Withal its maudlin sentiment (surely more acceptable then than now) it was generally recognized not only as a melodrama which pleased both audiences and critics but also as a powerful drama of reconciliation which did much to reunite the two widely different and strongly-opinionated sections of the nation which only a few years before had been split asunder by the bloodiest civil conflict in modern history. Moreover, in an era when European productions had all but taken over the American stage, *Alabama* made a place for itself as an American play written by an American for Americans. For these two unique reasons, if for none other, Augustus Thomas' *Alabama* deserves to be remembered.

"... people is more like hogs and dogs..."

Alias Simon Suggs: The Life and Times of Johnson Jones Hooper,
Chapter I, University, Alabama: University of Alabama Press, 1952.

Willis Brewer says that in going from his father's home in Wilmington, North Carolina, to his brother's home in frontier La Fayette, Alabama, Johnson Jones Hooper "journeyed through the Gulf States, and remained in Tuscaloosa several months." To have reached this West Alabama community, on the opposite side of the state from Chambers County, he would have had to come by ship from Wilmington, *via* Charleston and Savannah, to Mobile, and thence up the Mobile, Tombigbee and Black Warrior rivers—a long, slow and circuitous voyage which would have ultimately deposited him yet many miles from his known destination. As Alabama's capital, Tuscaloosa doubtless held a charm and opportunities not to be expected in the county-seat of La Fayette, and Hooper might well indeed have wished to "look the field over" from that vantage point. But this is not likely, in view of subsequent facts. Another writer, obviously following Brewer's lead, romantically states that Hooper "set out on a journey of the Gulf States, living by his wits, a few months here and a few there, until 1840 when he settled in La Fayette ... and read law under his brother, already a resident of seven years' standing." Another possible though highly improbable route would have been the Fall-Line Road all the way across the Carolinas and Georgia, a tedious stage-coach journey of approximately six hundred miles. And still another, even more improbable, would have been the northern road through western North Carolina, Knoxville, Huntsville and Tuscaloosa.

None of these routes seems plausible. As will be seen, Hooper was in East Alabama much earlier than 1840. Moreover, the logical and most attractive route for him to have followed from Wilmington to La Fayette was certainly not the longest way round.

By taking passage on one of the regularly scheduled schooners from Wilmington, Hooper could have reached Charleston in less than two days. There he could have boarded the newly-constructed, 136-mile

South-Carolina Rail-Road, then the longest in the world, and have arrived in Hamburg, across the Savannah River from Augusta, in a matter of hours. In Augusta, Georgia's principal stagecoach terminal, he could have taken the Fort Mitchell route directly west, through Sparta, Milledgeville, Macon and Columbus, across the Chattahoochee River to Fort Mitchell, Alabama, and thence to Opelika and La Fayette, a distance of but two hundred and sixty miles. This route, from Middle Georgia westward a part of the old Washington-New Orleans Federal Road and because of surveyors' markings commonly called the "Three Chopped Way," was the most frequented southwestward highway of its time. Immigrants from the Carolinas and Georgia who settled in Alabama, as well as those who pushed farther on, to Mississippi, Louisiana and Texas, had used it extensively and long. Moreover, Chambers County, one of Alabama's most easterly counties, strategically situated near famous Fort Mitchell on a chief pioneer thoroughfare, was widely known as one of the state's gateways. It is wholly logical to assume, therefore, that Hooper journeyed this way, rather than the longer and more circuitous route *via* Tuscaloosa.

At the time of Hooper's arrival, La Fayette was a mere frontier crossroads, a muddy-streeted, log-cabin village of scarcely two hundred inhabitants. Chambers County, of which it was the "chief city," contained not more than twenty settlers to each of its 620 square miles, almost one-half of whom were Negro slaves, and an unknown quantity of Muscogee Indians of the Creek Nation who still roamed the countryside, frightening women and children and in general adding no pleasure to an already rugged pioneer existence. Scarcely three years old, the county had been created December 18, 1832, carved out of territory ceded to the United States at the Treaty of Cusseta the preceding March. Already, however, settlers from Georgia, the Carolinas, Tennessee, Virginia and the older counties of Alabama to the west were pouring into the new land, staking claims, clearing the piney-woods, building log houses and trading posts, planting crops, and otherwise slowly converting the backwoods wilderness into a livable outpost of civilization. By 1840, five years after Hooper's coming and the year of Chambers County's first census, 17,333 had arrived. Within another decade thousands more were to come, dotting the red clay hillsides with better and better homesteads, cultivating the bottomlands along Osanippa and High Pine creeks and the rich valleys that eastward led into the historic Chattahooche River and westward to the Tallapoosa.

Hooper, doubtless through the good offices of his brother George, now one of the county's leading attorneys, adjusted himself quickly to East Alabama's pioneer life. He moved about the region easily, sharing his time between La Fayette and the nearby villages of Dudleyville, Dadeville and Wetumpka, making friends wherever he went.

The Indians especially fascinated him, their councils, ball games, sham battles, dances, and hilltop camp-fires remaining sources of unending pleasure. "It was a right beautiful sight to look at," he once stated, "the camp fires of five thousand Indians, that burned at every point of the circular ridge . . . and it was thrilling to hear the wild whoopings, and the wilder songs of the 'natives,' as they danced and capered about their respective encampments."

Quick to see the Indians' many faults, their drunkenness, stupidity and general undesirability as citizens in a white man's country, Hooper nevertheless lamented the ill-treatment these naive and unlearned people received at the hands of land-sharks, speculators, and traders. "There are few of the old settlers of the Creek territory in Alabama," he wrote, "who do not recollect the great Indian Council held at Dudley's store, in Tallapoosa County, in September of the year 1835. In those days, an occasion of the sort drew together white man and Indian from all quarters of the 'Nation,'—the one to cheat, the other to be cheated. The agent appointed by the Government to 'certify' the sales of Indian lands was always in attendance; so that the scene was generally one of active traffic. The industrious speculator, with his assistant, the wily interpreter, kept unceasingly at work in the business of fraud; and by every species and art of persuasion, sought—and, sooner or later succeeded—in drawing the untutored children of the forest into their nets. If foiled once, twice, thrice, a dozen times, still they kept up the pursuit. It was ever the constant trailing of the slow-track dog, from whose fangs there was no final escape!"

According to contemporary accounts, however, the Creeks were as a whole a revengeful, lazy lots of individuals who mostly lurked on the edges of the forest, a constant menace to the settlers. With "whiskey too much" they either lay about the piazzas of the village stores or, accompanied by "miserable-looking squaws" and filthy, naked children, begged food from white house-wives, "gobbling up their supper of hominy" and sneaking off into the shadows. Easily persuaded and largely controlled by intriguing settlers with the smoothest tongues, they remained constantly a disturbing element of Alabama's backwoods civilization. For years, until the Creeks were finally transported, the white man never dared let down his guard.

Yet the catalogue of the white man's frauds against the Indians was long, too, "as long almost, as the catalogue of Creek wrongs." He exploited them in every way, seduced their maidens, married them to get titles to their lands and left them, cheated and tricked them and laughed in their faces, refusing them at last even the beneficence of a horse and wagon in which to travel to the promised new lands in the West. Many a Creek, once self-sufficient and, after his fashion, proud, "was compelled to wait until the Government removed

[61]

his people; and then he went in one of the 'public' wagons, among the *'poor'* of his tribe.

Against these unscrupulous, conniving settlers Hooper, the "Champion of the Creeks," vented his special anger. With apparent great glee he rejoiced when "those lords of the soil!—the men of dollars—the fortune-makers who bought with hundreds what was worth thousands!" fell victims of "retributive justice." Within ten years, he declared, nine out of ten of the cheaters had "lost money, lands, character, every thing! And the few who still retain somewhat of their once lordly possessions, mark its steady, unaccountable diminution, and strive vainly to avert their irresistible fate—an old age of shame and beggary. They are cursed, all of them—blighted, root and trunk and limb! The Creek is avenged!"

As he moved about the countryside in these early, formative years, when life itself leaned heavily on the rifle, the axe and the froe, Hooper observed not only the white man's treatment of the Indians, but also the white man's treatment of himself.

To begin with, the old Southwestern frontier was a mecca for every sort of American, the good, the bad and the indifferent. Some who came, the large majority, no doubt, were hard-working, honest pioneers who desired more than anything else to exchange their old, worn-out soils back east for fresh, to build homes, churches, schools and to better themselves and their families for all time to come. They were steady, sturdy farmers, carpenters, mechanics, blacksmiths, merchants, printers, saw-millers—the numerous little people, largely unlearned but, like true pioneers everywhere, God-fearing folks filled with zeal to carve a homeland out of a wilderness. With them of course travelled some few already well-to-do planters and their families who rode in comfortable carriages, their slaves trailing behind in wagons sagging with Sheraton and Hepplewhite. Doctors, lawyers, editors, teachers, surveyors and other professional men came too, partly for adventure, perhaps, but largely because of man's eternal faith in the pot at the other end of the rainbow. Many were college graduates, men who had flung aside profitable careers and enviable reputations to join the southwestward caravan. Once on the frontier, however, they pitched eagerly into the practice of their professions, posting their shingles, opening schools or starting newspapers. Frequently they also tried their hands at farming or trading, but always they found that the last river they crossed had been their Lethe . . .

But not all who came were angels on horseback. A loud-voiced minority were shiftless ne'er-do-wells, the parasites of progress, hangers-on to whom the other fellow's grass seemed always greener and freer. Not a few were fugitives from justice. For reasons never discussed they somehow felt that Alabama's climate might be particularly healthful. Convicts emptied from the bowels of prisons in the old states cut paths westward, also. Indeed, some of all the flotsam and jetsam of a fabulous America, for one reason or another stifled by the too-sweet aromas of organized society, found their way to the backwoods of Alabama in the 1830's.

Once this adventuresome medley of the clean and the unclean reached their destination, they were strangely bound together by a common denominator of necessity. The frontier was America's greatest leveller. There were Indians to master and forests to clear, homes to raise and roads to build, crops to plant and food to gather. From sun-up to sun-down—from *can* to *can't*—was a day and each was hard and sombre. The unlearned farmer plowed around his stumps and shot the panther on his doorstep. The learned doctor, forced to spend the night on a shuck-and-straw mattress in a settler's chinked-and-daubed cabin, remote and not infrequently filthy, or the learned lawyer, obliged to hobnob with ignorant, drunken, tobacco-spitting clients or rascally land speculators, or the learned politician, making merry over a pewter piggin full of red-eye in a crowded, itchy, foul-smelling roadside tavern, came face to face with a happy breed he might possibly have considered many notches beneath his dignity. If he did, he could not afford to have the fact known. And so it came to pass that, for all his homespun jeans, his rawhide galluses and his bare feet a man was accepted for what he was, not what he had been, and no questions raised. It might have been frontier etiquette to ask a settler whence or even how he came to Alabama—but never *why.*

If life was bleak and rough, it also had its fun and frolics. Like the Pilgrim two hundred years before him, Alabama's pioneer shouldered old Silver Heels and trekked through the virgin forest to take part in a neighbor's log-toting, house-raising, wood-chopping, corn-husking, picking-bee, or that most social of all socials, the break-down. Funerals, too, though solemn to tears, were eagerly anticipated as gala occasions, important both to business and society. Usually they were preached weeks or months after the actual burial and were publicly advertised in the press and by widely distributed announcements. Few people passed up the opportunity for such get-togethers: at them office-seekers saw votes, horse-traders horses, creditors uncollected debts, farmers land, oxen or mules. All saw a good, rowdy time. "Brethering, as being as I'm here," announced one preacher as he opened a service for a colleague, "I'll open the meetin' fur Brother Buncomb, an' then he'll preach the funeral sarmint accordin' to previous a-p'intment. But while I'm before you, I want to say as how my main business over here is a-huntin' of some seed peas, and if anybody here has got any to spar', I'd like to know it after meetin'."

Like funerals, weddings were all day or all night affairs where corn whiskey flowed freely down the throats of celebrants of both sexes, including the Man of God who frequently relied upon a dram or two for added inspiration. Homemade white-lightning was as common as homemade cornbread. There were week-long religious camp-meetings held under the trees, quilting parties, cock and dog fights, shooting and cotton-picking bees, horse-racings, wrestling matches, local militia musters, house-warmings, goose jousts and gander-pullings—all keyed more or less to the tune of frontier rowdyism. Every crossroads had its "tippling house," "confectionary" or "grocery" where rot-gut and bust-head licker, peach brandy and other "sperrits" were sold by the keg, jug or dipperful. Along with their men-folks women smoked, chewed or dipped unceasingly, so much so that ministers railed from their make-shift pulpits against the evil of the "filthy weed." But to no avail. For it was considered quite an art to hit the bucket at twenty feet: apparently few were so accomplished, however, judging from the sluices of tobacco juice that found the floors or trinkled down the walls of stores, homes and public buildings.

Yes, Hooper's Alabama was a rough, tough, swearin', gamblin', heavy drinkin', fist-fightin' country and physical prowess, not mental, was usually its own reward. The "champeen" of any activity, be it shooting, wrestling or corn-shucking, easily crawled up the ladder of social prestige—and not the least affluent was the champion drinker, the man who could take on the most and walk away. It was, as the oft-quoted Henry Watterson once stated, "the good old time of muster days and quarter-racing, before the camp-meeting and the barbecue had lost their power and their charm; when men led simple, homely lives, doing their love-making and their law-making as they did their fighting and their plowing, in a straight furrow; when there was no national debt multiplying the dangers and magnifying the expenses of distillation in the hills and hollows, and pouring in upon the log-rolling, the quilting, the corn-shucking, and the fish-fry an inquisitorial crew of tax-gatherers and 'snoopers' to spoil the sport and dull the edge of patriotic husbandry."

Crude and lewd through it was, Alabama's backwoods society had it virtues. Chief among these was a deeply ingrained sense of friendliness, or better still, of neighborliness. When trouble threatened, as it often did, a community became instantly a big family: it was a poor dog indeed that wasn't worth whistling for. Withal his roughness the real frontiersman was at heart an altruist, quick to come to the aid of his friends. Independence of thought and action he had, to be sure, and frankness and forthrightness and a lightly borne spirit of belligerency, but seldom did he covet a reputation in his region higher than that of being a staunch friend. Fist fights were routine affairs, along with drinking and church-going, but it was against the frontier's code of ethics for a man to carry concealed weapons, fight

[64]

with a gun or a knife or attack an opponent smaller than himself. Locks on cabin doors, even in remotest sections, were taboo, and untaught pioneers had to take them off. It was insulting not to have the latchstring always on the outside. Man's faith in man was abiding and everyone was accepted as four-square until proved otherwise. Then, it often happened, it was too late.

In this simple but austere life, where free thought, speech and action was the unwritten law, American democracy found it finest testing-ground. Nowhere was ever more completely democratic, more wholly American than the frontier.

For Hooper, the young, aristocratic North Carolinian, who saw this pioneer Alabama during its most uncouth era, the illiterate, tough settler was a source of wonder and amusement. As the brother of an established attorney and a neophyte lawyer in his own right, Hooper had access to the homes of the affluent, slave-holding and not infrequently aristocratic planters, some of whom maintained, as far as was possible on the bewildering frontier, the standards of refinement once enjoyed in the old states. But these families were few and far between. The majority of associates with whom Hooper was of necessity thrown were small farmers, storekeepers, blacksmiths and their like, backwoodsmen all, a curious motley of men, crude, unpredictable and incongruous. Their society, so numerous throughout the Old South's ever-shifting frontier, instead of oppressing Hooper and his kind, however, served as comic relief in an otherwise bleak and boring existence. As a result, the peckerwood, cracker, sandlapper, hill-billy, red-neck, tar-heel, clay-and-dirt-eater, and piney-woods tackey, to list but a few of the well-known synonyms for the Southern poor-white, became soon and have been for more than a century a stock-in-trade for countless humorists, down to and including the renowned latest, William Faulkner and Erskine Caldwell.

If this seems incongruous, it must be remembered that the writing man on the frontier was himself recording the incongruous. Hooper and his fellow humorists in the antebellum Southern hinterland, had at best only three or four levels from which to choose their subjects—the wealthy, cavalier-minded landowner, his Negro, the Indian, or the po' white.

Withal his fine feathers, the planter-aristocrat offered nothing particularly unique. His chattel, the slave, was at best but chattel, and if his songs and antics were comic, as they doubtless were, he was after all hardly worthy of literary effort. His time in American letters, as well as that of his master, was to come in the romantic future. The Indian, of course, was mildly exciting, but not book-worthy, except for such hair-raising episodes as "captivities" (of which there were many) or for slushy, "noble-savage" sentiment.

The po' white, on the contrary, the illiterate, shiftless, malaria-ridden

[65]

backwoodsman was a real find, coarse, native, a comic of the first water and a perfect subject to laugh *either at or with*. He was in short a social anomaly. Whether seen as a scheming politician, a big-muscled bully, a Hard-Shelled Baptist preacher, a mock-heroic Davy Crockett, a conniving, shiftless rogue, a ludicrous horse-trader, a crooked faro dealer or, at his worst, a lazy, vermin-ridden squatter in his windowless, floorless, doorless and filthy log-cabin in the hills, he was the Great Common Man. If he belonged to the "half-agricultural, half-piscatory . . . sinewy, yellow-headed whiskey-loving set" in Tallapoosa County, or dwelt in Butler where "ther is no society nor no nothing . . . [and] the people is more like hogs and dogs than they are like folks," or in Barbour County where "we hain't ben eatin' nothin' but dried beef so long we've wore ur corn-grinders down to the gums, and we want suthin' else by way of change," he was nevertheless appealing as a pioneer, and Americans have always loved the pioneer. He was ignorant, but not pathetic and mainly he was *odd*. He was typically "Southern," unlike any class in any other section of the nation. But most of all he was humorous, a primitive comic, and as such he became the main stock of humor in the South for a hundred years, from Thomas Singularity to Jeeter Lester. Out of him or by means of him sprang a truly American literature, the most indigenous this country has ever produced. No doubt, Bret Harte, himself famous as a humorist throughout the English speaking world, had him in mind when he declared, "It is to the South and West that we really owe the creation and expression of that humor which is perhaps most characteristic of our lives and habits as a people. It was in the South, and among conditions of servitude and the habits of an inferior race, that there sprang up a humor and pathos as distinct, as original, as perfect and rare as any that ever flowered under the most beneficent circumstances of race and culture. It is a humor whose expressions took a most ephemeral form—oral, rather than written. It abode with us, making us tolerant of a grievous wrong, and it will abide with us even when the conditions have passed away. It is singularly free from satire and unkind lines. It was simplicity itself. It touched all classes and conditions of men. . . ."

The writers who so naively portrayed the ludicrous aspects of frontier life were not professional humorists. Rather, they were respectable doctors, travellers, surveyors, schoolmasters, preachers, printers, planters, merchants, politicians, soldiers, actors, country squires, or—like Hooper—lawyers or country editors who had keen eyes for the grotesque and the knack for putting it down. Crackerbox philosophers they have been called, amateurs who had the skill to blend horseplay with horse-sense to make horse-laughs and by so doing to create unconsciously, a distinctly national type of literary expression, the so-called Big Bear School of American Humor. As

Franklin J. Meine has admirably written, they "were quick to seize upon the comic aspects of the rough life about them, and graphically sketched the humorous and colorful happenings, the oddities in rustic or pioneer character, and the tall tales that were going the rounds of the locality. These spontaneous, hilarious pencillings, from an academic point of view, may indeed be considered nothing more than rather charcoal sketches. Yet in their way they are masterpieces: realistic, racy, written in a vein of rollicking humor, and thoroughly characteristic in tone, color, and action of that forgotten era. The age, one of the most vivid of American experiences, has no other authentic record in our literature. Nothing is more essentially American than the frontier; and these sketches, humble enough in intent, were the earliest literary realization of the frontier, and, remain its most revealing expression."

Many of the recorded yarns and tales were doubtless apocryphal, first heard on horseback in the wide open spaces or around the fireplaces of isolated taverns on winter evenings. Their *locale* was the country store, the village courtroom, the river steamboat, the squatter's cabin, the backwoods camp-meeting, the stagecoach or the hunter's camp. Their *subject matter* was the teller himself and his neighbors, the uncultured, unsophisticated Common Man. And their *style* was the frank, leisurely and often irreverent venacular of the comic backwoodsman, spiced with anecdotes, repetition, trick-endings and crude, homespun dialogue. As a result, the stories are strongly provincial, genuinely Southern and in most respects wholly unlike the humor produced in other parts of the nation. Certainly, their authors staked no claim to academic respectability. But nowhere in American letters is there anything more really American. Their eyewitness portrayals of life and character on the ante-bellum Southern frontier, exaggerated though they may be, are quite likely to be nearer the truth than those of the better-known Lavender and Old Lace School. From them American literature has inherited a realism, an earthiness and balance which has helped it steer a middle course these many years. As William T. Porter stated in his 1845 Preface to *The Big Bear of Arkansas*, "a new vein of literature, as original as it is inexhaustible in its source, has been opened in this country within a very few years, with most marked success . . . [The authors are mainly] country gentlemen, planters, lawyers, &c., 'who live at home at ease'. . . . Most of them are gentlemen not only highly educated, but endowed with a keen sense of whatever is ludicrous or pathetic, with a quick perception of character, and a knowledge of men and the world: more than all, they possess in an iminent degree the power of transferring to paper the most faithful and striking pictures with equal originality and effect. In this respect they have superiors on neither side of the Atlantic."

To these tongue-in-cheek raconteurs, of whom Hooper is a recog-

[67]

nized example, everything was grist for the mill. Without them our social history would be but dull drivel of a pseudo-chivalric past, a ruffled record of dyspeptic lords and crinolined ladies—as un-American as five o'clock tea. With them is an almost inexhaustible treasury of information about the early frontier—gambling, horse-racing, courtroom scenes, hunting and fishing, backwoods courtships and weddings, murders, burlesque revivalists' meetings, camp life, descriptions of the weather and the country, local customers, and hundreds of subjects typically American. "They rubbed elbows daily with the vigorous life of their times and reported it with shrewdly humorous insight. In laughing at the hurly-burly of America, *they knowingly laughed at themselves as part and parcel of it.* That is the core of our native sense of humor."

Nearly always these authors wrote anonymously, not for profit but for fun, publishing their products in local newspapers wholly for local consumption. If, as in the case of Hooper, their efforts were somehow forced upon a wider audience, they were frankly astonished. "If what was designed, chiefly," Hooper stated in the Preface to his first book, "to amuse a community unpretending in its tastes, shall amuse the Great Public, the writer will, of course, be gratified. If otherwise, the mortification will be lessened by the reflection that the fault of the obtrusion is not entirely his own." Several of the humorists, including Hooper, either tried later to suppress their works or denied having written them, fearing that such fame was detrimental to their rightful pursuits of politics, law, medicine, or preaching.

A few of them are well-known: Davy Crockett, George Washington Harris ("Sut Lovingood"), Augustus Baldwin Longstreet, whose *Georgia Scenes* (1835) has been called "the cornerstone of this early humorous literature," William Tappan Thompson ("Major Joseph Jones"), Joseph Glover Baldwin ("Ovid Bolus, Esq."), Sol Smith, George W. Bagby ("Mozis Addums"), Thomas Bangs Thorpe ("Tom Owen, the Bee Hunter") and William Trotter Porter who, although not a humorous writer himself, admirably served by collecting and publishing many tales in his *Big Bear of Arkansas* (1845), *A Quarter Race in Kentucky, and Other Tales* (1846), and—most important—in the *Spirit of the Times*, a weekly sporting journal of which he was for many years editor and proprietor. And of course Samuel L. Clemens, who unquestionably owed a great debt to his predecessors in the field of American humor, satire and realism.

Until lately the contribution of these homespun stalwarts to the literature of the region and, for that matter, of America, has been pretty much overlooked, "elegantly ignored," as Meine put it a decade ago, "by most of our writers on American history... and students of American literature, who have been, for the most part, either ignorant of the field or superior to it." More recently, however, they have attracted increasing attention as a highly important element of our native literary heritage.

And it's high time. If the literary Old South has been too long reflected in the glorious fuss-and-feathers of all the old-line make-believers—Simms, Kennedy, Caruthers, Poe, Augusta Evans Wilson and their ilk, to say nothing of foreigners like Thackeray, Mrs. Hemans, Bulwer and Sir Walter Scott—it is indeed time to lift their veil of smug respectability for a refreshing view of the real thing. Perhaps the Old South wasn't Sir Walter Scottland, after all.

Then, in ever clearer outline the predominant literature of the antebellum South slowly comes into focus—a simple, homemade literature, but a complete one because it is folk-literature of the people themselves and native to the core. In it is embodied the many aspects of society from the high-and-mighty cavalier to the wooden-nutmeg pedlar, a coarse, colorful, satirical, climatic literature, extremely masculine and frequently as funny as all *git-out*. It was the frontier in action, a literature as indigenous as camp-meetings-with-dinner-on-the-ground, corn-shuckings or house-warmings. It is the old Southern frontier looking at itself, laughing at itself, and talking about itself. It is as near as America has come to a literature all its own.

ELYTON AND THE CONNECTICUT YANKEE

Birmingham [Alabama] *News Monthly Magazine*, January 4, 1970.

Had it not been for the Connecticut Asylum for the Deaf and Dumb, there would have been no Elyton, Alabama. And thereby hangs an intriguing tale that begins 1,200 miles away and 150 years ago...

William H. Ely was a Connecticut minister's son and a graduate of Yale University. Before he was fifty he had earned a fortune and had dedicated his life to helping his fellow man. In 1819 he was instrumental in persuading the United States Congress to deed a township of land (that is, a tract equal to six square miles) to the Connecticut Asylum, a charitable institution in Hartford. This vast acreage was to be chosen from the public lands of any state in the Union and all money derived from sales was forever to remain "to the use of the said asylum, for the education and instruction of deaf and dumb persons."

The asylum trustees immediately appointed Ely their official agent, granting him full responsibility of selecting and selling the lands and crediting the proceeds to the institution. Agent Ely carefully studied a map of the United States, chose the newly-created state of Alabama as the best location and shortly after Christmas, 1819, left Hartford on his long and hazardous overland journey south.

Ely arrived in Huntsville, Alabama, on Feb. 20, 1820, after having ridden for seven days in a cold, driving rain on horseback from Knoxville.

Three days later, he set out, again on horseback, for Florence, 70 miles away, to seek aid and advice from General John Coffee, Surveyor General of Alabama.

Together, they laid plans for "an exploring tour thro the Country." By now, however, the gentleman from Connecticut was thoroughly disgusted with the "joyless, profligate" Alabama frontier and homesick to "fly to the Bosom of (his) dear family." But his sense of duty drove him forward. "Having put my hand to the Plough," he wrote his wife, April 4, 1820, "I must not look back: And I have consolation to think that, while enduring Privations and hardships, I am promoting the important Interests of a most interesting Charity."

From Huntsville, Ely and the General rode south to Jones Valley, where they staked off 2,560 acres—all Ely "thought expedient to select at that place ... (his) expectations not being realized on seeing the Land." Moreover, he was disappointed in General Coffee. Although earning $25 per day for his services, the General had quit the job suddenly after the fourth day. Ely, not to be outdone, registered his holdings at the United States Land Office and, before returning to Huntsville, sold two tracts of 160 acres each in the heart of Jones Valley for $16.50 and $15.00 per acre, respectively.

In mid-May Ely was back in Jones Valley, still pursuing his "researches after land." He selected additional lands for the asylum and succeeded in selling "a few Quarter sections" at "great Sacrifice." On April 20, from Carrollville (Jefferson County), he wrote his wife that he was "weary with traveling over Mountains, thro Swamps & Mud & living in the Piles of Logs with no other windows than the large spaces between them (there not being a Pane of Glass to 5,000 People in the Country) and living on Hog and Corn."

Later in the year Ely again returned to Jones Valley. Since his last visit several months before, the progressive citizens of that growing region had taken a decisive step. They had voted to make of their unnamed village an incorporated town which, with the proper consent of the state legislature, would become the county seat of Jefferson County. But—alas!—the very spot upon which they most wished to lay off streets and erect a courthouse had been deeded to that "Connecticut Asylum man." Everybody knew that William H. Ely gave nothing away—and yet ... well, there couldn't be any harm in trying.

The county commissioners—William Prude, Reuben Reed, William Erwin, John Adams, and John Cochran—approached Ely cautiously. They treated him most cordially—in "a most respectful & friendly manner," Ely later wrote his wife—informing him of their wishes. They tactfully outlined their plans for a courthouse, casually mentioning that somehow they had not yet been able to agree on a fitting name for the new town, but hoped to get around to that detail pretty soon now.

Ely chewed his lower lip and his eyes took on a far-away stare, glassy-like. For a split second he must have envisioned a colorful map of Alabama with his name emblazoned on it in large letters. Suddenly, his eyes brightened. Yes, he'd do it. He'd give the county a tract of land—8.66 acres to be exact—just where they wanted it, provided they'd build that courthouse right in the middle of it!

At the next meeting of the legislature, on December 20, 1820, the little muddy-streeted, log-cabined village in Jones Valley was incorporated as the Town of Elyton, Alabama. And William H. Ely proudly wrote his wife that through the "influence" of "respectful & friendly" citizens the legislature had "passed an act incorporating this place as a Town with, to me the complimentary name of Elyton, which is established as the Seat of Justice or County Town, of this County."

But the honeymoon was of short duration. Less than two months later, Ely, now fed up with the "famous Town of Elyton," as he sarcastically called it, wrote his wife that he had "no interesting Society" there and "little variety of employment or Scenery." He was tired of living in a log hut, waiting to sell land to people "who are all from Interest, combined against me ... cabaling & laying all Plans they can devise, to get the advantage of me in my Bargains, and I find it necessary to be wide awake & guarded at all Points & not only to be shrewd & watchful but to walk uprightly and circumspectly. . . ." Then he confidently added that he considered himself their "match," however, and was sure the people would never be able to "take" him, "as they do Uncle Sam . . . at the public Sales."

By late February Ely had disposed of a large part of his land in Jones Valley at from $3.15 to $10.00 an acre. One day in March he deposited $25,000 in cash and drafts in a Huntsville bank. Throughout April and May he continued selling at highest possible prices, carefully depositing all money to the asylum's credit in Tuscaloosa, Mobile, Huntsville and elsewhere.

But his opinion of Alabama never improved. He deplored constantly the "despicable rough dirty & uncomfortable" cabins built just high enough off the ground "for Hogs, dogs, Cats & fowls to go under." Their "growling, squealing, barking, squalling & cackling" kept him awake nights! Horses and cattle, he stated, frequently favored him with a visit by "running their heads into the Window, to say how'de." Alabama's tippling and gambling houses, cockfights, shooting scrapes, hunting and fishing caused him great concern. Alabamians are "a very avaricious People," he wrote his wife. "Money is their God, & Cotton the Idol of their devotions."

By June, 1821 Ely had got "enough of Alabama" and was eager to quit it "forever." Shortly thereafter he returned to the Nutmeg

State, taking with him a fortune made out of Alabama land sales. In his eighteen months in the new state he had found little or nothing to please him—except Alabama money. And behind him he had left nothing but his name—a town name which has been perpetuated for a century and a half and is today one of the principal areas of Birmingham.

SUPPLYING RESEARCH NEEDS
IN THE HUMANITIES

Florida State University Library School Workshop Proceedings, 1958.

I have heard with pleasure Dr. Sarah Herndon's summary of the new methods of research and investigation which presently impinge upon the ancient and honorable citadel of the humanities. I join you in applauding her for her keenly perceptive analysis and, although I lack the intuition to follow her predictions precisely, I do indeed appreciate the fact that she and I are kindred spirits. I am sure that, as fellow holders of the doctorate in English, we agree on the total impact of the theme, even though we might not choose to put our exclamation points in quite the same places.

Now that she has so admirably described—from the standpoint of the scholar-teacher—the changing trends and directions toward humanities research, I, as a scholar-librarian, am charged with the counter-responsibility of suggesting some of the problems librarians face in attempting to anticipate and supply the research needs of these new trends and directions.

In attempting to do this I could readily call the roll of some of the better bibliographic sources in the fields of literature, music, philosophy, fine arts, religion and perhaps even history (for in many ways history belongs to the humanities), and thus perhaps discharge my obligation to the conference. However, I shall not follow this simple procedure. It is a checklist you desire, I suggest you take copious notes on Lester Asheim's *The Humanities and the Library,* recently published, or read the small print in the latest editions of Constance M. Winchell's *Guide to Reference Books,* or re-study the last chapter of *Basic Reference Sources,* by our distinguished friend and colleague, Louis Shores. As for myself, I should rather look somewhat further or deeper, as the case may be, at some of our truly pertinent problems. And in so doing I shall confine my remarks to three topics, which in my opinion, largely determine the destiny of library research in the harassed humanities.

The first alone could easily consume all of my allotted time—the need for funds. This primary problem all libraries have faced forever. Libraries simply cannot keep apace without money, ample sums of money. Ever-increasing amounts of money must be budgeted for books old and new. And I hasten to explain that mere dollar count is not the criterion, for inflationary costs during the last two decades have hit libraries hard and painfully. The purchasing power of the 1939 dollar, for example, is only 48¢ today and in 1968, according to best estimates, will be little more than 40¢. This means that a library which in 1939 had a $100,000 book budget would now require $208,333 and within the next ten years, $250,000, just to break even on its purchases.

But that is not all. During the last twenty years several other insidious situations have been developing within the library. Let us look at a few of them. First, significant portions of the library's book budget have of late been siphoned off, wisely or unwisely, into the purchase of miscellaneous materials which with an embarrassing lack of inspiration we call "non-books." Whether you agree with Louis Shores in believing that these are to be assigned the same prestige as books or whether you decry their very existence, as does Leland Hazard, you cannot deny the fact that their emergence has noticeably diverted funds away from our original and basic stock in trade, the book. Second, considerable increases have of necessity been made in librarians' wages. Here, too, inflation has been hard at work. Today a beginning salary of $4,000 is really only $1,920 in terms of the 1939 dollar, and before many months have passed will be worth only $1,600. If these facts disturb you, look further. In 1939 the average library budget was usually divided roughly into 55% for salaries, 35% for books, and 10% for other expenses. Now, in 1958, the percentages are much more likely to be about 65, 20, and 15. Thus, even as we inch forward in the overall total, necessarily channelling more funds into salaries and operating expenses, it is at long last the book fund which suffers. In fact, in 1939, 35% of $100,000 was $35,000; but the buying power of 20% of today's $200,000, fairly equated, is less than $20,000. In short, out of a budget twice as great, the present-day librarian has only about one-half the amount his predecessor had twenty years ago to spend for books. Do you see why I earlier used the word insidious? Third, many automatic devices have flooded the library market in recent years, some of exceedingly doubtful value, but none inexpensive. Now, I hasten to add, I am not inherently anti-machine. Actually, I get along peaceably with the things, once we get used to each other. But I somehow never forget, as I twist their dials and push their buttons, that there but for the grace of God am I, a robot librarian in all my chrome and plastic splendor, impersonal and impermanent. But more than that, because I am at heart a humanities book-man, I see hundreds of dollars being filched from the library's book fund every year for electrical appliances of this and that sort. And I ask myself, how will it all end? When will the librarian be mechanized

[73]

out of his usefulness? When will the librarian go the way of the black-smith, the miller, the family doctor and the dodo bird?

I could lead you into a maze of other problems that thwart the librarian's plan to supply the needs of his humanities patrons—the growing demands for highly specialized and little-used but expensive materials, the need for a greater variety of foreign journals (and their translations), our embarrassing shortages of bibliographical guides (one of the researcher's chief complaints against us is our almost total lack of knowledge about where things are), the constantly rising prices of processing (our classification schemes and card catalogs are still most inadequate indexes to the material the research scholar needs) and, of course, the overall fact that with his 48¢ dollar, the 1958 librarian is expected to acquire and to service, in addition to books and periodicals, a welter of miscellany from postal cards to phonographs and, withal, to be patient, gracious and ever-pleasant.

Now, I would suggest a second problem which the librarian faces in his attempt to fulfill his obligation to the humanities researcher. Here I need be very brief and very blunt. If I were convinced that the librarian's potential responsibility to the scholar consisted solely of being a literary midwife, I suspect I should long ago have returned to the classroom. Heaven grant that our profession be above the level of a delivery service! Certainly, neither you nor I wish to spend our lives as mere checkboys in the parcel room of culture. But we have come dangerously close to that appellation. If not, why should the subject be so often broached, even in our professional literature? The librarian's "planning must be that of a teacher and scholar, not a curator or technician," states the Commission on Institutions of Higher Education of the Middle States Association of Colleges and Secondary Schools. And the idea that the contents of books should be given ever-increasing emphasis in library school curriculums, instead of library practices, has long been voiced, even in the aforesaid study of the integration of the library with the humanities.

I doubt if I need to elaborate upon the thought that our profession may be doomed to mediocrity, if we should fail to heed these ever-recurring warnings. For it is no secret that across America and at all levels many librarians have experienced considerable difficulty in obtaining desired professional recognition, to say nothing of con-comitant pay scales. Certainly, this cannot be because the innate intelligence of librarians is second to that of other educators. I for one believe and believe very strongly that the academic status we so much want will come to us when we earn it, not before, and that we will never earn it until we stop studying books as artifacts and stop reducing "research" in librarianship to the level of time and motion studies of janitorial services.

Much has been written in recent years about the efficacy of bib-

[74]

liotherapy. I agree with almost every word of it—but I am also equally convinced that the curative power of books is as beneficial for the librarian as it is for his patrons. Indeed, with his office the librarian assumes the responsibility for exploiting books to the best of his ability. His ultimate success depends, therefore, not on his skill in marking them or paging them, but on reading them, not on what he does to the outsides of books but what the insides of books do to him. In no other way, as I see the problem before us, can the librarian ever hope to discharge his full responsibility to the research scholar and at the same time render his profession both indispensable and ennobling.

The responsibility of the librarian to supply the research needs of the humanist in this mid-century suggests a third vitally important problem for our consideration. You will not be surprised when I say that our generation is living in the most interesting and in many ways the most terrifying era in world history. During our lifetime military, political, social and scientific crises, coming fast upon us in bewildering succession, have had profound effect upon your life and mine. The impact of such swift, climactic changes has been severe. Our world has become unlike anything we have ever known before, or ever dared dream of. And today, a stranger to yesterday, foretells an uneasy tomorrow.

Out of this turbulence have emerged many strange and dramatic proposals to assail our peace of mind, strike at our ways of life, yes, even to shake the very foundations of our national security. Not the least, and one which was re-born full-grown on sputnik day, consists of the theory that somehow we can manufacture happiness out of steel and synthetics and bring peace and good will to earth by splitting an atom. This theory has made a sudden but deep impression on many Americans and its repercussions have reached far and wide, even into our schoolrooms and libraries. Today there are actually many men and women across the land who tell us that the physical sciences will save us, that science will right our wrongs, that science is the summum bonum. Laboring under the hypnotic spell of technocracy, they would all but strip our curriculums of the humanities and thus turn our schools into powerplants for placing perpetual motion machines in outer space, for sending submarines around the world without refueling, for building bombs to blast mankind from the face of the earth forever. These, too, are the very pragmatists we librarians must surely watch—for in their power-mad confusion they would have us build our libraries into bastions of science, channelling all but a pittance of our book funds away from the humanities and social sciences into mathematical equations, scientific formulae and how-to-do-it treatises.

To them we must address a resounding NO. These things they

would sponsor are but temporal as sounding brass and tinkling cymbals. Deep inside, man is faith and lovingkindness. He longs to give goodness to his learning. He knows that the only realities of life are the *un*-realities, the things he cannot see or hear or touch, but only feel. He knows that in the end mankind struggles not against each other, not against flesh and blood, not against principalities nor powers, but against hate, prejudice, intolerance, ignorance and all the other unseen, elusive, imponderable but very, very real enemies of the human spirit.

I say to you, my library friends, our true and abiding strength lies not in robots or rockets, however they may steal the current headlines, but in a much deeper dedication—the meaning we finally give our researches and the direction in which we turn our discoveries. Art is long, but life is fleeting. Have you noticed that we say the Battle of Waterloo *was*, but David Copperfield *is?* That Queen Elizabeth *said*, but Shakespeare *says?* Which has had more enduring impact upon our lives these last thousand years—Archimedes' principle or the Apostles' Creed? And who knows but that the recently-discovered Dead Sea scrolls of the ancient Essenes, so faded and so fragile, might yet be a more potent force in the progress of mankind than Albert Einstein's theory of relativity.

This, then, is the spirit of the humanities: from the days of Socrates their fundamental aim has been self-knowledge, self-realization, self-improvement. The good life is not something apart from men, but something in the midst of men, something to be achieved by men of good will everywhere, working together for the good of all men everywhere. The true end of a generous education, therefore, stripped of all its ancillaries, is to mold men and women into mature beings of understanding and integrity.

As we librarians go about our daily business, therefore, let us not be duped or misled. Our task is both of today and of tomorrow, both of the real and the un-real. Let us strive to sponsor man's eternal yearning for peace, and truth and beauty, for beauty is truth, truth beauty, and that is all we know and all we need to know. Let us build our libraries, then, not for prowess or for power, but only for the eternal benefit and betterment of mankind.

ON THE BOOK REVIEWER

Waco [Texas] *Tribune-Herald*, "Sunday Book Corner," December 25, 1938.

This is going to be what is known in impolite circles as a "personal" review-confession, if there is such a thing. But that doesn't matter. If a fellow can't get personal on Christmas, when can he? So, pull up your chair and light your new pipe; I don't mind the odor of varnish.

Besides, I've got a little private matter to talk over with you. It concerns book reviewers, and if you follow book reviews regularly, you'll be glad to get some inside dope on the genus.

In the first place, book reviewers (hereafter referred to as we) are a hierarchy of unmitigated, overweaned egotists, a weak-kneed host of self-appointed angels who day by day flap their self-preened wings up and down the corridors of a celestrial hennery of conceit called, for lack of a better name, "critics' heaven." I have heard that you think of a reviewer as a sort of catalytic agent for good, an altruist with a passion for improving the mind of man; one, let us say, who drops himself into the murky liquid of a book and comes up puffing and sputtering and blowing, and—bless his heart—modestly hands over to you "the best that has been said and thought in the world." There are, to be true, some critics like that. The bad ones. The ones you don't (or shouldn't) read.

And I'll tell you why. No critic worth his weight is satisfied with merely diluting another man's thoughts and passing them on to you in broken doses, like a protracted siege of tenth-grain calomel followed by a flushing of epsom salts. A good critic is motivated by no such pedagogical notions; he leaves that to the college professors. A good critic is prompted to make his own yapping heard around the world. Granted, he may take his immediate cue from the book at hand, and to that extent he is playing second fiddle; but the reviewer who demands readers is as effervescent with ideas and as eager to propagate them as the so-called creative artist. In fact, a good critic is just as surely a creative artist as the creative artist himself in that his chief aim is to couch his own thoughts into the pleasantest possible phraseology and cram them with the least face-making down the mouths of an unsuspecting public. The honest reviewer will tell you that he burns with two desires: (1) to emit his own ideas with a finesse or a flourish and (2) to see his own name in print. A cricket may chirp at sunset because his music blends beautifully with the song of the katydid, but I am inclined to believe that he likes mostly hearing himself rub his legs together.

Reading a first-rate review is like sipping champagne. You can sit with it. You can watch its clear, amber-colored bubbles rise and sputter, and you can feel your drafts slowly hitting bottom. It's not until you've drunk the bottle that you realize that you don't think exactly about things as you did before. Every good reviewer knows this. And capitalizes on it. For every critic you show me whose thoughts never pass the printed pages before him, I'll show you the dullest pedant in the profession. Criticism is the one business I know of in which it does not pay to stick too close to the trade. I suppose it may be a far-fetched parallel, but every time I think of a reviewer bound

[77]

by the margin, I think of the Jivaro Indians down in Peru. The Jivaroans have a drink called yucca. They make it this way: the women all sit around a campfire and chew yucca roots. One by one, as they get up big, juicy wads, they lean over and spit in the pot. By and by, when the pot gets full, they boil it and let it ferment, yucca, spit, juice and all. Then they cool it and drink it. It's a great drink—for the Jivaroans. You see, everybody has had a hand (or mouth) in it, and it tastes alike to all; at least that's the assumption. I suppose you might call that process communal distillation, and by the same reasoning Jivaroan reviewers (I am assuming that Jivaroans would tolerate anything so antiseptic as a reviewer) might, I rather like the idea, be communal critics: each would read the same book and get the same impressions of it. To be true, I dare not speak too emphatically, not knowing how you feel about yucca, but, all things considered, I believe I should prefer champagne.

Then there's another thing. I think I mentioned it above. It concerns the Grant Wood's Gothic type of reviewer who flutters back and forth across the back alleys of book criticism, shouting that criticism to be good must be constructive. Such a man assumes that he knows more about the subject than the author does, and hems him up to tell him how he should have done it. Rufus Griswold was one. He told Edgar Poe that he'd never get to first base writing short stories. Sidney Smith was another. He told William Wordsworth that his poetry was trash.

The book columns of America are bulging with starving reviewers who spend half their lives showing successful artists how they ought to do their work. I doubt if there is an essayist, poet, novelist or biographer in the world today who has become a better writer because of a reviewer's constructive criticism. If a reviewer were that good, he shouldn't be a reviewer. Fact of the matter is, he won't—not for long. The creative writer invariably starts out as a critic, makes a springboard out of some literary guinea pig, and ends up with an original contribution upon the same or a similar theme. If he is exceeding good (that is, if the urge within is more valuable to art than the suggestion without), he will usually wind up by doing what the man he is criticizing has done, namely, write first-hand about life rather than secondhand about books. Then, I scarcely need say it, he automatically becomes the guinea pig, and, consequently, the laboratory specimen of still another critic who will, if he is a good critic, make a springboard out of him. And so it goes.

But my space is up. Indeed, I marvel that you have followed me this far (or did you skip?). It's all your fault; you had no business beginning in the first place! There is one more thing I'd like to tell you, though:

Merry Christmas and a Happy New Year!

[78]

MAGDALENE CHRISTIAN

Not previously published.

I came to Radlington thirty years ago this September. I was young then, plump, and fired with zeal to make good as an English teacher. Except for one year I have been here ever since.

The day I arrived Mr. Sudbury Ford met me at the station. He was a member of the Board of Trustees, he said, a steward in the Methodist Church and a widower. We drove around Radlington for an hour before he put me out at Gussie Comfort's boarding house on Radlington Street.

A week later Mr. Ford called to ask how I was getting along. I told him I was quite happy in Radlington. Miss Gussie smiled and said that Sudbury was from one of the best families in Radlington, and well-to-do.

In the fall Sudbury and I took long rides in the country, often stopping at Mineral Springs. He loved the riot of colored leaves on the hillside there and the broad-leafed bays and the cool clear water.

In April we picnicked at Mineral Springs. New leaves were pushing old ones off the trees and green grass could be seen beneath a dust-brown carpet of pine needles. You could almost hear the stillness. As Sud carved our initials on the wooden bench, I watched the soap ferns nod along the water's edge. Now and then a robin would call his wandering mate far in the forest. And once a startled gray squirrel flattened himself on an oak limb above us, his tail tossed back over his head in camouflage. Feeling much, we said nothing, Sud and I, until almost dusk. Then he broke the silence, "Madge, do you think you could always be happy with me?"

All I needed to say I said with a smile and he pulled me quickly, tightly to him and kissed my lips and face and neck until I could scarcely breathe. Neither of us knew what happened after that. I cried softly and Sud took my hand in his and told me he would love me, endlessly. Dark fell before we left, but in that brief hour I had traded flesh for spirit and spirit for peace.

As my cheeks flushed and my dresses tightened and I began to show, I went to visit my aunt in Knoxville. Everyone thought I was working for my master's at the university there. Sud saw no reason to say otherwise and until I had completed the adoption I had no choice.

When I returned to Radlington, Sud was married to Virgil Radlington, daughter of Mayor Radlington whose forebears had founded Radlington. They live on Radlington Street now, just down from Gussie Comfort's. He is chairman of the Board of Trustees and I was long ago promoted to principal. Every time I see Sud he tips his hat politely and asks me how things are at school. He has kept our secret.

[79]

Over the lorn, lonely years I have taught three of Sud's children, two boys, both endearing and full of life, and a girl, moody, quiet, brooding, with her father's eyes and black curly hair. Her name is Robin.

Radlington has been the only home I really know. A little of my life has gone into the molding of hundreds of Radlington's boys and girls (my boys and girls, I call them), even to the third generation. Like Ozymandias, I have become a name—I am "Miss Madge."

Now and then, when mail comes from Tennessee, I drive out to Mineral Springs and sit on the concrete bench overlooking the shrinking stream (the wooden bench with M.C. and S.F. intertwined rotted down long ago). Away, in the stillness of the deep, dark woods I can hear a robin's call and to myself I say: Truth is not a monolith, standing alone, separate from all truths. Truth is a circle, embracing all truths. Who then is to say what is chaste or unchaste, who among us knows right from wrong?

Be still, my heart, and listen to my voice.

THE DAY TECUMSEH SPOKE

Birmingham [Alabama] *News Monthly Magazine*, February 2, 1969.

The greatest orator who ever addressed an Alabama audience was not an office-seeker or an evangelist or a paid entertainer, and the town he spoke in has long since been wiped off the map. Yet his powerful address, delivered 156 years ago, started a bloody war against the United States which cost thousands of lives and millions of dollars and catapulted two victorious American generals into the White House.

In 1812 unscrupulous white settlers in Alabama were slowly edging the Creek Indians off their lands, by hook or crook swindling them out of choicest riverbottom soils with worthless specie or a few tawdry trinkets. Lacking a forceful leader, the Creeks seemed powerless to fight back.

Far away to the north, however, Tecumseh, a Shawnee chief, heard of their plight and resolved to save them—Tecumseh, twin brother of Ellskwatawa the prophet, a warrior whose hatred for Americans and whose cruelties were known far and wide.

Tecumseh's father was a Shawnee, but his mother, born and bred at Souvanogee, on the Tallapoosa, near Old Augusta, Alabama, had been a Creek. As a lad of 19 Tecumseh had visited her people, spending two years in Alabama, hunting, fighting, learning the Creek language. Now, as the most famous Indian chief of his day, he would revisit his old haunts and persuade his mother's kinsmen to join the Great Confederacy in one all-out assault on their common enemy, the greedy, grasping Paleface.

[80]

Accompanied by a coterie of Shawnee braves, Tecumseh moved slowly southward from his home near the Great Lakes. Miles ahead of him runners spread the news of his coming. In Alabama the Creeks called a grand council of welcome at the ancient town of Tookabatcha on the Tallapoosa. On the great day more than 5,000 Indians assembled to hear their blood relative and friend from afar, Tecumseh—"the Cougar Crouching for His Prey"—whose every word could stop the sun or cause the winds to roar and whose footstep could shake the earth. Ellskwatawa the Prophet, his twin brother, had so willed...

Tecumseh, more than six feet high, erect, dignified, and dressed in kingly splendor, marched down between two dense masses of Creeks. Behind him, in single file, like a procession of ugly devils, followed 24 massive Shawnee warriors, their faces painted red and black, their naked bodies profusely decorated with silver ornaments. Each man carried a rifle, a tomahawk, and a war-club.

As the frightful procession approached the center of a huge square, Big Warrior, the Creek chief, stepped forward and handed Tecumseh his peace pipe. Slowly the visitor smoked it and started it down the long line of Shawnees. Not one word was spoken.

From his leathern pouch Tecumseh lifted a handful of tobacco and sumach and tossed it on a small ceremonial fire. Each of his tribesmen in turn did likewise, solemnly. Three times was this ritual performed slowly and in complete silence, as ten thousand Creek eyes followed every gesture. Then, man by man, the Shawnee braves lined up, facing Big Warrior and his tribal dignitaries.

Suddenly, Tecumseh's mighty voice broke the silence with a warwhoop, a most diabolical yell. Each of the Shawnees shouted likewise. Tecumseh then produced his pipe, a large, long one elaborately covered with shells, beads, painted eagle feathers and porcupine quills. Lighting it, he handed it to Big Warrior, who puffed it and passed it among the Creeks.

Meantime, not a word was uttered—everything was as still as death: even the winds slept and there was no noise in the forest save the gentle rustling of the autumn leaves.

At last Tecumseh spoke. Like a succession of thunderbolts his voice roared over the multitude. His eyes burned with supernatural lustre. His fine, powerful body trembled with emotion. His expression changed with his words from anger to hatred to defiance to vengeance.

"Accursed be the race that has seized our country and made women of our warriors," he shouted. "Our fathers, from their tombs, reproach us as slaves and cowards. The Creeks were once a mighty people. Once, the maidens of my tribe, on distant lakes, sang the prowess of your warriors and sighed for their embraces.

"Now your very blood is white; your tomahawks have no edge; your bows and arrows are buried with your fathers. Oh! Brethren

[81]

of my mother, brush from your eyelids the sleep of slavery. Once more strike for vengeance—once more for your country. The spirits of the mighty dead complain. Their tears drop from the weeping skies. Let the white race perish!"

His Creek listeners, up to now stoic in silence, were electrified. Thousands of tomahawks brandished the air, war-whoops punctuated his words, resounding through the primeval Alabama forest. Tecumseh, the world in his palm, continued:

"They seize your land; they corrupt your women; they trample on the ashes of your dead!

"Back, whence they came, upon a trail of blood, they must be driven.

"Back! back, aye, into the great water whose accursed waves brought them to our shores!

"Burn their dwellings! Destroy their stock! Slay their wives and children! The Red Man owns this country and the Palefaces must never enjoy it.

"War now! War forever! War upon the living! War upon the dead! Dig their very corpses from the grave. Our country must give no rest to a white man's bones.

"All the tribes of the north are dancing the war-dance. Two mighty warriors across the seas will send us arms."

Tecumseh paused dramatically, held high his rifle. The audience, drugged by his magnetic oratory, in awful stillness waited his next word. Then, slowly, they heard this dramatic prophecy:

"Tecumseh will soon return to his country . . . When the white men approach you, the yawning earth shall swallow them up!

"Soon shall you see my arm of fire stretched athwart the sky. I will stamp my foot at Tippecanoe, and the very earth shall shake."

As Tecumseh concluded his address, the Shawnees leaped to their feet with one blood-curdling yell and began their tribal war-dance. In pantomime they scouted, ambushed, and scalped the enemy, annihilating him with their clubs and tomahawks, all the while screaming in terrifying concert their hatred for the usurping Paleface.

When the mighty Tecumseh started his long trek back to the Ohio country, long lines of his newly-won allies cheered his departure. Soon he would signal the time of attack by stretching his mighty arm of fire athwart the sky. The very earth would shake with his footstamp. Had not he so prophesied?

All along the Coosa, the Tallapoosa, and the Warrior war-whoops echoed and re-echoed from village to village. Armed by the Spaniards at Pensacola, and egged on by the crafty British, the Creek Red Sticks —the war party—made ready for a fight to the death. Had not the Tecumseh foretold of help from over the sea?

Suddenly, Tecumseh the Prophet flashed his signal! Across the autumn sky he stretched his mighty arm, dazzling the world with a flame 132 million miles long—visible to the naked eye as far away as Europe. Earthquakes, the most powerful ever known on the American continent, shook the Mississippi Valley from the Missouri to the Gulf. Dreadful disease followed in the wake of torrential rains, flooded rivers overflowed fields and forests, and—oh! year of miracles—countless multitudes of common squirrels, in such numbers as had never before inhabited the earth, devoured crops and food-stocks and even ate babies alive in their cribs!

Tecumseh the prophet had stamped his foot at Tippecanoe ...

Now, stealthfully, the Red Sticks began their vicious attacks. At first they burned isolated wilderness cabins, scalping white families and leaving their bodies for the wolves. Gradually, they grew bolder, striking throughout Alabama, now here, now there, then quickly slinking back into the dark forests.

On July 27, 1813, led by Peter McQueen, a fanatical half-blood, they surprised a company of U.S. militia on the banks of Burnt Corn Creek. In frenzied panic the soldiers fled into the swamps, a mere handful living to tell the sad tale of slaughter.

A month later, at high noon on August 30, the Creeks, this time led by Red Eagle, another half-breed, struck again—at Fort Mims on Lake Tensas. In less than five hours 501 men, women, and children were mercilessly shot, tomahawked, and clubbed to death in one of the bloodiest massacres ever to occur on American soil.

One brutal attack followed another in rapid succession. The frontiersmen hurriedly erected forts at strategic points, herding their families and cattle behind high stockades. For months terror reigned, as helpless, out-numbered families were slaughtered, their bones left to bleach in the Alabama sun ...

At long last, after weeks of anxiety and death, help came—led by General Andrew Jackson and his volunteers. The tide of battle slowly turned—at Econachaca, (the Holy City), at Tellasehatche, Talladega, Hillabee, Tallassee, and elsewhere the war raged. And at Cholocco Litabixee—the Horseshoe Bend of the Tallapoosa—on March 27, 1814, the inimitable "Old Hickory" broke the back of the Red Sticks and sent them reeling into ignominy.

Defeated, stripped of their lands, and at last driven from Alabama, the superstitious Creeks never learned that Tecumseh's great "arm of fire stretched arthwart the sky" was a natural phenomenon, a comet which British astronomers had calculated would arrive in October and had shrewdly instructed Tecumseh to use to dupe his southern kinsmen into war.

And Tecumseh—what became of the fabulous Shawnee?

As General Tecumseh of the British Army he was killed gallantly

[83]

leading his warriors against General William Henry Harrison at the Battle of the Thames, near Detroit, October 5, 1813, one brief year after his "arm of fire had stretched arthwart the sky."

In 1829 General Andrew Jackson became the seventh president of the United States. And General Harrison followed him, as the ninth, a few years later.

So blow the fickle winds of fate.

ALABAMA TORIES: THE FIRST ALABAMA CAVALRY, U.S.A., 1862–1865
Prologue and Chronology

Confederate Publishing Company, Tuscaloosa, Alabama, 1960.

When the victorious army of the Ohio, Major-General Don Carlos Buell commanding, swept down into North Alabama in early April, 1862 several thousand citizens who held little or no devotion to the Confederate States of America, rallied around the invaders for aid and comfort. Huntsville, which was occupied by 8,000 troops of the Third Division and was designated as military headquarters, soon became the center of activities disloyal to the South.

Variously described as "Unionists," "Loyalists," "Tories," "Moss-backs" or "Conscripts," the disaffected were for one reason or another revolting against Confederate authority. Some, no doubt, were sincere in their allegiance to the Union. Others were in all probability opportunists whose loyalties shifted with the fortunes of war. Nevertheless, in mid-1862, as their own little, hilly, red-clay farms were fast becoming Federally-occupied territory, they found it neither difficult nor unprofitable publicly to profess their devotion to Old Glory.

In the North the Tories were hailed as "the abused and persecuted" and citizens' meetings were held in their honor, but among their fellow Southerners they were known as "mountain whites" or, to use a modern term, "hillbillies," a poor, often underprivileged people who had long been isolated on their rocky highlands, suspicious of intruders and generally antisocial. Blindly hating the affluent slave-holder and his "nigger" alike, they had first refused to support the cause of secession and, afterwards, ignored all Confederate civilian and military conscription laws. Forming themselves into bands of so-called "Destroying Angels" or "Prowling Brigades," they occasionally swept down out of their piney-wood strongholds to raid their more fortunate neighbors in the valleys. Not infrequently, they burned cotton, gin-houses, jails, county court records, public buildings, and dwellings, willy-nilly "confiscating" food and other properties as they went. By their depredations thousands of Confederate sympathizers were driven from their homes—some to be stripped and whipped by the marauding guerrillas and not a few to be murdered or raped. Even

[84]

to the Union conquerors, their so-called friends, the Tories were sometimes "as vicious as copperheads." And, as one Confederate colonel,
who had captured a small band of them in the Tennessee Valley,
wrote his commander, "They are the most miserable, ignorant, poor,
ragged devils I ever saw." As early as July 16, 1862 Colonel Abel
D. Streight, of the Fifty-first Indiana Volunteers, then stationed at
Mooresville, Alabama, described them as the "mostly poor" who
"came into our lines begging [for] protection and a chance to defend
the flag of our country." He added, "the tale of suffering and misery,
as told by each as they arrived, was in itself a lamentable history
of the deplorable position of the Union people of the South."

Altogether, in North Alabama there were thousands of Tories—it
is impossible to determine the exact number. Brigadier-General
Gideon J. Pillow reported in September, 1862 that at least ten
thousand, including some who had deserted from the Confederate
Army, were hiding out in the hills. Seven months later General Gustave
T. Beauregard received word that North Alabama was "full of Tories,"
and that in late 1862 they had actually held a large "convention"
in the region of Winston, Fayette, and Marion counties at which they
had voted, while wildly waving United States flags, to remain
"neutral." In the spring of 1863 a similar convention was held in
Winston County and in 1864 a Confederate officer wrote Beauregard
that in Lawrence, Winston, and Blount counties Federal recruiting
agents were carrying on open correspondence with many disloyal
citizens. There was no doubt in his mind that to these "Alabama
Yankees" *neutral* meant supporting the Union. Colonel Streight, who
praised their courage in the face of the great odds, wrote that their
"examples of patriotism . . . are worthy of being followed."

> One old lady, Mrs. Anna Campbell [Streight continued], volunteered
> to ride thirty-five miles, and return, making seventy miles, with about
> thirty recruits, inside of thirty-six hours. When it is taken into considera-
> tion that these people were all hid away to avoid being taken by the
> rebels, and that the country is but sparsely settled, this case is without
> a parallel in American history. There are many cases of a similar nature
> that came under my observation, but I do not desire to weary your pa-
> tience with them. Suffice it to say, that I have never witnessed such
> an outpouring of devoted and determined patriotism among any other
> people; and I am now of the opinion that, if there could be a sufficient
> force in that portion of the country to protect these people, there could
> be at least two full regiments raised of as good and true men as ever
> defended the American flag. So confident am I that my views are correct,
> that if the Commanding General will grant me permission to do so,
> I will take my regiment, (the boys all want to go,) and two weeks' rations
> of bread, salt, sugar and coffee, (meat we can get there,) and five hundred
> extra stand of arms, with a sufficient supply of ammunition, and locate
> at least thirty miles south of Decatur, where I will rally around me
> a sufficient number of the brave mountaineers to protect the country
> effectually against anything except the regular rebel army, who, by the

[85]

way, would find it a difficult country to operate in. Never did people stand in greater need of protection. They have battled manfully against the most unscrupulous foe that civilized warfare has ever witnessed. They have been shut out from all communication with any thing but their enemies for a year and a half, and yet they stand firm and true. If such merit is not to be rewarded, if such citizens are not to receive protection, then is their case a deplorable one indeed.

Mostly, the disaffected were from the North Alabama counties south of the Tennessee River—Winston, Marion, Walker, Franklin, Fayette, Blount, Madison, Morgan, St. Clair, Lawrence, Marshall, Jefferson, Limestone, Randolph, St. Clair, Tuscaloosa, Cherokee, and Jackson—counties which (1) grew less cotton, (2) held fewest slaves and (3) without exception had sent Cooperationist delegates to the Alabama Secession Convention of January, 1861. That is, at the polls they had voted their preference for somehow compromising with the North rather than seceding and thus inviting the possibility of armed conflict (see Table A).

TABLE A

Election of Delegates by Counties, Dec. 24, 1860 to the
Alabama State Convention of Jan. 7, 1861
(Arranged Alphabetically Under Party Majorities)*

Cooperationist Counties (23)

County	Secessionist Vote	Cooperationist Vote	Cooperationist Majority
Blount	505	805	300
Cherokee	1,118	1,139	21
Conecuh	372	399	27
Coosa	898	1,126	228
DeKalb	—	600	600
Fayette	432	1,110	678
Franklin	348	1,372	1,024
Jackson	1,025	1,263	238
Jefferson	574	675	101
Lauderdale	505	1,197	692
Lawrence	—	—	—
Limestone	314	774	460
Madison	404	1,487	1,083
Marion	255	793	538
Marshall	327	906	579

*This tabulation was compiled from Clarence P. Denman, *The Secession Movement in Alabama* (Montgomery, 1933), 161–166, and Lewy Dorman, *Party Politics in Alabama from 1850 through 1860* (Wetumpka, Ala., 1935), 194–195, who secured the data from the official returns and other contemporary sources. It should be noted that there is an error of 1 in the total Cooperationist vote. The figure should be 28,630 instead of 28,631 (that is, 21,665 plus 6,965).

[86]

	Secessionist Vote	Cooperationist Vote	Secessionist Majority
Morgan	520	627	107
Randolph	1,109	1,303	194
St. Clair	499	763	264
Talladega	993	1,174	181
Tallapoosa	983	1,609	626
Tuscaloosa	718	1,270	552
Walker	143	796	653
Winston	—	477	477
	12,042	21,665	9,623

Secessionist Counties (29)

County	Secessionist Vote	Cooperationist Vote	Secessionist Majority
Autauga	626	603	23
Baldwin	91	1	90
Barbour	1,653	—	1,653
Bibb	245	—	245
Butler	695	—	695
Calhoun	1,574	558	1,016
Chambers	1,018	665	353
Choctaw	463	217	246
Clarke	733	170	563
Coffee	714	359	355
Covington	337	229	108
Dale	1,007	195	812
Dallas	1,015	358	657
Greene	823	530	293
Henry	763	—	763
Lowndes	990	—	990
Macon	1,549	258	1,291
Marengo	527	—	527
Mobile	2,297	1,229	1,068
Monroe	515	465	50
Montgomery	1,274	158	1,116
Perry	781	19	762
Pickens	1,001	300	701
Pike	1,571	—	1,571
Russell	554	—	554
Shelby	635	588	47
Sumter	665	31	634
Washington	64	6	58
Wilcox	676	26	650
	24,856	6,965	17,891

Nor is this difficult to understand. In 1860 Alabama's population numbered 964,201, of which only 526,431 (54.59 per cent) were white, 435,080 (45.12 per cent) slave blacks and 2,690 free blacks and Indians. The blacks were owned by only 33,730 whites (6.21 per cent)—an average of 13 per slaveholder—and these were mainly concentrated in the cotton-growing counties of South Alabama. The other 492,701 whites owned not a single slave (see Table B).

TABLE B

Alabama Population, 1860
(Arranged in Ascending Order of Percentage of Negro Slaves)

County	White	Free Black	Slave Black	Total	% Slave Black	No. 400 lb. Bales Cotton
Winston	3,454	0	122	3,576	3.41	352
Blount	10,193	6	666	10,865	6.13	1,071
Walker	7,461	0	519	7,980	6.50	2,766
DeKalb	9,853	4	848	10,705	7.92	1,498
Randolph	18,132	23	1,904	20,059	9.49	6,427
Marion	9,894	5	1,283	11,182	11.47	4,285
Covington	5,631	17	821	6,469	12.69	2,021
Fayette	11,145	2	1,703	12,850	13.25	5,482
Coffee	8,200	6	1,417	9,623	14.73	5,294
Dale	10,381	7	1,809	12,195	14.83	7,836
Marshall	9,600	51	1,821	11,472	15.87	4,931
St. Clair	9,236	9	1,768	11,013	16.05	4,189
Cherokee	15,321	37	3,002	18,360	16.35	10,562
Jackson	14,811	67	3,405	18,283	18.62	2,713
Calhoun	17,169	28	4,342	21,539	20.16	11,573
Jefferson	9,078	19	2,649	11,746	22.55	4,940
Coosa	14,050	11	5,212	19,273	27.04	13,990
Mobile	28,560	1,195	11,376	41,131	27.66	440
Tallapoosa	17,154	1	6,672	23,827	28.00	17,399
Shelby	8,970	26	3,622	12,618	28.71	6,463
Henry	10,464	21	4,433	14,918	29.72	13,034
Bibb	8,027	25	3,842	11,894	32.30	8,303
Morgan	7,592	37	3,706	11,335	32.70	6,326
Pike	15,646	4	8,785	24,435	35.95	24,527
Butler	11,260	44	6,818	18,122	37.62	13,489
Talladega	14,634	21	8,865	23,520	37.69	18,243
Lauderdale	10,639	44	6,737	17,420	38.67	11,050
Conecuh	6,419	10	4,882	11,311	43.16	6,850
Tuscaloosa	12,971	84	10,145	23,200	43.73	26,035
Franklin	10,119	13	8,495	18,627	45.61	15,592
Lawrence	7,173	14	6,788	13,975	48.57	15,434

Baldwin	3,676	140	3,714	7,530	49.32	2,172
Clarke	7,599	14	7,436	15,049	49.41	16,225
Chambers	11,315	50	11,849	23,214	51.04	24,589
Choctaw	6,767	16	7,094	13,877	51.12	17,252
Barbour	14,629	33	16,150	30,812	52.41	44,518
Limestone	7,215	6	8,085	15,306	52.82	15,115
Washington	2,119	56	2,494	4,669	53.42	3,449
Pickens	10,117	8	12,191	22,316	54.63	29,843
Madison	11,686	192	14,573	26,451	55.09	22,119
Monroe	6,916	46	8,705	15,667	55.56	18,226
Autauga	7,118	14	9,607	16,739	57.39	17,329
Russell	10,936	18	15,638	26,592	58.81	38,728
Perry	9,479	39	18,206	27,724	65.67	44,603
Montgomery	12,124	70	23,710	35,904	66.04	58,880
Macon	8,625	1	18,176	26,802	67.82	41,119
Lowndes	8,362	14	19,340	27,716	69.78	53,664
Wilcox	6,795	26	17,797	24,618	72.29	48,749
Sumter	5,919	25	18,091	24,035	75.27	36,584
Greene	7,251	10	23,598	30,859	76.47	57,858
Dallas	7,785	80	25,760	33,625	76.61	63,410
Marengo	6,761	1	24,409	31,171	78.31	62,428
	526,431	2,690	435,080	964,201	45.12	989,975

Of the 16 counties whose population was *less* than 25 per cent slave, 13 were in North Alabama and three (Covington, Coffee, and Dale) in the Wiregrass Region of Southeast Alabama, where the soil was not particularly suited to the cultivation of cotton; of the 19 counties whose slave population was *more* than 50 per cent, 17 were in South Alabama and two (Limestone and Madison) in the Tennessee Valley, both areas ideally conducive to cotton culture (see Table B). To be specific, the North Alabama county of Winston, which contained only 122 slaves (3.41 per cent of its total population) and which grew only 352 bales of cotton in 1860, was so pro-Union in sentiment as to threaten to secede from Alabama, if Alabama seceded from the Union. Even now the county is frequently referred to as the "Free State of Winston." Blount County's slave population was only 666 (6.13 per cent), Walker's 519 (6.50 per cent), DeKalb's 484 (7.92 per cent), and Randolph's 1,904 (9.49 per cent) and, in total, the four counties produced only 11,762 bales of cotton in 1860, as contrasted with 64,428 produced by Marengo County alone. Small wonder that, as war came in early 1861, Confederate authorities were gravely disturbed by the threat of several North Alabama counties to join with counties in East Tennessee and North Georgia in forming a new Union State of Nickajack.

On the contrary, the South Alabama counties of Marengo, Dallas,

Greene, Sumter, and Wilcox, where the soil was especially suited to cotton culture, had slave populations ranging from 24,409 (78.31 per cent) to 17,797 (72.29 per cent) and produced an average of 53,801 400-lb. bales per county in 1860.

Needless to add, the political sentiment of these heavy cotton-growing counties was unanimously in favor of immediate and straight-out secession from the Union. Indeed, in the Secession Convention the Cooperationist sentiment prevailed in almost the exact ratio that it had in the state-wide election of delegates the month before. When the final ballot was cast on January 11, 39 out of 100 delegates voted against the Ordinance of Secession—almost two out of five (see Table C). And seven of the 61 affirmative votes were cast by delegates who had been elected to the convention as Cooperationists—three each from Coosa and Talladega counties and one from Madison County. Had these seven *not* bolted their party, the vote against secession would have been 46–64—percisely the same as the test vote which on the first day of the convention had elected Secessionist William M. Brooks (of South Alabama's Perry County) president of the convention over his Cooperationist opponent, Robert Jemison, Jr. (of North Alabama's Tuscaloosa County).

Despite their opposition to secession from the Union, as evidenced by the popular vote of December 24, 1860 and the convention vote of January 11, 1861, the fact remains that, once the die was cast, the great majority of Alabamians remained loyal to their state and to the South. With few exceptions even the Cooperationists—those who had propagandized and debated and voted against the Ordinance of Secession—became devoted Confederates at last. Indeed, only three of the Cooperationist delegates to the Secession Convention deserted to the North—Jeremiah Clemens (Madison County), Charles C. Sheets (Winston County), and David P. Lewis (Lawrence County). Of these, Sheets was the most consistent: he voted against secession and he refused to sign the ordinance. Lewis likewise voted nay, but he later signed the document (as did 14 others). Clemens, the least consistent, vigorously opposed it but signed it, nevertheless. Shortly afterwards, the three men defected to the Union. Sheets was arrested as a traitor. (In 1872 and 1874 he represented Alabama in Congress.) Lewis quit Alabama and lived out the war in hiding in Tennessee. (In 1872–1874 he returned and was elected Scalawag governor of Alabama.) And the traitorous Clemens, after accepting the office of major-general in the militia of the Republic of Alabama, slipped away to Pennsylvania, where he conducted a vicious pamphleteering and speaking campaign against his native state. (Immediately after Appomattox he returned to North Alabama, but died within a month.)

In the final analysis, however, the firmest demonstrable test of the loyalty of Alabamians to the Union may be reflected in their willingness

TABLE C

Vote on the Alabama Ordinance of Secession, Montgomery,
January 11, 1861

	Secessionists			*Cooperationists*	
Autauga	(1)*	1	Blount	(2)*	2
Baldwin	(1)	1	Cherokee	(4)	3
Barbour	(3)	3	Conecuh	(1)	1
Bibb	(1)	1	DeKalb	(2)	2
Butler	(2)	2	Fayette	(2)	2
Calhoun	(3)	3	Franklin	(2)	2
Chambers	(2)	2	Jackson	(3)	3
Cherokee	(4)	1	Jefferson	(1)	1
Choctaw	(2)	2	Lauderdale	(2)	2
Clarke	(1)	1	Lawrence	(2)	2
Coffee	(1)	1	Limestone	(2)	2
Coosa	(3)	3	Madison	(2)	1
Covington	(1)	1	Marion	(2)	2
Dale	(2)	2	Marshall	(2)	2
Dallas	(2)	2	Morgan	(1)	1
Greene	(2)	2	Randolph	(3)	3
Henry	(2)	2	St. Clair	(1)	1
Lowndes	(2)	2	Tallapoosa	(3)	3
Macon	(3)	3	Tuscaloosa	(2)	2
Madison	(2)	1	Walker	(1)	1
Marengo	(1)	1	Winston	(1)	1
Mobile	(4)	4	Totals		39
Monroe	(1)	1			
Montgomery	(2)	2			
Perry	(2)	2			
Pickens	(2)	2			
Pike	(3)	3			
Russell	(2)	2			
Shelby	(2)	2			
Sumter	(1)	1			
Talladega	(3)	3			
Washington	(1)	1			
Wilcox	(1)	1			
Totals		61			

Compiled from William R. Smith, *The History and Debates of the Convention of the People of Alabama . . .* [January, 1861] . . . (Montgomery, 1861), 21–22, 118.

*(Figures in parenthesis represent the number of delegates from each county.)

to bear arms in its support. According to the official *Compendium of the War of the Rebellion,* only 2,678 Alabama white men actually enlisted in the United States Army, 1861–1865. Of these, 345 (339 men, 6 officers) lost their lives—killed, 50; died of disease, 228; died as prisoners, 22; died of accidents, 5; and died of other non-battle causes, 40. Many of the soldiers served in miscellaneous Northern companies, mostly Indiana and Tennessee, but the large majority—2,066, as nearly as may be ascertained—saw service in the First Alabama Cavalry, the only white Union regiment from the state and the subject of this study.

This is not to suggest that the day-by-day service record *per se* of the First Alabama Cavalry, U. S. A., justifies its being singled out for monographic treatment. In fact, a close examination of its chronology reveals otherwise—that by comparison with hundreds of other Union regiments it was not conspicuous in either accomplishments or attitudes. True enough, General William T. Sherman selected the unit as his "headquarters escort" in the march to the sea, but mostly it was employed in scouting, recruiting, raiding, and guarding the flanks. Only rarely in its three years of existence was it engaged in actual combat with the enemy.

Nevertheless, it may be safe to suppose that the very *existence* of the First Alabama Cavalry entitles it to special consideration. First, it was doubtless typical of the 85 Southern *white* regiments whose members voluntarily chose to fight *against* rather than with their own compatriots during the War Between the States—Alabama, 1; Arkansas, 10; Florida, 2; Georgia, 1; Louisiana, 10; Mississippi, 1; North Carolina, 4; South Carolina, 0; Tennessee, 51; Texas, 4; and Virginia, 1. And, second, so far as this writer has been able to discover, this study of the First Alabama Cavalry is also unique in that it is the only one ever undertaken of a *Northern* regiment composed of white *Southerners*.

As has been stated, 2,066 men joined the First Alabama Cavalry, U. S. A., at one time or another. Of these, the birthplaces were recorded for only 1,432 (those for 634 were unrecorded), as follows:

Alabama	712	Kentucky	6
Georgia	271	Missouri	5
Tennessee	150	New York	5
South Carolina	98	Pennsylvania	3
North Carolina	76	Arkansas	2
Mississippi	65	Texas	2
Illinois	10	New Jersey	1
Virginia	9	Indiana	1
Ohio	7	Michigan	1
		Foreign countries	8

The 712 Alabamians were natives of the following counties:

Walker	90	Limestone	12
Morgan	86	Shelby	11

Marion	83	Bibb	10
Fayette	54	DeKalb	9
Franklin	33	Calhoun	8
Winston	33	Chambers	6
Blount	32	Coosa	5
Marshall	29	Tallapoosa	4
Madison	25	Greene	4
Lawrence	24	Perry	4
Jefferson	22	Montgomery	3
Jackson	18	Dallas	3
Lauderdale	17	Bullock	1
Cherokee	16	Henry	1
St. Clair	16	Mobile	1
Pickens	15	Sumter	1
Randolph	15	Talladega	1
Tuscaloosa	15	County unspecified	6

It will be noted that almost exactly one-half of the 1,432 men whose birthplaces were recorded were native Alabamians. Using the same ratio, it may be assumed that one-half of the 634 men whose birthplaces were unrecorded were also native Alabamians, thus hypothetically bringing the total to 1,029 out of 1,432, or 72 per cent. Moreover, in the light of the ante-bellum westward migration trend, it is not unreasonable to reckon that an additional several hundred enlistments were *living* in Alabama in 1862–1865, even though they had been born in Georgia, Tennessee, Virginia, or the Carolinas. Altogether, therefore, it may be concluded that at least 75 per cent of the 2,066 men were residents of the state at the time they joined the regiment.

Of the 2,066 enlistments 1,987 are identifiable by dates and places (79 are unidentifiable), as follows:

1862 (Total 376)

July	- Huntsville	3	Oct. - Corinth	40
Aug.	- Huntsville	192	Glendale	1
	Nashville	1	Nov. - Nashville	1
	Corinth	6	Dec. - Corinth	112
Sept.	- Nashville	10	Glendale	8
			Chewalla, Tenn.	1
			Camp Davies	1

1863 (Total 953)

Jan.	- Corinth	69	Sept. - Glendale	73
	Glendale	7	Corinth	4
Feb.	- Corinth	74	Chewalla	4
	Memphis	6	Rome	1

[93]

	Glendale	9	Oct.	-	Glendale	148
	Camp Davies	1			Corinth	16
Mar.	- Corinth	51			Camp Davies	2
	Glendale	24	Nov.	-	Glendale	1
	Chewalla	2			Memphis	5
Apr.	- Corinth	27			Camp Davies	6
	Glendale	5			Corinth	2
May	- Glendale	5			Rome	2
	Corinth	3	Dec.	-	Corinth	105
	Nashville	1			Camp Davies	99
June	- Glendale	7			Memphis	9
	Corinth	2			Rome	1
July	- Corinth	6			Nashville	1
	Glendale	7			Glendale	1
Aug.	- Corinth	162				
	Huntsville	2				
	Chewalla	1				
	Glendale	2				

1864 (Total 544)

Jan.	- Corinth	3	July	-	Rome	4
	Camp Davies	8			Decatur	1
	Memphis	2			Larkinsville	1
	Rome	1	Aug.	-	Rome	28
Feb.	- Memphis	113			Louisville, Ky.	1
	Nashville	3	Sept.	-	Rome	35
	Pulaski	4			Louisville	1
Mar.	- Decatur	67	Oct.	-	Rome	47
	Memphis	48			Huntsville	2
Apr.	- Decatur	86			Glendale	1
	Rome	8	Nov.	-	Rome	14
	Memphis	1			Glendale	1
May	- Decatur	7			Chattanooga	1
	Rome	3	Dec.	-	Savannah	2
	Memphis	2			Monticello, Ga.	2
June	- Decatur	43			Nashville	2
	Rome	1			Corinth	1

1865 (Total 114)

Jan.	- Nashville	3	Apr.	-	Nashville	51
	Huntsville	3			Huntsville	3
	Savannah	3	May	-	Nashville	13
Feb.	- Nashville	23			Huntsville	1
	Memphis	1	Oct.	-	Huntsville	6
Mar.	- Memphis	1				

During the 3-year service of the First Alabama Cavalry 279 men deserted and 88 were captured by the Confederates. When the regiment was deactivated at Huntsville on October 20, 1865, only 397 remained to be discharged.

This study is based almost entirely upon primary source materials, particularly *The War of the Rebellion: A Compilation of the Official Records of the Union and Confederate Armies* (Washington, 1880 –1901), 128 volumes, *A Compendium of the War of the Rebellion . . .* (Des Moines, 1908), 1796 pp., and the collection of original manuscript records of the First Alabama Cavalry volunteers, U. S. A., on deposit in the National Archives, Washington, as Record Group No. 94, Records of the Office of the Adjutant General, a microcopy (No. 263, 11 reels) of which is in the University of Alabama Library. The manuscript "Compiled Service Records" consists of hundreds of jackets or envelopes, each containing the record (often incomplete) of a soldier—name, place, and date of birth, occupation, enlistment, rank, company (or companies), separation from service (with reason), and certain other data relating solely to that particular individual. In addition, the files contain monthly "Records of Events" and "Regimental Returns," written in camp or field, various reports, some personal correspondence and not infrequent notices of discharges, desertions, and deaths. All of this material has been carefully "carded," arranged and indexed alphabetically under the soldiers' surnames (see Chapter II, pp. 53ff.). The whole is described as "The Compiled Service Records of Volunteer Union Soldiers Who Served in Organizations from the State of Alabama: First Alabama Cavalry."

Chronology of the Regiment

The earliest official mention of the "volunteers from Alabama," who were later to compose the First Alabama Cavalry, U. S. A., appeared in Special Orders No. 100, issued by Major-General Don Carlos Buell at "Headquarters Army of the Ohio, Huntsville, July 12, 1862." The day before, Colonel James B. Fry, chief-of-staff, had written Major-General George H. Thomas at Tuscumbia:

> Some 80 or 90 citizens from [Madison] county about 25 miles south have come in to enlist in our army. As many more are represented as trying to get in but [were] prevented by the rebel cavalry and guerillas. [Brigadier] General [Thomas J.] Wood is today ordered to sent a regiment of infantry with the cavalry, without baggage, to cover the approach as such as desire to come in. The regiment will not go more than 25 miles nor be absent more than three or four days.

On July 13 Thomas advised Major-General Henry W. Halleck at Corinth, Mississippi that "a good deal of dissatisfaction" had been reported among Confederate troops in his area, causing "desertions . . .

from the Alabama, Mississippi, and Tennessee regiments." Three days later Thomas added that several deserters had come in, all destitute and "many barefooted." By July 18 a sufficient number of Tories had enlisted to justify Buell's issuing Special Orders No. 106:

> The volunteers from Alabama will be organized into companies, under the direction of Capt. H. C. Bankhead [of the Fifth U. S. Infantry], who will enroll and muster them into the United States service in accordance with the laws and orders on the subject. Company officers will be selected from among the men and appointed by the general commanding conditional upon the confirmation of the President of the United States. The provost-marshal in Huntsville will give Captain Bankhead such assistance as he may require in this duty. All Alabama men now traveling with any of the regiments of this command will be sent or left at this place.

Within three weeks Assistant Adjutant-General J. M. Wright, Buell's aide-de-camp, wrote Major W. H. Sidell of the Fifteenth U. S. Infantry and acting assistant aide-de-camp in Nashville, that "Requisitions have been forwarded for a complete supply of Springfield or Enfield rifles and accoutrements for the Companies (180 men) of the Alabama Volunteers. Direct the ordnance officer to forward them without delay."

Meanwhile, throughout the late summer Union recruiting officers combed the hills of North Alabama for additional volunteers. The activities of one such official, a civilian named Joseph Palmer (who had been forced to "flee to the mountains" for murdering a Confederate soldier) have been recorded by one of his recruits, 18-year old Pinckney D. Hall of Franklin, who later became a corporal in Co. B, First Alabama Cavalry. Reminiscing as "A Loyal Southron" in 1899, nearly thirty-five years after the war, Hall declared:

> Palmer made his way back to the mountains of Marion and Franklin counties for the purpose of raising a regiment for the United States service. While in our midst a man—Marshall McLoud or McLeod—living in the outer edge of our village [on Bull Mountain Creek, Franklin County], a good spy for the rebels, who kept them around him and harbored them for the purpose of hunting Union men, himself got into trouble. One evening about sunset Palmer assembled nine men, the writer being one of them, armed with rifles, shotguns and two old muskets. We started for McLeod's, a distance of six to eight miles, determined to break up one den of marauders. We arrived on the ground, and found no soldiers there. Palmer, in maneuvering around, routed a gang of sheep in front of McLeod's gate. McLeod stepped out to the gate to see what disturbed the sheep. Palmer was within 10 feet of him, with a good double-barrel shotgun. He tried both barrels of his gun on McLeod, and they failed to fire, only bursting the caps. McLeod was loading wagons to leave, and there were bullet-holes through the door, from the small rifle to the largest musket. There was no more trouble from that quarter. Palmer continued recruiting. In the Autumn of 1862 he had made up a company of cavalry at Camp Glendale, Miss., an outpost for Corinth.

On September 8 Buell ordered the "new" companies of Alabama troops "lately organized at Huntsville" to report "without delay" to Colonel William B. Stokes, commanding the First [Middle] Tennessee Cavalry, a "post force" regiment stationed in Nashville. Within two or three months, however, the companies were described as the First Alabama Cavalry and assigned to the Army of the Tennessee, Major-General Ulysses S. Grant commanding. At the time, January, 1863, there were only two companies which, with seven regiments of the Sixty-fourth Illinois Cavalry, made up the Third Brigade, Sixteenth Army Corps, District of Corinth. The officers were Major-General Charles S. Hamilton, Brigadier-General Grenville M. Dodge, Major John W. Stewart, Captain William A. Lord, and Henry T. Sumner, captain of the First Alabama Cavalry.

The "Record of Events" for March—the earliest official "Regimental Field and Staff Returns" from the First Alabama Cavalry—reveals that the unit was then stationed at Glendale, Mississippi:

From the first formation the regt. has been engaged in scouting in N. E. Miss. and owing to the acquaintance, thorough and minute, which a large portion of both officers and men have with the Country, they have been almost universally successful. The first Cos. were formed in Nov. & Dec. 1862 and all have been engaged in continual service, since that time. A portion of the officers as [of this?] report are attached from other regts & Cos. are not aggregated, not having been dropped on their original rolls. By this direction Co. A loses one, B do, do, D 2, E do. Field and Staff all detached & not aggregated. The Cos. 'C' 'D' 'E' have never been reported on monthly returns before, but are put in column aggregate last monthly return in order to account in summing up for change in other companies.

Throughout the summer of 1863 the headquarters of the First Alabama remained at Glendale, from which the regiment made frequent scouting and foraging expeditions in northern Mississippi and Alabama. Frequent reorganizations, however, resulted in its transfer from one brigade to another. On April 30 it was transferred to Colonel Florence M. Cornyn's Cavalry Brigade and a month later to the Third Brigade (same officers). On August 20 it was attached to the First Brigade, Third Michigan Cavalry, Colonel J. K. Mizner commanding. Besides the seven Alabama companies, this brigade included the Seventh Kansas, Tenth Missouri, and Fifth Ohio regiments and, of course, the Third Michigan from which the organization drew its name. The brigade was at this time still in the Department of the Tennessee, Sixteenth Army Corps, Major-General Grant commanding; however, on August 31 two unidentified companies of the First Alabama were transferred to the newly-created Department of the Cumberland, Major-General William W. Rosecrans commanding, sent to Camp Spears near Nashville, and placed under Colonel William C. Pickens. Meanwhile, Rosecrans, eager to cut off all Confederate supply lines leading into Atlanta and Knoxville and thus to seal off Chattanooga, in April had ordered Colonel Abel E. Streight to conduct "an expedition to the interior of Alabama and Georgia, for the purpose of destroying the railroads in that country." Streight's provisional command for temporary purposes" consisted of about two thousand officers and men "of well-attested pluck and endurance," including the Fifty-first and Seventy-third Indiana, the Third Ohio, the Eightieth Illinois, and two companies of the First Alabama Cavalry, under Captain D. D. Smith—evidently the same two which on August 31 had been transferred from the Department of the Tennessee. As these cavalrymen swept through Moulton, across Sand Mountain, and into the Black Warrior River Valley near Blountsville, Streight wrote: "We are now in the midst of devoted Union people. Many of Captain Smith's men (Alabamians) were recruited near this place, and many were the happy greetings between them and their friends and relatives."

As a diversionary aid to Streight, an expeditionary force of the Sixteenth Army Corps, including the main body of the First Alabama Cavalry, commanded by Brigadier-General Dodge, had been ordered to "scour" the countryside for "all the horses and mules that could be found." Encountering the enemy on four occasions (at Bear Creek, Little Bear Creek, Leighton, and Town Creek), the 8000-man detachment captured 40 prisoners, 900 head of horses and mules, 60 bales of cotton, and cattle, sheep and hogs "by the thousands." It destroyed 1,500,000 bushels of corn, eight mills and tan-yards, 60 flatboats on the Tennessee River, broke up ferries from Eastport to Courtland, and took the towns of Tuscumbia and Florence. Wrote Dodge, "Nothing was left in the valley that would in the least aid the enemy."

As agreed, on April 26 Dodge met Streight at Tuscumbia and turned over to him 500 mules and 12 wagons. Dodge agreed to advance down the Decatur road as far as Courtland in hopes of distracting Forrest's cavalry, while Streight rode in the direction of Russellville, Moulton, Sand Mountain, and Blountsville. The two commanders parted on April 28, Streight leaving with Dodge several hundred men who had been declared "not fit for the arduous duties" ahead.

Returning toward Corinth, Dodge destroyed the railway bridges and telegraph lines between Courtland and Tuscumbia. Altogether, on May 3, he boastfully reported to Major-General Stephen A. Hurlbut, commanding the Sixteenth Army Corps, "[We] rendered useless the garden spot of Alabama for at least one year, besides inflicting a deserved chastisement upon a most unrelenting community of intense rebel sympathizers." Two days later he filed a second and more detailed report of his expedition. In it he praised the First Alabama Cavalry for bravely charging Colonel Phillip D. Roddey's Confederates at Bear Creek (April 17) with *unloaded* muskets:

Colonel Cornyn hearing firing in the rear, immediately fell back, and, with the First Alabama Cavalry, charged the rebels and retook the artillery and caissons, with the exception of one gun.....

The charge of the Alabamians with muskets only, and those not loaded, is creditable, especially as they are all new recruits and poorly drilled. In this charge, Captain [James C.] Cameron, the commanding officer of the Alabama cavalry, a deserving and much lamented officer, was killed.

However, Colonel Cornyn, who had been closer to the Alabama Tories in their baptism of fire than his Brigadier-General, was far less complimentary of his half-hearted comrades:

I ordered a charge by the First Alabama Cavalry, which I am sorry to say, was not obeyed with the alacrity it should have been. After charging to within short musket-range of the enemy, they halted for a cause I cannot account for, and the enemy escaped to the woods with one of the pieces and limber of the other, it having been previously thrown down the railroad excavation. Here Captain Cameron was killed, and a private ... of the First Alabama Cavalry, but not until they had desisted from the charge, when the enemy turned and poured a perfect hail of lead into our ranks.

Two days later, Sunday, April 19, the First Alabama Cavalry was transferred from Cornyn's brigade to that of Colonel Moses M. Bane (Fiftieth Illinois Infantry), which was hiding "in ambush near Buzzard's Roost Creek." For the next week the brigade escorted prisoners and constructed foot-bridges, while now and then firing at the rear guard of Roddey's Confederates. Then, "after four days' marching, during which time nothing worthy of note occurred," Bane wrote, "we reached Corinth about 4 p.m. Saturday, May 2. Our only casualty was one man of Company B, Seventh Illinois, who shot himself accidentally."

So ended the first brief but inglorious foray of the First Alabama Cavalry, U. S. A. For the month of April the regimental scribe summed up the events in simple confusion, thus:

From Apr 14 to Apr 17 the right was engaged under command of Gen'l Dodge in an expedition toward Decatur, Ala. Was engaged in battle Apr 17 & at other times in skirmishing. From acquaintance with the surface of the country, roads may be very efficient but is improperly armed, with arms unfit for this branch of service.

Upon its return to Glendale and for four months thereafter the activities of the First Alabama were virtually nil, or so the extant "Regimental Returns," very sparse, suggest. For May, June, July, and August they were left completely blank. The September report described the activation of two new companies, H and L—which were "recruited in field"—and Company K, which had been transferred back to the regiment from the First Middle Tennessee. On August

20 the First Alabama was attached to the First Brigade, Sixteenth Army Corps (Army of the Tennessee), under the command of Colonel Mizner. The unit also included the Third Michigan, Seventh Kansas, Tenth Missouri, and Fifth Ohio cavalry regiments. However, within two weeks two of the Alabama companies were transformed to the Army of the Cumberland, Major-General Rosecrans commanding, and with seven companies of the Third Tennessee were assigned an "unattached" status under Brigadier-General Alvan C. Gillem and Colonel Pickens.

Meantime, in July Captain George E. Spencer, Brigadier-General Dodge's assistant adjutant-general, had asked to be transferred to the First Alabama Cavalry, which up to this time had not had a permanent commander.

The War Department, upon Dodge's recommendation, granted Spencer's request and simultaneously promoted him to the rank of colonel. On September 11, in Corinth, Spencer took formal command of the regiment.

In less than a week Colonel Spencer was ordered by Major-General Hurlbut to proceed "through Jasper, Ala., to Montgomery or some point east . . . on the West Point railroad . . . , there to destroy [it and] its rolling stock, track, and depots, doing the most thorough amount of damage possible." Not unmindful of Cornyn's report of the First Alabama's ignoble behavior at Bear Creek, Hurlbut added, "You will see to it that your men are kept together and thoroughly in hand. . . . [They] will be carefully instructed not to interfere with private property further than is necessary for [sustenance]. . . ."

The First Alabama did not "move out" until mid-October, however. Meanwhile, the regiment whiled the weeks away by making short, inconsequential raids on the countryside, recruiting more "Alabama Yankees," training, and by preparing to move Brigadier-General Dodge's headquarters from Glendale to Camp Davies, near Corinth, Mississippi. Fully confident of Spencer's ability, Hurlbut wrote Ulysses S. Grant, his so-called "general-in-chief," as follows:

Colonel Spencer's regiment is wholly composed of refugees from Alabama. They have been in several engagements and behaved well. They are thoroughly acquainted with the country, well mounted and armed; have two light steel guns, take with them as volunteers 6 engineers who can either run or destroy railroads or steamers. The expedition is directed against the West Point Railroad, because it is a connecting link of great importance and of a different gauge from the other southern roads. Spencer is certain that he can get through the outer cordon without observation and if he does so, I am satisfied he will make his way to Montgomery.

On the twentieth the First Alabama Cavalry, "a force of about 650 men," moved out of Corinth, directly southeastward, towards Columbiana, Alabama—its first responsibility to destroy the railroad from Line Station to Elyton, a new line being built "for the sole purpose of getting out the railroad iron now being manufactured at these mills." Forty miles out of Glendale, however, at Jones's Crossroads, the regiment was attacked by 2,000 Confederates, commanded by Brigadier-General Samuel W. Ferguson, who "scattered the Alabama Tories over the country," killing 20, including two captains, the adjutant of the regiment and a lieutenant, and capturing the "two light steel guns," a larger number of horses, many supplies, and 40 prisoners. Several days afterwards, according to Major-General Stephen D. Lee, C.S.A., stragglers were "still being caught over the countryside—all from the First Alabama Tory Regiment." When Major-General Sherman, at his Iuka, Mississippi headquarters, received news of the defeat, he swore under his breath at that "erratic Alabama regiment of ours, which had gone off on some recruiting or other errand" and been "worsted."

Thus ended the First Alabama Cavalry's second major encounter with the Confederate forces in North Alabama.

After their disastrous day at Jones's Crossroads the men of the First Alabama one way or another, singly and in disorganized groups, made their ways back to Dodge's headquarters at Camp Davies. And once again, while replacements were being sought and the regiment reorganized and further trained, the records of its activities were left blank.

Colonel Spencer, himself, was in early December temporarily transferred from the First Alabama on "detached service with Gen. Dodge at Pulaski, Tenn. in S. O. 313, Hd. Qrs. 16 A. C." His brief command of the Alabama Tories had, to say the least, brought him little or no credit—but within six months he was destined to return to the regiment.

Meanwhile, following Dodge's transfer from Corinth to Pulaski, the celebrated Brigadier-General Benjamin H. Grierson had been appointed Dodge's successor and he, in turn, had reassigned Colonel Mizner to command of the First Alabama Cavalry, now in the First Brigade.

Colonel Mizner reassumed his former position in the Alabama Tory regiment with something less than gleeful enthusiasm. Nevertheless, at daylight on November 26 he led his First Brigade, consisting of "400 men from the Third Michigan [Mizner's own regiment], 300 from the Seventh Kansas, and 200 from the First Alabama," out of Corinth, marched 31 miles and encamped near Blackland. From that point the brigade rode cautiously southward to Chesterville where, in order to avoid Lee's cavalry, it "moved to a safer position near Molino [and thence to] Ripley." Meanwhile, the 35 prisoners, who had been picked up along the way, had become "a burden." Looking about for a solution to the problem and seeing "the First Alabama . . .

[101]

miserably mounted and wholly unequal to expected marches," Mizner ordered that regiment to escort the prisoners back to Corinth. Upon his return to headquarters Mizner filed a detailed report of the scouting expedition, declaring that "from sickness, after long exposure and loss of horses, I sent about 60 men to Corinth, also 30 men as escort to prisoners. The horses of the First Alabama, only 200 in all, were so poor that I was obliged to order them back to Corinth."

As 1863 ended, the First Alabama Cavalry was in camp at Corinth, inactive, recuperating, and again seeking replacements. By mid-January 600 new Tories had been enlisted, bringing the total to 800, thanks to the recruiting activities of Brigadier-General Dodge, who, he declared, took a personal interest in signing up the "loyal men who flock to my lines. . . ."

But up to now, after more than a year's service, the "erratic regiment" had done nothing of which really to be proud. Indeed, it had accomplished little more than opening the door for other Alabama Tories who might wish to "come down out of the fastnesses" of their mountain hide-outs to seek aid and comfort with the winning side. It had altogether proved a liability rather than an asset. Surely, the First Alabama had thus far added no prestige or glory to the United States Cavalry.

During the first four months of 1864 the main body of the First Alabama Cavalry remained in and about Memphis in Grierson's First Brigade, First Division, Sixteenth Army Corps, Army of the Tennessee, with Mizner as substitute colonel for Spencer, who had since December been on "detached service" with Dodge in Pulaski. From time to time the regiment or a picked patrol or perhaps a company from it was sent out on reconnaissance expeditions to Decatur, La Grange, Corinth, Hernando, Coldwater, Germantown, Mount Pleasant or other points, sometimes skirmishing with Confederate cavalry patrols. But the outfit lacked men, equipment and horses to "thoroughly mount the command." Not infrequently, because of the shortage of horses (the regiment had only 270 on March 20), the unmounted men were shifted from place to place by rail or water or assigned to the infantry. At least two "detached" units of the command were in these early months of the new year serving in Northeast Alabama, one with the Eleventh and one with the Fifteenth Army Corps.

On January 9 from his Tennessee headquarters Dodge, going over the heads of his superiors, wrote directly to Secretary of War Edwin M. Stanton, asking "authority to raise one or more regiments of cavalry from Alabamians." He claimed that he personally had recruited approximately one thousand men at Corinth in 1863 and had found the task easy:

There are large numbers [of Alabamians] coming in to our lines, and a better class of men than has ever come through before, being men

[102]

who have furnished substitutes upon being drafted for the rebel service. Several of them are anxious to raise a regiment and have no doubt that [this can] easily be done. I recruited one regiment, at Corinth, Miss.—the First Alabama Cavalry, nearly 1,000 strong—and that fact being well known in North Alabama nearly all the refugees from there seek my lines. I also desire that authority to be given me to appoint the officers, most of which I would select from the old regiments now in service. My advance is opposite Decatur and at points on the [Tennessee] river easily reached from the Alabama mountains, from which these men seek my lines. We have to feed them, and it is no more than right that they should enter the service. Most of them are anxious to do so, but prefer to go into an organization of their own. An early response to this would be great benefit to the service.

There can be little doubt that Colonel Spencer was instrumental in persuading his superior to write this letter, for three days later Dodge wrote Major-General William T. Sherman in Memphis that,

If we could make lodgement at Decatur it would give an outlet to a large number of Union people who are seeking our lines and who would join our Alabama regiments, and if Colonel Spencer's First Alabama Cavalry could be ordered to me, it would form a nucleus that would soon give us another mounted regiment.

Again, on January 29, Dodge pleaded for authority to organize the "Alabama Yankees" who were seeking haven at his headquarters.

The rebel conscription [he wrote Adjutant-General T. S. Bowers] is driving into our lines a large number of Union men, who furnished substitutes, and men who have always stood by us and keep out of the rebel army by taking to the mountains. They desire to go into our service, and prominent men among them think they can raise a regiment. Can you authorize me to enlist them, and have a regiment to be known as the Second Alabama Cavalry? I raised and officered the First Alabama Cavalry at Corinth, now 800 strong, and I have no doubt I can raise another. These men flock to my lines from this fact.

Nothing came of Dodge's appeals, although there is no doubt that many Alabamians continued to file down out of the hills to the Union lines.

After one expedition in the direction of Larkin's Landing, thirty-odd miles east of Huntsville, hundreds "who had been secreted a great part of the time for two years ... came out of the fastnesses of Sand Mountain." Some joined the cavalry, others enlisted in various infantry regiments. One Tory, McCurdy by name, was described by Brigadier-General Morgan L. Smith as having been so enthusiastic as to muster a company of his own "with a pencil on brown paper, christen it, assume command ... , advance into Sand Mountain and actually make captures of rebel Home Guards in the same hiding places they had themselves just vacated."

The loyal Alabamians are invaluable [Smith continued] and exceed in number and are equal in zeal to anything we discovered in Tennessee.... The results of the expedition I considered important. Many of the Home Guards, including one officer, have resumed their allegiance by taking the amnesty oath, and the always-loyal people of this part of Alabama have learned from the general good conduct of the men who their real friends are....

Small squads of Brigadier-General Nathan Bedford Forrest's Confederate cavalrymen likewise raided the Sand Mountain area, now and then "capturing some of the First Alabama Cavalry"—Alabamians *versus* Alabamians, neighbors *versus* neighbors in what might have been described as a local feud rather a small segment of a massive international conflict of arms.

On March 24 the First Alabama Cavalry, "one-half of the regiment dismounted," were ordered by Grierson from Memphis to Decatur, a distance of 250 miles. Because of the poor physical condition of the men and horses, however, the regiment was moved 600 miles on the steamer *Westmoreland*—northward up the Mississippi via Cairo, eastward up the Ohio via Paducah, thence southeastward up the Cumberland to Nashville. From Nashville the regiment marched overland to their destination at Mooresville, in North Alabama, arriving April 14.

Meanwhile, in the extreme northeastern corner of Alabama, across the state from their comrades at Memphis, another detachment of Alabama cavalry was in the making. On February 6 from Scottsboro Major-General John A. Logan, commanding the Fifteenth Army Corps, wrote Brigadier-General John A. Rawlins, his chief-of-staff,

> I leave for Huntsville this morning and Decatur as rapidly as possible. A great many Alabamians in the country desire to enlist in the Alabama regiment. They have shown themselves very useful men. If I had authority I could fill the regiment and use them to a good purpose. They are the best scouts I ever saw, and know the country well clear to Montgomery.

Almost simultaneously, another detachment of the First Alabama was serving with the First Brigade, Third Division, Eleventh Army Corps, in the vicinity of Caperton's Ferry, near Bridgeport, Alabama. A scouting party from this unit was sent out March 28 "to ascertain the truth as to the presence of enemy." Within twenty-four hours it came into contact with a contingent of Confederate cavalrymen, fired a few rounds—and fled. The Confederates chased the Tories back "to within three miles" of their camp. Colones James S. Robinson, of the Eighty-second Ohio Infantry, who was commanding the expedition, evidently suspicious, wrote:

> A patrol from the First Alabama Cavalry, which returned at 5 p.m. on yesterday [March 27], reported themselves to have been driven back from Caperton's Ferry to Island Creek by a detachment of about 50 rebel cavalry. They declared that they exchanged shots with scattering

bushwhackers ... and that the enemy suddenly afterward appeared in such numbers as to compel the retreat of the cavalry. Upon receipt of this news I immediately dispatched a detachment of 10 men and a lieutenant ... with orders to patrol the road.... This patrol returned at 7 a.m. this morning. The lieutenant commanding reported that he went as far as within 4 miles of Caperton's Ferry without seeing the enemy, and that he could not learn that they had been in the vicinity during the previous day, thus partly contradicting the story of the Alabama cavalry patrol....

When Major-General O. O. Howard relayed Robinson's message on to headquarters, he neatly explained that the First Alabama had "come in contact with about fifty rebel cavalry and exchanged shots with them. The rebels *followed* them to within three miles of camp, near Bridgeport."

Meanwhile, Dodge's headquarters had again been moved, this time from Pulaski to Athens, Alabama. Colonel Spencer moved with his superior. One of Dodge's first communiques, dated April 6 and addressed to Major-General J. B. McPherson at Huntsville, once more reflected his interest in recruiting North Alabama Tories. There was now a virtual "cavalry picket line" extending across the state from Guntersville to Courtland "to catch the deserters and refugees seeking our lines," he wrote. "The mountains are full of them, and they hold the mountain district in spite of all efforts of the rebels to catch them. I know of several companies of at least 100 men, each led by our scouts and members of the First Alabama Cavalry."

As the month of April, 1864 came to a close, Sherman's "desperate campaign" for Atlanta began to take shape. Late in March the Secretary of War, acting under the order of President Abraham Lincoln, had appointed Lieutenant-General Ulysses S. Grant general-in-chief of the reorganized United States Army, replacing Major-General H. W. Halleck. Simultaneously, Sherman had been assigned command of the Military Division of the Mississippi, now composed of the Departments of the Ohio, the Arkansas, the Cumberland, and the Tennessee. Of the last-named Major-General John A. Logan was placed in command. It contained the Fifteenth, Sixteenth, and Seventeenth Army Corps—132,508 officers and men, among whom, in the Sixteenth Corps, Major-General Stephen A. Hurlbut commanding, was Brigadier-General Grenville M. Dodge's First Alabama Cavalry, temporarily led by Major George L. Godfrey. (Colonel George E. Spencer was still on "detached duty" as Dodge's chief-of-staff.)

On April 15 the First Alabama was on scouting duty along the Tennessee River at Triana. Two weeks later, in company with the Ninth Illinois, it moved northward towards Huntsville, then eastward towards Stevenson. Another two weeks found the two regiments, now joined by others, slowly working their devious ways across the Coosa River to Cedartown, Dallas, and Rome, Georgia—their destination (as was the destination of the entire Left Wing of the Sixteenth Army Corps) Burnt Church Crossroads, some forty miles northwest of Atlanta. The Ninth Illinois served as an advance guard, while the First Alabama rode the flanks. Between them were mostly ordnance trains, supply trains, and ambulances. Up to now, June 20, the regiments had not come in contact with the enemy except in brief inconsequential skirmishes on patrol.

Colonel Spencer, who had been absent from the regiment for several months, returned to active duty in early July. Under his leadership the First Alabama retraced its route through Rome, Gadsden, and Guntersville, rear-guarding railroad supply lines and scouting against the enemy. Upon its return to Rome the regiment was sent out on foraging parties (feed for horses, mostly) across the Chattooga River and elsewhere, during which it picked up a few prisoners. In early August it reached back westward again, this time to Cedartown, Cave Spring, Blue Mountain (now Anniston), Jacksonville, and as far south as Tallapoosa County, Alabama where it "destroyed a quantity of corn and wheat [and] burned a steam cotton factory."

By September the Confederates under Brigadier-General James H. Clanton, including the First Alabama Cavalry, C. S. A., had somehow managed to work themselves up to Etowah, wedging themselves between Cedartown and Cave Spring—and the First Alabama Cavalry, U. S. A., was sent out to "follow them." But their leader, Lieutenant-Colonel Godfrey (who had recently been promoted from major) "saw nothing, neither could they hear of any Rebel force in that direction." As September passed into October the Tories continued their monotonous routine of scouting, foraging, guarding bridges and railroads, now to Summerville, now Cedar Bluff, now Dirt Town, now Coosaville, but always circling back to headquarters at Rome. On October 4 the entire regiment was ordered to move to Kingston, 20 miles southeast of Rome on the Cartersville road, "supplied with three days' rations." A week later, "feeling for the enemy" in the direction of Cave Spring, the "Alabama Yankees" "ran into a picket... [and] were compelled to fall back," although from local citizens they gathered "valuable information." Wrote Brigadier-General John M. Corse, "I am largely indebted to the activity and gallantry of the First Alabama Cavalry in procuring information for me [about General John B. Hood's movements in Northeast Georgia and Northwest Alabama] since [arriving] here." Sherman likewise acknowledged his debt to the scouting activities of the First Alabama during the campaign for Atlanta.

On October 30 the First Alabama Cavalry, Colonel Spencer commanding, was transferred to the Army of the Tennessee (Right Wing, Major-General O. O. Howard) and the next day moved with the Seventeenth Army Corps (Major-General Frank P. Blair, Jr.) southward from

[106]

Rome via Cedartown to Marietta, arriving November 5. The corps remained at Marietta eight days and then, by-passing Atlanta, circled toward Milledgeville (which surrendered on November 20), destroying its railroad and depot. En route, however, the Tories had become so wantonly destructive of personal property as to cause Major-General Howard, at his headquarters "In the Field, Ga.," to direct his adjutant to write Colonel Spencer:

> Colonel: The major-general commanding directs me to say to you that the outrages committed by your command during the march are becoming so common, and are of such an aggravated nature, that they call for some severe and instant mode of correction. Unless the pillaging of houses and wanton destruction of property by your regiment ceases at once, he will place every officer in it under arrest, and recommend them to the department commander for dishonorable dismissal from the service.

Evidently, Howard was unaware of the fact that his commander, William T. Sherman, had personally ordered the First Alabama Cavalry to "Burn the country within fifteen miles...," an order which had made even Dodge wince because he "knew what that meant; it was a license under which other things besides burning could be done."

No mention of the First Alabama's outrages were recorded in its own "Regimental Returns," however. At the end of November, as the Seventeenth Army Corps crossed the Ogeechee River between Gordon and Millen, the scribe summed up the month's activities in these few words:

> In the Field, Ga. Regiment on duty every day scouting the country around Rome, Ga. Skirmishing with Wheeler's (Rebel) Cav. up to the 11th when it broke Camp and moved in the direction of Atlanta, Ga. arriving there the evening of the 14th. Was there assigned to duty with the 17 A. C. Took the advance of the Corps and moved on the 15th in a southeasterly direction and kept the advance. Had several brisk skirmishes with the enemy at every point with slight loss. Continued in the advance of the Corps until the last of the month.

Between December 1–7 the Seventeenth Corps, now east of the Oconee, advanced southward towards Savannah, destroying the Georgia Central Railroad and bridges as it went and skirmishing occasionally with the enemy. On December 18 the corps encamped at Midway Congregational Church in Liberty County, tearing up an 18-mile stretch of the Atlantic and Gulf Railroad and its trestles and bridges across the Altamaha River. Three days later, upon receiving word that Savannah had fallen, Major-General Blair marched his troops through the conquered city and pitched camp three miles east. After Christmas he established his command headquarters at Fort Thunderbolt, a former Confederate stronghold on the Wilmington River, five miles south of the city.

[107]

As 1864 came to a close, Major-General Sherman reviewed his victorious armies as they paraded through the streets of Savannah—the First Alabama Cavalry forming "on Price Street with its right resting on Bay Street."

On the night of December 31 the First Alabama's scribe wrote:

> Regiment left Millen, Ga. the 1st of the month moving down the Ga. Central R.R. in advance of the 17th AC having a brisk skirmish on the 4th at Bush Head Creek. Had slight skirmish every day until the 9th, when we came to the enemy's outer works at Savannah. We drove them two miles over a road where torpedoes were buried, which exploding mortally wounded Adjutant Tupper and six men slightly, also killing six horses. We drove the enemy to their main works when the Inft. and Artillery came to our assistance, we guarding the flanks until the 13th, when the Regt. moved with the 1st Div 17th AC to destroy the Gulf RR. Returned to camp on the 21st and moved into Savannah 22nd. Go into Camp four miles South of the City at Thunderbolt Battery, where we [are] at this time living without rations for men or forage for animals, on account of which a number of horses have died and men have suffered extremely.

And thirty-five years later, with tongue in cheek, former Captain Mortimer R. Flint, Company E, First Alabama Cavalry, reminiscing before the Minnesota Commandery of the Military Order of the Loyal Legion of the United States, declared,

> ...of the 1st Alabama Cavalry, of which regiment, by the way, I have heard delicate hints, that seemed to me at the time were intended to convey a suspicion that they believed in the axiom, that self-preservation is the first law of nature and so preserved themselves for the good of their country, by never going hungry in that of the enemy.
>
> I cannot vouch for this from personal knowledge, for although I had the honor of belonging to the regiment, was most of the time absent on staff duty; but this I do believe, that being mostly southern men, they enjoyed a special faculty of divining the most likely locality that a southern rebel would choose for secreting provisions and to be strictly just and truthful, I never knew a 1st Alabamian who would not share with a rebel sympathizer when that locality was discovered; as to the proportion that the rebel got—well, you know how that was yourselves.
>
> The 1st Alabama cavalry was composed mostly of men from the northern portion of that state and their love and devotion for the union and the old flag, was not excelled by any who wore the blue.
>
> They were terribly in earnest and the story of their privations and sufferings for the cause that they espoused, can never be fully described.

Following their victorious march through Georgia, Sherman's forces were reorganized. In January, 1865 the Seventh Army Corps was merged into the Tenth, Fourteenth, Fifteenth, Twentieth, and Twenty-third, and a new Third Cavalry Division, composed of four brigades, was created and placed under the leadership of Brigadier-General Judson Kilpatrick. The Third Brigade, commanded by Colonel

Spencer, included the First Alabama Cavalry (Major Francis L. Cramer and Captain Jerome J. Hinds), The Fifth Kentucky, the Fifth Ohio, and the Thirteenth Pennsylvania, altogether 5,068 men. Kilpatrick's first command to the First Alabama (and the Ninth Illinois), written "Near Savannah," ordered them to report with their wagon trains for supplies and "bring ammunition, as we expect to have a little fight...."

The First Alabama, now numbering 18 officers and 292 men, departed Fort Thunderbolt with the Third Cavalry Division on January 28. Five days later the troopers crossed the Savannah River into South Carolina, driving one of Major-General "Fightin' Joe" Wheeler's brigades ahead of it, and "laid the town of Barnwell in ashes, in spite of every effort of Brigadier-General Kilpatrick to prevent it." At Blacksville the Third Brigade destroyed the tracks of the South Carolina Railroad and advanced northward towards Columbia, the state capital. On February 7–8, near Williston, the brigade engaged the enemy in a "spirited fight, in which six regiments of Brigadier-General William W. Allen's division of Wheeler's cavalry... were totally routed."

> Colonel Spencer alone conducted the fight [Kilpatrick wrote] display-ing much skill and great gallantry. Several hundred stand of arms were abandoned by the enemy and left scattered along the road. One officer and many men were killed and a large number wounded. Several pris-oners were taken. Colonel Spencer pressed the enemy so close for a distance of seven or eight miles that he was finally forced to leave the roads and scatter through the woods and swamps in order to escape. Colonel Spencer brought back as trophies from the fight five battle flags....

Major Sanford Tramel likewise praised Spencer's "rout" of the Con-federates as "the most complete I ever witnessed. Guns, sabres, can-teens, haversacks, saddle-bags, hats, and everything which would impede the flight of the affrighted and flying enemy were abandoned and completely strewn over the ground.... The conduct of the officers and men of my regiment on this occasion was praiseworthy in the highest degree. The loss of the regiment was four men wounded, one mortally, who afterward died."

After reading Tramel's account, Spencer himself described the Williston fight, using almost the same words:

> Then commenced one of the most thorough and complete routs I ever witnessed. The ground was completely strewn with guns, haver-sacks, &c. Five battle-flags were captured, including the brigade and four regimental flags, and a large number of horses and over thirty pris-oners. After a charge of about seven miles from this point the enemy dispersed and went in every direction through the woods.... The force we had the encounter with proved to be the Alabama brigade of Allen's division, Wheeler's cavalry corps, commanded by Colonel [James]

[109]

Hagan, and consisting of the First, Third, Fifth, Ninth, Twelfth, and Fifty-First Regiments of Alabama Cavalry.

On February 11 the First Alabama Tories resumed their march northward, participating "in all the different scenes through which it passed, crossing the Edisto, Saluda, Broad, Wateree, and Great Pee Dee Rivers, via Lexington, Alston, Black Storks, Lancaster, and Sneedsborough, nothing of special importance occurring." Activities for the month were summed up in the "Regimental Returns" thus:

> In the Field, S. C., except Co. H. On the 3d inst. the Regiment being connected with the 3d Brig. 3d Cav. Div. Mil. Dis. Miss. started from Sister's Ferry Ga. on the Campaign through the Carolinas. Continued with the Brigade until the last of the month. Participated in all the hardships which Gen'l Kilpatrick's Cavalry was exposed to, often working all night crossing the numerous almost impassible swamps and streams. Was engaged with the enemy at various points, sustaining but little loss. Both officers and men have conducted themselves in all their arduous duties in the most notable and creditable manner.

The First Alabama crossed over into North Carolina on March 7, reaching Monroe's Crossroads two days later. At sunrise the next morning, according to Major Tramel, the regiment was suddenly "aroused from sleep by the whistling of bullets and the fiendish yelling of the enemy, who were charging into our camp." A "bloody hand-to-hand conflict" followed, lasting more than three hours. At last, the Fifth Kentucky and the Fifth Ohio rushed to the rescue and "in connection . . . we succeeded in driving the enemy from our camps." Later it was learned that the enemy had consisted of three divisions of Confederate cavalry, led personally by Generals Wheeler and Wade Hampton.

During the brief but fierce affray both Majors Cramer and Tramel were captured, leaving the First Alabama in command of Captain Jerome J. Hinds—but Tramel soon escaped and, "after three days lying in the swamps and traveling nights," succeeded in rejoining his command. Colonel Spencer's description of the early morning skirmish was complete:

> Simultaneously on the morning of the 10th of March with our reveille the camp of the dismounted men and our camp was charged by three divisions of the enemy's cavalry, viz, Butler's, Hume's, and Allen's, General Hampton personally leading the charge of Butler's division and General Wheeler leading the charge on the right with Hume's division. The camp of the dismounted men was instantly captured; also the headquarters of the division and brigade, and with the wagons and artillery. In the cavalry camp the firing became very severe, and for a time the enemy gained and held nearly two-thirds of their camp, when, by desperate fighting behind trees, the men succeeded in driving the enemy

[110]

entirely out of camp and partially away from the headquarters. About this time Lieutenant Stetson succeeded in creeping stealthily to his section of artillery and unlimbered one of his guns and fired upon the enemy. This was a rallying signal for the entire command, and immediately a sufficient force was placed in support of the battery and a withering and deadly fire of grape and canister was opened upon the enemy. Three successive charges were made by the enemy to recapture our artillery, but each charge was unsuccessful and cost them dearly.

About 7:30 the enemy retreated in confusion, leaving their dead and wounded in our hands. One hundred and three of the enemy's dead were left on the field, also a large number of wounded and about thirty prisoners. Our men were too much exhausted and fatigued to follow the enemy, and nearly all were out of ammunition. For two hours and a half three small regiments, numbering in the aggregate less than 800 men, had successfully resisted the oft-repeated charges of three entire divisions numbering not less than 5,000 men. We remained on the field of battle till 3 p.m., burying the dead and taking care of the wounded, when we moved about five miles in the direction of Fayetteville, and joined the other two brigades and camped for the night. Our loss at the battle of Monroe's Cross-roads was 18 killed, 70 wounded, and 105 missing.

Among the killed and wounded were some of the best officers of the command. Adjutant Mitchell, of the Fifth Kentucky, was killed. The First Alabama Cavalry lost eight officers, including both of its field officers, Major Cramer being both wounded and a prisoner.

It is impossible for me to speak in too high terms of the conduct of the officers and men of my command in this fight, and it would be invidious to mention any, although I cannot let the gallant conduct of Lieutenant Stetson go without mention, who, unaided and alone, crept through the ranks of the enemy and unlimbered and fired one of his guns. To this fact, more than to any other, I ascribe a terrible disaster turned into a brilliant victory.

After Monroe's Crossroads the First Alabama once more moved with the Third Brigade. On March 16 near Averasborough, the regiment briefly skirmished with the enemy, but in the decisive Battle of Bentonville, March 19–21, took no part, except to "guard the left flank."

As the Campaign of the Carolinas ended, the Third Cavalry Brigade—that is, the First Alabama, the Fifth Kentucky, and the Fifth Ohio regiments—went into camp on March 24 at Faison's Depot, North Carolina.

In 55 days the brigade had marched more than seven hundred miles, crossing seven large rivers and many small streams. It had suffered 179 casualties: killed, 26 officers and men; wounded, 85; captured, 68. It alone had captured 207 prisoners and with the division had shared in the destruction of 80 railroad bridges, 200,000 bales of cotton, 411 cotton gins, 170 saw-mills, and 70 grist-mills, to say nothing of rolling stock, water tanks, wagon shops, and countless quantities of miscellaneous supplies.

Colonel Spencer generously thanked all commands of the Third

Brigade "for their energy and zeal upon every occasion," but Major Tramel, besides presenting a brief chronology of the activities of the First Alabama Cavalry, stated simply that the regiment had during the campaign "captured something over 100 prisoners and over 200 horses. . . ." Captain John Latty, Company C; First Lieutenant George W. Emerick, Company A; and First Lieutenant Joseph H. Hornback, Company K, and four inlisted men had been killed in action, he added. Major Cramer, Second Lieutenant George₁ C. Jenkins, Company M, and 28 men had been wounded, and Surgeon J. G. C. Swaving, First Lieutenant John P. Moore, Company E, and 46 men had been captured. Of horses, he concluded, 215 had been lost—"some by being captured, others by being worn out and abandoned."

At his field headquarters near Mount Olive, Major-General Kilpatrick was jubilant. On March 22, after visiting Major-General Sherman, "our great chief," he issued this special circular to the men in the Third Cavalry Divison:

> The campaign is over and we are promised rest. . . . This day I met our great chief on the field of battle, amid the dead and dying of our enemy, who has again fled before our proud, advancing banners, and my ears were made to tingle with the grateful words of praise spoken in admiration of the cavalry.
> Soldiers, be proud! Of all the brave men of this army you have a right to be. You have won the admiration of our infantry, fighting on foot and mounted, and you will receive the outspoken words of praise from the great Sherman himself. He appreciates and will reward your patient endurance of hardships, gallant deeds, and valuable services.
> With the old laurels of Georgia entwine those won in the Carolinas, and proudly wear them.
> General Sherman is satisfied with his cavalry.

Within one week after General Joseph E. Johnston's surrender of the Army of Tennessee (April 26, at Greensboro, N.C.), the First Alabama Cavalry, now commanded by Lieutenant-Colonel George L. Godfrey and Major Tramel, was briefly attached to the Department of North Carolina, Army of the Ohio. In mid-April the regiment had moved from Faison's Depot to Raleigh to Durham to Hillsboro, where it had "remained during the negotiations and armistice between Gens Sherman and Johnson [sic], and the final surrender of Johnson [sic] until the last of the month." On May 4 Sherman ordered the regiment to Knoxville to report to Major-General George A. Thomas, commanding the Department of the Cumberland, and afterwards to "march without delay" to the Huntsville-Decatur area "to assist in keeping the District of Northern Alabama." Moving by way of Hillsboro, Greensboro, Salisbury (where it remained a week shoeing horses), Lincolnton, Rutherforton, Asheville, and Bull's Gap, the regiment arrived at Knoxville on the last day of May. As the regimental scribe reported for the month, "the 400 miles passed over [were] some very rocky and mountainous country, but as a general thing the roads were good. Forage was very scarce so much so that the animals were compelled to travel seven days without any grain, and being very poor when the march was commenced, a great many were wore out and abandoned. The men are in good health but are in great need of pay and clothing."

The First Alabama left Knoxville June 2. Passing through Bridgeport, Stevenson, and Larkinsville it arrived in Huntsville June 14 and reported to Major-General Robert S. Granger, commanding the District of Northern Alabama. At this time the regiment was re-joined by Colonel Spencer, who had been on leave since April because of "important private business involving the loss of a large sum of money" that required his personal attention.

Within a few days three companies of the Tories were sent across the Tennessee to Courtland and three to Moulton. The four others remained in Huntsville, where they were soon joined by their comrades-in-arms, the Fourth Alabama Colored Infantry, which had been organized at Decatur on March 31, 1864. Together these Alabamians, white and black, were assigned the duty—as occupational troops —of policing their own neighbors, both friend and foe.

On July 5 at Huntsville the regimental reporter wrote that Companies B, C, E, F, G, and M were bivouacked in that town and that all others, except H and K (unaccounted for) were at Moulton. A month later all companies, except B, H, and M, were at Courtland. Company M was at Pikesville (Marion County), and H—the lost company, which had somehow got separated from the regiment in South Carolina or North Carolina back in January, 1865—was at Blountsville.

Colonel Spencer resigned as colonel of the First Alabama on July 5, "the war being practically ended and my private business demanding my immediate attention." He added, "I have been in service nearly four years, and as long as there was an enemy in arms against the government I was willing to sacrifice every other interest to the public good. I now believe my duty requires me to bestow my entire time and attention to my private affairs." His resignation was immediately accepted and on August 22 he was appointed "Brigadier-General by Brevet of the Volunteer Force, Army of the United States for gallant, and meritorious services during the Campaign through Georgia and the Carolinas."

On October 16, 1865 the First Alabama Cavalry, U. S. A., ten companies, was officially mustered out by the Adjutant-General's Office, War Department, Washington, D. C., along with all cavalry companies east of the Mississippi River. From its humble beginning in October, 1862 it had served exactly three years.

[113]

THOMAS MIDDLETON'S USE OF *IMPRESE* IN *YOUR FIVE GALLANTS*[1]

Studies in Philology, University of North Carolina, Chapel Hill, April, 1934.

In *Your Five Gallants* Thomas Middleton employs the following characters: *Frippery*, the broker gallant; *Primero*, the bawd gallant; *Goldstone*, the cheating gallant; *Pursenet*, the pocket gallant; and *Tailby*, the whore gallant. These men, each a master in his chosen field of "gallantry", have designs on Katherine, a wealthy orphan, and wish to present themselves to her in a masque. Realizing their inability to arrange a proper performance, they secure the services of Ralph Bouser, supposedly another gallant but in reality Fitsgrave, a gentleman in love with Katherine, to prepare for them a series of suitable devices.[2]

This procedure suggests the popular use of *imprese* and devices in the sixteenth and seventeenth centuries. Henry Green has stated that before 1616

> the Emblem literature of Europe could claim for its own at least 200 authors, not including translators, and that above 770 editions of original texts and of versions had issued from the press.[3]

Elsewhere Green quotes a letter from William Drummond of Hawthornden to Ben Jonson, in which there is much praise of Mary Queen of Scots for her knowledge of and interest in emblems.[4] Spenser's *Shepherd's Calendar* is embellished with devices, each eclogue

---

[1] For the loan of books of *imprese* and for other valuable assistance I wish to express my thanks to Professor Allan H. Gilbert.

[2] *Goldstone*. By my troth, a good jest! Did I not commend his wit to you, gentlemen? Hark, sirrah Ralph Bouser, cousin Bouser, i'faith, there's a kind of portion in town, a girl of fifteen hundred, whom we all powerfully affect, and determine to present our parts to her in a masque.
Fitsgrave. In a masque.
Goldstone. Right, sir: now, a little of thy brain for a device to present us firm, which we shall never to able to do ourselves, thou knowest that; and with a kind of speech wherein thou mayst express what gallants are, bravely.
Fitsgrave. Pooh, how can I express 'em otherwise but bravely? Now for a Mercury, and all were fitted (IV, viii, 289–300, *The Works of Thomas Middleton*, ed. A. H. Bullen, London, 1885, vol. III).

[3] Henry Green, *Shakespeare and the Emblem Writers* (London, 1870), p. 102. Green adds in a footnote: "Since the above was written I have good reasons for concluding that the fact is very much understated. I am now employed... in forming an Index to my various notes and references to Emblem writers and their works: the Index so far made comprises the letters A, B, C, D... and they present 330 writers and translators, and above 900 editions."

[4] *Ibid.*, pp. 123–124. This letter is also quoted by Joan Evans, *Pattern in Western Europe, 1180–1900* (Oxford, 1931), I, 156–157. Miss Evans quotes directly from Hawthornden's *Works* (Edinburgh, 1711), p. 137, a volume which has not been available for this study.

having a motto expressive of the leading idea. In the original version of Sidney's *Arcadia* four devices are used; in the 1590 edition nineteen, most of them in connection with a battle or tournament.[5] While imprisoned at Woodstock by her sister, in 1554, Elizabeth busied herself in working on black silk devices expressive of her condition.[6] *Imprese* were embroidered on her clothes;[7] later in her career she was presented with gifts upon which were "graven emprezes",[8] and in *Gesta Grayorum; or, The History of the High and Mighty Prince Henry*, a masque performed for her pleasure in 1590, the following "Impresses which the Maskers used upon their Escutcheons, for their Devices", formed an impressive part of the ceremony:

H. Helmes. In a bark of a cedar-tree, the character E engraven. *Crescetis.*
W. Cooke. In a plain shield, as it were *Abrasa tabula. Quid ipsa velis.*
Jarvis Tevery. A tortoise, with his head out of the shell. *Obnoxia.*
Joh. Lambert. A torch by the sun. *Quis furor.*

---

[5] Philip Sidney, *The Countesse of Pembroke's Arcadia*, ed. Albert Feuillerat (Cambridge, 1922), pp. 63–64, 101, 105–106, 107, 108, 284, 285, 286 (2), 350, 415–416 (2), 423, 430, 445, 454, 455, 462 (2). A few of these will serve as admirable examples: "His *impresa* in his shield, was a fire made of Juniper, with this word, *More easie, and more sweete*" (pp. 105–106); "... his device he had put in the picture of *Helen* which hee defended. It was the *Ermion*, with a speach that signified, *Rather dead than spotted*" (p. 108); "His *Impresa* was a sheepe marked with pitch, with this word *Spotted to be knowne*" (p. 285); "His *Impresa* was, a mill-horse still bound to goe in one circle; with this word, *Data fata sequutus*" (p. 286); "His shield was beautified with this device; A greyhound, which overrunning his fellow, and taking the hare, yet hurts it not when it takes it. The word was, *The glorie, not the pray*" (pp. 415–416); "In this shield (as his owne device) he had two Palme trees, neere one another, with a worde signifying, *In that sort flourishing*" (p. 423); "In his shielde for *Impresa*, he had a beautifull childe, but having two heades; whereof the one shewed, that it was alreadie dead: the other alive, but in that case, necessarily looking for death. The word was, *No way to be rid from death, but by death*" (p. 445); "His *Impresa* was a *Catoblepta*, which so long lies dead, as the Moone (whereto it hath so naturall a sympathie) wants her light. The word signified that *The Moone wanted not the light, but the poore beast wanted the Moones light*" (p. 455). One of Sidney's *imprese*, "the fish Torpedo faire" (pp. 350, 415) has been skillfully discussed by Emma Marshall Denkinger, "The *Arcadia* and 'the Fish Torpedo Faire,'" *Studies in Philology*, XXVIII (1931), 162 ff.

[6] John Nichols, *The Progresses and Public Processions of Queen Elizabeth* (London, 1823), I, 10–11. "The covers are of black silk; on which she had amused herself with curiously working, or embossing, the following inscriptions and devices in gold twist. On one side, on the border, or edge, *Coelum patria. Scopus vitae xpus. Christo vive.* In the middle a heart; and about it, *Eleva cor sursum ibi ubi E. C.* (i.e., *est Christus.*) On the other side, on the border, *Beatus qui divitias scripturae legens verba vertit in opera.* In the middle a star, and about it, *vicit omnia pertinax virtus. E. C.* (i.e., *Elisabethae Captivae;* or *Elisabetha Captiva.)*"

[7] *Ibid.*, III, 503, 508.

[8] *Ibid.*, III, 49. "The gifts which the Vestall Maydens presented unto her Majesty, were these; a vaile of white, exceeding rich and curiously wrought: a cloke and safeguard set with buttons of gold, and on them were graven emprezes of excellent devise; in the loope of every button was a Nobleman's badge, fixed to a pillar richly embrodered."

[115]

Molineux. A river with many turnings, running into the sea. *Semper ad mare.*
Crimes. A flag streaming in the wind. *Famamque fovemus inanem.*
Paylor. A sail and an oar together. *Fors & virtus miscenter in unum.*
Campnies. A flag of fire wavering upwards. *Tremet & ardet.*[9]

Green also lists more than four hundred of Shakespeare's references to emblematic material.[10] Perhaps the best counterpart of Middleton's use of *imprese* in *Your Five Gallants* is to be found in Shakespeare's employment of them in *Pericles;* direct knowledge of emblem books is apparent, and, says Green, "may be taken as evidence to show that the Emblem writers were known and made use of between 1589 and 1609 by the dramatists of England."[11] The scene represents a pageant, or triumph, held in honor of Thaisa, daughter of Simonides, King of Pentapolis:

> *(Enter a Knight; he passes over, and his Squire presents his shield to the Princess.)*
> Simonides. Who is the first that doth prefer himself?
> *Thaisa.* A knight of Sparta, my renowned father;
> And the device he bears upon his shield
> Is the black Ethiope reaching at the sun;
> The word, *Lux tua vita mihi.*
> *Sim.* He loves you well that holds his life of you.
> *(The Second Knight passes.)*
> Who is the second that presents himself?
> *Thai.* A prince of Macedon, my royal father;
> And the device he bears upon his shield
> Is an arm'd knight that's conquer'd by a lady;
> The motto thus, in Spanish, *Piu por dulzura por que fuerza.*
> *(The Third Knight passes.)*
> *Sim.* And what's the third?
> *Thai.* The third of Antioch;
> And his device a wreath of chivalry;
> The word, *Me pompae provexit apex. (The Fourth Knight passes.)*
> *Sim.* What is the fourth?
> *Thai.* A burning torch that's turned upside down;
> The word, *Quod me alit, me extinguit.*
> *Sim.* Which shows that beauty hath his power and will,
> Which can as well inflame as it can kill. *(The Fifth Knight passes.)*
> *Thai.* The fifth, an hand environed with clouds,
> Holding out gold that's by the touchstone tried;
> The motto thus, *Sic spectanda fides. (The Sixth Knight passes.)*
> *Sim.* And what's
> The sixth and last, the which the knight himself
> With such a graceful courtesy deliver'd?
> *Thai.* He seems to be a stranger; but his present is
> A wither'd branch, that's only green at top;
> The motto, *In hac spe vivo.*

---

[9] *Ibid.,* III, 319.
[10] Green, *op. cit.,* pp. 531 ff.
[11] *Ibid.,* p. 158.

Sim. A pretty moral;
From the dejected state wherein he is,
He hopes by you his fortunes yet may flourish.[12]

In contrast to Shakespeare's serious use of the *imprese,* however, Middleton's adaptation of them is humorous or satiric. Even this was not a complete innovation: Samuel Daniel writes that "a ridiculous mot or posie is not to be used but in some occasion of maskes, or to quip an enemy,"[13] and Sidney, in the Arcadia, adapts the device to comic purposes:

> Then gave he order to a painter for his device; which was, a plowe with the oxen lewsed from it, a sword with a great many armes and legges cut of; and lastly a great armie of pen and inke-hornes, and bookes. Nether did he sticke to tell the secrete of his intent, which was, that he had lefte of the plowe, to doo such bloudy deedes with his swoorde, as many inkehornes and bookes should be employed about the historifying of them: and being asked, why he set no worde unto it, he said, that was indeede like the painter, that sayeth in his picture, Here is the dog, and here is the Hare: & with that he laughed so perfectly, as was great consolation to the beholders. Yet remembring, that *Miso* would not take it well at his returne, if he forgat his dutie to her, he caused about in a border to be written:
>
> Miso *mine own pigsnie, thou shalt heare news o' Dameatas.*[14]

In somewhat the same humorous fashion Middleton has Ralph Bouser take advantage of the five gallants by producing for them a series of *imprese* and mistranslations that will reveal to Katherine the true nature of the imposters. In the process of devising the plan, Bouser renders two distinct translations of the mottoes;[15] the first, which freely renders the correct meanings, is given to two gentlemen and Bungler, men whom Bouser has taken into his confidence; the second translation is given to the imposters themselves, and is decidedly misleading, being in the serious vein the gallants expect of him. The devices and translations are as follows:

> For *Pursenet:* "the device, a purse wide open, and the mouth downward: the word, *Alienis ecce crumenis!"* Fitsgrave translates:
>   1. "One that lives out of other men's pockets."
>   2. "Your bounty pours itself forth to all men."
> For *Goldstone:* "three silver dice," "two cinques and a quarter." "The word, *Fratremque patremque."* Fitsgrave translates:
>   1. "... he will cheat his own brother; nay his own father, i' faith."

---

[12] *Pericles,* II, ii, 17–47. For a similar masque, with *imprese,* see Marston, *The First Part of Antonio and Mellida,* V, i, 173–238.

[13] *The Complete Works in Verse and Prose of Samuel Daniel,* ed. A. B. Grosart (The Spenser Society, 1896), IV, 22–23. In illustration Daniel describes a device with a motto *(Crucifixux etiam pro nobis)* which like those of Middleton, is serious in itself but ridiculous in its setting.

[14] Sidney, *op. cit.,* p. 430.

[15] *Your Five Gallants,* V, i, 78–113, 144–237.

2. "Fortune of my side."
For *Primero:* "The device, an unvalued pearl hid in a cave; the word, *Occul[t]os vendit honores."* Fitsgrave translates:
    1. "One that sells maidenheads by wholesale."
    2. "A black man's a pearl in a fair lady's eye."
For *Frippery:* The device, "a cuckoo sitting on a tree; the word, *En avis ex avibus!"* Fitsgrave translates:
    1. "One bird made of many; for you know as the sparrow hatches the cuckoo, so the gentleman feathers the broker."
    2. "I keep one tune, I recant not."
For *Tailby:* "For the device, a candle in a corner; the word, *Consumptio victus.*"[16] Fitsgrave translates:
    1. "My light is yet in darkness till I enjoy her."[17]

Middleton's employment of these burlesque *imprese,* and others of a similar nature,[18] not only confirms the belief that emblem literature was known to the English dramatists, but also indicates that Middleton was well aware of the popularity of the *imprese,* and realized that a burlesque of them would be readily understood by his audience.

In an attempt to determine the sources and analogues of the *imprese* in *Your Five Gallants,* an investigation of forty-one volumes[19] of

---

[16] Possibly a misprint for *virtus,* as given at V, i, 211: "... *cujus virtus consumptio corporis [corpus]."* This part of the play is exceedingly corrupt, says Bullen, *ibid.,* p. 234.

[17] *Ibid.,* V, i, *passim.*

[18] *The Black Book,* VIII, 18. "... the gentlewoman, wondering it was so long a-kindling, at last she caught the miserable conceit of it, and calling her man to her, bade him seek out for a piece of chalk, or some peeling of a white wall, whilst in the meantime she conceited the device; when taking up the six former coals, one after another, she chalked upon each of them a satirical letter; which six were these,

                    T. D. C. R. U. S. ;

explained thus, .

            These dead coals
            Resemble usurers' souls."

Father Hubburd's Tales, VIII, 74–75. "To conclude, I took the pen first of the lawyer, and turning it arsy-versy, like no instrument for a ploughman, our youngster and the rest of the faction burst into laughter at the simplicity of my fingering; but I not so simple as they laughed me for, drew the picture of a knavish emblem, which was a plough with the heels upward, signifying thereby that the world was turned upside down since the decease of my old landlord, all hospitality and good housekeeping kicked out of doors, and all thriftiness and good husbandry tossed into the air, ploughs turned into trunks, and corn into apparel.

"Then came another of our husbandmen to set his mark by mine: he holding the pen clean at one side towards the merchant and the mercer, showing that all went well on their sides, drew the form of an unbridled colt, so wild and unruly, that he seemed with one foot to kick up the earth and spoil the labours of many toiling beasts, which was fitly alluded to our wild and unbridled landlord, which, like the colt, could stand upon no ground till he had no ground to stand upon."

The Black Book, VIII, 33–45. The gallants here depicted strongly resemble those of *Your Five Gallants.*

[19] Andrea Alciati, *Emblematum flumen abundans,* etc. (Lyons, 1551); Andrea Alciati, *Emblemata* (Lugdini, 1614); Andrea Alciati, *Emblematum Fontes Quatour,* ed. Henry

[118]

imprese and emblem literature has revealed corresponding ideas and similar engravings, but nothing that may be termed an exact duplication. Though without doubt Middleton was working independently in transferring the *imprese* to comic use in the drama, it yet appears reasonable to assume that his devices are composites of those that he saw in actual use, or read about in emblem books. For instance, Pursenet's "purse wide open, and the mouth downward" has its counterpart in Ripa,[20] Ruscelli,[21] and Cornhertio[22]—each of which depicts a purse turned bottom-upwards and spilling its gold. Goldstone's dice are frequently encountered in devices: Bargagli[23] and Alciati[24] depict them, the former showing "five" and "three", and the latter showing three separate dice. The translation, "Fortune of my side", is sugges-

Green (London, 1870); Harold Bayley, *New Light on the Renaissance* (London, 1909); Scipion Bargagli, *Dell' Imprese . . . etc.* (Venice, 1594); Jean Baudoin, *Inconologie ou la Science des Emblemes* (Amsterdam, 1698), 2 vols.; Antoine Bourgogne, *Mundi lapis lydius*, etc. (Antwerp, 1639); William Camden, *Remains Concerning Britain* (London, 1674); Joachim Camerarius, *Symbolorum et Emblematum, etc.* (Norbergae, 1590); Jacob Cats and Robert Farlie, *Moral Emblems*, ed. Richard Pigot (London, 1862); Jean Cousin, *Le Livre de Fortune* (Paris, 1883); Theodoro Cornhertius, *Emblemata moralia et oeconomica, etc.* (Arnhemi, 1609); *The Complete Works in Verse and Prose of Samuel Daniel*, IV, 4–27, V, 297–304; Lodovico Dolce, *Imprese nobili et ingeniose di diversi Principi* (Venice, 1578); Hen. Englegrave, *Lux Evangelica sub velum Sacrorum Emblematum* (Coloniae, 1655); *Emblems and Hieroglyphicks on . . . a Variety of Subjects* (London, 1753); Paolo Gavio, *Dialog dell' imprese militari et amorose* (Lyons, 1574); Henry Green, *Andrea Alciati and His Emblems* (London, 1872); P. Leenheer, *Theatrum stultorum Joco-serium, etc.* (Brussels, 1669); *Les Emblems d'armour divin et humain ensemble* (title page missing); Jacob Masen, *Speculum imaginum veritatis occultae*, etc. (Kinchii, 1681); Andres Mendo, *Principe perfecto y Ministros aiustados, Documentos Politicos, y Morales En Emblemas* (Leon, 1662); Francois Menestrier, *L'Art des Emblemes* (Lyons, 1662); Francis Quarles, *Divine Emblems* (London, 1635); Francis Quarles, *Emblemes* (London, 1676); George Richardson, *Iconology; or a Collection of Emblematic Figures, etc.* (London, 1779), 2 vols; George Riley, *Emblems, natural, historical, etc.* (London, 1779); Cesare Ripa, *Della Novissima Iconologia, etc.* (Padova, 1625); Cesare Ripa, *Inconologia del cavaliere, etc.* (Perugia, 1764), 5 vols.; R. Rooleeuw, *Schat der Zielen, of te Begeerder*, etc. (Amsterdam, 1699); Ieronimo Ruscelli, *Le Imprese Illustri* (Venice, 1584); Faxardo Saavedra, *The Royal Politician: One Hundred Emblems*, etc. (London, 1700); Joan Sambucuis, *Emblemata et Aliquot nummi antiqui operis* (Antwerp, 1566); Florent Schoonhon, *Emblemata* (1630 c.); Jacobius Typotius, *Symbola Divina et Humana, Pontificum*, etc. (Arnhemi, 1609); Jan van der Veens, *Zinne-Beelden oft Adams Appel* (Amsterdam, 1642); Octavio van Veen, *Amoris divini emblemata* (Antwerp, 1660); Octavio van Veen, *Amorum Emblemata, Figuris Aeneis Incisa* (Antwerp, 1608); E. Veeryke, *Zederyke Zinnebeelden* (Amsterdam, 1713); George Wither, *A Collection of Emblems, Ancient and Modern* (London, 1635); Geoffrey Whitney, *Choice of Emblems*, ed. Henry Green (London, 1866). I have given the date of the editions I have consulted. Some of those here dated later than Middleton's play first appeared before it and the others present much that is traditional.

[20] *Op. cit.*, I, 290.
[21] *Op. cit.*, p. 16.
[22] *Op. cit.*, pp. 10, 26, 28.
[23] *Op. cit.*, pp. 359, 366.
[24] *Op. cit.*, p. 51.

[119]

tive of *E mia fortuna* and *Comite fortuna* by Ruscelli.[25] Goldstone's *Fratremque patremque* resembles *Ex patri et patriae* of Typotius.[26] Primero's "unvalued pearl hid in a cave" may have a distant connection with the pearl hid in an oyster, as given by Saavedra.[27] Frippery's "cukoo sitting on a tree" has various parallels: Ruscelli,[28] Typotius,[29] Whitney,[30] and Camerarius[31] give examples. *Ille meos* and *Mens eadem* as used by Ruscelli[32] suggests, "I keep one tune, I recant not." "A candle in a corner" as it appears in Tailby's *imprese* is a variant adaptation of a popular and frequently used idea. *Emblems and Hieroglyphicks*[33] lists at least six uses, Ruscelli[34] gives two, and Verryke[35] depicts a candle being covered with a cloth, with the word, *Et obducta lucet.* Various other distant parallels can be drawn, such as the resemblance of Middleton's mottoes to passages in the classics.[36] But though Middleton was obviously familiar with emblems and *imprese* in books and in actual use, he seems to have devised for himself those in his play; moreover, his elaborate employment of them for ridicule is not frequent in the drama.

---

[25] *Op. cit.*, pp. 131, 459.

[26] *Op. cit.*, p. 235. With Goldstone's "He will cheat his own brother; nay, his own father" compare Baligny's speech to King Henry in Chapman's *The Revenge of Bussy D'Ambois:*

> Your highness knows
> I will be honest and betray for you
> Brother and father . . . (II, i, 29–31).

[27] *Op. cit.*, I, 234.

[28] *Op. cit.*, p. 32.

[29] *Op. cit.*, p. 36.

[30] *Op. cit.*, p. 29.

[31] *Op. cit.*, II, 48, 60, 64.

[32] *Op. cit.*, pp. 170, 20.

[33] *Op. cit.*, pp. 178 ff.

[34] *Op. cit.*, pp. 331, 429.

[35] *Op. cit.*, p. 247.

[36] Pursenet: *Aliena vivere quadra.* (Juvenal, *Satires*, 5, ii).
> *Et mundus victus non deficiente crumina.*
> > (Horace, *Epistles*, I, iv. xi).
Tailby: *Vis concili expers mole ruit sua.* (Horace, *Carm.*, III, iv, 65).
> *Virtus omnia in sese habet.* (Plautus, *Amphitryon*, II, 652).

POET IN UNIFORM

Sir, New York City, August, 1944.

Poor, starving Edgar Allan Poe, author of *The Raven* and *The Gold Bug*, is probably America's best-known poet and short story writer. His "Once upon a midnight dreary..." is quoted by verse-loving children from six to sixty—yet it is doubtful if one in ten thousand knows that the sentimental author voluntarily enlisted in the U.S. Army at the age of eighteen, served a two-year hitch and was honorably discharged as an "exemplary" soldier, "prompt and faithful in the discharge of his duties."

And those who insist on picturing the poet as a liquor-loaded gutter-snipe will be surprised to learn that his commanding officer recorded his habits as "good and entirely free from drinking"—a fact proved by his rapid promotions, as any soldier will testify. Entering a private, he was discharged as sergeant major—a jump of six ranks, according to present Army Regulations, in only nineteen months' service!

Poe, violently censured by his parsimonious foster father, John Allan, a well-to-do Richmond merchant, for spending too much money while a student at the University of Virginia, ran away from home in March, 1827. Penniless, but with a sheaf of verses tucked under his tunic, he worked his way to Boston on a coalship. There he fell in with Calvin Thomas, a 19-year-old printer, whom he persuaded to publish a few copies of *Tamerlane and Other Poems* on cheap, yellow paper. This 40-page booklet, Poe's first volume, sold for about 25c. Today less than a half-dozen copies are known to exist. They are valued at $10,000 each.

But in May, 1827, there were no takers at any price and Poe, hungry, broke and too proud to go sniveling back to Allan, joined the Army under the name of Edgar A. Perry. He was immediately assigned to the First U. S. Artillery, Colonel James House commanding, and stationed with Battery H, Fort Independence, Boston Harbor.

Late in October, during Poe's fifth month of service, Battery H was ordered to Fort Moultrie, Sullivan's Island, Charleston, S. C. On November 8 Pvt. Poe boarded the brig *Waltham* and eleven days later began "garrison duty" in the southern seaport.

Devotees of Poe who maintain that he lived in a poet-world, eerily set apart from ordinary mankind, would do well to consider his "dream works" in the light of his experiences as a hard-boiled U. S. trooper. He was stationed at Fort Moultrie for thirteen months during one of America's longest eras of peace, midway between the War of 1812 and the Mexican War. He was for once completely free from debt and the problem of earning three square meals. He was in a strange, semi-tropical environment, a section of the country reeking with folk- and piratical-lore and only three miles from an exotic old city steeped in aristocracy and tradition. As a coast-guardsman in an isolated post, he had time on his hands to roam the island, swim in the warm surf, visit the city's libraries, and to attend the Charleston Theatre where his father, David Poe, had starred as "The Lover" in *The Old Soldier* and his mother, as a member of a traveling troupe sixteen years before, had played "Jacintha" opposite the famous John H. Dwyer's "Ranger" in *The Suspicious Husband*.

To say the least, this strange interlude of Army life made a lasting impression on the young trooper. Fifteen years after his discharge he set the scene of *The Gold Bug* on Sullivan's Island and called his chief character "Legrand" (Legare, pronounced Legree, is a Charleston name). *The Balloon Hoax* is centered on "the low coasts of South Carolina" and in *The Oblong Box* and *The Man That Was Used Up*, as well as in his poetry, many lights and shadows appear which unquestionably reflect his sojourn in Carolina.

On May 1, 1828, after a year's service, he was promoted to battery artificer (supply sergeant), a rank which doubled his pay and carried with it "one ration of whisky or rum per day."

However, by now the sensitive poet-soldier was, despite rapid promotions, tiring of Army life. Swallowing his pride, he wrote his foster father asking for permission and money to buy his leave from the service (as was then customary) and try for an appointment to the U. S. Military Academy at West Point. Allan, still adamant and believing this merely a ruse to get out of the Army, shelved the letter.

Meanwhile, as the hot summer months dragged by, Poe carried on as battery artificer, spending his leisure time playing cards and polishing up a poem called *Al Aaraaf*—the longest he ever wrote. It was with great glee that he and the other troopers of Battery H received orders on December 11, 1828, to embark for new duties at Fortress Monroe, Old Point Comfort, Virginia.

Arriving four days later on the *Harriet*, Poe at once reopened negotiations with Allan. Weary with the monotony of Army routine and dead set on entering West Point, he appealed to Lieutenant Howard who complimented him on his performance of duty and presented him to Colonel House. Both officers felt that Poe had a good chance if only Allan would use his influence. But Allan sat tight.

Shortly after Christmas, Poe fell ill with fever and was placed in the Fortress Monroe Military Hospital under the care of Dr. Robert Archer, Surgeon, USMC. Archer, sensing the soldier's unusual aptitudes, offered to help him with the Academy scholarship by appealing directly to Allan, whom, as Fate would have it, he knew through mutual friends in Richmond. Under the stimulus of this encouragement, Poe quickly recovered, eagerly resumed his duties and early in January, 1829, was promoted to Regimental Sergeant Major—the highest non-commissioned rank in the Army and a position demanding executive ability and complete trustworthiness.

Allan, meanwhile, yielded to the pressure of the colonel, and lieutenant and the doctor. He agreed to put up the necessary cash to buy Poe's discharge and to pull whatever strings he could to help him into West Point—after all, that *was* a convenient way to provide for his "son's" upkeep at public expense! Poe, therefore, was ordered discharged on condition that he could furnish "an acceptable substitute" and $75. On April 15, 1829, both regulations complied with, ex-Sergeant Major Poe walked out of Fortress Monroe a private citizen. Under his arm he carried the manuscript of *Al Aaraaf*.

In less than a month, armed with recommendations from his officers and a half-dozen of his "father's" influential friends and an introduction from Allan to John H. Eaton, Secretary of War, Poe went to Washington to seek the scholarship in person. He was told that he might expect an appointment in September.

With that off his mind, he set out for Baltimore to see his Aunt Maria Clemm and her daughter Virginia (later his wife) who were living with several other members of the family in semi-poverty on Milk Street. From that vantage point, and with an allowance of $8 per month from Allan, Poe spent the summer peddling *Al Aaraaf* among Baltimore and Philadelphia publishers. September passed and no word came from West Point. If Poe was disappointed, Allan was heartbroken—it looked as if he might have to support the young whippersnapper after all! To make matters worse, in December Hatch & Dunning of Baltimore printed *Al Aaraaf*, and the author, his mission accomplished, left the Clemms and returned to Richmond. Allan, determined to get Poe off somewhere again—anywhere—persuaded a business associate, Charles Ellis, to write his brother, Powhatan Ellis, U. S. Senator from Mississippi, to come to the rescue. Senator Ellis obliged by personally recommending Poe to the Secretary of War and, as usual, a senator's letter did the job.

On June 28, 1830, Poe entered the Academy as cadet-at-large on a special appointment from President Andrew Jackson. There he remained until February 19, 1831—but that is another story.

THE SOUTHERN ASSOCIATION AND COLLEGE LIBRARIES: AN HISTORICAL REVIEW

Southeastern Library Association Proceedings,
Asheville, North Carolina, 1946.

The Southern Association of Colleges and Secondary Schools was organized November 6, 1895, by a small group of college and university representatives who assembled in Atlanta at the request of a committee of the faculty of Vanderbilt University. At this initial meeting a constitution and by-laws were adopted and the following threefold purpose of the association approved: (1) to organize Southern schools and colleges for cooperation and mutual assistance, (2) to elevate the standard of scholarship and to effect uniformity of entrance requirements, and (3) to develop preparatory schools and cut off this work from the colleges. From a charter membership of but six institutions the Association has grown to include 202 colleges and universities and 1285 secondary schools in eleven states, and after a half-century of service to education in the South is today generally recognized as one of the foremost educational bodies in the nation.

During the early years of its struggling existence, however, this small body of colleges fought hard to enlist members, institutional and individual, to achieve organization and mutual cooperation among rival colleges and universities, and it fought hard to drive home to sometimes recalcitrant educators the need for certificating and accrediting systems, standardized college entrance requirements, the development of better secondary schools, the proper recognition of junior colleges and women's colleges, and the urgency of the need for better teaching methods, better faculties, better laboratories and better libraries.

Those of us who have begun our affiliation with the Association in recent years are prone to accept its influence as born full-grown, unless we take time to go back through the files of *Proceedings*, reading the yearly record of combat against ignorance, prejudice and educational orneriness in the South.

We are here primarily concerned, however, with the Association's interest in college and university libraries and although it requires stoic courage to omit the many enticing and tellable stories about other educational matters, the remainder of this essay will be devoted to the role the Southern Association has played during the last fifty years in the improving of library facilities of institutions of higher learning in the region.

The *Proceedings* of the Association for the first two decades of its existence reveal no attempt by the membership to establish definite standards for the college library. During these years books and their use in the upper levels of learning were apparently of small concern. In 1898, at the 4th annual meeting, in Athens (Georgia), Miss Anne Wallace of the State Library of Atlanta briefly outlined the need for Southern librarians to participate in the affairs of the American Library Association and emphasized "the importance of the library to the college and the need of efficient, especially trained librarians to successfully administer library affairs." Except for this pioneering effort the library emphasis throughout these early days was on the secondary school level entirely. Inasmuch as a separate Commission on Institutions of Higher Education, organized to study the particular affairs of colleges and universities, was not created until nineteen years later, this is not difficult to understand. Meanwhile, the Association of necessity dealt largely with problems doubtfully greater but more pressing, perhaps—certificating and accrediting of both schools and colleges.

It was not until 1901, at the 7th conference, that the Association received its first blast on the inadequacies of college libraries. In an address entitled "The Problems of the Small College in the Southern States," Professor E. H. Babbitt of Sewanee outlined the many difficulties facing institutions of higher learning, commenting on libraries as follows:

> There is not a college library in the South which has 30,000 up-to-date volumes, and there are many, in colleges whose work is to be taken seriously, which have not 5,000. If some millionaire with a library habit would give even moderately in this direction, would it not do more good than providing novels for growing boys and factory girls?

A year later Professor F. W. Moore of Vanderbilt University declared that library facilities for the study of history in the South were "only fair, though improving." Teachers, he maintained, were frequently forced to put their private libraries into the hands of students and only a few institutions were located near enough to public or state or historical association libraries to call upon them for books. Moreover, he added, "College libraries are small and the income insufficient to enable them to keep up with the new literature and the best modern authorities. Thus it is sometimes the case that a library fairly large in numbers contains many books which are out of date, and accordingly has a disproportionately low grade as a working library."

Between 1902, the date of Professor Moore's address, and 1916 the *Proceedings* contain no record of discussions regarding the college library. At the 22nd annual meeting, however, the President of the Association, Professor Bert E. Young of Vanderbilt University, delivered a significant and prophetic address, entitled "Taking Stock." Summing up the work of the Association, he pointed with obvious pride to the successes which had been accomplished during two decades of endeavor, and then asked. "What are our shortcomings?" They were many, he declared. One section of his address dealt with the college library:

> We have too many weak members—too many that are weak in equipment, in library, in endowment, in faculty, in requirements for graduation to be voted as standard colleges... We should now begin to require a certain minimum of income, of library facilities, of academic preparation of members of faculties, *et cetera*, of all our colleges... We are not going ahead so rapidly in higher education as we should. Our colleges

[125]

have not altogether kept pace with our secondary schools, nor with the astonishing economic development of the Southern states. Too many of our colleges are still holding fast to antiquated methods and worn-out ambitions. Many of us are spending more on various forms of advertising than on the library. I believe in democratizing the college, but not in vulgarizing it ...

Professor Young then turned his attention to a subject which somehow has a familiar ring—the lack in the South of "scientifically organized libraries" and "centers of graduate study." Written thirty years ago, his words still hold solid meaning:

It should be entirely possible for us to establish half a dozen—not more—reserve centers of higher education in the Southern states. We already have two or three institutions that have gone far on the road. This will mean not necessarily large institutions, but choice institutions that specialize. It will mean as many great libraries—not large, but choice; not mere accumulations of books, but collections scientifically selected and correlated.

Apparently, these remarks did not pass unheeded, though, action came slowly. In November, 1917, the Commission on Institutions of Higher Education was organized, and two years later, at the 24th meeting in Louisville, a Committee of this body presented the first "Standards for Colleges." As adopted, they include the following Library Standard:

10. Library.—The library should contain, exclusive of periodicals and public documents, at least 7,000 volumes bearing specifically upon the subjects taught, and should be kept up by means of an adequate annual appropriation.

This standard was revised at Chattanooga the following year (1920) as follows:

10. *Library.*—The library shall contain, exclusive of periodicals and public documents, at least 10,000 volumes bearing specifically upon the subjects taught, and shall have an adequate annual appropriation for permanent additions.

At the Birmingham meeting in 1921, however, the standard was again changed—this time mainly through the efforts of Chancellor J. H. Kirkland of Vanderbilt University, then President of the Association and long a colorful and dynamic figure in its affairs. Chancellor Kirkland was at the time Chairman of a Committee on Accreditization of the National Commission on College Standards, sponsored by the American Council of Education. The Committee had lately (October, 1921) met in New York City and adopted a report called "Principles for Accrediting Colleges" which contained eight cardinal standards for the improvement of national higher education.

When the Southern Association assembled two months later, President Kirkland delivered an address outlining the work of the National

[126]

Commission. Without a dissenting vote new regulations, in general based on those of the National Commission, were adopted, including the following which was devoted to the college library:

Standard No. 10. Library.—The college library should have a live, well distributed, professionally administered library of at least 8,000 volumes, exclusive of public documents, bearing specifically upon the subjects taught and with a definite annual appropriation for the purchase of new books in keeping with the curriculum.

For several years thereafter the *Proceedings* contain references to the revised standards. In 1923 a special committee of the Commission on Institutions of Higher Education, which had been appointed to investigate the practical application of the new rules, reported that the fifty-eight fully accredited member colleges and universities had pronounced the 1921 Standards satisfactory, and that "all institutions report the minimum 8,000 volumes or more." However, it was found, "in a number of cases the funds set apart for library purchases are meager, though, in compliance with the Association's standard. A definite appropriation seems to be made in every instance." Two years later the investigating Committee again reported, this time stating that "the general expression... is that member institutions are endeavoring to keep faith and meet the standards," but that "in many cases funds set apart for library purposes are very meager. Both in purchase of books and in subscriptions to journals, some of our member institutions make showings far from creditable."

But the 1925 annual meeting was a noteworthy one, nevertheless. That year divisions for Teachers Colleges and Junior Colleges were created, admitting those types of institutions, which had previously been excluded, into the Association. Standards for each were immediately established. The Library Standard for Teachers Colleges, as adopted, was the same as that for Arts and Science Colleges (i.e., the 1921 Standard); but the Library Standard for Junior Colleges, as follows, was a modified version of that of the American Association of Junior Colleges:

Standard Number 9. Library.—A working library, adequately catalogued, of not less than 2,500 volumes, exclusive of public documents, shall be maintained and a reading room in connection with the library. A definite annual income for the support of the library shall be provided.

Comparison of this standard with the original from which it came reveals the omission of "appropriate current periodicals," keeping the library "open to students throughout the day" and this significant sentence: "A trained librarian shall be in charge of the library."

Junior College officials were obviously not satisfied with their first try, however; for the following year it was modified, as follows:

Standard Number 9. Library.—The junior college shall have a modern, well-distributed, catalogued, and efficiently administered library of at least 2,500 volumes, exclusive of public documents, selected with special reference to college work, and with a definite annual appropriation for the purchase of books and periodicals. It is urged that such an appropriation be at least $500.

One supposes that a paper, "The Growing Importance of Libraries," read at this meeting by Dr. Louis Round Wilson, Librarian, University of North Carolina, had an effect on the assembled delegates of this, the 31st conference.

In 1927 Dean W. D. Hopper of the University of Georgia, Chairman of the Commission on Institutions of Higher Learning, delivered an address in which he declared that "we believe the time has come for greater emphasis by our Commission on the general atmosphere of the college under consideration, as shown ... in the use of the library, in encouraging students to go on for graduate study, etc. These standards have been lightly regarded in the past, or some institutions would not have been admitted." But that year and the following saw no changes in the Library Standards as adopted in 1921 and 1926 for senior and junior colleges, respectively.

At the 1929 meeting, however, action was taken. Up to this time the standards for Arts and Science Colleges and those for Teachers Colleges, even though identical in many instances, such as in the Library Standard, had been recorded separately in the *Proceedings*. Now they were merged into one series and many changes made.

The revised Library Standard as adopted at this conference was largely the work of a joint Committee, composed of members from the Southeastern Library Association and the Southern Association. Dr. Louis R. Wilson was a leading figure in this movement also. Following the 1928 meeting of the Southern Association he, Dr. D. R. Anderson (Randolph-Macon College), Dean Theodore Jack (Emory University), Dr. Duncan Burnet (University of Georgia), and Charles H. Stone, Librarian, North Carolina College for Women had met to study the possibility of creating better standards for the college library. As a consequence and upon their recommendations, in 1929 the 1921 Library Standard was discarded and the following substituted by the Commission on Higher Education:

The college shall have a live, well distributed library of at least 12,000 volumes, in addition to duplicates and public documents, bearing specifically upon the subject taught and administered by a professionally trained librarian. For a college of approximately 300 students and a minimum number of departments, there should be spent annually for the library, exclusive of the care of the building, not less that $5,000, with proportionate increase for larger student bodies and a larger number of departments. Leading periodicals in the difference fields covered by the curriculum should be taken as well as those of more general cultural interest. There should be a catalogue of approved type. The library should be open not less than ten hours per school day. The building should be well lighted, protected as far as possible against fire, and equipped with adequate working quarters for the staff. Seating capacity for at least 15% of the student body should be provided in the reading rooms. Arrangements should be made through freshman week, orientation courses, or otherwise, for the student to receive instruction in the use of the library.

The Junior College Library Standard of 1926 remained unchanged.

From 1929 to 1939 the senior college Library standard was recorded annually without further modification. During these years little concerning college libraries was reflected in the *Proceedings*, although in 1931 Dean Paul P. Boyd of the University of Kentucky raised important questions "concerning the use of the library by faculty and students and the place which the library service occupies in the life of the college." And five years later, at the 41st annual meeting in Richmond, the Commission on Institutions of Higher Education incorporated into its report two recommendations submitted by the Southeastern Library Association. One of these dealt with school libraries; the other, quoted below, concerned the libraries of institutions of higher learning:

Inasmuch as a wide acquaintance with books and a working experience of the library and its tools are essential to rich personal development, it is recommended to the Southern Association of Colleges and Secondary Schools that generous contacts with books and other reading materials as well as instruction in books and reading, library resources and use, be considered a criterion in the accreditation of colleges.

The recommendation bore immediate fruit. At the next meeting (1938) the Committee on Standards submitted a long report, including a revised standard for senior college libraries, which was unamiously approved. As was customary, however, the changes were not presented to the Association for final action until the following annual session.

The new Standard, which was officially adopted by the 43rd conference, Memphis, March 29, 1939, was as follows:

Standard Nine. The Library.—Since in many respects the library is the heart of the college, its effectiveness is one of the surest tests of institutional worth. The collection of books and periodicals should be tested frequently by comparison with the Shaw list or other standard guides. The building should be well lighted, protected as far as possible against fire, and equipped with adequate working quarters for the staff. There should be a live and well distributed collection of at least 12,000 volumes exclusive of duplicates and government publications. There should be an expenditure of an average of five dollars per student for books, periodicals, and binding. The librarian or librarians should be well trained and experienced, and should have faculty rank. The salaries for the staff should average not less than the equivalent of five dollars per student enrolled in the institution. In case of graduate work, professional training, or other specialized services are attempted, heavier expenditures than those above permitted should be expected. A careful record should be kept to show the use of the library by faculty and students; and arrangements should be made so that all students may receive instruction from time to time in the use of the library.

This Standard is still in force at the present time.

No changes were made in the Junior College Library Standard in 1939, but a new one was proposed and, the following year, officially adopted by the Association. This standard, as quoted below, is also currently in force.

> *Standard Ten.* The Library.—The collection of books and periodicals should be compared frequently with the Mohrhardt's list or other standard guides. The library building should be well lighted, have reading room space for at least twenty per cent of the student enrollment, be fireproof, if possible, and have adequate quarters for the working staff. For a small junior college, there should be a collection of books, adequately catalogued, carefully selected with reference to the subjects taught, and professionally administered, of not fewer than 4,000 volumes, exclusive of public documents. At least fifty magazines and periodicals should be taken each session. Attention shall be given to the possession of standard works of general and special reference, their number and recency.
>
> The librarian should be a full time library employee, have a degree in library science, and have faculty rank.
>
> There should be an annual expenditure of an average of at least two dollars and fifty cents per student for books, periodicals, and binding. All students should receive at least elementary training in the use of the library. A careful record shall be kept of the use of the library by faculty and students.

The 1940 conference was noteworthy in yet another respect regarding college libraries. At this meeting a report of a newly-appointed Library Committee of the Commission on Institutions of Higher Education, headed by Dr. A. F. Kuhlman, Director, Joint University Libraries, was presented by Mrs. Brainard Cheney. Entitled "Development of Sound and Practical Criteria for Measuring the Adequacy of the College Library: A Preliminary Statement," the paper outlined for the Southern Association six-fold essentials for the college library, developed methods of measuring resources and personnel, and discussed buildings, budgets, and integration of library materials with the curriculum. Among other needs the report emphasized the desirability of improved reference and periodical collections in college libraries. As a result, Dr. Kuhlman's Committee was requested to proceed with the preparation of two checklists, one of essential and desirable reference books, the other of periodicals, which could be used by Association colleges in the strengthening of their libraries.

Dr. Kuhlman enlisted the aid of many librarians and teachers throughout the Southern region in the compilation of these booklets, *The Classified List of Reference Books for College Libraries* and *The*

Classified List of Periodicals for College Libraries, which were published by the Association in the summer of 1940. Copies were distributed to all member institutions, and it is generally agreed that this cooperative effort was of great benefit to the building up of college libraries in the South.

In July, 1941, the Commission on Institutions of Higher Education and the Commission on Curricular Problems and Research, under the sponsorship of the General Education Board, held at Sewanee, Tennessee, the first of three scheduled Work Conferences for the purpose of studying the many problems confronting higher education in the South. Unfortunately, no librarians were invited to attend, and meager attention was paid to the role of the library in college and university programs.

However, at the second Conference held the next summer, six librarians, led by Dr. A. F. Kuhlman, were in attendance as consultants. For the better part of a week they discussed with college professors, deans, and presidents ways and means by which the library might be improved and more effectively coordinated with the instructional program. These topics received major attention: 1. Functions of the Library in the College Program; 2. The Responsibility of the College Administration; 3. Role of the Faculty in Promoting Library Use; 4. Book Collections; 5. The Library Staff. The resulting study, "The Relation of the Library to Instruction," incorporated in the report of the Committee on "The Improvement of Instruction," has since been widely distributed and well received.

Six months later, at the 47th annual meeting of the Association, an address emphasizing the Work Conference report as a means of effectively using the library in higher education was delivered before a joint meeting of the Commissions on Institutions of Higher Education and Curricular Problems and Research, but no further college library activity was recorded in the 1942 *Minutes*.

Because of the war no full meetings of the Association were held in 1943, 1944 and 1945 and the third Work Conference, which had been scheduled for the summer of 1943, was postponed. Meanwhile, however, the Committee on Work Conferences continued its study and, when the Association assembled for its 50th annual meeting (March, 1946), reported that a small group of educators had in the interim issued a book, *Studies of Higher Education in the South*, which was to be used as the *agenda* for the third Work Conference. "It is hoped," the Committee stated, "that as a result . . . of the deliberations of the members of the forthcoming work conference this tentative report may be revised, rewritten, and published before the end of this year in such form and manner that it will serve as a directing influence in southern education for some time to come."

The *Minutes* of the 50th meeting contain another decision of significance to college libraries. The classified lists of reference books and periodicals originally sponsored by the Association in 1940, it was agreed, had served a very worthy purpose. However, the passage of time and new emphases on education brought about by World War II had rendered the compilations incomplete and the Commission on Institutions of Higher Education, in executive session, March 27, 1946, approved and appropriation of $2,500 for the publication of revised editions.

Studies in Higher Education in the South, published in the Spring of 1946, contains eleven chapters covering many phases of college and university endeavors—administration, student and community work, general and special education, the humanities, social and natural sciences, teacher education, and others. Of special interest to this paper is the fact that Chapter VII is devoted entirely to "The Library in Higher Education."

This chapter, though compiled by one librarian, is actually the work of many librarians and many teachers throughout the Southern region. To begin with, "The Relation of the Library to Instruction," as conjointly developed at the 1942 Work Conference by a large group of administrators, professors, and librarians, was used as the point of departure. Since the integration of library materials with the teaching processes of an institution, like the strengthening and building of the library collection itself, calls for the cooperative effort of almost everyone on the campus, it was decided that any study involving library use should include the viewpoints of many people in the hierarchy of learning. Consequently, no revision or re-study of the 1942 report was attempted before librarians and faculty representatives of the two hundred higher institutions within the Southern Association had been extended the opportunity of offering criticism and advice.

In July, 1945, therefore, two letters outlining the proposed plans for a third Work Conference and asking for candid comments were addressed, one to the Librarian of each affiliate college or university and the other to the President with the request that it be placed in the hands of the Chairman of the Library Committee or a selected faculty representative.

From librarians 121 replies were received; from faculty members of Chairmen of Library Committees, 88. A large number of the answers —roughly one-fourth—offered no specific suggestions or criticisms. Rather, many of them expressed sincere appreciation of the 1942 report and stated that it had done much to clarify viewpoints regarding the place of the library in the instructional program and to stimulate interest in the use of local facilities. However, from the other correspondents minute and sometimes lengthy analyses and criticisms were obtained. All were extremely helpful in determining the extent to which the report was meeting specific needs throughout the area.

Part II of the chapter, the "Analysis," is in a sense a declarative statement, of necessity opinionated, of the roles that must be played by all members of the campus family, if the usefullness of the college library is to be nourished into full fruition.

And Part III deals with specific recommendations directed toward the administrator, the teacher, the librarian and, finally, to the Association itself. Included in the last are recommendations for (1) studying and improving the present junior and senior college library standards (which have been in effect since 1939 and 1940), (2) developing more effective standards for the education, working hours, tenure and salaries of librarians, and (3) for the creation of a standing committee on libraries, either separately or as a division of the Commission on Institutions of Higher Education, to study and report continuously, according to Association policies, on all matters relating to the libraries of institutions of higher learning.

At the third Work Conference, held in Spartanburg last July, *Studies in Higher Education in the South,* as had been originally planned, was used as the basis for one week's study by a group of approximately 150 educators. Those librarians who so generously gave of their time and wisdom in the preparation of the library chapter will doubtless be pleased to know that it was unanimously approved by the Conference. Bearing this stamp of approval and after necessary redirection, the chapter, as a section of the final version of *Studies in Higher Education in the South,* will be officially presented to the Association at the next December meeting. Doubtless it will fare well there. Meanwhile, work continues, even at this meeting of the Southeastern Library Association. For here now seven of our members are by request studying the chapter, offering their criticisms. And when the completed work is at long last published, "The Library in Higher Education," representing the cummulative thinking of many teachers, administrators and librarians, should serve for some time to come as a guide to the continued improvement of college and university libraries in the South.

Meanwhile, work on the revised editions of *The Classified List of Periodicals* and *The Classified List of Reference Books* has gone forward.

In the Spring of 1946 the Editor invited fifteen outstanding librarians in the South, thirteen of whom reside within the area of the Southeastern Library Association and all whom reside within the area of the Southern Association, to serve as members of Advisory and Editorial Committees in the task of revision. It is tribute to the eternal willingness and altruism of librarians that none declined the invitation, although each was aware of the tremendous amount of unremunerative labor involved.

The Reference Committee, headed by Mrs. Brainard Cheney, first met in Chattanooga in May and the Periodicals Committee, under the leadership of Miss Virginia Trumper, Librarian, Woman's College of the University of North Carolina, in Knoxville, in June. Using the original lists as guides, the Committees have since carried on their work unceasingly, studying curriculum needs, seeking advice from other librarians, teachers and specialists, analyzing new titles and editions, deleting and adding, weighing this book or magazine against that, until now the revised lists are well in hand and nearing completion. At present, indications are that they will be slightly longer than the first editions, somewhat differently arranged, more detailed and thus more complete, and will appear in an entirely different format. Moreover, it is very likely that the two lists will be bound in one volume, rather than separately, as before. Unless some unforseen obstacle arises, the new editions should be in print before Christmas.

Needless to say, the librarians who have so generously given of their time truly hope that the revised lists will enable college and university librarians in the South to take yet another step forward in the systematic strengthening of their periodical and reference collections.

Glancing back over the college library activities of the Southern Association for the last half century, we have seen humble beginnings develop slowly into respectable achievements. One dares not say whether these achievements be altogether sufficient: fifty years is a long, long time and progress, especially library progress, seems sometimes slow. Yet, by comparison, library standards today are higher, interest keener and activity greater now than at any time during the last five decades. All this augurs well for the future; but much remains to be done.

Library standards need not only immediate improvement but continual study and moderization. Stricter enforcement in many of our colleges of present standards, including especially those regarding the status and salaries of librarians and expenditures for books, periodicals and binding, is obligatory. Future progress depends largely on the cooperation of all concerned, the official associations, the institutions, the administrators, teachers, and librarians. Only by joint effort will we reach our common and ultimate goal—more effective institutions of higher learning geared to keep pace with the ever-advancing South.

ALABAMA AND W. GILMORE SIMMS

The Alabama Review, Alabama Historical Association,
University of Alabama, and Auburn University, April & July, 1963.

William Gilmore Simms, of Charleston, the foremost literary figure of the Old South and next to James Fenimore Cooper the best known

American novelist of the early Nineteenth Century, had an unusual and enduring affinity for Alabama. He toured the state twice, in 1824 –1825 and 1834–1835, he used it in 1838 as the locale of one of his most popular frontier romances, and he delivered an address at the University of Alabama in 1842. So well received was he on that occasion that the Board of Trustees called a special meeting to vote him an honorary degree, the President gave him a public dinner, the faculty joined with the students in paying for the publication of his oration in an elaborate brochure, and the charmed citizens of Tuscaloosa persuaded him to delay his return for a week and deliver two additional addresses in the Methodist Church, both open to the general public.

Simms, the son of an Irish emigrant who had settled in South Carolina shortly after the Revolutionary War and Harriet Singleton Simms, the granddaughter of one of General Francis ("Swamp Fox") Marion's captains, was born in Charleston on April 17, 1806. His mother died in 1808 and his distraught father—it is said his hair turned white overnight—put his two-year-old son under the care of his maternal grandmother, Mrs. Jacob Gates, and left for parts unknown. Within a few years, however, he had established himself in Tennessee and formed a fast friendship with General Andrew Jackson. When the Creek Indian War mounted in fury, Simms joined General John Coffee's brigade and fought with distinction in the Battle of Horseshoe Bend and, later, in the Battle of New Orleans. After the war he moved to Georgeville, Holmes County, Mississippi, a rough-and-ready frontier village in the Chocchuma District about sixty miles north of Jackson, staked out land recently ceded by the Choctaw Indians, prospered quickly, and began to plan, as it were, to "repossess" his son and namesake whom he had not seen in almost a dozen years.

According to the best authority, the elder Simms hurriedly dispatched his brother James, armed with a power-of-attorney, to seize the boy and "escort" him to Mississippi. Uncle James acted none the less precipitately: he tried bodily to take the boy as he played in a Charleston street. But the ten-year-old threw himself to the ground and kicked and screamed until the neighbors rushed to his rescue. Several days later the problem was placed before a local city court for decision and the judge, after much deliberation, finally decided to let the boy choose for himself whether he would go to his father in faraway Georgeville or remain with his grandmother in Charleston. Carefully coached by Mrs. Gates, the boy chose the latter.

Later, when he learned that the "kidnaping" had miscarried, the elder Simms, remorseful, himself journeyed to Charleston personally to beg his son to move to Mississippi. Again, young William refused—but the decision was not easy. For his father's tales of the wild experiences on the Southwestern frontier, of hairbreadth adven-

[135]

tures, of blood-curdling border warfare, of Indian cruelties and daring and danger thrilled the adolescent boy beyond words. Indeed, to the day of his death, William Gilmore Simms, the distinguished American novelist, was at his best in his descriptions of guerilla warfare, Indian border fights, hand-to-hand combat, of scalpings, gory murders, highway robberies, and the like, all done with realistic robust and all reminiscent of his father's tales of frontier bravadoes. In an age of sentimental romances, written mostly by nice lady authors who, Simms wrote, dared not use such words as "legs, or thighs," Simms the Realist told factual stories that often shocked his readers, even his reviewers. His "Loves of the Driver" (1843), for example, portrays a Negro raping an Indian squaw. To his disturbed clientele Simms explained, "A writer is moral only in proportion to his truthfulness."

Simms's decision to remain with his grandmother was an agonizing one. For the motherless boy, long separated from his father and with no brothers or sisters, the adolescent years were years of gloomy brooding. Alone he walked the historic streets of Charleston, companionless, or hour after hour secretly glowed and shivered in turn (as he later wrote) over *The Pilgrim's Progress* or *The Vicar of Wakefield* and the novels of Scott and the odes of Byron. At the age of eight he was writing verses. At twelve he had completed a drama. At sixteen he was publishing poetry. At seventeen he was editing a juvenile magazine and had written a thousand-line poem. Such were the literary attainments of the precocious youngster who at an early age succeeded in substituting a fantastic world of make-believe for his own solitary world of sad, unrelenting reality.

At the age of eighteen Simms, now a budding young author-editor of considerable local fame, voluntarily decided to visit his father in North Mississippi. From Charleston he travelled by stagecoach through Augusta to Milledgeville (Georgia) and Fort Mitchell to Montgomery (Alabama), then down the Alabama River to Selma and Mobile and up the Tombigbee to Demopolis and up the Black Warrior to Tuscaloosa. The last 160 miles westward from Tuscaloosa to Georgeville he made overland, via Columbus, Louisville and Kosciusko (Mississippi). On this long and tedious journey young Simms saw at first hand and for the first time the wild Southwest that he was later so effectively to use in his three "border romances"—*Guy Rivers: A Tale of Georgia* (1834), *Richard Hurdis, or the Avenger of Blood: A Tale of Alabama* (1838), and *Border Beagles: A Tale of Mississippi* (1840). More important, perhaps, was his personal association with his father, the experienced frontiersman, an Indian fighter, a fire-eating individualist, and a yarn-spinner par excellence. With him (and Uncle James) the impressionistic young author travelled far and wide through the Indian country, one time riding horseback west of the Mississippi, living in the primeval forests, hobnobbing with hardy pioneers, and

[136]

bargaining with the Choctaws for food and drink—all of which became a golden vein of experience he was destined to mine the remainder of his long life. Some of his most significant writings, in novels, short stories, poetry, and drama, portray the life he saw in the Old Southwest —Georgia, Alabama, Mississippi—and his firm belief in the influence of the frontier on American history and literature anticipated that of Frederick J. Turner and Lucy L. Hazard by almost a hundred years.

Time and time again during his long visit (he stayed in Mississippi almost a year) the elder Simms tried to persuade his son to remain with him, to make the most of the opportunities that were everywhere to be found in the new, fast-growing, fascinating frontier country. "Stay here," he begged. "Study your profession here, and pursue it with the energy and talent you possess, and I will guarantee you a future, and in ten years a seat in Congress." Young Simms listened respectfully, but in time he made the long journey back to Charleston—this time by stagecoach, directly east from Georgeville through Columbus or Cotton Gin Port and down the Warrior River to Mobile. (Years later, although he had become one of the most celebrated writers of his generation, Simms is alleged to have regretted his failure to follow his father's advice—the profession of *belles-lettres* was not a lucrative one in the Old South.)

Upon his return to Charleston in early 1825 Simms went to work in a pharmacy (his grandmother hoped that he would become a physician), but he was soon pulled away by a sudden ambition to read law and, after an apprenticeship under Charles R. Carroll, a distinguished Charleston attorney, he was admitted to the South Carolina bar in 1827. Law failed to hold his attention for long, however: too strong was his love for literature. Already, in 1825, he had published his first poem, *Monody on the Death of Gen. Charles Cotesworth Pinckney*, a Revolutionary War hero. Two years later two more volumes of poems appeared, in 1829 a fourth, in 1830 a fifth, in 1832 a sixth—and William Gilmore Simms the unsuccessful young attorney had emerged as the affluent young author and editor of a literary weekly, *The Album*, and part-owner and editor of a daily newspaper, the Charleston *City Gazette*.

Meantime, in October, 1826, the ambitious young littérateur had married Anne Malcolm Giles, daughter of a local civil employee, and taken her to nearby Summerville where living expenses were lower than in Charleston and where he could find the peace and quiet so necessary to his profession.

On March 28, 1830 Simms's father died and several months later the son made his second trip into the Old Southwest, presumably to settle the dead man's estate and to acquire whatever property was now his own. This journey he carefully reported for the readers of his *City Gazette* in a series of letters entitled "Notes of a Small Tour-

[137]

ist." Leaving Charleston in late February, 1831, Simms travelled overland via Savannah, Macon, Augusta, and Milledgeville. On March 6 the stagecoach broke down near the west bank of the Flint River, midway between Macon and the Georgia-Alabama boundary, and Simms was invited to spend the night in the home of Captain Henry Crowell. Simms entertained his hosts—and they charmed him with their courtesies. He expressed complete surprise "at finding so much intelligence, refinement, and taste so far away ... from civilization and society." And he questioned the Crowells at great length about frontier legends, the vernacular of backwoodsmen and "the wild stories then in circulation of daring adventure and wild lawless life on the frontier." When he retired at midnight, he asked for pen, ink and paper and, as he said goodbye the next morning, he gave little Ellen Crowell the poem he had written, "Flowers in the Wilderness," for pasting in her album.

From the Crowell's home Simms moved on to Columbus (Georgia) which, he wrote, had "had no existence" when he had "trod the same site six years ago." After pausing briefly at Fort Mitchell, he arrived in Montgomery about March 15.

> Montgomery [he told his *City Gazette* readers], a town of some business in Alabama ... is situated upon the river Alabama, and possesses a steam boat trade to Mobile.... It contains probably, fifteen hundred to two thousand inhabitants; a Court House, Post Office, and a few stores, having a decent capital. Two newspapers are published in the place, one of them the *Alabama Journal*, conducted by Turner Bynum, Esq. formerly of our city. The town is situated upon a bluff of some elevation above the river, and is reputed to be not unhealthy—a reputation which I should, from its locality, be greatly disposed to call in question.

Simms's voyage down the Alabama River, from Montgomery to Mobile, took almost a week—much to his displeasure, he stated, for it should have been "effected in two days." As the steamboat "glided down the serpentine waters," he "dozed away the better portion of the six days (!) of [his] confinement, in the solitary companionship of [his] berth."

> We stopped at every landing to take on cotton and passengers ... [he wrote]. There are several little townships upon this river—some in a declining, and others in a prosperous condition. The first of any note after leaving Montgomery, is 'Selma'—containing about four to five hundred inhabitants, and principally known as a chief depot for cotton after Montgomery. There were about five thousand bales at Selma, on our arrival, and it is said to have sent, last year, nearly twenty thousand to market at Mobile. Selma, is said however, to be rather upon the decline. The number of small townships daily starting up, on the river and its neighborhood, take from one another in importance, and thus, create a common level or standard of size among them. They are always at low water mark. In Selma there is published a small weekly newspaper called the 'Courier.' Even in this secluded part of the world politics

and politicians have penetrated with their poisonous commodities, and a great antimasonic excitement is on foot, and made to affect the local concerns of the country.

From Selma Simms's riverboat drifted slowly downstream to Cahawba, "another stagnated depot; more used as a ferry, than for any other purpose," and thence to Claiborne which he described as "next to Montgomery in point of size, on the Alabama River . . . , [and containing] about six or seven hundred houses." Throughout the trip, he added, he was impressed by the large number of little places, "distinguished sometimes by very large and sonorous names, but dwindling upon inspection to a range of log-houses, a tavern, cotton, and possibly, a meeting-house."

Since his first visit to Mobile six years earlier, the city had "grown into importance." Many houses and businesses were "large, elegant and durable structures of fine red brick, built in most cases, in solid blocks—the squares duly and evenly laid out by measurement, and perfectly uniform."

> The city is multiplied two fold [since 1825, he wrote], in population, as in extent, and were I asked, what place in this region had progressed the most within the last five years in every species of improvement, my reply, without hesitation should be, Mobile. . . . The only public place, which, in the short stay, I made, I took occasion to visit in Mobile, was the grave yard, about a mile from the city. It is spacious, and well filled. . . .

From Mobile Simms took a stage to Pascagoula (Mississippi) and thence a steamboat to New Orleans. There he remained a week or ten days, visiting points of interest and attending both the French Theatre and the American Theatre. Leaving about May 1, he crossed Lake Pontchartrain to Madisonville, bought a horse and rode to Covington, Louisiana ("a respectable looking settlement") and then to Columbia (Mississippi) which, he stated, had a "population of one hundred or more inhabitants and is on the decline." At Columbia Simms began a long and hazardous horseback journey northward into the Yazoo River region. And although he did not report his personal problems to the *City Gazette*, it was there, in Georgeville, that he reached his destination and saw after the proper settlement of his father's estate.

> I have just returned [he wrote] from a journey on horseback, of seventeen days into the Yazoo purchase, over and through swamps, and creeks and bayous, half the time swimming and wading through mud and water waist deep. . . . Innumerable little villages are springing up in every quarter, averaging in population about three hundred, and stagnating at that. The great rage at this time in Mississippi is the possession of the new Indian purchase, the Choctaw lands. Many of the Choctaws have already gone to the Arkansas, and more are upon the go. I cannot but think the possession of so much territory, greatly inimical to the

well being of this country. It not only conflicts with, and prevents the formation of society, but it destroys that which is already well established. It makes our borders mere Ishmaelites, and keeps our frontiers perpetually so. Scarcely have they squatted down in one place, and built up their little 'improvement', than they hear of a new purchase, where corn grows without planting, and cotton comes up five bales to the acre, ready picked and packed—they pull up stakes and boom off for the new Canaan, until they hear of some still better, whence they commence the same game—death not unfrequently stopping them on the road....

On February 19, 1832 Simms's wife died. He sold the *City Gazette*, gathered up his unpublished manuscripts and left for an extended trip to the North where, during his meteoric rise as a youthful journalist and author, he had made many literary connections—among them William Cullen Bryant, Nathaniel P. Willis, James K. Paulding, and Fitz-Greene Halleck. In Philadelphia he met Willis G. Clark who introduced him to James Lawson of New York, the well-known dramatist, journalist, and businessman, who became Simms's life-long friend, literary agent, financial agent, critic, and confidant. From that summer's sojourn in the North may be dated Simms's most remarkable success as a poet, dramatist, editor, and novelist, a national success which was to endure for thirty years—until it was abruptly ended by the Confederate War.

Simms's popularity skyrocketed upon the publication of his first novel, *Martin Faber: The Story of a Criminal* (1833), a gruesome blood-curdler that found sympathetic treatment at the hands of a young critic named Edgar Allan Poe. Immediately, Simms conceived the idea of capitalizing on his travels through Georgia, Alabama, and Mississippi by writing a series of "Border Romances" based on historical facts and incidents of the locale he now knew so well—the Old Southwest. *Guy Rivers: A Tale of Georgia* was the first. Appearing anonymously in July, 1834, it enjoyed sudden popularity. A second edition was published later in the year, a third and fourth in 1835 (one of these in London), a fifth in 1837—and at least sixteen more were destined to appear. Now the twenty-eight-year-old author was everywhere lionized—even in his home town: the usually reserved Charleston *Courier* devoted three praiseful columns to him who now had "entered a new field for his labors, whose untrodden paths afford a large scope for his fine imaginative mind.... [He] has used the materials spread so plentifully around him, with a master's hand." The rival *Mercury* was "sincerely gratified" at the success of the young Charlestonian. "We admire the energy of his devotion to literary pursuits, and thank him for his contribution to Southern Literature."

Now that his fame as a novelist had suddenly reached the heights, Simms pressed on as never before. In 1836 he married Chevilette Roach, daughter of a wealthy plantation owner, and thereafter the

[140]

couple divided their time between Simms's Charleston "town-house" and her 3,000-acre estate, "Woodlands," in nearby Barnwell District. Blessed with leisure and free from financial worries, Simms produced an amazing number of short stories, poems, essays, and novels. *Guy Rivers* had proved that the public would buy and read historical romances, and he set about to pursue the idea with all his energy. Within a few months he had issued two full-length books, *The Partisan: A Tale of the Revolution* and *Yemassee: A Romance of South Carolina* (which has since proved to be his best-known work), and many other works.

In 1838 and with obvious gusto he returned to his "Border Romances of the South"—this time with *Richard Hurdis, or The Avenger of Blood: A Tale of Alabama.* Again, as in *Guy Rivers,* he published anonymously, his tale based largely on a continuation of the sensational exploits of the famous "Mystic Confederation" of land-pirates who in the early 1830's had menaced the Old Southwest, leaving behind a frightful record of highway robberies, counterfeiting, kidnapings, and coldblooded murders. The leader, a vicious desperado named John A. Murrell, posed as a Methodist preacher and envisioned himself as the dictator of a vast empire. His fantastic scheme included, among other things, the seizure of thousands of Negro slaves whom he planned to arm and turn loose to burn, sack, pillage, and loot Southern towns and homes while he, the Great Conspirator, would rise "in omnipotent magnificence, to rule his pirate kingdom." At long last, after countless shocking depredations, Murrell was trapped and captured near Muscle Shoals, Alabama by a mild-tempered little Georgian named Virgil A. Stewart who risked his life by joining the "Mystic Confederation" incognito as "Adam Hues" with the avowed purpose of bringing the arch criminal to justice. In Murrell's saddlebag the authorities found a catalogue of scores of "friends and members" of "Murel's Mystic Clan" in thirteen Southern States. Among them were listed the following from Alabama:

Alabama:—H. Write, J. Homes, E. Nolin, three Parmers, two Glascocks, G. Hammons, R. Cunagen, H. Chance, D. Belfer, W. Hickel, P. Miles, O. More, B. Corhoon, S. Baley, four Sorils, three Martins, M. Hancock, Capt. Boin, Esq. Malone, G. Sheridon.

Having travelled widely in Georgia, Alabama, Mississippi, and Louisiana during the apex of the Murrell crime wave, Simms was familiar with the madman and his missions. Indeed, he had actually known Stewart personally and had interviewed him and others who knew Murrell and, as he explained in detail, he had based *Richard Hurdis* on the facts he had obtained directly from eyewitnesses on the frontier. In the preface of the first edition (1838) he assured his readers that his story was far from make-believe:

[141]

Here, gentle reader, you have a genuine chronicle of our border. This story is truly named, a story of our own country. The events are real, and within the memory of man, though names have been changed, and, in some respects, localities altered, that living and innocent affections should not be outraged. In the arrangement of my narrative, I have suffered myself to conduct it, as if the events had been told according as they became known to the narrator; but, for the easier comprehension of the reader, I have stated them, as if after subsequent consideration, putting each in its connection with its fellow for the sake of more coherence. The hero and the author become, under this plan, identical—though I would not have any of my friends suppose the author and narrator to be one.…

In the 1855 (sixth) edition Simms, having meanwhile failed to convince his readers that *Richard Hurdis* was a realistic tale, reassured them in no uncertain terms:

[*Richard Hurdis*] is a genuine chronicle of the border region where the scene is laid [he wrote], and of the period when the date is fixed. Its action, throughout, is founded on well-known facts. Its personages were real, living men; being, doing, and suffering, as here reported. Nothing has been 'extenuate,' nothing has been 'set down in malice.' A softer coloring might have been employed, and, more frequently, scenes of repose might have been introduced for relieving the intense and fierce aspects of the story; but these would have been out of place in a narrative so dramatic of cast, and where the action is so rapid. Some doubts have been expressed touching the actual existence of the wild and savage confederation which I have described; but nobody, at all familiar with the region and period of the story, can possibly entertain a question of the history. There are hundreds of persons, now living, who knew, and well-remember, all the parties.… I knew Stewart, the captor of Murrell, personally; and had several conferences with him, prior to the publication of this narrative. I also met certain of the *dramatis personae* [of *Richard Hurdis*] during my early wanderings in that then wild country. The crimes here recorded were then actually in progress of commission; and some of my scenes and several of my persons, were sketched from the best local authorities. I repeat, briefly that the facts here employed are beyond question, and still within the memory of living men.…

As a novel *Richard Hurdis* is a sensational, suspenseful, episodic, picaresque tale of adventure, filled with hair-raising escapes, murders, gambling—and love. Loosely put together, the scenes shift rapidly and there is considerable repetition. The dialogue, while in the vernacular, is often stilted. The characters are conventionally wooden. But, all told, the romance, crowded as it is with melodramatic situations, comic interludes, and the author's sermons on a variety of subjects, manages somehow to hold the reader to the end. For, never doubt it, William Gilmore Simms was a born storyteller, a scene-builder par excellence, and his narratives, with all their faults, have seldom been equalled in the history of American romance.

The complicated plot of *Richard Hurdis* centers about the activities

[142]

of the hero, a native Alabamian, who, after a violent quarrel with his brother John over the "finely proportioned" Mary Easterby, daughter of a neighboring planter, leaves his Marengo County home for the Chocchuma region of Mississippi in the company of a friend named William Carrington, who is in love with Catherine Walker. On their circuitous journey via Tuscaloosa and Columbus towards the Choctaw Purchase of Mississippi the travellers confront almost every conceivable frontier danger. When Carrington is killed from ambush by land-pirates of the "Mystic Confederation," Richard hurries back to Marengo to notify his family—a trip which happily affords him the opportunity to patch up his quarrel with Mary. However, despite her tearful pleadings, Richard in true dramatic style is honor bound first to return to Mississippi to seek revenge for the death of his friend.

On this, Richard's second journey from Marengo into Mississippi, he rides alone to Mobile, sells his horse for $180 in Alabama notes, grows a beard and otherwise disguises himself as "Mr. Williams," a riverboat gambler complete with "sundry bunches of seals, a tawdry watch, a huge chain of doubtful gold, and some breast-pins and shirt-buttons of saucer size." Then he boards a Tombigbee River steamboat and begins the eleven-day up-river trip via St. Stephens, Coffeeville, Marengo, and Demopolis to Columbus, "a wild-looking and scattered settlement of some thirty families, within a mile of the Tombeckbe." En-route he makes friends with several gamblers, among them Clement Foster, a psalm-singing Methodist preacher of the Alabama Conference (i.e., John A. Murrell), and several of his cut-throat confederates and, upon their arrival in Columbus, they invite Richard to ride eastward with them to a gathering of the Mystic Brotherhood at a "Day Blind" in Alabama's Sipsey River Swamp.

> It was near noon when we reached our place of destination [the narrative continues], and such a place! Imagine for yourself, a thousand sluices over a low boggy ground running into one, which, in time, overflowing its channels, sluices all the country round it, and you have some faint idea of the borders of the Sipsey River. Nothing could we see but a turbid yellow water, that ran in among the roots of the trees, spread itself all around for miles, forming a hundred little currents, some of which were quite as rapid as a mill-race. The road was lost in the inundation; and but that our men were well acquainted with the region, we should have been drowned—our horses at least—in the numerous bays and bogs which lay everywhere before us. Even among our party a guide was necessary.... For a time we seemed utterly lost in the accumulating pits and ponds, crossing currents and quagmires in which our path was soon involved, and I could easily conjecture the anxiety of our company from the general silence which they kept. But our guide was equal to the task, and we soon found ourselves upon a high dry island, within a few yards of the opposite shore.

As the meeting of the Mystic Brotherhood convenes, Clement Foster

[143]

announces that "more than fifteen hundred men" have sworn allegiance to the organization and now stand ready to answer his summons. Next, he reads aloud numerous letters received from absent members in Mobile, Montgomery, Tuscaloosa and elsewhere, each suggesting a plot for a major crime. One dwells on the simultaneous robbery of all the banks; another, the wholesale burning of plantation houses; others on burglary, horse stealing, and Negro stealing. But a plan to rob the United States mails of money known to be on its way to the Choctaw Indians wins Foster's wholehearted approval and is immediately adopted. Not long afterwards, under a ruse, Richard disappears, dashes off towards Tuscaloosa, passes en route the very spot where William Carrington had been killed, and hours later pulls up at the Tuscaloosa County home of a wealthy planter, whom he met on his first trip to Mississippi. There the men form a posse, invade Sipsey Swamp and ambush the land-pirates, killing seven and capturing two. Foster outwits the good men, mounts a horse and gallops into the thickets. Richard pursues him "through the bog and branch, over hill, through dale," but to no avail. Unlike the real-life story of Murrell and Stewart, Foster escapes the clutches of Richard Hurdis in this most remarkable fashion:

> There was a pile of cotton, consisting of ten or fifteen bags, lying on the brink of the river, and ready for transportation to market whenever the boats came by [Richard states]. Foster threw himself from his horse as he reached the bags, and tumbling one of them from the pile into the stream, he leaped boldly upon it, and when I reached the spot, the current had carried him fully forty yards on his way, down the stream. I discharged my pistol at him but without any hope of touching him at that distance. He laughed good-naturedly in return, and cried out . . . 'Farewell—we shall meet some day in Arkansas, where I shall build a church in the absence of better business, and perhaps make you a convert. Farwell!'

Richard Hurdis: A Tale of Alabama is, of course, replete with descriptions of persons and places reminiscent of the author's visits to the state. For instance, Mary, Richard's sweetheart, is the daughter of Squire Easterby whose plantation is seven miles away, "a matter of no importance in a country where, from childhood, the people are used to fine horses and long distances."

> Her person was tall, but not slight; it was too finely proportioned to make her seem tall, and grace was the natural result, not less of her physical symmetry, than of her maiden taste and sweet considerateness of character. Her eyes were large and blue, her cheek not so round as full, and its rich rosy color almost vies with that which crimsoned the pulpy outline of her lovely mouth. Her hair was of a dark brown, and she wore it gathered up simply in volume behind, a few stray tresses only being suffered to escape from bondage at the sides, to attest, as it were, the bountiful luxuriance with which nature had endowed her.

[144]

Fourteen miles west of the Warrior River and eleven off the main Tuscaloosa-Columbus road, Richard and his travelling companion stop at the frontier home of Colonel John Grafton. ("We are all colonels at least, in the Southern and Southwestern states," he quips.) There the author is afforded ample opportunity to describe the home life and "good breeding" of Alabama's affluent settlers:

Hospitality was a presiding virtue, not an ostentatious pretender in that pleasant household; and, in space of half an hour, we felt as comfortably at home with its inmates as if we had been associates all our lives.... A something of complete life—calm, methodical, symmetrical life—life in repose—seemed to mark [Colonel Grafton's] parlor, his hall, the arrangements of his grounds and gardens, the very grouping of the trees. All testified to the continual presence of a governing mind, whose whole feeling of enjoyment was derived from order.... Yet there was no trim formality in either his own or his wife's deportment; and, as for the arrangement of things about his house, you could impute to neither of them a fastidious nicety and marked disposition to set chairs and tables, books and pictures, over and against each other of equal size and like color. To mark what I mean more distinctly, I will say that he never seemed to insist on having things *in their places*, but he was always resolute to have them *never in the way*. There is no citizen of the world who will not readily conceive the distinction.

After a warm supper, Grafton's daughter Julia entertains the company by reading "The Deserted Village." And the next day, bright and early, Hurdis and Carrington wind their "way down from gorge to gorge among the pile of hills," westward toward the Mississippi border.

Shortly after leaving Marengo, Hurdis and Carrington encounter a cavalcade of North Carolina emigrants, slowly plodding their way across Alabama. After sharing their hospitality, Richard (i.e., Simms, the Charlestonian) philosophizes:

... The wandering habits of our people are the great obstacles to their perfect civilization. These habits are encouraged by the cheapness of our public lands, and their constant exposure for sale. The morals not less than the manners of our people are diseased by the license of the wilderness; and the remoteness of the white settler from his former associates approximate him to the savage feebleness of the Indian, who has been subjugated and expelled simply because of his inferior morality. These thoughts force themselves upon you as you behold the patient industry of the travellers while they slowly make their way through the tedious forests. Their equipage, their arrangements, the evidence of the wear and tear inevitable in a long journey, and conspicuous in shattered vehicles and bandaged harness, the string of wagons of all shapes, sorts, and sizes, the mud-bespattered carriages, once finely varnished, in which the lady and the children ride, the fiery horse of the son in his teens, the chunky poney of the no less daring boy, the wriggling jersey—the go cart with the little negro children; and the noisy whoop of blacks of both sexes, mounted and afoot, and taking it by turns to ride or walk—however cheering as these may seem at a first sight, as

[145]

a novelty, removing the sense of loneliness which you may have felt before, can not but impress upon you a sentiment of gloom, which will not be lessened as you watch their progress.... Will their hopes be confirmed? Will the dreams so seducing to them now, be realized? Will they find the fortune which tempted them to new homes and new dangers? Will they even be secure of health, without which wealth is a woful mockery? These are doubts which may well make the thoughtful sad, and the doubtful despondent.

Nevertheless, Richard Hurdis finds warm hospitality in the emigrants' camp, albeit he laments their "Mississippi madness." With him they share their food and their good cheer, however primitive.

They travel slowly [Richard narrates], but twelve or fifteen miles a day, and by night they encamp upon the roadside, hew down a tree, clear the brush, and build up fires that illuminate the woods for miles around.... The watch-dog takes his place under the wagon by night. . . . The men crouch by the fire, while rude and temporary couches of bush and blanket are made for the women and children of the party.... Before the dawn of day they are prepared to renew their journey with such thoughts as their dreams have rendered most active in their imaginations.

Among the travellers the Negro slaves are the most care-free, "particularly famous," according to Hurdis, "for the lightheartedness of their habit while journeying in this manner."

You will sometimes see ten or twenty of them surrounding a jersey wagon, listening to the rude harmony of some cracked violin in the hands of the driver, and dancing and singing as they keep time with his instrument, and pace with his horse. The grin of their mouths, the white teeth shining through the glossy black of their faces, is absolutely irresistible.... Sometimes the whites hover nigh, not less delighted than their slaves, and partaking, though with a less ostentatious show of interest, in the pleasure and excitement.... Sometimes the grinning Momus of the group is something more than a mere mechanician, and adds the interest of improvisation to the doubtful music of his violin. I have heard one of these performers sing, as he went, verses suited to the scene around him, in very tolerable rhythm, which were evidently flung off as he went. The verses were full of rough humor which is characteristic of all inferior people. In these he satarized his companions without mercy; ridiculed the country which he left, no less than that to which he was going; and did not spare his own master, whom he compared to a squirrel that had lived upon good corn so long, that he now hungered for bad, in his desire for change.

As Hurdis and Carrington ride westward from Tuscaloosa to the Black Warrior River, they come upon a group of four Alabamians on their way from market. One, a foul-mouthed little fellow with a pug-puppy nose, wears a long black coat and swears like a trooper. The other three are local farmers returning from a market trip to Tuscaloosa.

Like the people of all countries who live in remote interior situations and see few strangers who can teach them anything [Hurdis states], these people had each a hundred questions to ask, and as many remarks to make upon the answers. They were a hearty, frank, plain-spoken, unequivocal set, who would share with you their hoe-cake and bacon, or take a fling or dash of fisticuffs with you, according to the several positions, friend or foe, which you might think proper to take. Among all the people of this soil, good humor is almost the only rule which will enable the stranger to get along safely.

Tuscaloosa, itself, several times affords Hurdis the opportunity to express his opinions of village life in frontier Alabama. First, when Carrington suggested going forty-odd miles off their direct Marengo-Columbus route to see the town, Hurdis argues that he sees "no reason to go that way—the town is new, and has nothing worth seeing in it." Later, however, when they reach the place, they enter their "strange lodgings in Tuscaloosa, with feelings of satisfaction amounting to enthusiasm." The site of the town, high on the Black Warrior River, a branch of the Tombigbee, was once Chief Black Warrior's best village, Hurdis moralizes:

[But now] there is no remnant, no vestige, no miserable cabin, to testify to what he and his people were. The memorials of this tribe, like that of all the American tribes, are few, and yet the poverty of the relics but speak the more emphatically for the mournfulness of their fate. Who will succeed to their successors, and what better memorials will they leave to the future? It is the boast of civilization only that it can build its monument—leave its memorial; and yet Cheops, could he now look upon his mausoleum, might be seen to smile over the boast.

And the village itself the travellers find "little more than hewn out of the woods":

Piles of brick and timber [the narrator continues] crowded the main, indeed the only street of the place, and denoted the rawness and poverty of the region in all things which could please the eye, and minister to the taste of the traveller. But it had other resources in my sight. The very incompleteness, and rude want of finish, indicated the fermenting character of life. The stagnation of the forests was disturbed. The green and sluggish waters of its inactivity were drained off into new channels of enterprise and effort. Life had opened upon it; its veins were filling fast with the life-blood of human greatness; active and sleepless endeavors and a warm sun, seemed pouring down its rays for the first time upon the cold and covered bosom of its swamps and caverns.

In Tuscaloosa Hurdis and Carrington are forced by the landlord, "a turbulent sort of savage," to share a small room in the town's only inn with two other transients, in spite of vigorous opposition. They choose cots near each other, put their saddlebags in a corner, place their "dirks and pistols in readiness, some on the table and some under [their] pillows," and prepare to go to bed. But they do not find retiring so easy or simple in this "poor lodging-house."

Before we had entirely undressed [Hurdis continues] our two other occupants of the chamber appeared, one of whom we remembered to have

[147]

seen in the bar-room below.... They were, neither of them, calculated to impress me favorably. They were evidently too fond of their personal appearance to please one who was rather apt to be studiless of his. They were dandies—a sort of New York dandies—men with long coats and steeple-crowned hats, great breast-pins, thick gold chains, and a big bunch of seals hanging at their hips. 'What the deuce,' thought I to myself, 'brings such people into this country? Such gewgaws are not only in bad taste anywhere but nowhere in such bad taste as in a wild and poor country such as ours. Of course, they cannot be gentlemen.'

And Hurdis is right. The strangers prove to be Yankee gamblers whose mode of operation is "as ingeniously indirect as the cowpaths of Boston." In the whist game which soon follows, Hurdis catches one of the strangers cheating, challenges him to a fight and gives him a good tongue-lashing, after which the Alabamians go quietly to bed. (Later, these gamblers reappear as members of the Mystic Brotherhood.)

In *Richard Hurdis* the beauties of nature in Alabama also receive considerable attention. Sleepless because of his love for Mary, for example, Richard sits by a window and looks out upon a scene "lovely beyond comparison.... The night in the forests of Alabama was never more beautiful.... There was no speck in the heaven—not even the illuminated shadow of a cloud—and the murmur of the wind swelling in gusts from the close curtaining woods, was a music, rather than a mere murmur."

The next day, as Richard rides from Marengo to Tuscaloosa, he finds loveliness in the leaves, flowers, and wild creatures of the Alabama autumn:

> The afternoon ... was one of the loveliest among the lovely days so frequent in the Alabama November. The glances of the oblique sun rested with benignant smile, like that of some venerable and single-hearted sire, upon the grove of the forest, which ... had put on all the colors of the rainbow. The cold airs of coming winter had been just severe enough to put a flush-like glow into the cheeks of the leaf, and to envelop the green, here and there, with a coating of purple and yellow, which served it as some rich and becoming border, and made the brief remains of the gaudy garb of summer seem doubly rich, and far more valuable in such decorations. Dark brown and blooded berries hung wantonly from bending branches and trailing vines, that were smitten and torn asunder by premature storms of cold, lay upon the path and depended from overhead.... Thousands of flowers, of all varieties of shape and color, came out upon the side of the path, and, as it were, threw themselves along the thoroughfare.

Continuing, Richard describes the "thousands of trees ... [which] stood like mourning ghosts or withered relics of the past," the "melancholy spider, her web now completely exposed in the absence of the leaves," the "nimble squirrel, who skipped along the forests, making all objects subservient to his forward motion," and "the timid rabbit stealing out from the long yellow grass beside the bay, would bound and crouch alternately" along the roadside which abounded in "pale blue and yellow flowers . . . and flaunting berries."

Among the many critics of *Richard Hurdis* was a twenty-five-year-old resident of Alabama named Alexander Beaufort Meek who, in 1839 in Tuscaloosa, was editing a short-lived magazine called *The Southron: A Monthly Magazine and Reivew*. Devoting more than seven thousand words to the novel and its anonymous writer, Meek stated:

> Whoever the author is,—even if it is the De'il himself; and there *is* much that is Satanic about the book,—he may now pride himself upon having written a successful novel. . . . But the author has done something more. He has written a bold and original romance,—in a new field, and in some respects, after a new fashion,—which will stand the scrutiny of criticism, as well as entertain the superficial reader. This we say though we think the book, in addition to many good qualities,—many excellencies,—has many faults, and is deficient in some of the most important properties of a good novel.

After summarizing the plot (quoting liberally) and pointing "out the chief beauties and excellencies of this fine, manly novel," Meek proceeded to draw his objections. Chief among them was its "moral tone and temper."

> It is objectionable [he stated] because it represents the hero . . . as cherishing the most fiend-like antipathy to his brother,—insulting, disgracing and beating him, for having dared to love the same girl, with himself; and finally—although unknown to himself—pursuing him with the felonious purpose of taking his life.

As for characterization, Meek continued, the author had completely failed in the delineation of his females. Mary Easterby, Catherine Walker, Julia Grafton and all the others are "of the same stamp. . . . We defy any reader to designate a difference, if we except the mere *physique,* of one having blue eyes, and another dark ones, and their hair not being of the same color." And, according to Meek, the author of *Richard Hurdis* was "totally deficient . . . on humor and wit."

> Though some of the strictures of William Carrington upon 'your sober-sided, drawling croaking, methodists,—fellows that preach against good living, yet eat of the fat of the land, whenever they can get it; who never refuse a collection, however small the amount, and say a long grace at supper till the meat grows cold,'—may excite a faint smile,—yet they but poorly relieve the sombre and intense seriousness of the other four hundred and eight-five pages. The encampment of the 'Mystic Brotherhood,' in Sypsy Swamp, afforded a fine opportunity for those scenes of merriment, that, in nature, would always be found under such circumstance. It would have greatly relieved the monotonous gravity of the novel, and added much to the impression and effect of all its parts.

Nevertheless, the long review of *Richard Hurdis* ended on an encouraging, indeed, a prophetic—note:

To the author we need say no words of encouragement. He will receive that from the ready and extensive sale, with which his 'first production' has met. If, however, he will go on in the career he has commenced—the delineation of Southern scenes and incidents,—if he will avoid the faults we have pointed out, and supply the deficiencies; if he will individualize his personages better,—particularly his females; if he will infuse more humor and gaiety into his pages, and abandon his evident partiality for the intense and horrid,—he will become,—what we have no doubt he is capable of becoming,—in many respects, decidedly the first of American fictitious writers.

In *Border Beagles: A Tale of Mississippi*, the 1840 (first) edition of which is dedicated "To M— L—, of Alabama," Simms concluded the story of John A. Murrell and his Mystic Brotherhood begun in *Guy Rivers* (1834) and continued in *Richard Hurdis* (1838). The action of the third romance takes place largely in the Big Black or Chitta Loosa River area of Mississippi, east of Grand Gulf, in the very same region through which Simms had travelled in 1831. In this book Murrell is Edward Saxon, a fugitive from justice who is being hotly pursued by Mississippi Regulators, one of whom is William Badger, an old man who had served in Coffee's Brigade and fought in the Battle of Horseshoe Bend (obviously, Simms's father). Wearing the remnants of an ancient uniform he had worn many years before, "when he followed Andrew Jackson down from Tennessee to his Indian battles in the Southwest," he carried "the same pistols in his holster, the same belt about his waist, and the same long rifle in his grasp." Other chief characters in *Border Beagles* are Harry Vernon (Simms himself?), a lawyer who had come to the Yazoo Purchase to seek information about the Choctaw Indians, and Gideon Badger, gallant old William's son (Simms himself?), who, alas, turns out to be a member of the Mystic Brotherhood. His arraignment before his own father affords the author ample room for the pathos he so apparently relished:

> The ancient leader, however, made a far less ludicrous appearance than his men.... At another time, the appearance of this regiment would have moved [the Regulators] to unrestrained merriment; but... the thought that the venerable old man was marching forward to behold his own and only son, bound as an outlaw, and destined to all the penalties of such a life, filled them all with a sorrow that was not less deep because it was speechless. The very unconsciousness of the old man as he drew nigh—the rigid and pompous erectness of his carriage, and the swelling dignity of his manner—contributed to increase the solemnity of their feelings. Who should convey the truth to the father? It tasked the boldest heart and the best mind of the troop.... When the truth was fully shown —when the tale was fully told—there was no more visible emotion in [the old man's face], beyond a slight quiver of the lips, than if he had listened to the most ordinary intelligence. His keen eyes, from under their shaggy brows, ... dropped quietly upon the ground. His lips opened but to exclaim:

'Son of mine! son of mine! Oh, God! thou hast indeed stricken me with thy wrath. Verily, thou hast terribly rebuked the pride that was shooting upward like a rank weed within my heart.... After this ... who will believe in education?'

That William Gilmore Simms was deeply influenced by his visits to the Southwest is evidenced in his poetry, as well as in his Border Romances. *Southern Passages and Pictures* (1839), for instance, includes "The Western Emigrants" a long narrative poem about an old man and his "Mississippi-mad" family, "all moving on to the new land of promise, full of dreams of western riches," and "The Indian Village" which contains a neat reference to Old Federal Road across South Alabama and another to a more northerly route to the Choctaw Purchase:

> Nature and freedom! These are glorious words
> That make the world mad. Take a glimpse at both,
> Such as you readily find, when, at your ease,
> You plough the ancient military trace,
> From Georgia to the 'Burnt Corn' settlements—
> Or, higher up, if, happily you speed,
> Where the gaunt Choctaw lingers by the swamps
> That fence the Yazoo, or the Chickasaw
> Steals his hog nightly from the woodman's close....

"The Story of God's Judgment," a long poem about murder on an Indian trail, contains the following description of three men on their way to Alabama to buy prairie land:

> 'Way down, for Alabam', my child,
>   A-seeking lands, one day,
> Three strangers, to the old men's house
>   Came riding on their way—
> Two were rough men, with grisley beards,
>   And coarse and rude of speech,—
> But the other was a gentleman,
>   And far above their reach....
> To buy the lands in Alabam',
>   The richest prairie there,
> With thoughtless hand he opened wide
>   The wallet that he bare—
> Nor mark'd the eyes, so full of sin,
>   They fixed upon the book,—
> Nor, sudden, how they cast them down,
>   Lest he should see the look.

In his short stories and novelettes Simms also frequently employed his knowledge of the Southwest, as this autobiographical passage from "The Last Wager, or The Gamester of the Mississippi," in *The Wigwam and the Cabin* (1846) testifies:

The circumstances [surrounding this story] were picked up when, as a lad of eighteen I first wandered over the then dreary and dangerous wastes of the Mississippi border. Noble, indeed, though wild and savage, was the aspect of that green forestry country, as yet only slightly smitten by the sharp edges of the ranger's axe, I travelled along the great Yazoo wilderness, in frequent proximity with the Choctaw warriors. Most frequently I rode alone. . . . Very few white men were then settled in the country; still fewer were stationary. I rode forty and fifty miles without sign of human habitation, and found my bed and supper at night generally in the cabin of the half-breed.

In "Oakatibbee, or the Chocataw Sampson" he again relied upon his first-hand knowledge of Alabama and Mississippi:

It was in the Year 182-, that I first travelled in the vallies of the great South-west. Circumstances, influenced in no slight degree by an 'errant disposition,' beguiled me to the Choctaw Nation, which, at that time, occupied the greater part of the space below the Tennessee line, lying between the river Tombeckbe and Mississippi, as low, nearly, as the town of Jackson, then, as now, the capitol of the State of Mississippi.

Among Simms's friends and correspondents were several Alabamians of repute. The one with whom he enjoyed the longest and closest relationship was Alexander Beaufort Meek, mentioned previously, editor, lawyer and author of *The Red Eagle: A Poem of the South* (1855), *Songs and Poems of the South* (1857), and *Romantic Passages in Southwestern History* (1857). Eight years the younger, Meek looked to Simms for literary advice, describing his as "one of the first—we may say the very first of our native writers." In 1839, when Meek was struggling with *The Southron* in Tuscaloosa, Simms contributed three pieces to it—a poem, "River Serenade," an essay, "Southern Literature," and "A Story of the Sea." The two men agreed completely "in pure literature as opposed to literature with a purpose." Simms wrote favorably of Meek's literary efforts in his *Southern and Western Monthly Magazine and Review* and the two men exchanged frequent letters in the 1840's. As for Meek, he repaid his mentor for his encouragement and courtesies by contributing several articles and poems to the various journals Simms himself edited in the 1840's and 1850's and by "cordially" inscribing his *The Red Eagle* to "W. Gilmore Simms, LL.D., the Historian, Novelist and Poet." Simms returned the favors by including Meek's essay entitled "Americanism in Literature" in his *Views and Reviews in American Literature, History and Fiction* (1845). And in 1854, when Simms was helping Evert A. and George L. Duyckinck prepare copy for their *Cyclopedia of American Literature . . .*, Simms wrote the former:

Meek is now an editor in Mobile, graduated at the University of Alabama, a Lawyer-politician-Editor—now of a newspaper, formerly of the *Southron*, a monthly magazine. Wrote a good sketch of the Hist. of Alabama. Served as a volunteer ensign in the Florida war;—tall 6 ft. 4 inches perhaps—good looking fellow,—versatile—but lazy. Might become a distinguished Orator or Politician if he would work. Is now about 42.

Despite his high regard for Meek as a poet and editor, Simms nevertheless criticized him as a politician. When Meek and William Lowndes Yancey were sent as delegates from Alabama to the Democratic Convention in Charleston in April, 1860, Simms wrote a friend:

The Charleston Convention was a great good so far as it went. But the men who made the movement were not competent to use it. Never did men show themselves more feeble & indecisive. Had Yancey been a wise man as well as an eloquent one—had he not been so much under the bonds and shackles of an old party harness, from which he was not bold enough to cut loose,—and what is said of him applies equally to . . . Meek, and nearly all the rest—they could have done at that time, what now will require four more years of struggle & vexation. But the fruit will mature the better perhaps, & the throes of birth will be less difficult for the new organization [of Southern states].

Simms's third and last visit to Alabama was at the request of the faculty and students of the University of Alabama in Tuscaloosa. Arriving on December 10, 1842, while the state legislature was in session, he became the guest of Benjamin F. Porter who was serving Butler County in the House of Representatives. Three days later, under the sponsorship of the Erosophic Society, Simms addressed a large audience on "The Social Principle: The True Source of National Permanence." In his opening remarks he recalled his first visit to Alabama in the early 1820's:

It is now nearly twenty years, my friends, since [I] first made [my] acquaintance with your city. . . . Little did I imagine that the rude and scattered hamlet which I then surveyed . . . was, in so short a space of time, to become so eminent a city;—her dwellings informed by intellect and enlivened by society;—her sons refined by education,—her daughters ennobled by sentiment;—Learning at home, with an allotted and noble mansion in her high places, and Taste secure in her dominions of equal peace and prosperity. . . .
Then—a decapitated Colossus—the forest lay prostrate before her threshold,—the wild vine swung luxuriantly across her pathway,—and, at the close of evening the long howl of the wolf might be heard, as he hungered upon the edges of the forest for the prey that lay within her tents. Scarcely less wild, in its unpruned, uncultivated condition, was the mind of that youthful spectator,—cumbered by fragmentary materials of thought,—choked by the tangled vines of erroneous speculation, and haunted by passions, which, like so many wolves, lurked, in ready waiting, for their insuspecting prey.

Continuing, the speaker traced the progress of American society from the days of Hernando de Soto, emphasizing the "social principles" which had secured peace and prosperity and preserved freedom for all. Two hours later he concluded:

Millions rise every morning in Europe, with an overpowering apprehension, that day, that they shall get no bread,—neither for themselves nor for their little ones. Nobody contents himself, in America, with so humble a desire;—and were we to form any idea of our prayers, in this country, from our complaints, we should be seen, morning and night, before the throne of God, supplicating, not for bread, but fortune. The mere bread of life seems but a sorry object of prayer; and yet, without this prayer, no better future awaits us. Certainly, peace, security, happiness, are not ours, with all our toils, and with all our prayers to fortune. Gentlemen, we must pray to God, and not to fortune!

The next day, at the commencement services, the University conferred the honorary degree of Doctor of Laws upon Simms and President Basil Manly gave him a dinner in Steward's Hall (now the Gorgas Home) which was attended by "some 40 persons, including the Trustees and Faculty." That night Manly wrote in his diary, "A sumptuous affair," adding that he had personally footed the bill.

> I can discern, beyond question [he concluded], that the University is gaining every year on the public estimation. The number and quality of the Audience, on such occasions [as Simms's oration], are manifestly improving; & the attention, order, & interest, likewise. If we can be let alone a few years we shall have friends enough.

Stephen F. Miller, editor of the Tuscaloosa *Monitor*, described Simms's oration in glowing terms:

> ... Mr. Simms appeared before a large audience in the Rotunda, at the University, 13th inst. and delivered one of the most eloquent and polished Discourses ever listened to in the South-West. Public expectation was very high and decidedly in his favor previous to his late introduction here, so much so that his effort, however masterly, could, it was believed add but little to his fame, while the chances were indeed hazardous. In South Carolina he had won for himself great distinction as a native author, and the popularity of his works throughout the Union sufficiently attested the high rank and merit which the reading public assigned him. Besides, he was confessedly at the head of criticism, in the South, in the department of elegant literature; and as a poet, novelist, and reviewer, his pre-eminence has long been settled. With all that weight of character which such considerations gave him in the public mind, Mr. Simms undertook the task with which he had been complimented by the Erosophic Society; and it is but justice to say that the manner in which he executed that task, gained fresh laurels to his brightly encircled brow.
> Of the topics embodied in the address, we shall not venture to speak at present. They were judiciously chosen, and treated in a style worthy of his distinguished reputation for scholarship and elevated humanity. In a reasonable time the address will be published, when we shall present such fragments and beauties from it as will convey to our readers the most conclusive proof that our commendations are more than justified.

Upon the insistence of his friends and admirers, Simms agreed to extend his visit in order to deliver two public orations, December 14–15, as a special guest of the Tuscaloosa Lyceum. About the orations, which were presented in the Methodist Church in order to accommodate the crowds, including members of the legislature, the *Monitor* stated:

> On Thursday and Friday evenings succeeding, Mr. Simms ... delivered a lecture before its members and a crowded audience at the Methodist Church, on the subject of 'American History, and the Uses for which It is Employed by Art and Fiction.' Much of the intelligence of the State was present, in the members of the Legislature, and there was no dissenting voice as to the ability of the performance. During the ten days Mr. Simms remained in the city, he received every attention, public and private, which could gratify a generous mind. His drawing room was thronged with visitors, all anxious to improve his acquaintance, and to testify their respect.... As a man of genius, pure taste and high cultivation, to which may be joined exalted personal character, it was eminently due Mr. Simms that he should receive the attentions which, unsolicited, were rendered him in this city.

Simms's own reactions to the occasion were mixed. Upon his return to Charleston in early January, he wrote a friend, "I have just got back from delivering an oration before the Erosophic Society of the University of Alabama, at Tuscaloosa where I was well received. The citizens gave me a public dinner and the faculty conferred on me the degree of LL.D.— [A]t the dinner ... I acknowledged the authorship of the Hurdis & other novels." Five months later, in his *Magnolia*, he editorialized: "We remember with prolonged satisfaction, a week of delightful sojurn in Tuscaloosa, amidst elegance, intellect and a graceful hospitality, which left nothing to the stranger to desire!" However, on May 20, 1845, writing to former Governor James H. Hammond (of South Carolina), on whose staff Simms had been named an honorary colonel, Simms declared:

> While in this frank mood let me beg that you will forbear giving me any title other than those which are in ordinary use.... I respect the wish that I may neither be called Dr. or Col. I am no military man, and have long since learned to smile, at your parade soldiers, of whom when the season of action comes, we seldom hear anything. I confess too it always seems to me to degrade the man to dress him up like a monkey or a peacock.... I have as little claim to be a Dr. of Laws as any literary man in the country. Never was education so worthless as mine,—i.e. in a classical point of view. I am very little of a linguist, am versed in no sciences, cannot play with chemistry as you do, and exult in agriculture.... I must submit to be called Dr. or Col. by that silly class of persons who attach much importance to these things. To you I may safely declare myself & I do so.

Despite his objections to the "Dr. of Laws," Simms's 1842 visit to Alabama seems to have increased his admiration for the state and its people. Besides continuing his correspondence with Meek, he afterwards exchanged letters with Augustus Julian Requier, of Mobile, who in 1844 dedicated his blank verse drama, *The Spanish Exile*, to the eminent South Carolinian. The play, which is alleged to have

[155]

been first staged in Mobile's Old Dock Street Theatre in 1842, was actually performed in the Charleston Theatre on March 28 and April 1, 1844, with Simms in attendance as the honor guest. However, when Requier deserted literature for the more lucrative law, Simms wrote, "Requier is now one of the most distinguished Lawyers in Mobile, Ala. highly successful & making a fortune. His wooings of the Muse are now all *sub rosa*."

John Archibald Campbell of Alabama, one-time associate justice of the United States Supreme Court and assistant secretary of war for the Confederate States, and Simms were friends in the late 1840's and 1850's. As editor of the *Southern Quarterly Review,* Simms published Campbell's three articles on "British West India Island," "The Rights of Slave States," and "Slavery Throughout the World." Further evidence of the respect Simms held for Campbell may be seen in his dedication of the 1855 (second) edition of *Border Beagles: "To Hon. John A. Campbell, of Alabama.* My dear Sir—It will not fall within your official province to consider the case of the *Border Beagles* ads. *The State;* but you will suffer me to become the client of friendship, entreating as favorable a judgment, upon the reported case before you, as is consistant with critical justice and the rights of Literature."

In 1847 Simms wrote several letters of encouragement to Albert James Pickett, urging him to go ahead with his *History of Alabama, and Incidentally of Georgia and Mississippi.* The Carolinian supplied him with a useful bibliography and in a long letter, dated March 18, 1848, advised him:

> If your aim be reputation, you should go over your manuscript twice or thrice. If money, you can afford no such thing. But as a young beginner & for the first ten years after beginning, you should rewrite every syllable before publishing.

Simms also advised Pickett to limit his history to a single volume:

> One volume is far to be preferred over two and you *can* condense your material into one. Beware of a big book in these days when the shelves are groaning, and the idea of a big cumbrous book devoted to the history of a small state only two hundred years old, is an absurdity.... The great secret is to know where you can dilate with advantage, & when to contract, in order to spare your reader from fatigue. But this is a point upon which an author must teach himself.

Pickett failed to take Simms's advice—his *History of Alabama...,* published in Simms's own Charleston (one suspects with Simms's aid) in 1851, contains two volumes totalling 820 pages of small print. Nevertheless, Pickett included Simms among his dedicatees "as a token of my sincere esteem ... as well as in consideration of the deep interest which [he] has taken in my literary enterprises." Simms reviewed the work favorably in his *Southern Quarterly Review,* once upon the publication of the first volume and again, at great length, when the second appeared.

On April 18, 1856, after the publication of the *Cyclopedia of American Literature*, Simms wrote Editor Evert A. Duyckinck, lamenting the fact that he had failed to include "several of our Southern men," among them the following authors who were one way or another identified with the State of Alabama: Johnson Jones Hooper (*Adventures of Captain Simon Suggs*, 1843), Joseph G. Baldwin (*The Flush Times of Alabama and Mississippi*, 1853), F. A. P. Barnard, one-time professor at the University of Alabama, William T. Hamilton of Mobile (*The Friend of Moses*, 1852), Joseph Clarke Nott, professor of medicine in the Medical College of Alabama, and Henry W. Hilliard, Alabama lawyer whose *Speeches and Addresses* had been published in New York in 1855.

As the Confederate War approached, Simms's interest in politics, which had lain dormant since his days as a youthful attorney, mounted steadily. He strongly supported the withdrawal of South Carolina and other Southern states from the Union, believing that each had the constitutional right to secede, if it so elected. As early as January 28, 1858 he wrote his friend Hammond, now a United States senator, to hold fast to his Southern principles:

> In the conflict between the South & the North, the great object with us, is the extrication of the former from the folds of the latter. If we could get our Southern representatives up to your standards & mine, the game would be an easy one; for we are stronger in the sinews of war, really, in fighting men & wealth, than our enemies....

From 1858 through 1859 and 1860 Simms kept up a constant correspondence with Hammond and others, especially William Porcher Miles, each letter of which teemed with politics, secession, and such terms as "a Southern confederacy" and "Black Republicanism." On October 16, 1860 Simms wrote James Lawson: "If Lincoln is elected, a convention will be immediately called, and South Carolina will secede..., even though she goes alone. But she will not go alone. She will be followed by Alabama, Mississippi, Georgia, Florida, Louisiana, & more slowly by North Carolina, Virginia, Tennessee, Kentucky, &c." A month later he told his friend, John J. Bockee, of Brooklyn (New York):

> Never was a people so thoroughly aroused and resolute before.... South Carolina will secede first, Alabama and Mississippi, Georgia and Florida, in order next, and before the 1st of February, all these States will be out of the [Union].

Simms never faltered in his belief that Alabama would "justify and demand disunion," following rapidly in the path of his own South

Carolina—as would Georgia, Mississippi, Louisiana, and all the other "Cotton States" in due time.

When war came, Simms was fifty-five years old. Too old to fight, he volunteered his services in preparing the defenses of Charleston. His oldest son, Gilmore, Jr., served as sergeant in the Sixth South Carolina Cavalry, was wounded in Virginia and nearly died. In 1863 Simms's wife died and, grief-stricken beyond description, he all but lost his reason. In 1865 the United States Army under General William T. Sherman burned "Woodlands," including sixty-five early American paintings and Simms's personal library of more than ten thousand books, considered the finest private library in the South.

After 1865 Simms, a widower without a home, slaves, plantation equipment, or money, sold his beloved collection of personal and historical documents, which had somehow been saved, in order to rebuild one wing of "Woodlands" which with several outhouses sheltered him and his several young children. In that crowded space he wrote books, essays, poems, one after the other in rapid succession—"the amount of work [he did] would have killed an ordinary man." He contributed to any periodical, old or new or North or South, that would print his products—*Southern Society, Southern Home Journal,* and *Southern Review* (Baltimore), *Lippincott's Magazine* (Philadelphia), *Illuminated Western World (New York), Rural Carolinian* and *XIX Century* (Charleston), and many more, as well as to three Charleston newspapers, the *Courier, Mercury,* and *Daily News.*

Among his many efforts was the publication in late 1866 of a 490-page anthology, *War Poetry of the South,* for which the New York firm of Richardson & Company advanced him a much-needed $300. In the Preface of this volume, as he had always done, Simms strove to stress the importance of an indigenous literature, a Southern literature, an American literature, one which, "though sectional in its character... is essentially... the property of the whole.... [This volume] belongs to the national literature, and will hereafter be regarded as constituting a part of it, just as legitimately to be recognized by the nation as are the rival ballads of the Cavaliers and Roundheads, by the English, in the great civil conflict of their country." The anthology contains 207 poems "carefully selected from contributions which [had] poured in upon [the compiler] from all portions of the South," including seventeen written by eight Alabamians, as follows: "Our Faith in '61," "Clouds in the West," and "Ashes of Glory," by Augustus J. Requier; "Wouldst Thou Have Me Love Thee," by Alexander B. Meek; "The Good Old Cause" and "Ye Men of Alabama!" by John D. Phelan, "Zollicoffer," "The Legion of Honor," and "Jackson," by Henry L. Flash; "Cleburne," by M. A. Jennings; "Only One Killed" and "The Soldier in the Rain," by Julia L. Keyes; "Eulogy for the

Dead" and "Ye Cavaliers of Dixie," by Benjamin F. Porter; and "Pro Memoria," "Gendrone Palmer, of the Holcombe Legion," and "Mumford, the Martyr of New Orleans," by Ina M. Porter. The volume also contains a poem entitled "John Pelham," by James R. Randall (of Maryland, author of the famous "My Maryland") and "No Land Like Ours," by J. R. Barrick (of Kentucky), which had originally appeared in January, 1863 in the Montgomery *Advertiser*.

The last four years of Simms's life, before his death on June 11, 1870, were spent (as had been the previous forty) in writing hour after hour, day after day, unceasingly, partly because his economic needs were great and partly because he was determined to regain his own lustrous position, even though a Southerner, in the field of post-bellum American literature. "I have been literally hors de combat from over work of the brain—brain sweat—as Ben Jonson called it . . . ," he wrote Paul Hamilton Hayne on December 22, 1869. "I [concentrated] myself at my desk from 20th Oct. 1868 to 1st July 1869—nearly 9 months, without walking a mile in a week, riding but twice and absent from work but half a day on each of these two occasions." Truly, grinding toil and declining health pursued him to his grave. But he never lost sight of his goal—"putting himself on record for posterity by providing the South 'with jewels of song and story' all its own," as his most recent biographer so aptly expressed it.

And Simms never forgot the glory and the grandeur of Alabama nor the "elegance, intellect and graceful hospitality" of its people. Indeed, in 1868, twenty-five years after his last visit to the state, he paid final tribute to its beauty in these stanzas:

Midnight on the Tombeckbe River

It is a solemn, but a lovely night!
　The soft and breathing firmament of June
Swells out with a voluptuous flood of light,
　In all the glow of the meridian moon:—
Far o'er the stretch of waters round us spreading,
　Her long and levell'd streams of silver flow,
Netting the waters into smiles, and shedding
　All her sweet-soothing on the waves below.

The dark and ever-murmuring Indian water,
　Murmuring as if it still bewailed the fate
Of the wild tribes destroy'd by waste or slaughter,
　Leaving both land and river desolate:—
What memories rise of hamlets in the wildwood;
　Of hunters darting headlong through the grove;
Of simple songs to suit the simpler childhood,
　And, it may be, to lesson it to love!

[159]

These pass from thought, as through the foliage darting,
    That wan, sweet mistress maiden of the night
Sends shaft on shaft, the dark green foliage parting,
    To sweeten the black waters with the bright.
She wakes more touching reveries with the feeling
    Of those vague, spiritual fancies, caught
'Twixt dream and waking, other worlds revealing,
    Precious to Fancy, though unseen of Thought.

Oh, night! what wondrous fancies of bright meaning,
    Even with the whispering silence, joy to come,
Making all sunshine;—all the present greening,
    And setting forth each blighted bower with bloom!
Will they depart us when the strife is ended—
    The circle made—the spirit on its flight,—
The glory and the darkness strangely blended,
    As are they sweet and solemn, beautiful night!

MY DAUGHTER'S FATHER

Childhood Education, Washington D.C.,
November, 1943.

I remember how helpless I felt when Doctor Simpson told us that he looked upon all babies as vegetables until they were two, at least. After that, he added as he prized a tongue depressor between our Marcia's gums and spotted her tonsils with his headlight, they slowly become human beings.

That was eight years ago. Time enough for me to think it over and conclude that Doctor Simpson was right. He simply omitted an intermediary stage: vegetable becomes animal, then human being. The process is exasperatingly slow and clumsy. Its importance is not so much in the change itself as in the fact that it is as sure as sunrise. With this development comes the opening of a thousand new windows of the mind, the closing of old, and the emergence of personality, that imponderable which in the end brands the breed.

It has taken me much less than eight years, I assure you, to become convinced that every day in a child's life is a long day, an eternity of learning for the parents. Nor do I mean the part the child's dawning cognizance contributes toward pulling and holding the family together, oft-discussed and invaluable as this may be. There is another role in the drama of childhood, one played with less fanfare, silently, forcefully: that of quietly setting up for parents to weigh the many and varied responsibilities of Today against the clear, sharp relief of To-morrow's values.

In experienced hands the responsibilities my eight-year-old has etched upon my consciousness would doubtless be tagged as sociological, economical, educational—or by other equally high-sounding names. For a plain man, however, these are too academic and they are strangely shopworn. Levelled off, they mean that my daughter deserves of me more than anything else an accordant pattern of living.

And upon what, you ask, does my pattern of living depend? Let me be brief. The keystones of my pattern, simply put, are a happy home, good schooling, and security. Like the foundation of a house, these pillars may be separable one from another; yet they tie in together and all are necessary to hold the structure firm. They may be examined one by one. Our only bother in examining them here lies in remembering that we—you and I—are not discussing (except of course in awkward, backhand fashion) the rearing of children: we are bringing up father!

I am not one of those timid souls whose parental pride seeks a new low when his offspring addresses him by his given name. There is something almost beatific about "Father"—surely I must glow when I hear it. And "Daddy" has a ring of reverence that I like; but when my daughter and her dog-eared copy of *Peter Rabbit* sidle up against me on the divan and she says, "Bill, let's read about Peter," I know I am what I want most of all to be—her friend. By virtue of birth alone she is my daughter and that is taken for granted. But friendship is a far different thing and must be cultivated.

All the attributes of a happy home—natural confidence in and regard for others, shared responsibilities, ethical standards, cooperation and the rest—are predicated on friendship. If I would guide my child, I must do so by example and by winning her respect for my better judgment and straight shooting. I must remember that patience is a by-product of sympathy; that the emotional wounds of childhood are often scars for the grave. That means I must be her friend. Among adults, restrictions which fail to balance the rights of the individual we call downright un-American; in the kingdom of childhood, discipline which ignores the nature of the child is no less tyrannical. I would rather come to intelligent compromise with my daughter, thereby earning her comradeship and strengthening her own belief in herself as a person, then to browbeat her with the combined authority of a thousand parents.

Good schooling is an ever-widening circle which takes in much more than mere going-to-school. Of course my daughter shall go to school, but let it be a public school where she can rub elbows with her kind and learn that life is give and take and that nothing is worth having unless it is worth fighting for. Then, if she merits it, I want her to go to college. Not a large college—a small, old one, steeped in the traditions of right living, where it is not old-fashioned to believe that God is still in His heaven and where the masters are gentlemen before they are scholars. One never remembers much he learned in college; one never forgets the personalities who taught him.

[161]

To see that my daughter gets these advantages is, however, but part of a larger responsibility. If much is learned in school, much more is learned outside. At home I must point the way toward a love of truth and beauty, the real stabilizers of a good life; but this I cannot do until I make them important in my life, too.

I must encourage her in the art of graciousness and goodness which, taken together, spell charm. But she will not be a lady unless I am a gentleman.

I must instill into her a love of good books; but I must hasten to tell her that one mark of an educated person is his refusal to believe a thing simply because he saw it in print.

I must instruct her to discriminate among values, to know much so that little will mean more; yet I need not let her fail to understand why many of life's victories are won around the banquet table and on the ballroom floor. Whether it is well, I dare not say, but no one denies in these days that success depends almost as much on one's ability with a knife and fork, as on one's agility with a slide rule.

Realizing that intellectual capacity accrues with normal growth, I must grant her freely the benefits of my superior wisdom. I must teach her what I know. But I must caution her that my beliefs are not valid for her generation until she has proved them so. Meanwhile, she must know that it is not wisdom to be only wise: the tender beam of faith often dims the cold light of reason. And I on my part, mindful of all, must ever be on guard against a too-close supervision that breeds contempt. I must teach her to think for herself.

Now what are my financial obligations to Marcia? Why, you say, that's easy! To leave her a million dollars. And I reply that you are unfair and outside my range. I shall never have that much money. Besides, it may not be wise, even if I did. I am but an average man on a modest income and I must set my sights accordingly.

Let me approach the idea from the rear: childhood is the one time in life for joyous, carefree play. Soon enough will come worry and when it does, you know, it comes riding a snorting, double-headed beast. Seeing every day how it tramples grownups, I want for as long as possible to keep it away from my child. Unsavory debates about the rent or the food bill should be staged when she is in her sandpile or asleep. This is nothing but just. If I have the right to demand of her respect for my parenthood, it can be grounded on nothing short of my equal respect for her childhood.

Do not presuppose that my daughter should be kept in ignorance about money. Far from that, I think, I am obliged as a good father to teach her what money is and will do, to encourage her to save, not niggardly but thriftily, to spend wisely, not foolishly. Unfortunately, wheels on the car of progress are still made of coins and she must know how to keep them turning. Her ten cents a week is a lesson in both marketing and accounting. What's more, it drives home the fact that she, though not so large and not so tall, is nevertheless a full-fledged member of our family—and that is the important thing. In my short career as father nothing has impressed me more than the abiding faith my daughter has in what she and playmates can call "turn about is fair play." And I believe in it, too.

My daughter and I like nothing better than to read together. We try the newer books from time to time, but for our best-loved we always go back a very, very long time—2,500 years, in fact—to Aesop's Fables. It's the one book I know as good for parents as for children. We read here and there among the fables, skipping at will. It seems better that way. But at last we always come back to one story—"The Boy Bathing." Remember it? A boy, in danger of being drowned in a river, yells for help to a passing traveler. The man, instead of holding out a helping hand, stands on the bank and scolds the lad for his imprudence. "Oh, sir!" cries the youth, "pray help me now, and scold me afterwards."

There the story ends—except for the pay-off. We are not told whether the traveler rescues the lad. My daughter, strong in childish faith, says the man was a kind man and couldn't let the boy drown, could he, Daddy? I, grown-up and worldlier, hide my doubts behind a smile. Somehow, all I can think of is another traveler who, like Aesop, whispers to himself, "Counsel without help is useless." And by his side, hand in hand and looking ahead, walks a little girl—just turned eight.

THE MADAME WAS A LADY

Birmingham [Alabama] *News*
Monthly Magazine, May 3, 1970.

This is the story of Louise C. Wooster, one of the most heroic women in the annals of Birmingham and, by all odds, the most intriguing.

Lou Wooster was a lady of easy virtue whose flourishing house of harlotry was in the early years a mecca for many Magic City men.

She was author of *The Autobiography of a Magdalen,* sponsored by a minister and printed in 1911. It is one of the rarest and most fascinating books ever published in Birmingham.

She was an actress of merit, at one time a member of a theatrical troupe which travelled up and down the Mississippi River.

She was, according to her own declaration, the fiancee of John Wilkes Booth, the notorious murderer of President Abraham Lincoln.

And she was, most of all, a charitable Angel of Mercy who, during Birmingham's woeful, tragic, cholera-ridden days of 1873, converted her bawdy house into a hospital, risking her life night and day, nursing the sick and comforting the dying.

Louise C. Wooster was born in Mobile on June 12, 1842, the daughter of ultra-respectable parents, a South Carolina French Huguenot mother and a New England father. When she was a small child, her father died, leaving her mother with six young girls to support, the eldest only fourteen. Lou, the third daughter, was less than ten. Living here and there with relatives who did not want her and lacking the love and the security of a home, she was not yet in her teens, she recorded in her *Autobiography*, when she yielded to the seductive charms of a much older man, an old family friend whom she had known "from earliest recollection." Thereafter, one affair followed another in New Orleans and Mobile and finally, in desperation, she accepted the good-natured hospitality of Madame Jennie Garborough in Montgomery, Alabama. She was then nineteen.

At this time John Wilkes Booth, her "ideal man, handsome, generous, affectionate and brave," walked into her life. She fell in love with him and he, loving her, advised her to become an actress. Under his tutelage she rehearsed many parts, perfecting herself for such roles as his management would in time secure for her. But her hopes were soon blasted: the bullet which Booth fired in Ford's Theatre on the night of April 14, 1865, sending President Lincoln into eternity, also plunged pathetic Lou Wooster back into the slough of barren despair.

But not for long. For John P - - - -, one of "nature's noblemen," she called him, offered her marriage and a happy home in his native Virginia. Before joy came, however, Mr. P - - - - was murdered, "cruelly, foully murdered by a crowd of drunken, bloodthirsty ruffians" as he stood in the doorway of Montgomery's historic Exchange Hotel.

Lou now turned to the theatre for surcease. And Ed B - - - -, a smooth-tongued theatrical agent, accompanied her to Richmond on promise of finding her work. He soon walked out on her, however, and again in despair she returned to Montgomery.

There, for many years, she declared, she had been secretly loved by Sam R - - - -, son of one of Alabama's most prominent attorneys, who now established her in a "small cottage, very secluded," rather than see her return to Madame Jennie's house of ill repute. A few days later, however, Mr. R. - - - - was assassinated and Lou attempted suicide by swallowing fifty cents worth of pure morphine picked up at the corner apothecary. "I could not feel kindly towards those who saved me," she wrote in her *Autobiography*. "I felt that they had done me an injustice, that it would have been more merciful to have let me die . . . I have suffered more than I ever dreamed mortal could suffer . . ."

A few weeks later, earnestly seeking respectability, Lou joined a small theatrical troupe in Little Rock, Arkansas. The cast, which included Sol Smith Russell, began tour on the *Belle of Memphis*, a side-wheeler playing the river-town circuit. Soon Lou, the company favorite, earned the leading female roles. At St. Louis, Missouri, Charles C - - - -, one of the actors, proposed to her, but she declined: she loved him too deeply, she later explained, to ruin his life. You see, Louise C. Wooster had joined the company as a poor but virtuous widow, wholly dependent on the theatrical talents for support. Not one of the troupe ever suspected that her profession was really older than theirs. . . .

At the season's end Lou returned to Mobile where Frank ----, "a good, true and worthy gentleman . . . kind, affectionate and very impulsive," bought her a small home. With him she lived as wife, save only in name. But Frank lost heavily at cards and, while drinking to excess, murdered a man. Lou, again heartbroken, returned to Montgomery, trying desperately "to forget the past, to forget myself."

Now it was 1872 and papers throughout the South were full of news about a little Alabama "railroad crossing with . . . about twenty or thirty houses." And there, to new-born Birmingham, despondent, ambitious Lou Wooster—just turned thirty—decided to cast her lot.

Never had she seen such hustle and bustle. "All was life and money was plentiful," she penned, as old friends sought her out and new ones followed them. Throughout the fall and winter and into the spring of 1873 Lou prospered in the prosperous, mushrooming Magic City.

Never had a little town grown so miraculously. Scarcely two years old, its lots were selling at a fast clip, bringing fabulous prices.

And Madame Louise C. Wooster prospered with it.

Then, suddenly, amidst plenty, cholera struck the Magic City, dragging death in its wake. All building ceased as carpenters laid down their tools and fled. Men, yesterday thriving, closed their shops and businesses, barred their doors, and ran for their lives. Property values fell to zero. Businesses stagnated. Bats and owls frequented stores and houses. Muddy streets were empty. Like a dark pall, gloom and silence—except for the moans of the dying—settled over the young city.

In less than a month only 1,500 citizens remained, including the ill and dying. More than 2,000 had fled and an estimated 500 had died before they could quit the city limits.

Hearses hauled the dead away—four and five deep, according to eyewitnesses. No time for ritual: the stricken fell in the streets, or were laid there, and dreary, creaking wagons carted them away to unmarked graves. Reverend J. D. Anthony, a Methodist minister, wrote that he counted seventeen bodies in less than five hours. There were "over five hundred deaths in the city in the space of two weeks," he added, "and perhaps that number or more who left the city . . . died within a few hours after leaving."

Only the poor, the sick, the dying, and the brave were left behind. And among the brave was the Lady known as Lou.

At first afraid to offer her services because she was known to be a "fallen woman," Lou timidly gave freely of her money, her clothing, her bedding, and helped prepare the dead for burial. Then, boldly, she threw open the doors of her "house" to the sick and the homeless, her "girls" serving as nurses. To the poor they also contributed generously. All that Lou had she gave to those in need, day after day—except her name. That, she later told, "I never gave to anyone who did not already know me."

Cautioned by friends to quit the stricken town before she, too, died of the dreaded scourge, she determinedly stayed on to nurse the sick and suffering. Now, wherever she went, to the well-to-do home or the hovel, she was welcomed by rich and poor alike. In almost Biblical language she recorded her work:

"Gladly accepted they my service, for there were but few now left to care for the sick.

"My doors were thrown open to the homeless. My purse strings were loosened and all that I had to give was for those in need...

"Quietly, I did what I believed to be my duty, and was happy to think that I was for the time at least doing only good....

"I did not fear death: I rather courted it."

After the epidemic Birmingham was dead, as dead as a doornail. For the boom price of a single lot a man could have bought the whole town. Madame Wooster rested and travelled. To every state and territory in the Union, to Canada, the British Isles and across the European continent she went, mingling everywhere, she wrote, "with the best and most aristocratic people of England, France, and America."

Five years passed before she returned to the Magic City, once more busy, expanding, and prosperous beyond belief. Old friends of the Cholera Days greeted her heartily. The many she had nursed and supported extended her far more praise, she modestly declared in her book, then she rightly deserved. Newspapers and citizens complimented her heroism—so much so, she added, "until I might have appeared vain. . . ." Men and women alike told her that she had carved her "name in stone that time and tide cannot efface." But Lou insisted to the end that she had only done her duty, that and nothing more.

Among her many friends now was an un-named man, one who had given freely to the building of Birmingham's schools, churches, and hospitals. He knew of Lou's past, of her trials and heartaches, but he asked nothing of her save friendship. She accepted his kindness. His financial advice enabled her greatly to increase her income from wise investments. With ample to give to the downcast, she was now happier than she had ever been in her life.

Thus did she spend her last years, giving almost lavishly to poor, suffering people, always helping the needy. She sought out the sick, especially those afflicted with dangerous, contagious disease—that was her one way, she religiously believed, of atonement "before the only just and merciful Judge of all our doings." To her house at 1909 Avenue D (now 4th Avenue, S.) came the lame, the halt, and the blind, year after year, white and black alike. And none went away unhelped.

On May 16, 1913, in her seventy-first year, Louise C. Wooster died and was buried in beautiful Oak Hill Cemetery. The next day *The Birmingham News* told a callous, fast-forgetting world that she had "long been known for her heroic work" during the cholera epidemic, when "she remained, working and caring for the sick and spending her own money freely."

A simple headstone marks her grave. But for those who know her story she truly "carved her name in stone that time and tide cannot efface."

WERE WHITE MEN HERE IN 1232?

Birmingham [Alabama] *News*
Monthly Magazine, Oct. 11, 1953.

One hundred and thirty-seven years ago Thomas Scales, one of Alabama's first white settlers, was clearing new ground along the north bank of the Warrior River six miles below present-day Tuscaloosa. Suddenly, at the mouth of Big Creek, he came upon an embankment four of five feet high which arched across the small peninsula forming a triangular fortress. On top of the broad earthworks grew great, ancient trees.

At the foot of one very large old tulip tree Scales noticed a lone, cone-shaped sandstone half imbedded in the ground. Brushing off the dirt of the years, he made out this rude inscription:

HISPAN ET IND REX
1232

Brought to Tuscaloosa village, the curious discovery was found to measure 21½ inches in height, 18 in breadth and about 12 in thickness, and to weigh 204 pounds. For several years it stood in front of Squire Levin Powell's office, a subject of constant speculation.

In 1824, eight years after its discovery, the stone was given to Silas Dinsmore, of Mobile, who promptly shipped it to the American Antiquarian Society in Boston, an organization of which he was a trustee. The society, puzzled but pleased, catalogued the item as "The Alabama Stone" and later published a long description of it in their official proceedings. Today, almost 130 years later, the society still exhibits the stone as one of the earliest evidences of white man's explorations in North America.

As for the translated inscription—"King of Spain and the Indies,

1232"—one distinguished authority has declared that the figures "may be" intended for a date, but he doubts it. An archeologist has suggested that 1532 was probably meant, dismissing the error as "innocent blundering." Another historian maintains that the Alabama Stone is without question a relic of Fernando De Soto's march across the region in 1540. He points out that the renowned discoverer left behind many evidences—a four-inch brass cannon found on the Coosa River, near Rockford, Ala., for instance, as well as brass kettles, silver crosses and other objects which have been picked up here and there.

Since it was after Columbus discovered America that the King of Spain assumed the added title of "King of the Indies," all historians generally conclude that the stone's inscription must have been carved after 1492. However, one insists that 1232 may indeed be correct, after all, because several old coins bearing dates as early as 1114 have been found in the vicinity of Valley Head, Ala.

The mystery of the Alabama Stone will doubtless never be solved. At best, it will remain a thing of wonder, forever conjuring up visions of the long ago.

Only one thing seems sure: Massachusetts has had this ancient relic long enough! Surely as one of Alabama's earliest historical records, it belongs in Alabama. Shall we petition the Boston society to send it back home?

MUSIC IN A COLLEGE LIBRARY

School and Society, New York City,
March 7, 1942.

Librarians, both public and college, have never come to full agreement on the scope and content of their collections. Beyond obvious printed materials, the latter, especially, have up to now drawn no common denominator of understanding. Almost all consider manuscript material valid, but comparatively few make any efforts in this field, leaving it rather to the larger university or public libraries. Thanks to the generous distribution of art sets by the Carnegie Corporation of New York, a number now service pictures and prints. Filmstrips, slides, motion pictures and microphotographs have received increasing attention within the past few years. And music, in both graphic and recorded form, thanks again to the corporation's generosity, has found its way into a selected group of institutions. There have, of course, been other innovations. Generally speaking, however, it is true that most college libraries have not ventured far beyond the book-magazine-pamphlet stage.

Under certain conditions and in peculiar localities this omission of non-book materials is desirable. Yet no one, we suppose, will doubt the place of importance these have earned in the modern college curriculum. For example, not long ago, the well-known English scholar, Ernest Bernbaum, delivered on our campus an address entitled "The Motion Picture in the Teaching of History"—a talk which was reflected immediately in the library by requests for "Northwest Passage," "Drums Along the Mohawk," "Gone With the Wind" and other historical films for classroom showings. Parallels could be drawn for the calls for prints, pictures, slides, and filmstrips. But more than any other non-book material has been the demand in our library for music—so great a demand, in fact, that a separate Music Library had to be established, a specially trained librarian added to the staff and the budget for non-book materials juggled and, finally, enlarged.

We doubt if North Texas State Teachers College students are unusual in their desire for music. To be true, under the leadership of W. C. Bain, the department of music has grown remarkably during the past four years (yet we in the library like to think that at least a small part of this success may be attributed to the fact that the library's music program has been constantly expanded to meet the needs of the department). Again we say we doubt if our students are unique in their love of music. The facilities of the library are, of course, open to all students and faculty, and non-music majors are quite in evidence. It must be stated, however, that much has been done by the department of music and by the library to stimulate interest in music; but this we know to be a legitimate angle of our work, as important as stimulating interest in reading. Music is a language—the language of emotions, but a language nevertheless—and deserves a place in the college library. With us, recorded music takes its place side by side with recorded speech.

The department of music has necessarily accomplished a great deal toward making the campus music-conscious. The college symphonic orchestra gives frequent concerts; the band plays often for assemblies and other gatherings, both indoors and out; the chapel choir and the A Cappella choir, besides touring the Southwest annually, offer programs frequently on the campus; and last spring the first college-sponsored musical of its kind in this region was consummated when ninety voices, accompanied by the College Symphony Orchestra, presented a three-day Bach festival. Music critics pronounced it "the largest and perhaps the most important musical program ever put on by a Texas college" and stated that it set "a new standard of achievement for the Southwest." Upward of 10,000 persons were in attendance at the three performances—at least half of these were students of the college.

The chief contribution of the library in creating interest in music has been its well-balanced collection of books about music, books on music appreciation, biographies of musicians, scores, orchestrations, sheet music and phonograph records, both classical and popular—a list which includes folk-songs, dances, opera scores, music for solo instruments, vocal, orchestral and chamber music, miniature scores, choruses and practically all forms of the art. Then, too, the library, in cooperation with the department of music, has for more than a year sponsored a weekly "Listening Hour." Until more suitable accommodations were provided in Music Hall, these programs were presented in the library auditorium. For the occasions, a regular schedule is adopted in advance and appropriate publicity given in the local daily newspaper, in the college weekly, in the library's mimeographed fort-nightly and by placards and signs. This plan is usually followed: a professor from the department of music delivers a brief talk on the life and works of the composer of the afternoon—let us say, Schubert. An assistant then plays phonographic recordings of the "unfinished Symphony." At appropriate intervals, the inter-locutor explains certain movements, describes instruments, offers interpretations, clarifies the author's intentions, etc. Afterward, he answers questions. The library anticipates the demand for books and music by having on display a suitable selection, not only of Schubert's works but also those of his contemporaries. Suffice it to say that this scheme has played no small part in bringing music to the lay student, for the discussions are purposely non-technical. A third evidence of the cooperation between the library and the department of music is the course entitled "Music Libraries," offered by the department of library service. Taught by the music librarian, this class places special emphasis on the correct selection of all kinds of music, acquisi-tion, classification, cataloguing, preservation and distribution. Some attention is also given to music appreciation. Because of the general nature of our college, the philosophy behind the course of necessity aims at the elementary- and high-school levels; but it is populated by library majors as well as by music majors (credit may be earned in either department), and occasionally an outsider matriculates. The syllabus for the course is approved by the heads of both the music and library-service departments—so far, there has been not the slightest room for dissatisfaction on the part of either. In fact, harmoni-ous cooperation has been in large measure responsible for the increas-ing success of the endeavor. The work is proving beneficial to prospec-tive secondary-school band leaders, chorus directors and music teachers, as well as to school librarians and teacher-librarians.

The contents of the Music Library may be divided roughly into three types of materials—books and periodicals, records, and music itself. That these are interdependent need scarcely be stated; yet their very natures make it necessary to discuss them separately.

Of books and periodicals little need be said. The more than 2,000 books are catalogued and circulated according to generally accepted library methods, and, as is also true of periodicals and scores, are on open shelves. Reference works are of course not permitted to circulate, nor are current or bound periodicals. There is a small official "Reserve," always kept at a minimum, for it is the policy of those concerned to tax with immobility as few items as possible. Since the college furnishes texts to all students (there are approximately 5,000 music books in the Textbook Library), the library has no problem in this field. All other books have a 7-day loan limit and are renewable. Twenty-one magazines are received currently. In addition to these books and periodicals devoted to music exclusively, there is in the main library a generous supplemental stock of materials which combine music with other subjects, such as music education, physical education and public-school teaching.

Music itself constitutes the main body of the library. The 5,000 items in this group cover almost all phases of musicianship. The work of the department of music, as would be expected, dictates largely the composition of the collection. Miniature scores for orchestras, opera scores, octavo scores for choruses, including men's, women's and mixed voices, both sacred and secular, and piano music, have a prominent place. The orchestral masters are well represented by Bach, Beethoven, Brahms, Schubert, Chopin, *et al.*; and music from many countries, including Finland, Italy, Norway, Russia, England, Germany and France, are much in evidence. Because of our geographical location some emphasis also has been placed on the works of Latin-American composers in both orchestrations and piano music. Sheet music has received considerable attention; and the collections of chamber and organ music, folksongs, dances, art songs, concertos for piano, violin and violoncello, oratorios and cantatas, mainly with piano accompaniment, make up a large portion of the items. Materials for the practical teacher, the public-school musician, the student of theory and those interested in rhythmic music for children are also included; and there is an adequate collection of seasonal music, such as Easter and Christmas songs. In this connection we should mention the popularity of opera scores before and during the annual Dallas Civic Opera (Dallas is but 40 miles away), and at other periods when local or nearby musical programs are rendered. The majority of scores, miniature and orchestral, are bound and offer no circulation problem; music in parts is prepared for circulation by the College Bookbindery, which has perfected a cloth-covered, board portfolio with pockets. This enables the whole score to be kept together on the shelves, yet permits use of separate units. Larger pieces with many parts are likewise housed in special box-board cases made by the bindery, and smaller pieces are bound in pamphlet binders, carrying additional end-flaps. Sheet music is kept in regular music file-boxes, and is issued separately in manila envelopes. All music is catalogued by composer only in the central catalogue in the main library, and in the Music Library by composer, title, form and medium. The Dewey System of classification, prefixed by "M," is used throughout the collection.

The basis for the records division of the Music Library is the Carnegie phonograph, which, with 1,000 discs, was presented to the college a year or two ago. To these have been added two smaller machines and some 1,500 records. This collection, which runs the gamut from Bach to Benny Goodman, is housed in albums and single envelopes. Under the combined supervision of the music librarian and the head of the department of music, regular concerts are still offered to the public at specified hours, and at other periods throughout the day the machines are in constant use by music classes and individuals. Checking the records out for home use has as yet presented no problem, for few students have machines upon which to play them. In special instances, however, the discs are signed out and a record-carrier, resembling a small suitcase, designed by the College Book-bindery, is brought into use. The Music Library catalogue contains a composer-title card for each record, and with the records themselves there is a complete set of cards covering composer, title, medium, form and performer.

Several methods of coordinating the library with the department of music have been outlined. One further plan deserves mention: the rôle of the College Book-bindery. Besides making portfolios, cases and record-carriers, as already stated, the bindery does all repairing, mending and reinforcing of music, and makes albums for the records. Upon this division of the library program also rests the printing of hundreds of placards, signs and posters for publicity purposes. Here, of course, is also centered all bookbinding for the entire library program, to say nothing of the private binding done for students at nominal costs. Perhaps the most original function of this department, however, lies in the assistance it renders in the realm of photography. By means of microphotographic equipment complete symphonies have been recorded on 35-mm. films for classroom showings and orchestra practices—the library even supplying screens. For rehearsals the bindery has also made numerous photostatic copies of scores, when sufficient originals were not on hand to serve.

If it is the opinion of college administrators generally, and we believe it is, that the library "should be the coordinating center of the institution . . . , a place of emanation, not simply one of impingement," certainly music, as well as other non-book materials, must be given ever-increasing attention. With us, the correlation of library policies with those of the music faculty not only has proved profitable for both, but also has laid the groundwork for a corresponding cooperation

[172]

between the library and other departments. Someone has said, Rabindranath Tagore, if we remember correctly, that music begins where words leave off. We like to think we have gone the Bengalese one better: we have put them side by side.

WILLIS BREWER AS A NOVELIST*

The Alabama Review, Alabama Historical Association,
University of Alabama and Auburn University, July, 1965.

Willis Brewer was one of the most versatile, successful, and influential Alabamians of his day. Born at Brewersville, Sumter County, March 15, 1844, he was a printer at fourteen, a newspaper editor at seventeen, a soldier in the Confederate States Army at eighteen, a licensed attorney at twenty-one, and at twenty-two an honorary colonel on the staff of Governor Robert M. Patton. In 1865 he became part-owner of the weekly *Wilcox Times* (Camden). Three years later he moved to Hayneville, Lowndes County, to establish his own paper, the *Examiner*. There he married Mary Baine, daughter of the late Colonel David W. Baine, C.S.A., and as his paper became "one of the most powerful engines in the state in the exposure of the corruption of Reconstruction," his prestige spread far and wide as an able editor, lawyer, planter, businessman, and politician. In 1876 he was elected president of the Alabama Press Association in recognition of his prowess as a forthright and fearless journalist. Between 1876 and 1897 he served two terms as state auditor, three as a state representative, and three as a state senator. In 1892 he was presidential elector for the state-at-large on the Grover Cleveland ticket and in 1897–1901 he twice served Alabama in the United States Congress. As his personal fortune increased, he invested wisely in cotton plantations and in such businesses as the Montgomery, Hayneville & Camden Railroad. By the time he was forty he was independently well-to-do. Nevertheless, he was a strange, singularly reticent man, formal at all times and, as one who knew him wrote, "very chesterfield in his manners." In 1902 Brewer moved from Hayneville to "The Cedars," a 1,684-acre plantation on Catoma Creek near Montgomery, where he spent the remaining ten years of his life in patriarchal retirement as one of the most controversial Alabamians of his day. In 1910 he had a life-sized portrait of himself, dressed immaculately in a knee-length coat and

---

*This paper was read at the annual meeting of the Alabama Historical Association, Florence, April 24, 1965.

a wide brim hat and holding a large curved-stemmed pipe, painted by Samuel Hoffman, a well-known local artist. And visitors recall his entertaining them as he sat cross-legged on the floor, puffing away at a water-cooled Oriental nargileh. Upon his death on October 30, 1912 at age sixty-eight, he was buried in a $16,000 marble mausoleum he had personally designed and built on his own land. In his will he left $10,000 to his wife, a 440-acre farm at Hayneville to a grand-daughter, $1,000 to a friend, $5.00 to his son, and the balance of his estate, valued at $200,000, to Miss Estelle H. Manning, his secretary, whom he had earlier adopted as his daughter. Among other properties Miss Manning received $10,000 in cash and a house in Washington (as "compensation for her faithful help in business, in turns of ill health and for slanders she suffered for her attendance on me") and the 1,684-acre plantation at Montgomery ("because she had been my most devoted attendant and secretary and business manager and book-keeper and reader and in many ways indispensable to me.") The will was contested and, after much litigation extending over a two-year period, a settlement was reached out of court. Miss Manning-Brewer, as the will names her, was at last required to share her properties with Mrs. Brewer and her two daughters.

Sporadically, between 1872 and 1910, as he was able to put aside his many and varied responsibilities, Brewer turned his hand to his most compelling avocation—writing. Somehow, in addition to many newspaper stories he found time to complete and publish four books, each completely unique, each totally different from the others. Two of them, the last two, published in 1895, when Brewer was fifty-one and a state senator, and in 1910, when he was sixty-six and retired, are downright bizarre, revealing their author's marked penchant for the peculiar and surely confounding his contemporaries as much as they now do his successors. One of these, *The Secret of Mankind with Some Singular Hints Gathered in the Elsewheres of After-Life, from Certain Eminent Personages as Also Some Brief Account of the Planet Mercury and Its Institutions* (1895, 428 pages), a weird, metaphysical study of man's relation to man and to the universe, was issued by G. P. Putnam's Sons, New York City. It was once alleged that this book "won such praise as to cause it to be compared to the works of Tacitus and Swedenborg" and that it became so popular as to be translated into German. The other, a 548-page volume, equally ponderous, but more fantastical, bore the self-explanatory title, *Egypt and Israel: An Inquiry Into the Influence of the More Ancient People Upon Hebrew History and the Jewish Religion, and Some Investigation Into the Facts and Statements Made as to Jesus of Nazareth.* Published in 1910 by the Torch Press of Cedar Rapids, Iowa, it was reviewed as "a scholarly production of philology, [showing] a remark-able knowledge of the language of the ancient Egyptians and He-

[174]

brews." Both of these books have long been relegated to the limbo they so rightly deserve; therefore, it is upon his first two works that Brewer's fame as an author must inevitably depend.

His first book, *Alabama: Her History, Resources, War Record, and Public Men,* a massive 712-page compendium of military, political, social, and economic data, is one of the landmarks of the state's literature. Published by Barrett & Brown of Montgomery in 1872, it was designed, according to Brewer, "to familiarize the people with many events and facts which should not escape the memory of Alabamians" and especially to perpetuate the names and deeds of the "brave sons of Alabama whose triumphs make such a luminous chapter in the annals of mankind." In his *Bibliography of Alabama* Thomas M. Owen devoted five full pages to his book, calling it "the most valuable general contribution to the history of the state. . . . The War Record presented is the fullest account that has been published about Alabama troops in the several wars." Today, ninety-three years after its publication and sixty-seven after Owen's criticism, Brewer's *Alabama* . . . is still a major and reliable source for the study of antebellum Alabama and Confederate biography and history and perhaps the one most frequently quoted book ever published in the state.

The Children of Issachar, Brewer's second book and only novel, was published by Putnam's in 1884. Sub-titled *A Story of Wrongs and Remedies,* the 303-page narrative is based on the author's ample knowledge and understanding of the bitter-sad days of Reconstruction through which he and his generation of conquered Southerners had so recently suffered—that Tragic Era, when Carpetbaggers and Scalawags and freed Negroes controlled the states of the crushed Confederacy, ruling by armed might, plundering, stealing, over-taxing, and putting the bottom rail on top, all under the banner of a Black Republican Party which, alas, had too soon lost the charitable leadership of Abraham Lincoln. Brewer had known the stoic courage of his people and their patient but over-powering determination to break the political shackles which bound them. He had seen them fight back with fair means and foul to restore the democratic government which was their inalienable right under the Constitution of the United States. And he, himself, as a fire-eating lawyer and fist-slinging editor, had personally shared with them the threats, insults, and assaults of the hated and unholy triumvirate of intruders. Against this turbulent background Brewer wrote *The Children of Issachar,* a story of vivid contrasts, Southerner versus Northerner, Republican versus Democrat, white versus black, and hate versus love, all spiced with the night-riding activities of the Ku Klux Klan, the treachery of former slaves, violent passions, intrigue and—murder. And throughout, as the title indicates, he drew a clever parallel between the noble men and women of the South and the children of the Tribe of Issachar, those "mighty men..." of old who three thousand years before had rallied 'round King David to resist the Philistines and drive them from their land (1 Chronicles, XII;32).

In his preface Brewer directly acquaints his readers with his dominant motif:

> This small volume [he states] is meant to expound a principle as applied to a particular fact or state of facts. This fact is a part of American history, some true incidents of which are herein set forth, laid in the years 1867 and 1868, but limited and localized as becomes the romantic features of the story. A whole people were, perhaps are, misjudged because of the response they made to that fact.... It is often ignorance, not the absence of charity, that renders men censorious.
>
> When war, clad in civil robes, devotes extensive states to pillage and rapine, resistance becomes the loftiest virtue. The proudest chapter in a people's annals may be that which tells of their embattled ranks sweeping over fortified crests, or their attenuated lines standing emaciated and in rags behind beleaguered ramparts; but the courage and fortitude which steadfastly resist lawless and dominate power are the attributes which should most surely link the names of men and of peoples to earthly immortality.

And, as if to drive home his intent, he concluded that it was "high time" to remove "the veil of falsehood" that had so long obscured the truths about Reconstruction in order that the virtue of the Southern people, "constant and inflexible in their adherence to the clearest principle of natural right, should be made manifest to those who, in an age of trade and gain, love peace but honor manhood."

The locale of *The Children of Issachar* is Granby, a postbellum Alabama town (obviously Hayneville) into which like rats had swarmed a pack of Carpetbaggers who, in collusion with local Scalawags and Negroes, are intent upon nothing but graft and greed for personal gain. Typical of them are the Reverend Nehemiah Silsbee and a former Yankee sutler named Watson. Considering all white Southerners as traitors, they organize "the niggers" against them under the banner of "equality," meantime cheating them and capitalizing on their ignorance and superstition for every possible impious purpose.

> I and Brother Silsbee have come to live in this country for your good... [Watson shouts to a midnight gathering of Negroes on the outskirts of Granby]. The Republican party found [you] slaves, and it struck off [your] shackles.... The Democrats want you placed back in slavery.... And if they can beat the Republicans at the elections they will put you back into slavery; and sell off your wives and children; and lash your bare backs, and run you down with bloodhounds again.... If one of these 'Rebels' tries to keep you from voting, or tries to make you vote the Democratic ticket, he had better never been born.... If one of them insults you, insult him; if he strikes you, strike him back. The government will protect you; the soldiers will be here to keep you out of danger.

[176]

Amid shouts of "Go on, boss!" and "Go on, Jesus!" Watson continues his harangue, telling his black listeners that they are the "equals" of the whites and can "out-vote them," if they will each pay him fifty cents "to defray the expenses" and swear to support the Loyal League, even with their lives.

Now [he concludes], if you want to keep the overseer's lash off your naked backs; if you want to keep the teeth of the hounds out of your flesh; if you want your wives and children to stay with you to take care of you in sickness and old age; if you want to learn how to read and write; if you want churches and schools, you will vote the loyal Republican ticket in all the elections. If the Republicans get control of the offices they want to give every voter a good mule and forty acres of good land.

To challenge this sort of fanatical appeal and to protect their own families and property, the oppressed white citizens of Granby organized themselves into a "counter movement" called the Ku Klux Klan. Led by a young lawyer, Sam Ormond, the secret lodge includes members from all social strata and is pledged to strike back "with the double energy of virtue and despair."

With the mere political opinions of men we cannot interfere [Ormond tells his comrades], or even with their legitimate political actions. But when they become firebrands and incendiaries, fomenting hatreds and instilling prejudices and vicious ideas into the heads of the poor simple negroes; and when the tendency of their villainous teaching is to cause strife and bloodshed, and to reduce our fair land to a condition of anarchy and consequent desolation; it becomes our duty, perhaps, to strike, and to strike with the double energy of virtue and despair.

Although this conflict between two opposing political idealogies is the dominating theme of *The Children of Issachar*, there is an intriguing secondary narrative which runs parallel. In a moment of girlish imprudence Catherine Vinnell yields to the passions of Hal Neilson, an unprincipled ne'er-do-well who promises to marry her. Later, when she has won the love of Alfred Rowe, Hal threatens to make public certain letters which she had written him during their intimacy. One day, suddenly, Hal dies from poison and Catherine is arrested for murder. She is tried and found not guilty—but her sorrow in the sad after-time clearly symbolizes the South during the agony of Reconstruction and subtly reveals the author's ability as a first-rate narrator. Despite the appeal of this subordinate romance, however, it cannot be said that *The Children of Issachar* has either a hero or a heroine. Hal and Catherine, as well as two or three other characters, are cleverly drawn, to be true, but they are personifications of a mightier struggle, an epic subject of American history, one which even now, a century later, continues to plague not only the South but the entire nation. Willis Brewer was wiser than he knew: he wrote

[177]

not of a child of Issachar but of the children of Issachar, even unto generations yet unborn.

Beyond his skillful interweaving of parallel plots and his selection and juxtaposition of characters, Brewer's artistry is also evident in his description of the socio-historical climate in which his narrative moves and, particularly, in his adroit use of dialects and other homely but effective literary mannerisms. For instance, Lawyer Sam Ormond, Squire Baffles, and Mildred Ormond are direct contrasts of Preacher Silsbee, Watson, and Catherine Vinnell. Hal Neilson, the scheming, brutish Southerner, stands in apposition to Harrod, the altruistic Northerner and former Union soldier who sympathizes with the plight of the conquered Alabamians and befriends them at every opportunity.

> I must tell you plainly [Harrod states] that I came down here to live among this people, and to try to make something out of my labors... [I] have lost within the past two years more or less of the capital [I] brought here. But our Southern friends have fared no better, though they understand cotton-raising better than we do. I don't lay blame on any one for what I have lost.... But, as I was saying, I came here for the purpose of identifying myself with the people. I have been treated well generally; in most cases with cordial kindness; certainly far more kindly than I could, as a Northerner and a stranger, have expected from a proud people, humiliated by defeat, and sore under a sense of injury in the loss of their slaves, the depreciation of their landed property, and the rule of the military army (p. 36).

And, of course, the Southern Ku Klux Klan and the Northern Loyal League represent two completely contradictory points of view regarding the political rehabilitation of the old Confederacy following the War Between the States.

Brewer's use of dialect is also exemplary. Baffles, the humorous, semi-literate, but shifty country squire; Silsbee and Watson, the conniving Yankees; and Jim, the fawning Alabama Negro, are readily discernable by their peculiarities of speech. For example, Squire Baffles' reaction to the nefarious activities of Silsbee and Watson is cleverly couched in the lingo of the uncultured backwoodsman:

> Uv course, Sammy, ef you boys honestly believe thar's eny thin' goin' on thet's ergin the peace en dignerty uv the State uv Alabamy, why uv course we ought ter know what it are. But, uv course, ef ye go whar they're holdin' ther meeting's yer mus' n't git up any disturbence, nur commit eny breach o' the peace under the statuts in sich cases made en pervided, as uv course I ain't got er right ter serpose ye would. It 'ud be er heap better fur yer not ter go thar than fur yer not ter behave yerselves arter ye git thar; en maybe ef 't was foun' out thet ye was thar, ther'd be trouble, en per'aps, under the circumstancs, it 'ud be better fur ye ter stay away altergether.

Watson, his *r's* rolling, speaks the language of the Downeast peddler, as he replies to Silsbee's suggestion that they enlist Southerners in the Loyal League:

Oh, bother! Silsbee, do you reely think what you're saying? Don't you know that these God-forsaken rebels would never do in a business of this kyind? I don't want one of them in with us. Heer I've been among them for over a year and a half, and I've had no treatment but that of a dog. And now, that we've got a good thing of it, I reely don't see the sense of taking them in with us.

And Jim's dialogue with his master, Hal Neilson, concerning the delivery of a letter to Miss Vinnell, illustrates not only the paternalistic white-black relationship of the period but also Brewer's masterful use of the Negro's dialect:

'Jim! Jim!' cried Mr. Hal Neilson at the top of his voice as he stood at the window looking into the garden.

'Sah!' shouted the black, dropping his hoe, and appearing in Hal's room a minute later. 'Here I is, Mos' Hal.'

'Why don't you answer when I call you, you black rascal, and not have me whooping for you all day?' said the irate young man.

"Fore God, Mos' Hal, I nebber hear ye tell dis minit,' replied Jim.

'If you'd keep your mouth shut and your ears open you'd hear better. Take this note.'

'To Mizzes Winell's, Mos' Hal?' inquired Jim.

'Yes, and bring me an answer to it.'

'Yes, sah; I be dar in a jiffy,' said Jim, picking up his hat as he passed out of the rear door....

'Mos' Hal.' The negro again appeared.

'Well,' answered Neilson, gruffly.

'She say she sen' a answer soon es she git time ter write it; en she say she want yer to come roun' dar.'

'Humph! Is that all?'

'En she say fur yer to let her know when yer comin'. Dat's all.'

'Well, get out of here!' replied Neilson.

In *The Children of Issachar* Willis Brewer also emphasizes local color by putting homely aphorisms into the mouths of his characters and by occasionally interposing Southern Negro ballads into the main stream of the narrative. Among the best of the pithy sayings, selected at random, are the following:

A dollar's a good thing in the pocket, but a better thing when it's circulating.

Go to the sluggard, thou ant, if you want to find rest, and the pass that pieceth all understanding.

Whenever yer see er man whose notions is habiterly ergin public erpinion ye may set him down es er man thet ye can make money by swappin' horses with.

They are an unfruitful tree that cumbers the ground.

I guess you are guaging my wheat by your own bin.

He'd turn his stocking inside out to catch a flea.

It's a long row that's got no balk, and if we'll stick together, as they do, they'll find that it's lightning agin blackjack.

Ef grit's worth eny thing in the piece it's worth er heap more in the lump.

I have not seen any dogs choked to death with butter.

Brewer's use of Negro songs in dialect is also impressive, as the following selections indicate. While Negro Jim chops weeds in Hal Neilson's garden, he sings in "full clear voice" the following melody.

> My ole Missus, an' two or free mo'
> Went down de hillside to jump Jim Crow;
> An' when da jump up to jump Jim Crow
> Da wheel 'roun' free times, an' do jes' so.

On his way to the Silsbee-Watson midnight meeting of the Loyal League, he squats down under a sweet-gum tree and breaks out in this "low lively song":

> Adam wus de fus' man, Ebe wus de tudder
> Cain wus er wicked man 'case he killed he brudder.
>   Oh, grab de cotton peddycoat,
>   Nab de cotton gown;
>   Shoes and stock's in de han',
>   En feet on de groun'.

And as the Ku Klux "ghosis" ride through the dark, quiet streets of Granby Jim moves nervously down a back alley, singing boldly:

> Raccoon, raccoon, yer better pray,
> Raccoon, raccoon, yer better pray;
>   For I'm de chile ter fight,
>   For I'm de chile ter fight;
> My eyes am bright an' shine at night
> When de moon am gone away.
>   Oh, rock de cradle, Jo,
>   Oh, rock de cradle, Jo;
> I cannot rock, I will not rock,
> De chile am not my own.

It is not surprising that *The Children of Issachar,* voicing Brewer's condemnation of the violence and lawlessness of Reconstruction, should have received little or no praise in the Northern press. Only one major magazine noticed the novel, *The Literary World* of Boston—and it damned the book with faint praise:

Brewer has evidently drawn on real life and actual facts for materials [the reviewer stated], and in more delicate and at the same time more powerful hands they would have yielded a better result. As it is, the picture made from them is commonplace and of little value. Some things about it are positively unpleasant. There are negroes in it and carpet-baggers, midnight harangues and protective associations, incendiary speeches and warning of lynch law, Northern reprobates and Southern fire-eaters. There are some exciting stories about intemperate cardplayers. There is an unhappy love-story of a girl who was seduced, who was afterwards ground under the heel of her betrayer, who was arrested for causing his death by poison, as was supposed, to head off his threats to make her shame public, and who was acquitted after a sensational trial. The truthfulness of many of the incidents related is probable, but that does not make them pleasant, and the book does

[180]

not lead in elevating directions, or familiarize one with crime and violence to any very good purpose.

On the contrary, the Montgomery *Advertiser and Mail,* October 21, 1884, hailed *The Children of Issachar* in a 1,100-word review as "by far the most notable Southern book of the day, one that cannot fail to attract attention from the higher literary world." Describing it in "many respects a remarkable book," the critic continued:

> Truth is unquestionably the foundation for this thrilling recital of carpetbagger tricks, negro ignorance, man's heroism, man's evil passions, and woman's love, all woven together with a golden thread of romance whose force in many places quite takes one's breath away. We find ourselves giving the real name to the country town of Granby and to many of the characters who figure in the book. Very evidently the author is native here, for there is not a scene that is not true to life. . . .
> Out of cold, hard, unsentimental facts the author has made a beautiful chain of pearls in which heroism and murder, innocence and brutality, pathos and bathos, romance and sentiment, are all reflected with the skill and ingenuity of a George Eliot.

And, taking direct issue with *The Literary World,* the reviewer added that the purpose of *The Children of Issachar* was lofty, "for it tells in its own charming way the story of a people's wrongs and preserves in immortal type many of the incidents of the Age of Corruption and Thievery."

The Mobile *Weekly Register,* however, on October 4 reviewed Brewer's book with mixed emotions. It failed, the writer paradoxically stated, "to convey a correct idea of Southern society," although the author was an "active politician in Reconstruction days and knows whereof he writes." Brewer's use of Catherine Vinnell as an "immoral heroine" was also condemned as indelicate:

> Of course [the reviewer added] Southern society, like society elsewhere, is made up of various grades and conditions, and no doubt the author intended to portray what may be exceptionally true while not typical. In our opinion, however, it is unfortunate that he adopted a sensational plot. . . . The carpetbagger, the negro leader, the lawyer and the justice of the peace, are very well drawn. The incentives that led to acts of violence in 1867–'68 are depicted with master skill. The author has given us a historical romance, which, while it exhibits in some respect the crudity of a pen unused to story telling, possesses value as a correct record of the resistance offered to oppression by a conquered people.

In conclusion, the Mobile critic hoped that "the author will give the public another and more elaborate production from his pen, for the ability which he possesses as a writer should not be lost in a law office."

Three weeks later, on October 25, the *Register* published a letter, written by a citizen of Hayneville, which voiced keen displeasure at the unfair treatment the paper had given his fellow citizen. Signing

[181]

himself "Plain Facts," the correspondent defended Brewer's portrayal of the unfortunate Catherine Vinnell, contrasting her to Effie Deans in *The Heart of Midlothian,* Tessa in *Romola,* Hester Prynne in *The Scarlet Letter,* Little Emily in *David Copperfield,* Hetty Sorrel in *Adam Bede,* and Becky Sharp in *Vanity Fair.*

> Are we to discard these masterpieces [he asked] because there is in them the story of a misled woman? Does not our best society listen with rapture to Rhea when she plays Camille? And do we take Camille as a type of French women, or Becky Sharp as the type of English wives? Why should you then speak of Kitty Vinnell instead of Mildred Ormond as the type of Southern women as presented by *The Children of Issachar?*

"Plain Facts" also took issue with the *Register's* attack on Brewer's "picture of village life." "It may not describe the social features of Mobile or other large towns," he wrote, "but I boldly maintain the realism of the picture which it presents of our Alabama villages." Then "Plain Facts" went on to reveal his true discernment as a critic. Willis Brewer, he suggested, had never meant to present a pleasant panorama of Southern life or a moonlight-and-magnolia picture of fanciful days of yore. His satirical observations were too obvious for even the most casual reader to suppose that he had intended to describe an ideal existence. Such was out of the question, he added, for Brewer was a realist—not a romanticist—and fidelity to facts was his most appealing attribute.

> The day of idealism in literature is gone [he ended], or remanded to the poets. Men and women of flesh and blood have faults. They find out how to correct them when you hold up before them the mirror of nature. There can be little good in depicting to them an ideal to which they can· not hope to attain. 'Paint me as I am,' said Cromwell to the painter, who wished to leave the mole off the face of the portrait. It is not honesty but flattery which draws a picture of Southern life, and omits to show us our faults.

"Plain Facts" was a prophet. Following the Confederate War—one of the bloodiest of all fratricidal wars, and fratricidal wars have always been the bloodiest of all wars—a new type of naturalistic fiction arose in America to challenge the old but lingering romances of long-gone days. Across the re-united nation such novelists as William Dean Howells, Henry James, and S. Weir Mitchell advanced their theories of realism by boldly describing life, not as it might have been but as it was. In the South Albion W. Tourgee, an Ohio Carpetbagger who had settled in North Carolina, led the vanguard of true-to-life fiction. He saw no need for a "Lost Cause" nostalgia even in the confused and unsettled conditions of the Tragic Era. Rather, in three remarkable novels he boldly described the interbreeding of whites and blacks (in *Toinette,* 1847), the evils of Carpetbagging (in *A Fool's*

Errand, 1879), and the need for education of Negroes as the only hope of racial peace in the South (in *Bricks Without Straw,* 1880). After him came George W. Cable, a former Confederate soldier, whose novels were based on building a New South through tolerance, education, and a non-agrarian economy. His *John March, Southerner* (1894) recounts, for instance, an attempt to establish in Louisiana a cooperative all-Negro community. Walter Hines Page, distinguished North Carolinian, and Ellen Glasgow, a distinguished Virginian, likewise chided their countrymen for trying to perpetuate an outmoded, provincial caste system and for pursuing a blind obeisance to Old South traditions. His *The Southerner* (1909) remains today one of the most outspoken presentations of New South needs—crop rotation, manufactories, sanitation, and education—and her *Voice of the People* (1900) and *The Deliverance* (1904) make clear the South's need for initiative, vision, and industry, if the region would play a vital part in national affairs. Northern novelists, like John de Forest, Maurice Thompson, and Constance Fenimore Woolson, also realistically strove to describe the inevitable reconciliation of the North and South. De Forest's *The Bloody Chasm* (1881), for example, brings together in love a Rebel girl and a Yankee boy against a background of old hates and sorrows. Thompson's *His Second Campaign* (1883) depicts the love affair between a Georgia girl and a young Northern lawyer who had marched with Sherman. And Woolson, in *East Angels* (1886), tells the story of a New England school teacher who marries a Southern planter and tries, against almost insurmountable odds, to become a successful "Southern" housewife.

It is to this post-bellum school of realists that Alabama's Willis Brewer belongs. In *The Children of Issachar* he boldly depicts the down-to-earth actions and interactions of the several strata of post-bellum Southern society with which he was so thoroughly familiar: the gentile but land-poor aristocracy, the aggressive yeomen, the middleclass merchant, the professional man, the indolent, grabbing po' buckra, the ignorant, gullible Negro, the industrious but shrewd and crafty Carpetbagger, and the treacherous, irresponsible Scalawag. Each he presents in a startling, daring prototype who eloquently bespeaks the inherent philosophy of his class. Each he endows with befitting dialect, apt attitudes and genuinely appropriate mannerisms. Nevertheless, Brewer makes no attempt to propagandize at any level—a realist, he tells only what he sees and knows, not what he wished might be. He was clever and creative, but he was also very, very subtle.

To the extent that all first novels are autobiographical, *The Children of Issachar* is Willis Brewer's own story—or, better, his own story of Hayneville, Alabama and its people and himself in one of the dreariest decades in all of Southern history. He saw clearly and he wrote forthrightly in a crisp, terse, condensed style and with a naturalistic bravado uncommon in his day. It would be absurd, however, to class him as a first-rate American novelist, or a first-rate Southern novelist, or even a first-rate Alabama novelist—particularly on the basis of only a single volume. But he deserves recognition as an inventive writer who understood the peculiar post-war problems of his day and presented them with a keen and true sense of tragedy, irony, and wit. As such, he was one of the South's first local-color realists. He anticipated other and better known Southern realists who were to flower a generation or so later, in their own comparable post-war era of the 1920's and 1930's—William Faulkner of Mississippi, Erskine Caldwell of Georgia, Thomas Wolfe of North Carolina, and T. S. Stribling and William March Campbell and Andrew Lytle of Alabama.

THE I'S OF TEXAS

Sir, New York City, February, 1943.

Longhorns say that sooner or later everybody comes to Texas but nobody ever leaves. They come from everywhere, take one look at the sun-blistered, brush-spotted plains, and quote Phil Sheridan. They curse the Texas summers and droughts and winters and floods, but they keep coming. And once they arrive you couldn't rope 'em out, not even with a Texas cuttin' pony.

Boast of your Crossroads-of-the-World at Times Square or The Loop, if you've never seen Texas. Otherwise don't. More than 1,500,000 of the 6,414,824 Longhorns were born in the other States and 235,528 are foreign-born. There are close on to a million Negroes. All of which means that every other white person you meet on the streets of Dallas or Dime Box is not a native. And this excludes the Armed Forces. Before 1930 the "emigrants" came mostly from Oklahoma, Arkansas and the Old South—and that was okay. Now they come in greater numbers from Illinois, Ohio and points east and west. The Nawth is slowly taking over.

Texans will tell you that's bad very bad. To begin with, nobody's worth a pluperfect, if he wasn't born in Texas, but to be born above the Smith-and-Weston Line, why, Gawdamighty, you just as well not be born at all. Egged on by fierce State pride, love of boasting and the Yankee dollar, however, Longhorns muffle their resentment and keep on bragging. A man may come to Texas, wear tooled boots and call himself a Longhorn, but nothing short of birth can make him a Native. A Texan is one thing, a "native" another, and there's as much difference between them as there is between an FFV and an Eskimo. Texans speak of one another as a "second-" or "third-generation," meaning that one's father or grandfather was born in the State. Of course there are more seconds than thirds and fourths are museum pieces.

[184]

A newcomer has a hard time reconciling this importance of the geography of birth when he hears (and hear he will!) of the gallant handful of "Texans" who cashed in at the Alamo. Two of the leaders, Col. William ("The Lord is on our side") Travis and Lieut. James Bonham were South Carolinians. Col. James Bowie, shot as he lay on his sickbed, was a Louisianan, and Davy Crockett a Tennessee ex-Congressman. Of the 180-odd members of the suicide squad 145 were from seventeen United States. Tennessee sent thirty-one, Kentucky and Virginia ten each, Pennsylvania nine and South Carolina eight. The others came from Missouri, Louisiana, Georgia, North Carolina, Massachusetts, Ohio, Mississippi, New York, Alabama, Maryland and New Jersey. Foreigners were there too: fifteen from England, ten from Ireland, four from Scotland, two each from Germany and Wales, and one from Denmark. Birthplaces of the others have not been agreed upon. It is doubtful if any were "born Texans," though one, a boy of 19, is listed as a "native."

Rather than surrender to the Dictator of their day, the heroes of the Alamo went down with both barrels smoking. That spirit alone made them Texans. Today, Texans say, and news dispatches bear them out, wherever as many as a half-dozen men are fighting on land, sea, or in the air, you can bet your bottom dollar at least one of them is a Longhorn. In 1940 the State was first in voluntary enlistments in the Army. When the Royal Canadian Air Force was opened to Americans a couple of years ago, so many Texans joined that the authorities threatened to change the name to R. C. T. A. F.

If every state was taking the war as seriously as Texas, there'd be no need for all the dither about U. S. complacency. Maybe it's because nearly every man or woman wears a uniform. Or because you can't stick your head out of a Texas window without seeing a P-40, a B-24 or a Trainer. The Texan passionately, vehemently loves his land and will fight for it at the drop of a hat. It would be easy to name a half-dozen men who oiled up their 30–30's on December 7 and leaned them in their chimney-corners. One Negro janitor collected a one-ton truckful of silver paper before anybody ever said, "Remember Pearl Harbor." War-talk in Texas centers about Fredericksburg's Nimitz, Commerce's Chennault, Houston's Hobby, and Menard's Wheless. Now and then you might hear Douglas mentioned—after all, as the crow flies Little Rock is a scant eighty miles from the Lone Star State.

Since 1900 the population of Texas has more than doubled. The average increase per decade has been 24%—8% more than the U. S. as a whole. Don't get the idea the State is over-run, however. If the population were equally distributed, there would be only 24 people to each of the 265,896 sq. miles, as compared to 44 for the nation. But one-fourth of the people live in only four counties. Thirty-one counties hold more than 50%. This leaves 223 (238,870 sq. miles) with less than seventeen residents per sq. mile; 85 counties have less than ten and 29 have less than three. When a Longhorn says, "C'mon, y'all, thar's room fer ever'body down heah," you may know he's drawn a bead.

Nobody ever asks a man why he came to Texas. It's an unwritten law dating back into early State history. Besides, it's unhealthy. As long ago as the 1830's the ominous letters G. T. T., done by a suspicious creditor on a merchant's window meant only one thing: the Sabine or the Red had become his Lethe. In 1884, Tom Huges, writing the first book titled *Gone to Texas*, said, "When we want to say shortly that it's all up with a fellow, we just say 'G. T. T.,' just as you'd say gone to the devil, or the dogs." Texans themselves indulge in a sly chuckle over the somewhat dubious reputation of their antecedents, but they are more likely to ask a man what his name was before he came to Texas than to ask him why he came. Chances are they won't ask anything. In Texas a man is accepted for what he is, no questions asked. But he'd better be a right guy or keep moving.

Outside of profanity the most frequently used words in Texas are *most* and *biggest*. The Longhorn who told his Tarheel friend that Texas had flat land as high as Mt. Mitchell wasn't far wrong. On top of the ground Texas grows 30% of the nation's cotton, has more airports, beef cattle, sheep, goats, wool, pecans, roses and army camps than any State in the Union. Under the ground it has more oil, gas, sulphur, salt, helium and onions. In the sky more planes. It is bigger than Germany, France, or Spain, and has three times the area of England, Scotland, and Wales combined. An El Pasoan is nearer eight other states than he is his own capital at Austin. If you want a better idea, fold a map of the state along its borders—put Brownsville in Devil's Lake, N.D., El Paso on top of Charleston, S. C., and Texarkana 250 miles out in the Pacific Ocean!

Newcomers soon get used to the bigness and say nothing about it unless they are talking to newer-comers. What they don't get used to is Texas weather and Texas women.

The Longhorn will coyly tell you his weather is "unusual." When the thermometer hits 110, it isn't hot—just warm. The fact that one county may have 1.80 inches of rain in a year and another 109.38 isn't important. Texas has no spring and no fall. It just cools off one October day and heats up again in May. During the six-month summer the mercury climbs to 100 or more and squats. Long about Thanksgiving it climbs down again.

Stories about Lone Star summers and duststorms make dull telling, however—it's those about the famous "blue-northers" that always hold the candle. Meteorologists claim they are anticyclonic gales forced down out of the Rockies by high atmospheric pressure. Texans say that's a lie. They come fresh out of the North Pole because there's nothing to stop them but barbed-wire fence. You look up in the northern sky on a sunshiny, 60-degree day between October and March and see the blue-blackiest, murkiest cloud imaginable. You smell the cool, fresh air a-hurrying. "Here she comes," you shout, speed your car into the garage, throw a blanket over your dog and turn up the gas stoves. Before you've finished, she's hit; icy winds beat your windows and bend your trees; hail and rain blow over the threshold; the house groans and staggers. Your water pipes all but freeze solid and your dog howls. Within the hour the temperature has dropped 40 degrees. That old yarn about one horse of a team freezing to death while the other fell out with the heat is truer than it sounds, if you've ever wintered in Texas.

Bar none, Texas women are the best-looking in the world. God could not have done a better job elsewhere. The truth is, that's why He took off Sunday for a day of rest. He wasn't really very tired. He just wanted to sit back and look at the Longhorn women He'd made on Saturday.

One reason the Texas woman is prettier is because there's more of her to be pretty. You see none of those Dresden China things in the Lonestar State. Texas grows 'em big. The Longhorn woman is the best dancer, the straightest walker and talker, and has the best figger in the U. S. A. What's more, she's the friendliest female on earth. This thing about not speaking to a "strange man" passed out in Texas with the Indians. But to *her* man she's as loyal as the day is long, to say nothing of the night!

Perhaps, because Texas is just now emerging from the log-cabin era, its women are the lousiest housekeepers in the country. No use to fret your life away, they say frankly, over a little dirt and dust. Besides, tomorrow's winds will bring in more. Respectable families live in the rattiest, down-at-the-heels houses you could find anywhere. Yet the womenfolks drive powerful cars and wear diamonds the size of hummingbird eggs. Look closely and you might find an oil well in the back yard.

Don't come to Texas in the summertime, however, if you would feast your eyes on beauties. Or *do* come then—it's largely a matter of opinion. For Longhorn women wear less clothes between June and September that any others this side of the Fijis. Some folks say this is due to the hot weather; others think it's because Texas women have plenty to show and don't mind showing it. Lamour's sarong is winter wear by the side of what you see in August on Santone's Main Street, but it is on the campuses of the State that Nature really bares her breast. In halters, huaraches and shorts, or a mid-riff dress, they slouch in classes and populate the corner drugstore, sipping cokes. On special occasions they put ribbons in their hair. Sometimes one will doll up in a dirndl and a C-front blouse—the effect is the same.

[187]

But let somebody pass the word around that "there's gonna be a dance tonight" and they come out the prettiest, best-draped bevy of female flesh man ever set eyes upon.

The hallmark of the native Texan is friendliness. There might have been a time when their favorite greeting was "Hi-ya, Stranger," but today it's "Hi'ya, Neighbor." You may live in Detroit or Boston and not know your next-door neighbor, but if you move to Houston or Ft. Worth, you'll know everybody in the block in a week. They'll serve you cookies and coffee while you unpack, nurse your baby on your night out and keep your dog while you're vacationing. What's more, they'll get up a weiner-roast or a steak-fry for you and, seated around a sweet-smelling mesquite wood fire, they'll sing you songs that only folks who dearly love their land could ever sing. Everybody speaks to everybody in the Lone Star State and if you don't speak back you're a furriner and got no damn' business heah nohow. Texans may sit on top of the richest mineral deposits and own half the petroleum in the world, but it is their love of their fellow man that makes them what they are. A cheery "Howdy" is worth more than a barrel of crude oil to a real Texan any day.

Never was there a place where music meant more to folks than Texas. Children from six to sixty go to orchestra practice in every hamlet from Beaumont to Mule Shoe. But it's plain singing that they really go for. Wherever more than two get together, somebody's bound to start a tune. Tots that can't yet talk hum melodies and grownups drown out dance orchestras. Starting a song is the easiest thing to do in Texas next to starting a fight. W. Lee O'Daniel, cognizant of the ballotbox power of music, wrote a thing called "Beautiful Texas" and hired a hillbilly band to tour the State playing it. He's been twice elected Governor and twice U.S. Senator.

Longhorns never hit their singing strides until they start in on "Bury Me Not on the Lone Prarie." No "sing" ever closes, however, without "The Eyes of Texas," sung to the tune of "I've Been Working on the Railroad."

When you first hit Texas, you'll be warted (that's Longhorn for bothered) by the weather and the bragging of the people. You'll wonder why they make such a to-do over the State's having flown six flags and been a Republic, when Alabama fought just as many and it and South Carolina, were also Republics and had *their* own Presidents. You'll not understand why they árgue eternally over the whether they're "Texians," as the old-timers prefer, of just plain "Texans."

But you won't wonder long. Soon you'll catch yourself collaring a newcomer and swelling up about San Jacinto or Old Spindletop.

Maybe you won't be that bad. But before you know it you'll be warting an emigrant with yarns about horned toads and humming

"The Eyes of Texas" while you shave. What's more you'll have doubts about what to call yourself.

Ten-to-one it'll be "Tex-I-an."

LAWLEY COVERS THE CONFEDERACY
THE PREFACE

Confederate Publishing Company,
Tuscaloosa, Alabama, 1968.

Francis Charles Lawley, the fourth and youngest son of Sir Paul Bielby Lawley-Thompson, first Baron Wenlock, and his wife, Catherine Neville, daughter of Sir Richard, second Lord of Braybrooke, was born on May 24, 1825 at Escrick Park, East Riding, Yorkshire. After attending a preparatory school at nearby Hatfield, he entered Rugby School on May 24, 1837 and matriculated from Balliol College, Oxford, March 21, 1844. In 1848 he was graduated Bachelor of Arts with high honors in *literae humaniores* and, because of his brilliant record, was elected a fellow of All Souls' College. There, in addition to his superior scholastic achievements, Lawley gave vent to his enthusiasm for horseracing, a sport he had participated in since childhood. Although he was not permitted as a student to run horses in his own name, he and the Earl of Airlie, a long-time friend, entered a jointly-owned colt named Clincher in the 1850 derby. Clincher ran third and Lawley lost a large sum of money. As a result, he speculated in the stock market which, in turn, drove him deeper in debt. Nevertheless, he was able to hold high his scholastic standing and 1851 he was awarded the bachelor's degree *cum laude*.

Now resolved upon a career in politics, Lawley stood for Parliament as an advanced Liberal and in July, 1852 was elected to the House of Commons from Beverly, East Riding. Six months later, when William E. Gladstone, leader of the Liberal Party, succeeded Benjamin Disraeli as chancellor of the Exchecquer, he appointed his new, ambitious, young political colleague to serve him as private secretary. Lawley accepted and in the months following performed his duties to the complete satisfaction of his mentor.

On July 19, 1854, when Lawley's term had run less than two years, Sir Geroge Grey, Her Majesty's secretary for the Colonies, recommended his appointment to the office of governor of South Australia, replacing Sir Henry Young. After three days' deliberation Lawley accepted the offer and began preparing for his new duties on the other side of the world.

However, on the floor of the House of Commons on August 3, Sir George, who had but recently succeeded the Duke of Newcastle, claimed that in offering the post to Lawley he had not really known

[189]

the gentleman but that he had merely followed his predecessor's advice and honored his commitment, believing that the Duke considered Lawley's ability and character eminently fitted "a man of his position for colonial service under the Crown." Indeed, he added, the Duke had actually discussed the matter with Lawley before he, Sir George, had assumed office. The Duke had stated that he knew of no reason why Lawley should not be named, although he was thoroughly familiar with Lawley's propensity for horseracing.

> The Duke of Newcastle informed me [Sir George declared] that he thought it right to state the only drawback which in his opinion might be alleged against the appointment of Mr. Lawley arose from a fact which, under the circumstances, he did not consider to be a sufficient bar to his appointment....Like many young men I fear, in his position in society, Lawley had early in life been addicted to—I hardly know how to describe it in ordinary language, but all will understand what I mean—had been unfortunately 'on the turf.' He had, in early life, been inclined to horseracing...; but he [the Duke] submitted to me that, so far from thinking this circumstances a bar to the appointment of Mr. Lawley, or as constituting an objection to his appointment, it was, on the contrary, a recommendation under the circumstances....

The "circumstances" to which Sir George alluded were Lawley's own regretful confession of his youthful "horse-racing habits" and his earnest intention "to break off from them." As proof, Lawley had accepted the position as Gladstone's secretary with the view of engaging himself in "higher pursuits." Moreover, he firmly believed that his transfer to Australia would once and for all "remove him beyond the reach of temptation."

But the longer Sir George addressed the House the stronger his disapprovel of Lawley's appointment grew. He had "inherited" Lawley from the Duke of Newcastle, he continued: "He certainly is not a gentleman to whom ... I should have offered the government of South Australia, nor was his a name I should have submitted to Her Majesty for the Governor of an important colony." In the first place, he was too young—only twenty-nine, Sir George added. Furthermore, betting on horseracing during his college days had not been the only stigma attached to Lawley's name. More recently he had received information of "rumors of a much more serious character as affecting the conduct, position, and character of Mr. Lawley—namely, that Mr. Lawley had availed himself of the official knowledge acquired as private secretary to the right hon. Gentleman, the Chancellor of the Exchequer, to engage in extensive speculation in the funds [stock exchange]." Continuing, Sir George asked that, "in justice to Mr. Lawley, in justice to myself, in justice to the Government, and in justice to the colony to which he was to be appointed," the negotiations be suspended in order that Lawley "might have the means and opportunity which every man is justly entitled to, of knowing what had been said in regard to him, and having every opportunity of explaining or refuting the charges."

Lawley promptly presented Sir George "a clear, satisfactory, and conclusive denial" of the charge of having speculated in stocks upon official information. The Duke of Newcastle supported him whole-heartedly. But Gladstone told the House of Commons that, while he still took "a warm and affectionate interest" in his protegé, the thought that the young man should be "publicly broken." Sir John Pakington, the member from Droitwich, agreed. All together, their influence crushed Lawley's feeble remaining chance for confirmation. And as the final result, Sir George wrote Queen Victoria, advising her to revoke Lawley's appointment as governor of South Australia. Lawley promptly resigned his position as Gladstone's private secretary, receiving £400 as "special compensation" for his outstanding work, and returned to his ancestral home in Yorkshire. There, humiliated by the ill fortune which had been heaped upon him, he spent the next few years of his life in semi-seclusion.

In the spring of 1861 the London *Times* sent William H. Russell to the United States as "special correspondent" to report the American Civil War. After a tour through the newly-formed Confederate States he arrived in Washington just in time to witness the defeat and stampede of the Union army at the First Battle of Bull Run, July 21. His outspoken, all but gleeful account of that Rebel victory so angered the Federal military and civil authorities as to make Russell's position untenable. Thereafter, as the summer and winter passed, his name became increasingly opprobrious in the North—"Bull Run Russell" the Yankee press called him—until, finally, Secretary of State William H. Seward refused him permission to accompany General George B. McClellan on his expedition against Richmond in May-June, 1862. And, Russell, his effectiveness as a military correspondent gone, made hasty plans to return to London.

Meantime, Francis Lawley had been persuaded to journey to the United States as Russell's replacement on the *Times*. On March 25, 1862 Lawley called on the depressed Russell in his Washington quarters, comforted him by writing a "very kind and very able letter" in his behalf to John T. Delane, editor of the *Times*, and urgently advised Russell to get back home as soon as possible in order to "save the British legation any unpleasantness." A week later Lawley put his opinions in a letter to Russell, again insisting that he "stay away from the legation." Russell, realizing at last that he had no alternative, telegraphed New York for passage on the *China* and on Wednesday, April 9, sailed for Liverpool.

The responsibility of reporting the Southern side of the war for the London *Times* now his own, on September 23 (*Times*, Oct. 7, 1862) Lawley wrote from Baltimore his first, albeit secondhand account, of the battles around Richmond and elsewhere along the vacillating front. He described the sufferings of the wounded in the local hospitals, praised Dorothea Dix for her heroic work and, as best he could, generally endeavored to restore the prestige of the London *Times* in the United States.

Meanwhile, Lawley grew more and more sympathetic with the Southern point of view. After more than eighteen months of warfare, he stated, the power of the Confederacy was "much stronger" than it was in the beginning, while the North was "bleeding at every pore." Although the killing and the suffering would continue, he wrote, "I do not for a moment believe that they will lead to the subjugation of the South." But it was impossible, he concluded, "for anyone with eyes in his head to be blind to the invincible determination of the Southern people to attain their independence. They have already shown sufficient power of endurance to give an earnest of what they will do and dare."

Indeed, so ardent was Lawley's enthusiasm for the Confederacy that in late September he teamed up with Colonel Garnet Wolseley, a British officer on leave from Canada, for an excursion into Rebel territory. Hurriedly, the two men mapped their plans for the "underground passage" to the Confederacy. As Wolseley described it in *Blackwood's Magazine*, January, 1863, "Knowing how little reliance can be placed at any time upon the information published in American newspapers, I was very anxious, if possible, to get to the South, and judge for myself as to the condition of its people, the strength of its government, and the organization of its armies."

Leaving Baltimore in a rented two-horse buggy, Lawley and Wolseley traveled southward at a rate of thirty miles a day, enjoying the hospitality of the natives, many of whom boasted of their English ancestry. Upon reaching the Patuxent River they changed to a two-horse wagon and went on towards the Leonard's Town home of a rude and illiterate farmer who had recently taken to the more lucrative but more risky occupation of smuggling. Getting a boat proved difficult, however, and the two English gentlemen, accustomed to the luxury of a bed each, were required to sleep three-deep in the attic of the smuggler's "old tumbledown shed." The soldier managed to find a dirty sack for a pillow and, being accustomed to roughing it, soon fell off to sleep. The former Oxonian and member of the House of Commons, however, fared not so well:

> Roused [Wolseley later wrote in his autobiography] by some noise about midnight, I saw Frank Lawley with the end of a lighted candle in one hand and a stick in the other chasing the rats which swarmed there, and which had been, he said, running over him freely. I laughed and recommended him to take an old campaigner's advice and go to sleep, rats or no rats. . . . This was my travelling companion's debut in campaigning life, and the rats were a little too much for him.

[192]

But, he continued, Lawley's subsequent duties with the Confederate Army taught him to sleep well, "even when the rats ran freely about him as they had done the night we spent together in that horrid loft by the Potomac River."

The next morning, after much deliberation, the Maryland smuggler pulled the travelers five miles up the river in his bateau—to avoid a Yankee gunboat directly opposite—and then across, with favorable winds, discharging them on the Virginia shore shortly after mid-day. A five-mile walk took the Englishmen to a small village. Late that afternoon, after a long, tiresome drive in a cart without springs during which they dodged several Federal cavalry patrols, they reached Fredericksburg. The following morning they rented a two-mule wagon and with a Confederate cavalry escort drove to Beaverdam Station. There they boarded the Virginia Central Railroad which was already overloaded with hundreds of wounded Confederates from the Army of Northern Virginia.

> The road was extremely rough and jolting [according to Wolseley], and many in the crowd of wounded men on the train had recently had their legs amputated. That train opened Frank Lawley's eyes to the horrible side of war, made all the more in this instance because no chloroform or medical appliances of any sort were available.

Several hours later the travelers reached Richmond. Finding the Spottswood, Exchange, and American hotels filled to capacity, they were forced to pay an exhorbitant price for a "little double-bedded room up four flights of stairs." And to add to their misery they could buy no tea, no wine, no liquor, and only commonplace food, even bread and meat being "proportionately expensive."

In Richmond Lawley and Wolseley were joined by Frank Vizetelly, the well-known artist-correspondent of the *Illustrated London News*, who had himself but recently arrived in the Confederacy. The three Englishmen called on Secretary of War George W. Randolph, secured the necessary passes and letters of introduction to General Robert E. Lee, and on the morning of October 9 left for the headquarters of the Army of Northern Virginia near Winchester.

From his first meeting with General Lee and his lieutenants, Generals J. E. B. ("Jeb") Stuart, T. J. ("Stonewall") Jackson, and James Longstreet, Lawley was as ardent an admirer of the South and as loyal a supporter of the Confederacy as it was possible for a foreigner to be—perhaps, indeed, as it was for a native Southerner. During the next two and one-half years, until Lee's surrender at Appomattox, he was constantly with the Confederate fighting men, sharing their joys and sorrows, eating at their tables, sleeping in their tents, warming by their campfires, marching, foraging, singing, helping the wounded and comforting the dying—and telling the world about all of it through the columns of the most influential English-language newspaper in the world, the London *Times*.

All together, Lawley wrote about one hundred long, detailed letters from America for the *Times* between October, 1862 and April, 1865, usually sending them to London through the French consulate in Richmond via Paris. Of these, eighty-six—averaging approximately thirty-six hundred words each—appeared in print under the heading "The Southern Confederacy" or "The Confederate States." Always they were by-lined "From Our Special Correspondent." One letter was written from Baltimore, four from Hagerstown, and two from New York City. The others were from various places in the Confederacy, the largest number from Richmond.

In his communiques Lawley frequently included accounts of his interviews with such famous men as President Jefferson Davis and Generals Lee, Longstreet, Braxton Bragg, and P. G. T. Beauregard. His eyewitness descriptions of several major battles are considered classics of their kind. For instance, his "Account of the Battle of Fredericksburg," written from Lee's headquarters on December 8–13, 1862, was reprinted in *The Rebellion Record: A Diary of American Events* ..., edited by Frank Moore (1863), and later reissued in London as a separate pamphlet. Captain Justus Scheibert of the Prussian Army, who served with Lee's army in 1863, stated in his *Seven Months in the Rebel States* (1868) that Francis Lawley's "reports were at that time the best that appeared in Europe concerning American affairs. [He] excelled in tactful, restrained demeanor and in a calm view of things, ... [and] did more [than William H. Russell, his predecessor on the *Times*] to promote a true understanding of the facts." Markinfield Addey, in one of the first biographies of "Stonewall" Jackson (1863), quoted Lawley's account of the Battle of Chancellorsville verbatim, nine pages long, prefacing it thus: "The particulars of this battle have been so graphically narrated by the Special Correspondent of the London *Times* ..., who was present at the battle, that we have no hesitation in transferring it to these pages." Douglas Southall Freeman relied heavily upon Lawley's description of Lee's surrender and his account of the last meeting of Lee and Longstreet in his biography of the Confederate commander-in-chief. And Lawley's biographer in the *Dictionary of National Biography* considered his dispatches "admirable, both as to matter and to style."

The battles of Chancellorsville and Gettysburg Lawley had the rare opportunity of observing from the very spots selected by the Confederate high command. His accounts of both are masterpieces of description, beautifully embellished with scintilating sidelights and overtones of a sensitive, perceptive man to whom war was mostly suffering and dying. Lawley's reports of his visits to many important regions and cities in the Confederacy—Richmond, Charleston, Augusta, Vicksburg, Chattanooga, Columbia, Petersburg, and elsewhere—are replete with close observations of men, women, and children, the loyalty of slaves, roads, fortifications, crops, foods, hospitals, and his persistent, repetitious description of the determination of the Southern people to win their independence regardless of cost.

Not the least fascinating aspect of Lawley's adventures in the Confederacy was his personal association, on and off the battlefield, with other distinguished correspondents and with military observers from several nations of Europe. Besides his friendship, already mentioned, with Colonel Garnet Wolseley (later Viscount Wolseley) and Frank Vizetelly (who accompanied Lawley on the *Lillian* from Nassau to Wilmington in May-June, 1864), Lawley was closely identified with C. J. Cridland (British consul to Virginia), Prince Camille de Polignac of France, Captain Justus Scheibert and Colonel Heros von Borcke of Prussia, Captain Fitzgerald Ross (an English officer in the Austrian Hussars), Colonel St. Leger Grenfell, Lord Edward St. Maur, Lieutenant-Colonel Arthur J. Fremantle of the British Army, and others who visited the Confederacy during the war years. Scheibert, for example, described the good times the representatives of England, France, Prussia, and Austria had with their Confederate friends at Madame Zitelli's in Richmond. Laughingly, they called themselves the "Congress of the Five Great Powers." Several of these civil and military observers wrote articles and/or books about their adventures in the Confederacy and an exciting experience it is to read what they wrote about each other or what each of them wrote about a mutual associate, event, or escapade, or, for that matter, what their native Southern friends wrote about them. For example, Ross, Fremantle, Scheibert, and Lawley witnessed the Battle of Gettysburg together from Lee's headquarters and each described the conflict as he saw it. Lawley and Scheibert and von Borcke were together at the Battle of Chancellorsville—Lawley as an observer, the others as participants. Afterwards, each wrote his impressions, each telling in his own peculiar way the same story, now many times repeated, of Scheibert's amazing singlehanded capture of a half-dozen Yankees whom he marched back two miles to deliver personally to General "Jeb" Stuart.

Besides his close association with Generals Lee, Stuart, Longstreet, and Jackson, and his comradeship with other foreigners in the Confederacy, Lawley enjoyed the society of the elite of Richmond. By Mrs. Burton Harrison, for instance, he was cordially remembered long after the war as a staunch and loyal Confederate. T. C. DeLeon recorded that Mrs. Mattie Paul Myers described him as "one of the handsomest and more agreeable men I ever knew." Lieutenant-Colonel William W. Blackford, who once saw Lawley eating dinner with General Lee, described him as an unassuming, polite and thorough gentleman.

Lawley's unique descriptions of the wounding of Jackson at Chancel-

[195]

lorsville, Lee's surrender at Appomattox, and the farewell meeting of Lee and Longstreet are considered not only exemplary journalism but also authentic accounts even to the minutest details. He is believed to have been the only newspaper correspondent who eyewitnessed these three events.

No other writer, save perhaps Stephen Crane in *The Red Badge of Courage*—whom Francis Lawley surely anticipated—has brought the horrors of war closer to the heart of mankind. His talent for seeing the whole as well as its myriad parts was phenomenal. He delighted in chronicling the "unchronicled incidents of battles," as he put it in his essay of May 19, 1863, "the unconsidered trifles which await picking up and collecting." In one happy phrase he was capable of photographing a single fleeting battlefield incident—an infantryman stooping amid rifle fire to lace his shoe, a horse's whinny, the way smoke nestled in a valley leaving only the green treetops aglow in the sunlight, the spectrum of a hundred varicolored battleflags merging in the charge up Cemetery Ridge, the gelatinous mud after Gettysburg, mud that pulled retreating men's shoes off and sucked at the feet of their horses, the color of the sky at dawn, the eternal rain, rain, rain that pelted, punctured, and pestered, the mingling odor of dead men and horses and black powder smoke and the stench of hungry, filthy men at war—yet, in total he seldom failed to impress his readers with the overall sweep of armies moving, the monotony of camp life, or the panorama of mile on mile of entrenched infantrymen.

But Lawley the foreign correspondent was not without fault. He was, as a careful reader of his letters will quickly reveal, a very prejudiced reporter. From his very first communique to his last, from 1862 to 1865, he was in spirit, if not always in letter, a British propagandist for the Confederate States of America. That is not to say that he failed to describe what he saw accurately and brilliantly, for he did; but his interpretations of what he saw, his deductions and his conclusions must surely have sometimes been imponderable for his contemporaries. For example, he believed the South unconquerable—even as late as 1865, when Sherman was marching into North Carolina and Grant pursued Lee westward along the narrowing Appomattox River. To Lawley the men of the Confederate high command, Lee, Johnson, Longstreet, Stuart, and their lieutenants, were all but knights in shining armor. And after reading his descriptions of the men in the Confederate trenches below Petersburg, one is left with but a single thought: yes, one Rebel could indeed whip a dozen Yankees—and with one hand tied behind his back! Perhaps it would be fairer to say simply that in his boundless enthusiasm for the South Lawley sometimes premised his communiques more on hope than fact, more on wishful thinking than on reasoned logic. Or, better still, perhaps the blame should be put where it really lay—in

Printing House Square, the home office of the paper he served. As the anonymous *History of the Times* (1939) states,

> It had to be admitted behind the scenes that *The Times* had gone very far astray in its military and even its political estimates [during the American Civil War]. Charles Mackay [the *Time's* New York correspondent] and to some extent Lawley were blamed, but although there is no doubt that their pro-Southern sentiments had been misleading the paper for a long time, it is equally clear that the real responsibility lay upon those in Printing House Square who too readily accepted their judgment. There had never been any secret about the extreme partisanship of Mackay at least. Lawley was accused of no more than an error of judgment.

On January 31, 1865 Mowbray Morris, manager of the *Times*, questioned Lawley's one-sided conclusion about the "growing discontent" in the South. "I observe that you never notice the Opposition & always represent the Southern people as being unanimous. Are you sure that you are right in this?" he asked. Then he quickly went on to congratulate Lawley for the work he had done: "[You have] presented the public here with a continuous narrative which has served to correct the errors and exaggerations of the Federal Press, & has indeed been the only authentic record of the Southern side of the civil war."

Later, however, Lawley was made to share with Morris, Mackay, and John Delane, editor of the *Times*, the sharpest of criticism from Leslie Stephens and George H. Putnam, both of whom accused the *Times* of prejudicing their readers in favor of the South. Lawley's name was not mentioned in the attack—and none of the illustrations of bias used by the critics are directly traceable to Lawley's letters—but there can be no doubt that Stephens and Putnam were fully aware of the partisan reporting from "Our Special Correspondent in the Confederate States." As Stephen wrote,

> The *Times* began by sending out to America a gentleman for whom impartiality and power of description every one must feel a high respect. During 1861, his letters, although in my opinion frequently expressing erroneous judgments, were highly graphic, interesting, and invariably gentlemanlike. Mr. Russell, however, left America in the spring of 1862, on not being permitted to accompany McClellan's Peninsula expedition. Occasional letters were afterwards published from a Southern correspondent, of whom I shall only say that a little more information, with a few less sentimentalities about Lee and Jackson would have improved the substance of his writing, though they may have made his presence less acceptable to the Southern authorities. From the moment at which he commenced his letters, he became (if he had not previously been) a thorough partisan of the Southern cause. The *Times* also employed a special correspondent during part of 1863 and 1864. His letters were unfavourable to the North, but evidently candid, and, therefore, such as no Northern sympathizer should condemn.

Upon his return to England after the American Civil War Francis Lawley remained briefly with the *Times* before accepting a more lucra-

[197]

tive position as a special correspondent for the London *Daily Telegraph.* On December 18, 1869 he married Henrietta-Louisa-Amelia Zaiser, daughter of the Reverend Frederick Augustus Zaiser, former chaplain to the King and Court of His Majesty the late King of Saxony. When the Franco-Prussian War began in July, 1870, Lawley was sent to cover the conflict. While in Paris he began an association with Ambrose Dudley Mann, former Confederate commissioner to Belgium, who had remained in Europe following the defeat of the Confederacy. Of Lawley Mann wrote his son, Grayson Mann, on October 30, 1870:

> The circle of my French acquaintances is daily enlarging. Of Englishmen I see none any longer except Mr. Lawley, who is favorably known in the South for the services he conscientiously rendered as correspondent of the London *Times.* The charms of his tongue in social intercourse and not unsurpassed by the charms of his pen as a public writer.

At this time or shortly afterwards Lawley became interested in writing a biography of Judah P. Benjamin, former Confederate attorney-general, secretary of war, and secretary of state, the versatile and perhaps most outstanding member of Jefferson Davis' Cabinet. Off and on for the next thirty years Lawley hacked away at this task, corresponding with various people, including Benjamin himself and Mrs. Jefferson Davis. On one occasion he interviewed Benjamin, labelling the result as "Words taken down from Mr. Benjamin's own lips by F. L. early in 1870." But the manuscript was never completed and only fragments remain today as a sad reminder of Lawley's high hopes.

Any record of Lawley's accomplishments after the 1870's has all but vanished—if, indeed, any record ever existed. Present-day authorities of the *Daily Telegraph* remember his name but vaguely and F. L. Burham's *Peterborough Court: The Story of the Daily Telegraph* (1955) makes only brief mention of his work. Because of its longstanding "rule of anonymity" the London *Times* has virtually no account of his having ever been employed, except the few casual references to him in the official *History of the Times.* During the remainder of his life Lawley eked out a living for himself and his wife (they had no children) by continuing his connection with the *Daily Telegraph,* by contributing articles to *Bailey's Magazine* and to the London *Sportsman,* and by occasionally editing, co-writing, or writing books. For *Bailey's* he wrote such pieces as "The Late General J. C. Fremont" and "Some Old Sporting Periodicals" and a series on famous horses. Among the last-named were "Two Famous War Chargers" (the Duke of Wellington's Copenhagen and Robert E. Lee's Traveller), "Some Famous War Horses" (Ulysses S. Grant's Cincinnati, William T. Sherman's Lexington, Philip H. Sheridan's Winchester, and again Lee's Traveller and Wellington's Copenhagen).

In 1886 Lawley contributed to *Racing and Steeple-Chasing,* a volume in the "Badminton Library of Sports and Pastimes," written by Arthur Coventry and Alfred E. T. Watson and dedicated to His Royal Highness the Prince of Wales. His most successful literary effort was *"The Life and Times of "The Druid"* (1895), a full-length biography of Henry Dixon Hall, a distinguished sportsman and journalist and, incidentally, Lawley's friend and benefactor. In 1889 Lawley wrote a pamphlet entitled *The Bench and the Jockey Club* in defense of a controversial jockey named Charles Wood who had been arraigned for misconduct. In 1892 he co-authored with John Kent a book called *The Racing of Lord George Bentick.* To the *Dictionary of National Biography* (1897) he contributed a memoir on the life of Admiral Henry John Rous. And on one occasion, at least, he turned to his American experiences for subject matter: his *"The Story of Appomattox,"* a short account of Lee's surrender—thirty years before he had written on the same subject for the *Fortnightly Review*—appeared in the April, 1894 issue of *Bailey's Magazine.*

Francis Lawley's death in his London home at 6 Cornwall Terrace, Regent's Park, N. W. on September 18, 1901 received little notice in the press. Three days later the *Times* devoted about one hundred words to his obituary, stating that he had gone through the American Civil War "as a Special Correspondent of *The Times*"—this much and no more for the man whose hundreds of thousands of words had given the readers of the most influential newspaper in the world "the only authentic record of the Southern side" of the American Civil War.

The *Daily Telegraph* declared that "deep regret will be felt by a large circle of social, political, literary, and sporting friends at the death of the Hon. Francis Lawley..., the youngest son of the first Baron Wenlock, and an uncle of the present peer."

> After a distinguished career at Oxford [the *Telegraph* added], where he took honours in classics, Mr. Lawley turned to politics, and in 1852 entered the House of Commons for Beverly as a Liberal. During the two years he represented that constituency he also acted as private secretary to Mr. Gladstone, and between him and his 'chief' there existed a sincere friendship which lasted until death separated them. Politics did not, however, absorb the whole of his attention. He was a keen sportsman, and not only possessed an extensive acquaintance with men whose names were almost household words among followers of the Turf during the fifties and sixties of last century, but was associated with many events which have become famous in the history of racing.
>
> Subsequently Mr. Lawley turned his attention to literature and journalism in which his wide reading, his splendid memory, his clear and concise style, and his inexhaustible resources of anecdote and story gave him peculiar advantages and gained for his articles and sketches, and the volumes which he wrote or edited, a large share of popular favour.
>
> For many years readers of this journal have perused with pleasure

papers on past and present day sport from his pen, marked with care and accuracy in their facts and full of chatty and interesting reminiscences, such as few men could command.

In private life Mr. Lawley was a polished and agreeable companion and an excellent reconteur with a charm of manner and an affability which made him welcome wherever he went. His death creates a void among the veterans of journalism and of sport, and will be sincerely lamented by many accustomed in the past to his genial and urbane presence.

The Sportsman published a short account of his activities on September 20, but it remained for Bailey's Magazine forcefully to call the public's attention to the accomplishments of "The Late Honourable Francis Lawley," son of "the Yorkshire magnate, Lord Wenlock."

No more accomplished pen was ever set to paper than that of Honourable Francis Lawley [the writer stated]. He never touched a page that he did not adorn, and in all things that he wrote we saw the authority, the scholar and the gentleman. Born to much greater things, it was reserved for him to become the pleasant writer on the sport of the time in which he lived. Disastrous to him as was his connection with the Turf, his heart was as much in it when ... he [recently] backed Flying Fox for the Two Thousand Guineas, as it was when he had his many thousands of pounds on Clincher ... nearly fifty years earlier. . . .

He was [as a young man], sometimes more than the mere handsome, pleasant, dashing, man about town. He had taken high honours at Oxford, where he was at Balliol with his life-long friend, the late Duke of Westminister, with whom he was associated in his early school-boy days at Hatfield. He was a fellow of All Souls and, on being returned Member of Parliament for Beverly soon after he became of age, he seemed destined for political distinction on being appointed private secretary to Mr. Gladstone. . . .

In May, 1865 Lawley returned to England after passing nine years almost without intermission in the United States of America. It was during the latter part of his period that he was correspondent for The Times with the Confederate forces, and better newspaper work was never accomplished.

[He was] a handsome, intellectual, aristocratic and refined man. . . . His great power and charm lay in the fact that he was well behind the scenes in connection with much that he described. In this he had a great advantage over most of his contemporaries. He was a voluminous letterwriter, and a great reader. His letters, in fact, had almost the appearance of having been written with a view to publication. His writings never wearied the reader, but on the other hand left a regret that the chapter had come to an end. Now that the book is closed we pay our tribute to the memory of the man who, to use his favourite quotation, is forever 'blotted from the things that be.'

And then, at last, this appealing paragraph on behalf of the widow of the man who through his writings had meant so much to so many readers for so many years.

We understand that some of Mr. Lawley's friends are taking steps to try and obtain for his widow a grant from the Civil List, and the pleasure afforded by his voluminous writings to a vast number of readers more than justify this endeavour, which we sincerely hope may prove successful. Mrs. Lawley, as we learn with regrets, is in extremely poor circumstances, and such assistance would be a fitting recognition of the wide popularity and affectionate esteem in which her late husband was held.

THE TRUE END OF KNOWLEDGE

Saturday Review, New York City, June 8, 1957.

Last year you and I, progressive Americans all, consumed 45 million aspirin tablets daily. Each night we swallowed 20 million sleeping pills, the next morning chasing them with as many million "wake-up" pills. American doctors will this year write nearly 40 million prescriptions for the new anti-worry pills, called "tranquilizers," hoping to stave off the anxiety, depression, and fear that hamstrings our modern living. Juvenile delinquency is a common topic over our teacups. Seventy-five million Americans are chronic drinkers and 5 million of these are confirmed alcoholics.

Such is the price of our sagacity: one out of every two hospital beds in America is occupied by a mental patient; one out of every ten children born suffers a mental illness. Today the hallmarks of our civilization are stomach ulcers and heart attacks. Slowly but surely in our land of bounty we are driving ourselves to a sort of prosperous desperation. Like modern Frankensteins we are being devoured by our own alchemies, and many of us find ourselves American aliens, mentally and spiritually displaced in our own native land.

However did we come to believe that we could manufacture happiness out of steel and synthetics and bring peace and good will to earth by splitting an atom?

It is trite but true that our generation has made greater technological advances than all our ancestors combined since time began. We have indeed turned natural resources into heretofore undreamt-of power, power to send planes around the world without refueling, power to place perpetual-motion machines in outer space, power to blast mankind from the face of the earth forevermore. Yet, withal, we know we have failed to tap the greatest resource of all, the power of the human being for mutual understanding and respect, one for another, his benign ability to settle his difficulties and differences in peace. And until we do learn in lowliness of mind to esteem another as equal or better than ourselves, violence shall not cease to be heard in the world, nor wasting, nor destruction.

Perhaps our fault lies in our trusting nothing we cannot see or hear or feel—for we are opportunists, most of us. But the problem goes deeper. We have somehow taught ourselves that might makes right, that superiority is virtuous, that wisdom is found in gold and onyx and sapphires and topaz.

I am a librarian. There is prevalent opinion which holds that librarianship is a sort of Casper Milquetoast profession, and that our stock-in-trade—namely, the book—is an ineffectual artifact which serves primarily to collect dust on musty, dim-lit shelves. Therefore, the book is of no practical importance, we hear, for the busy, hard-driving man of the world.

But let me state that throughout all history man's recorded word has been more powerful than his most diabolical machines. And books —instead of being lifeless, static things—have been man's most dynamic, most explosive force in the world. No other has had so powerful an impact upon humanity, anywhere, anytime. If you doubt this, remember "The Prince," remember "Das Kapital," remember "Mein Kampf" and "Uncle Tom's Cabin," and remember the New Testament.

While I can do no more in this space than express a solitary opinion, I am convinced that the world we have made for ourselves is scheduled for sadder days unless we learn to capitalize on man's innate goodness and somehow to sponsor his eternal yearning for peace and lovingkindness, one for another. The deep, deep reservoir of the human spirit, powerful and everlasting, yet remains to be utilized for the preservation of all that mankind—in his sanest moments—really believes in and cherishes. I would address one general admonition to us all: consider the true end of knowledge—seek it not for pleasure or profit, not for prowess or power, but only for the benefit and betterment of mankind.

Librarians, teachers, preachers, statesmen, writers, and others have the vast advantage of communication. And we have easy access to the materials which man most needs to direct or re-direct his destiny and to strengthen his armor, intellectual, cultural, and spiritual. However, man and the materials so necessary to his beneficence do not just happily fall together, by chance. They must be brought together—and in my humble opinion this very act of bringing them together is the principal role of the librarian of the future. If our era is one of tragedy, terror, and maddening tension, it is also one of tremendous opportunity and unbounded challenge. The future promises even greater opportunity, even vaster challenge.

Up to now the library profession has put great stress upon acquiring materials and upon organizing them for their smooth flow into the hands of our patrons. But the time has come, or so it seems to me, for us to realize that these practices, however, important, are but means to an end. The end itself, we must know, is wisely interpreting these materials for the hosts of men, women, and children of all walks of life, who now more than ever come within our care, providing them proper guidance to the vast store of recorded knowledge which is our rightful province. Surely, our success in helping them survive their many ordeals, in making them better citizens of a world we

[202]

must all inhabit—whether we like it or not—may be measured in terms of our ability to translate into dynamic force the best that has been thought and said in the past and found only in our workshops. Therein lies the real, the only solid foundation for "The Library and Its Future."

ALABAMA'S WORLD WAR II
PRISONER OF WAR CAMPS

The Alabama Review, Alabama Historical Association, University of Alabama and Auburn University, April, 1967.

In early 1942 the United States War Department published a manual, *Civilian Enemy Aliens and Prisoners of War,* setting forth its basic policies for handling enemy personnel captured in World War II. The document largely paraphrased the permissive provisions which had been adopted jointly by the Geneva Prisoner of War Convention and the International Red Cross Convention in 1929. Included were regulations governing types and hours of work, rates of pay, rest periods, and other pertinent factors concerning the utilization and welfare of prisoners. Shortly after the publication of the manual, and following a reorganization of the United States Army, all prisoner of war operations were placed under the Office of Provost Marshal General (OPMG) which reported to the Chief of Staff of the Army Service Forces. An Assistant Provost Marshal was directly responsible for the administrative supervision of the Prisoner of War Division.

Meantime, as plans were formed for the immediate transfer to the United States of the first contingent of an estimated fifty thousand German prisoners from over-crowded camps in Great Britain, a nation-wide "Authorized Internment Camp Construction Program" was hastily inaugurated. The majority of these earlier camps were located in the Southwest (Eighth Service Command) in facilities which had earlier been built to house enemy aliens, but as the number of incoming prisoners slowly increased, all sorts of sites on military installations and emergency housing were temporarily used as construction of new PW camps were rushed to completion. By the end of 1942 thirty-three camps (ten of which were described as "temporary") with a capacity of 72,218 prisoners, were either completed or nearly completed. Of these, eleven were in the Southeast (Fourth Service Command): two each in Tennessee (Forrest and Crossville), Mississippi (Como and Shelby), and Louisiana (Livingston and Rushton), and one each in Georgia (Oglethorpe), Arkansas (Monticello), Florida (Blanding), North Carolina (Braggs), and Alabama.

Alabama's first prisoner of war camp was built two miles west of the center of the town of Aliceville (Pickens County) on land purchased by the Unites States Government from Dr. S. R. and Nannie S. Parker for an estimated sum of $29,295. Although rumors of the possible establishment of an "alien concentration camp" in the vicinity had been prevalent for several weeks, not until September 24, 1942 was the weekly *Pickens County Herald and West Alabamian,* published in Carrollton, the county seat, able to release the news:

> For more than six weeks several groups of engineers have been busy in or near Aliceville in surveying a large acreage of farm land, but no information was given out from any source till the last few days. It is definitely understood now that the project will be an alien concentration camp.... No idea as to the number to be located has been advanced, but the survey covers practically four hundred acres of the best farm land in the county.
>
> Such institutions are made to be self supporting, and all the land will be drained, stumps removed, and put in the best possible condition for intensive cultivation. Most of the land located in the project belongs to Dr. Parker and his wife and son, and includes the dairy farm operated by young Thomas Parker. The dairy has just been completed with new barns, tenant houses, pastures, and other improvement, and will upset Mr. Parker's plans for a big dairy farm. Much of the land has produced from one to one and a half bales of cotton each year for several years.
>
> The engineer to be in charge of construction will arrive soon and work will begin at an early date.

Within a month the contracting firm of Algernon Blair of Montgomery, under the supervision of Major Karl H. Shriver, Corps of Engineers, United States Army, had the Aliceville PW Camp well in progress. To the people of the town and surrounding area the impact of the construction was tremendous. According to the *Pickens County Herald,* October 22, 29, $75,000 a week was being "turned loose" in the community, "giving complete employment to all skilled labor ... and unskilled labor has shared much of the work at good wages." Farmers were selling their products at the highest prices and boarding and rooming houses in Aliceville and Carrollton (ten miles distant) were filled to overflowing.

> Farmers with fat calves and pigs are getting Western prices for native beef and pork, and eggs have jumped to 45¢ a dozen, and not half enough of them.... Every citizen of the county will prosper directly or indirectly by the construction of the camp.... After the camp has been completed, there will be eight or nine hundred guards, and most of them will spend their money in Aliceville. The people of Aliceville are fortunate to have such a large pay roll. Business is bound to thrive, and Aliceville will double its population before the next Federal census.

Construction of the Aliceville camp was completed ahead of schedule and activated on December 12, 1942. According to Major Shriver, it consisted of "400 frame, one story buildings, capable of housing 6,000 prisoners and 900 soldier guards." Also provided were several large mess halls, recreation areas, a hospital, a theatre, and many other miscellaneous buildings. Ample heat, water and toilet facilities were installed.

At first it was widely reported that the Aliceville compound would imprison "six thousand or more Japanese" and there was some concern in the vicinity as to the safety of the local citizens who "would be sitting on a powder keg," but fears vanished as week after week passed and no prisoners of any nationality arrived to occupy the new installations. Indeed, the expected large and immediate influx of enemy prisoners of war into the United States did not anywhere materialize, as had been expected, and it was not until June 2, 1943 that the first contingent—"three train loads of about one thousand Germans" arrived in Aliceville via the Frisco Railway which paralleled the camp along Highway 17. Virtually everybody in the vicinity lined the tracks to see the remarkable sight. The editor of the *Pickens County Herald*, on hand to describe the occasion, wrote the next day:

> The majority of the prisoners are very young, many look to be not over 16 years of age. There were tired but not sullen. There was a homesick look on the faces of many; but the majority were smiling and singing. There was a wave of sympathy that swept over the local citizens when they saw the age of the prisoners. . . . [But] they probably sat down to the best meal last night they have had in years.

Emmy Peebles Hildreth, special correspondent of the Birmingham *Age-Herald*, described the arrival of the "3,000 members of the famous Africa Corps" in these words, on June 10:

> After months of waiting, the splendidly built and equipped internment camp in Aliceville is at last occupied. . . . Suspense and excitement seethed through the town when the rumor spread that two train loads of the German Africa Corps would arrive at 4:45 p.m. on the Frisco. . . .
>
> I was disappointed with the appearance of the super-race. . . . About six looked above the average and not very 'super' at that. . . . They were mostly very young about 22, but some looked 17. A few older ones, officers maybe, looked hardened and serious. . . . All carried bundles of some kind. . . . One had what looked like golf sticks in a case, but it might have been a musical instrument. A jolly-looking one had a checker board in his hand, another carried a leather brief case. Their shoes were heavy. One was barefoot. . . .
>
> The spectators were quiet, watching and respectful. One lady said she didn't see how the prisoners could be so well behaved. She was reminded that they were looking down too many gun barrels to misbehave. . . . The Red Cross ambulance was there also. The barefoot prisoner was marched back to the ambulance and given a ride to the camp. Two of the prisoners had bandages on their heads. . . .
>
> Soon the Red Cross will notify the mothers where their boys are—safe in America—the land of the free and the land of plenty. Journey's end for them—in a clean, well-built, well-managed camp, away from all danger. Lucky, lucky prisoners, I think.

Another reporter for the *Age-Herald,* also in Aliceville for the momentous occasion, stated in the same paper, that the Germans gazed "in open-mouthed surprise" as they learned that the United States had not been "practically devastated by German bombs." The prisoners, "mostly boys in their 'teens," had been told that "this country had been blown to bits. They said they were surprised to see the Statue of Liberty still standing."

> Restrictions prevent a newspaper man from interviewing the prisoners [he continued], but from the smiles on the faces of these conquered soldiers, their expressions are self-explanatory. Words could add little to the comfort they are now enjoying, 4,000 miles from where the Allied forces are striking at the Axis back door.... As it is, though, these men will enjoy comparatively comfortable living conditions amongst peaceful surroundings for the duration. They will be joined by some of their comrades later. The cantonment here is prepared to handle two or three times the present number of 'guests'.

Three days later, on June 13, Jack House, a staff writer from the same paper, devoted column after column, including several hand drawings, to life in the Aliceville PW Camp. The Nazis, he wrote, "are obedient and happy ... and, soberly subdued by a superior foe," and are "now willing and anxious to help make this a better world in which to live." The Nazis received "fair and just treatment, better than one might expect, considering they are prisoners of war," the reporter continued.

> For instance, they still are permitted to carry on with many of their own customs. They still use the Nazi salute when addressing American officers. They are given the same privileges inside the compound (the fenced area) they could expect to have in one of their own camps. Many of them continue to wear the same battered and tattered clothes they wore when Tunisia fell little more than a month ago.... They have their work shops. They cook their own meals, getting the same kind and amount of food that the Americans get. They are allowed to write two letters and one card a week.... [Even though] all of the men are listed as Germans, actually they are a combination of nationalities—Germans, Rumanians, Bulgars, Hungarians, and a few, not many, Italians.... The German soldier is a perfect example of condition, despite the fact that he definitely isn't the superman his masters would have him be.

Later in June hundreds more Germans arrived at Aliceville, many seriously wounded. One man, it was reported, died the day after his arrival and was buried in a little cemetery adjoining the camp. By August the camp had taken on a "homelike" look, according to Henry C. Flynn, a syndicated columnist, whose description appeared in the Birmingham *Catholic Week*, August 20, 1943:

> There are men here who fought throughout the North African campaign, at Stalingrad, in the Balkans, in Norway and Dunkerque. Theirs are young faces, mostly, but they are tired young faces....
> They work regularly, at assigned tasks for which they are paid ... and in their free time they work voluntarily within their compounds. They have their own organizations and their own non-commissioned

officers direct their work, such as land-scaping, policing their streets, extending sanitary facilities, repairs.

They have formed song groups; they are exceptionally proficient at gymnastics, and they seem to take high interest in amateur theatricals.... A mild description of their games on the athletic field would employ the word strenuous. They really play for keeps and the one aim is to win, and little matter how.

Throughout the remainder of 1943 and into 1944 and 1945 prisoners continued to pour into the Aliceville compound in increasing numbers. On June 29, 1944, for example, 450 arrived from the battlefields of Europe, via Boston, "most of them very young men, some as young as 15 years," and many wounded. As of June 1, 1945 there were 3,485 prisoners, almost all Germans, within the military compound. The Aliceville camp was deactivated on September 30, 1945.

Generally speaking, the Nazis accepted imprisonment stoically. Many tried to escape. For instance, according to the Birmingham *Age-Herald*, August 27, 1943, two Nazi privates who tried to flee the Aliceville camp were killed instantly by the guards. On March 28, 1945 the same paper reported that two others had escaped from Aliceville and, in spite of efforts of the Federal Bureau of Investigation, were still at large. At other prison camps throughout the state the story was the same—but attempts always failed.

Incidentally, all accounts agree that the prisoners could be easily identified by their uniforms which consisted of blue denim trousers and shirt, with a large yellow PW stenciled across the back, and brown shoes.

Following the establishment of the Aliceville camp in the fall of 1942, the United States Government rapidly acquired land for the second basic prison site within the State of Alabama. It was situated near the southern limits of the City of Opelika (Lee County) on Highway 37, in the center of a 50-mile triangle formed by West Point and Columbus, Georgia and Tuskegee, Alabama. The scantily populated area of 840 acres (only fifty-five persons in seven families lived there) was acquired from A. M. Williamson, H. L. Hall, W. S. Collins, and F. J. Whatley, all of Opelika. The contracting firm of Smith, Yetter & Company of West Palm Beach, Florida began work in September, 1942 and in approximately six months—that is, by February 1, 1943—had virtually completed the job, despite annoying delays caused by labor shortages and a litigation over the removal of electric power lines owned by the Alabama Power Company and the City of Opelika. Designed to accommodate 3,000 or more men, Opelika PW Camp was activated on December 12 at a cost of $58,600, plus $18,000 for razing and clearing, and $5,000 annual property lease. The first contingent of "hundreds of Germans" arrived from North Africa via Boston during the first week of June, 1943, as Opelikans filled the streets to watch the excitement. Reporters from the Opelika *Daily News* talked to several of the prisoners who told them that their Nazi leaders had told them that the Japanese Navy had long ago destroyed New York City and the Unites States Navy. Most of all, the writers added, the Germans asked for cigarettes and chocolates. By June 1, 1945 2,772 men were imprisoned at Camp Opelika. Of these the majority were Germans, although there were a few Arab deserters from the French Foreign Legion who had, perhaps under pressure, joined the German Army. The Opelika PW Camp was officially closed on December 8, 1945.

The third camp established in Alabama was in conjunction with Fort McClellan, near Anniston (Calhoun County), a United States Army infantry post which had been in operation since 1917. It was activated on May 1, 1943 and closed three years later, on April 10, 1946. According to the Anniston *Star*, July 6, 1943, the first 2,000 "Axis prisoners" arrived in late June—"but no information about them could be released" to the news media. When questioned, the camp commander denied any knowledge of "just what the prisoners will do." By June, 1945 2,758 Germans were confined there, more than half of whom were non-commissioned officers. In October of the same year the total was 3,058—six officers, 1,672 non-commissioned officers, and 1,380 enlisted men.

A Washington *Post* correspondent, after visiting McClellan PW Camp, wrote on April 15, 1944 that it was "our largest and best," but that he and other newsmen could "feel the sneers of the prisoners as they passed through the place."

> They seemed cocky [he continued], even about their capture. Their attitude is reflected in the German legend which they put around a huge sun-dial they have built. It says, 'For us the sun never goes under. . . .' For the most part they are service troops, Nazi officers [having] evacuated their front line fighters first when they retreated, leaving the more easily replaced service force behind. They are goodlooking soldiers, but most of them are rather short. Nearly all carry that Aryan superiority look, which they were taught by the Hitlerites. . . .

The Montgomery *Advertiser*, March 11, 1945, described the McClellan prisoners as greatly depressed by the turn of the war, but still persisting that Germany was superior to all the world. Some of the prisoners, the older ones, had been "occupation troops" in France. "They were in excellent health, well-fed, and had bright, shiny uniforms." By contrast, the younger men, those who had been through the "bitter campaign" in France, Belgium, and inside Germany, were "bedraggled and worn"—and there was "some contention between the two groups, with the men who had seen action suspecting that those from Southern France had been rather agreeable to capture." On one occasion, however, in 1944 the "agreeable" McClellan prisoners

[208]

refused to work, when their request for certain special concessions was denied. "After two days of bread and water diet" for thus striking, however, all of them quietly returned to their respective tasks.

The fourth basic prisoner of war camp in Alabama was incorporated into the 65,000-acre Camp Rucker, in Dale and Coffee counties, midway between the towns of Ozark and Enterprise, which had itself been newly-created in April, 1942. The first contingent of "several hundred prisoners of war and a company of military police" arrived February 28, 1944, "bringing to life a small prison camp erected with all possible speed during the past two weeks." As of June 1, 1945 Camp Rucker held 1,718 prisoners. They were widely used in Southeast Alabama as farm and lumber labor until the camp was deactivated on March 31, 1946.

In addition to the four "base camps" at Aliceville, Opelika, McClellan, and Rucker, there were twenty so-called side camps, branch camps or labor camps, within Alabama. Obviously, these side camps were created for immediate, particular purposes and were often short-lived. In several instances they were merely tent-towns, hastily thrown up to meet an emergency need, such as harvesting peanuts or cotton, cutting timber, or preparing ground for sowing and planting. For example, 500 Germans from Camp Opelika were sent more than two hundred miles into the vicinity of Albany and Valdosta, Georgia in the fall of 1944 to pick cotton, gather peanuts, and drain resin. They were quartered in barracks of an old Civilian Conservation Corps and in "standard American army tents." Prisoners from Aliceville, stationed in a side camp at nearby Tuscaloosa were put to work in the kitchens and laundries of Northington General Hospital.

PW SIDE CAMPS IN ALABAMA

Place	Base Camp	Dates	No. Prisoners June 1, 1945
Abbeville	Rucker	8-30-45 to 10-2-45	
Andalusia	Shelby	8-30-45 to 10-22-45	
Chatom	Shelby	? to 12-15-45	247
Clanton	McClellan	? to 9-10-45	224
Clio		9-10-45 to 10-22-45	
Dothan		8-27-45 to 10-29-45	
Dublin		5-24-44 to 6-22-44	
Elba		8-30-45 to 10-2-45	
Evergreen		11-8-44 to 5-10-45	
Foley	Rucker	4-22-45 to 12-8-45	298

Place	Base Camp	Dates	No. Prisoners June 1, 1945
Geneva		8-30-45 to 11-17-45	
Greenville	Rucker	2-23-44 to 11-30-45	230
Huntsville	Forrest	11-1-44 to 3-7-46	655
Jackson	Shelby	4-6-45 to 3-12-46	253
Loxley	Shelby	? to 10-22-45	410
Luverne		8-25-45 to 2-10-46	
Montgomery	Rucker	8-15-44 to 12-8-45	248
Sibert (near Gadsden)	McClellan	? to 12-8-45(?)	379
Troy		9-10-45 to 11-5-45	
Tuscaloosa (Northington Hospital)	Aliceville	6-1-45 to 3-20-46	

They were housed in temporary wooden buildings, enclosed within barbed-wire fences, bordering on Fifteenth Street near the property now occupied by Shelton State Technical Institute. Aliceville prisoners were also transported to Dothan, Alabama (under a heavy guard of Japanese and Hawaiian volunteers from Camp Shelby, Mississippi) to gather peanuts.

It was also legal and customary for prisoners of war to be assigned under contract to private employers for certain types of non-military work, provided they were paid the prescribed wage rates, kept under strict surveillance, properly fed and clothed, and transported to and from the camps to their jobs. As a rule, however, PW labor proved only fairly satisfactory. For instance, according to the *Pickens County Herald*, September 9, 1943, fifty-three truck loads of Germans from Aliceville were transferred to peanut harvesting because they had proved to be so incompetent at picking cotton.

> [The] farmers say they are very poor help, and not worth the trouble to provide for their transportation [stated the paper]. But few could pick a hundred pounds in a day, and many not more than 50 pounds, where an ordinary negro could pick 200 pounds and not half try....

On the contrary, according to the Birmingham *News*, November 21, 1943, farmers in Oneonta, Alabama once petitioned the authorities for prisoner of war labor to replace the 3,500 men who had left the county for military service or defense work.

Personal welfare and morale of the prisoners of war were of great concern to the responsible authorities and countless efforts were made by both military and civilian agencies, particularly the American Red

Cross, the Young Men's Christian Association, and the Salvation Army, in agreement with the Geneva Convention, to assure the desired esprit de corps. Frequent inspections by officers of the Special Projects Division (SPD) of the Personnel Security Division (PSD) of OPMG were routine, each of which was followed up by a detailed written report on virtually every phase of camp life: clothing, physical plant, educational facilities (libraries, lectures, formal instruction), indoor recreation (motion pictures, workshops, chess, music, cards, pingpong, theatrical performances, etc.), outdoor recreation (badminton, soccer, football, gardening, sign painting, etc.), religious activities (Protestant and Roman Catholic), and many miscellaneous projects described as "Intellectual Diversion Programs." Special civilian agents, often religious, were also assigned the responsibility of visiting the camps regularly and advising SPD of needed improvements, as for example, did Rev. Otto Kothbackeberger on his visit to Camp Opelika, May 21–23, 1945:

Immediately on my arrival at Camp Opelika, I was introduced to the Commanding Officer.... He received us most hospitably and arranged that same evening I might visit for an hour with the pastor in the camp.

In the camp is an evangelical chaplain, Altpreussische [?] Union, Breslauer Kendestorius. A Catholic prisoner of war chaplain also serves the camp. No theological students are registered.

Spiritual Camp Survey. The spokesman is an intelligent and approachable man but without sympathy for religious life. The pastor himself is a young man, without wide experience, and his position is correspondingly difficult. Half of the prisoners of war are Catholic, half Protestant.

Church services are held every Sunday at 9 o'clock, the participants numbering about 80 to 100; Sunday afternoon, Bible studies, dealing with the Epistle to the Hebrews; Monday evenings, lectures on questions concerning the Christian religion; Thursday evenings, Bible class. A barrack has been furnished for the church services and is used by both confessions.

Equipment needed. A communion set. (Until now the Post Chaplain had kindly put his own set at the disposal of the prisoners of war.) 30 Bibles in German; Bible concordance; Greek dictionary for the New Testament; 'Einleitung in de bibl. Schriften,' 'Ethik', 'Seelsorge' (Brunner, Asmussen); history of the YMCA. For the church choir, music paper and composition books; good church music. 50 copies of the 'Kirchesboten.' Service order. There is no definite service order. The congregation has a church choir of fifteen members. No students of theology are registered. The United States Army Chaplain who had previously served the camp was recently transferred to Camp Benning. He still pays weekly visits to the camp, however.

Edouard J. Patte, another civilian agent, visited Camp Rucker in January, 1945 and again in the following May. His reports indicated that the camp chaplain was a Roman Catholic priest who was a "scholar and an excellent preacher," well qualified to conduct Bible study classes and prayer meetings.

[211]

I was impressed by the work of the Pastor [Patte wrote] and the response he is getting from the POW's. At an evening of old German music in the chapel I thought I was at the 'Salzburg Mozart Annual Festival.' The chapel was lit by thirty-six candles surrounding the string quartet; Mozart, Haydn, Bach were played in the finest style, while hundreds of men in uniform, in a complete silence, eyes half closed, were literally breathing the beautiful music, in a setting which was utterly devoid of camp life reminiscences.

Of particular interest in the United States Armed Forces was the education of prisoners of war. Great effort was devoted to the establishment of camp libraries, study groups, and formal instruction. Classes were offered at Camp Opelika and at Camp Rucker in English, Latin, French, German, Spanish, science, mathematics, physics, chemistry, geography, biology, shorthand, and law, taught either by selected prisoners or by instructors from Alabama Polytechnic Institute. Similar teaching programs were operated at Camp McClellan and at Camp Aliceville, sponsored by the University of Alabama. At McClellan instruction in English, history, and other subjects was well received and the attendance at classes "extraordinarily high." In December, 1945 Colonel George C. Neilson, the commanding officer, conducted "graduation exercises" for "a large group of prisoners of war" who had excelled in "English for advanced students."

Captain Myrvin G. Clark's report on the "educational classes" conducted at Camp Opelika "as a part of the Intellectual Diversion Program of the Special Projects Division for the time period of 15 January 1945 to 15 April 1945" states that 1,407 German prisoner-students received "graduation certificates" there. The classes in architecture, auto-mechanics, biology, bookkeeping, chemistry, commercial science, English, French, geography, geometry, German (both language and literature), history, Latin, mathematics, physics, and shorthand met a total of 1,885 times, all taught by the prisoners themselves, mostly by sergeants, technical sergeants, and master sergeants. According to the reporter, these instructors were "carefully selected" and as a result the program was "progressing with enthusiasm amongst the Prisoners of War."

At Camp McClellan a similar program met with less success, in the estimation of Inspector Edouard J. Patte. On February 23, 1945 less than one hundred students were enrolled in eight subject-classes. "The school is not prospering," he wrote on May 1–4 of the same year, but sports were "exceedingly popular":

...a championship tournament has been organized, with 300 contestants, in handball, 120 in faustball, 66 in ping pong, 70 in tennis, 45 in boxing and 42 in light athletics. The uniforms for the teams were made out of onion sacks, dyed in various colors, and tailored in camp.

Church activities are well attended, with Sunday and weekday services, which I attended. I was much impressed by the sense of devotion.

[212]

The camp is one of the most attractive bases in the U.S.A. The new German set-up seems to be eager to cooperate, and the Assistant Executive Officer has won confidence.

However, eight months later, on October 4–5, 1945, Captain Alexander Lake of OPMG, after a tour of inspection, found the situation at McClellan quite different and urged immediate action to "correct the deficiencies" there. He recommended that classes be commenced as soon as possible in American history, civics, and commercial geography, that 16mm. educational and visual aid films for prisoners of war "be shown at regular intervals," that "more musical recordings by American composers . . . be obtained," and that "loud-speaking equipment for the public address system be obtained so that daily news broadcasts, lecturers in American history, civics, and allied subjects can be presented daily to all prisoners of war in the compound." Immediately, the commanding officer of Camp McClellan notified SPD (OPMG) that the "recommendations set forth . . . will be complied with as limited facilities and funds will permit."

Closely allied with the formal educational program in all the PW camps were libraries and reading rooms. At Camp Sibert, a side camp of McClellan, eight miles southeast of the City of Gadsden, there were 500 volumes in the library on February 5, 1945—approximately 60 percent of which were in "constant circulation." Newspapers and magazines were in adequate supply. As a further move, the inspector, Captain William F. Raugust, recommended that "some of the better books in the Modern Library, Pocketbook Editions, and Infantry Journal-Penguin Series be placed in the canteen." At Camp Rucker, which in March, 1945 held approximately two thousand prisoners, the library contained only "850 volumes, mainly purchased from prisoner of war funds" and was in need of chairs and tables. There was a small collection of phonograph records and plans were made for establishing a "book repair project." By May of the same year the library had grown to 2,000 books. Opelika's library in April, 1944 numbered 45,000 volumes and was "completely equipped," according to M. Peter, an inspector for Red Cross International, who was obviously in error (perhaps he meant 450) because Edouard J. Patte reported in January, 1945 that there were only 600 books at Opelika, "divided between the three compounds" of the camp. In April, 1945 a list of books in that library was prepared and an "organized method of censoring inaugurated." All incoming books were examined ("without attracting the attention of the Prisoners of War") and, at one time, forty-seven were removed from the library as being on "the disapproved list of 'Authors and Books'" (again "without attracting the attention of the Prisoners of War to the action taken").

Creative work of various sorts was encouraged among prisoners of war in all American camps and indications are that the overall program was eminently successful. Amateur theatrical performances were popular, as were musicales, orchestras, painting, wood-carving, writing, publishing, and sculpture. Among the most interesting activities was the publication of camp newspapers, only a few copies of which are known to have survived. At Camp McClellan *Die Oase*, an 18-page, 8½″ x 11″ sheet was issued every two weeks, edited by PW Paul Metzner. It contained articles, stories, poetry, and "camp reports." On April 1, 1945 the military authorities described the paper as "poor" in make-up and content, "militantly Nazi" in political attitude and "very dangerous." No copy of *Oase* is known to have been preserved, but an idea of its contents may be gleaned from the remainder of the (unsigned) official report:

> The camp newspaper Oase consists of average articles of average quality: (Sports, recreation, novels, cartoons). The articles of general contents touch PW-care, the daily life of the prisoners and criticisms of performances within the camp. —A very active sporting life in the camp is revealed by abundant information concerning sports. A page with mixed contents and cartoons as well as short novels and humorous articles. The section 'Novels and Science' has scientific articles and answers to correspondents. The novels are taken from German authors, being well known in Germany, and approved by Nazi authorities.
> Very dangerous paper!

A weekly newspaper, *Der Zaungast*, was begun in early 1945 by the prisoners in Camp Aliceville. Two issues of this paper are extant, Numbers 22 and 26 (May 20, June 17). The masthead states: "Zeitschrift des Kriegsgefangenenlagers Aliceville, Ala." Neatly printed on 8½″ x 11″ sheets, *Der Zaungast* contains poetry, essays, humor, sports, several cartoons and other drawings, and a calendar of "Die Kulturellen Veranstaetungen der Woche." The issue of May 20 carries a lead article entitled "Ewige Mutterschaft" and a poem,"Mutter" (Mother's Day was May 13 in 1945). The front page of the June 17 issue is devoted to a reproduction of a wood-carving and an article called "Begegnung im Dschebel Aures." *Die Bruecke* was the name of one PW paper issued at Camp Opelika, followed by a second called *Der Querschnitt*, a 24-page news magazine, of which four issues in 1945 have survived. Fourteen issues of *Das PW Echo*, published at Camp Rucher in 1945–1946, are now available.

As has been indicated, strict surveillance of PW newspapers was of necessity maintained in all camps. This censorship often led to segregation of prisoners. For example, in February, 1945 at Camp Sibert the prison inspector recommended "that complete files be kept on those prisoners of war who are likely to interfere with the Intellectual Diversion Program." Notes were filed on individuals observed to be "organizers" or advocates of political trend. At Camp McClellan the commanding officer in February, 1945 requested Captain Walter

H. Rapp, the military inspector from OPMG, to interrogate six Austrian prisoners who claimed to be anti-Nazi.

> As a result of this interrogation [the inspector's report continues] Captain Rapp recommended to the camp commander that these six prisoners of war be immediately segregated from the rest of the prisoners of war population and that service command headquarters be requested to transfer these prisoners without delay to an anti-Nazi camp. Their personal safety seems to be in constant jeopardy because of the presence of three S. S. and Gestapo prisoners and it is recommended to the camp commander to request the service command headquarters to immediately transfer these prisoners of war to Alva, Oklahoma.

Moreover, the commander was reprimanded for lack of knowledge "about the latest segregation directives and policies" and ordered to "study them and comply with their contents."

Inspection of mail received by individual prisoners also gave the military an insight into their attitudes. For instance, 44-year-old Obersoldat Paul Metzner, the aforementioned editor of McClellan's *Oase*, was carefully eyed. A former high school teacher in Berlin, he apparently wielded considerable influence among his fellow prisoners. In February, 1945 he received mail, including a money order, from Ernest Metzner of Philadelphia, Pennsylvania—a fact duly noted in the local and national records. Indeed, in many instances recalcitrant German prisoners evidencing strong Nazi influences on their colleagues were transferred to Camp Alva (Oklahoma) or to Camp Aliceville. Carefully screened, these prisoners were classified as "segregated." On May 16, 1945 the Birmingham *Age-Herald* emphasized the "toughness" of the Germans at Aliceville, adding, however, that the commanding officers had boasted that they could "take them as tough as they come."

> When they go inside the wire at Aliceville, they say goodbye to privileges earned by prisoners who work at Army camps or on private contract for 80 cents a day in canteen coupons.... [They] get only 10 cents a day.... Many of the non-commissioned prisoners have been 'busted back' to privates because they could not furnish satisfactory credentials showing they were noncoms. Only a few score are permitted outside the [compound] were to bring supplies into the camp or work for the engineers.

As has been suggested, perhaps the best remaining accounts of World War II prisoner of war camps in Alabama (as elsewhere) are those written on the spot by the official Y.M.C.A., Salvation Army, International Red Cross, or church-affiliated inspectors. Few, indeed, of these reports have been preserved. In Alabama those of Edouard J. Patte, Otto Kothbackeberger, and Karl Gustof Almquist are most fruitful. Patte was a Y.M.C.A. agent and, as can best be determined by internal evidence, Kothbackeberger represented the Lutheran Church. Almquist was an inspector for both the Y.M.C.A. and the Ecumenical

Commission. All were most probably ministers or, certainly, churchmen of one kind or another.

Patte apparently roamed from one camp to another, recording as he went. On December 11, 1944, following a snowstorm, he appeared at Camp McClellan. He inspected the barracks which had been set aside as PW art studios "with self-made benches, old canvas frames, tin cans full of red, blue, yellow, and black and white [paint]." Around the walls hung "paintings of European landscapes, of marines, of winter-scenes, of still nature,—cheese, sausages and beer, or glorious bouquets of geraniums." There were also in abundance "portraits of soldiers, of Arabs, of nude women or of a child." But Patte overlooked the quality of the work, believing that in it, however doubtful, the "artists have found . . . the best outlet for their inner force." At McClellan, continued Patte, the University of Alabama "with twenty-five teachers has a one thousand two hundred student enrolment who are taught every conceivable subject." The camp newspaper, *Oase*, which had been issued weekly, was now issued monthly because of a shortage of paper—but, he wisely added, "I do not believe that the *Oase* is of such paramount importance for the camp morale to justify the expense as well as the contribution of a special contingent of paper."

One of the Germans at McClellan, a former circus attendant, had built a little zoo where he housed birds, snakes, alligators, turtles, squirrels, 'possums, and 'coons.

> The POW [wrote Patte] entered a small enclosure, moved a few stones, awoke a beautiful fox and tried with much skill, poise and persuasion, to teach him to obey his voice. It lasted ten minutes, all of them packed with tense interest. First frightened, then sneaky, then calmed, then obedient, at last the captive animal tamed by a captive man learned the lesson; but as soon as the POW had disappeared it certainly forgot it! The circus-man had a smile—or was it a grin—when he said to me: 'Sir, neither man nor animal can ever learn anything when being a captive!'

A year or so later, September 16, December 21–23, 1945, Patte was again at McClellan. This time his interest seems to have been especially directed toward the religious welfare of the prisoners. He attended the Lutheran services and later held conferences with the Roman Catholic priests. The sum of his visits revealed little change in the attitudes of prisoners:

> My meetings with the German pastor, with the Catholic German priest, with a young Dominican and two Lutheran students, was most illuminating [Patte wrote]. The religious life in the camp does not seem to have been greatly affected by the new situation in Germany. There is as much indifference as in the past, and a little bitterness; however, the influence of the Church is not negligible. . . . The students in theology have the possibility, at night, to study under the ministers in charge

and have access at all times, to the Catholic and Protestant library, in the Sacristy of the chapel.

At the end of 1945 McClellan was being deactivated and, according to Patte, "all activities had been stopped." Several of the prisoner-musicians who had belonged to the camp orchestra were still clinging to their instruments, hoping the American authorities would allow them to keep them. As Christmas neared, a prisoner decorated the church altar and the two remaining pastors philosophized for the reporter:

> Seriously they discussed the problem of whether the Church had failed in Germany during the last twelve years under the Nazi regime. Both pastors had suffered greatly during that time. The Lutheran pastor could not obtain any position and was obliged to move from one place to another. The Catholic priest was nearly taken to a concentration camp. It was a rather sad story about inhuman suffering and persecution for the reason only that they were steadfast in their faith. Systematically, the Nazi leaders tried in all ways to break down their courage. However, it always is impossible to fight against the true Christian spirit.

Now, concluded Patte, the men "hoped to found and built a new church at home, to help children, women and men in their great need." But most of all they wanted "the understanding and help from the Christians in America and other countries in this most difficult task." Added Patte: "I was glad to bring them greetings from the Church outside the barbed wire."

Three reports on Camp Rucker in 1945 have survived—one each by Reverend Kothbackeberger (May 14–17), Edouard J. Patte (September 19–21), and Karl Gustof Almquist (December 18–19). Kothbackeberger recorded that the official PW spokesman was "indifferent to the Church," adding, however, that "65 per cent of the prisoners of war are protestant, the rest Catholic." The former were served by only one pastor, an Evangelical, the latter by one priest, a man from the Bishopric of Meissen, Saxony, Prussia. Both worked under the aegis of the post chaplain, Captain Edward Mueller, and the camp military authorities. Kothbackeberger related, as did Patte at Camp McClellan, that several prisoners of war at Camp Rucker were busily studying theology in preparation for the ministry. Inspector Patte, agreeing in general with Kothbackeberger's summary of the conditions in Rucker, added that he was pleased with the new educational program in progress "with classes in English, Democracy and History, and the bi-weekly lectures on democratic ways of living, with the broadcasting of news and good music, and with the sports championship." Almquist, whose report was longer and more detailed than those of Kothbackeberger or Patte, was much impressed with the Nazi prisoners' eager preparations for Christmas:

The spokesman was hurriedly completing arrangements for Christmas in order to make all as nice as possible for his comrades. An important place on the program was given to a gramophone concert over the loud-speaker, the records to consist only of carols.... The pastors showed me the church program and I recognized all the loved hymns which the choirs (the Evangelical and the Catholic) were going to sing. Already the preparation of the programs means a great deal to the prisoners of war. It is strange to observe what power the Advent and the Yuletide have over men. You can see it in the external preparations of the Christmas tree, the Advent-wreaths and other decorations. Nobody could mistake the Christian character of the festival. But neither can anyone judge how far the inner influence will reach. No doubt there will be a great and wide-spread influence upon all in the camp. May that influence last long into the New Year!

Both Patte and Kothbackeberger inspected the Opelika PW Camp in May, 1945, their visits overlapping. The former (May 19–21), besides mentioning the prisoners' sports programs in progress, the 32-piece symphony orchestra, the theatrical club and other recreational activities, was most impressed with "the unique" plan of formal education employed in the camp. *"The school,"* he wrote, *"is managed by an 'advisory council' of German prisoners of war, who organize the examinations and keep the records of 1,200 students. Our [Y.M.C.A.?] publications are widely used by the camp, especially for foreign languages."* (A bold marginal note added "Camp Operations did not like!") Kothbackeberger's report (May 21–23) praised the prisoners' "splendid orchestra" and the theatrical performances which were "of the highest quality," but it consisted largely of an appeal for equipment for the prisoners, half of whom were Protestant, half Roman Catholic:

> ... a communion set. 30 Bibles in German; Bible concordance; Greek dictionary for the New Testament; 'Einleitung in de bibl. Schriften,' 'Ethik,' 'Seelsorge' (Brunner, Asmussen); history of the YMCA. For the church choir—music paper and composition books; good church music. Copies of the 'Kirchesboten'. Service Order.

The ubiquitous Patte paid a short visit to Camp Sibert, a small labor-camp branch of Camp McClellan, on September 15–16, 1945. There he renewed his acquaintance with an unidentified pastor whom he had known at Aliceville the year before. This man's transfer to Sibert with its "extremely limited possibilities for religious life" required of him a "thorough adjustment." At Sibert, in contrast to Aliceville, for instance, "the chapel is outside of the barbed wire, and consequently not accessible to the POWs without special requests." As a result, "the camp population is not vitally interested in religious matters, with the exception of a small group." Patte, greatly distrubed, appealed for an immediate correction of this situation and was assured that "we will try to remedy it, if at all possible." With other

[218]

activities (the educational program, the "very well furnished library," the phonograph-records service, and the "well taken care of" sports routines) Patte was highly pleased.

Three months later, December 17, Almquist also inspected the operations at Sibert, arriving just as "all were very busy moving the camp." Cordially received, he was introduced to the PW spokesman, a highly regarded German school teacher, who escorted him about and answered his questions. Among other things Almquist learned that Sibert, composed mostly of young German boys, had already made a "large donation" to the International Red Cross and had been collecting funds for the Y.M.C.A.

> The Church attendance at Sibert [Almquist recorded] was quite small. The pastor gave as an explanation that the inmates were rather young and were seeking their way in life. Many among them were not more than eighteen years old and had been captured only a few days after they had been inducted into the German Army. [They] were not accustomed to going to church and attending services. All were glad to have a pastor among them, which they demonstrated by looking him up for talks and advice on different matters. To the service came a faithful congregation which seemed to have good influence in the camp.

But Almquist was skeptical. Could the influence of a mere handful of Christians reach far among the larger group of youthful Nazis, heavily indoctrinated since their birth?

> To this an [Evangelical] theological student, gave me an answer. Once after a Bible class which only a few had attended he went through barracks and there his comrades were discussing the subject from the Bible class in a serious way and trying to grasp the meaning and trend of the pastor's teaching. This shows that the influence might be greater than we think or realize. That the Church is there, with its message, and looking for men ready to receive the message, is important and of great value. Faithful and hard work from the side of the pastor can bear fruit. The Evangelical student will contact the World Council of Churches, Geneva, when he is back home someday.

Satisfied, Almquist concluded his report with these hopeful words: "It was a visit to a camp which was closing and probably would move that same night; but it was a visit among men showing a good will to do their best in life."

In general, the accounts concerning the religious attitudes of the prisoners of war vary widely. The Birmingham *Catholic Week*, October 22, 1943, for instance, stated that a survey made at McClellan by a Catholic-Protestant committee revealed "42 per cent as Catholics, 57 per cent as Lutherans or Evangelical." Almost all of the prisoners were described as "definitely religious." A few said they believed in God but had no definite religious affiliation. Not more than ten out of the entire group gave National Socialism as their religion, and about three said they had no religion. On August 15, the Feast of the Assumption, the survey continued, according to Chaplain Robert J. Sherry, 675 men attended Mass and ninety-seven received Holy Communion.

At Camp Opelika the Germans were said to be "religious despite the Nazi culture. The efforts of Adolf Hitler to drive religion from his army were in vain...." Many of the prisoners "not only came into camp with their prayer book and rosaries, but use them in the most conscientious manner." On the contrary, the Germans clung doggedly to their faith in Hitler and the Nazi philosophy. Many were unhappy because they could not return to the battlefields to fight for the Fuehrer. At Opelika, as elsewhere, according to the Birmingham *News*, June 22, 1944, the Germans persisted in greeting American officers with the Nazi salute, shouting "Heil Hitler." And, although in captivity for two years, most of them continued to "bow before the shrine of German militarism." Stated another reporter, Jack House, early in 1945:

> German militarism is buried so deep in the minds of 15,830 German prisoners of war being in Alabama that two years of imprisonment has not fazed them, and this militarism may never wear off, at least not in this generation.
> Visiting the Aliceville cantonment, the writer was amazed to find so trivial a change in the mental attitude of the German prisoners. From all appearances, [they] are as militarily-minded today as they were the day they were interned....

Commenting on the camp itself, the reporter declared that it had changed "greatly... in scenery." The "one-time mudhole... surrounded by swamplands" was now a "well-irrigated and handsomely groomed village of green-painted baracks with green lawns."

> But the change is confined solely to the scenery. The prisoner himself hasn't changed a bit... [He] is polite in 1945—but he was also polite in 1943. He behaves well, as a rule, but he also behaved well, as a rule, in 1943. He is just as conservative on food now, two years later, as he was in 1943, when he scraped every bone and spared as much peeling from every potato as he possibly could....
> The prisoners still use the German Army (not Nazi) salute.... They still click their heels with the gusto of a Prussian general, and still talk their native tongue, although a considerably larger number now speak English....
> Despite good treatment... the prisoners are as much German soldiers now as they were when firing on British and American troops. They have no more love for Americans today than they did when they first came to this strange land.

After World War II and in accordance with the Surplus Property Act (1944), the War Assets Administration disposed of virtually all prisoner of war camp material in Alabama (and elsewhere) on a bid basis, in order of four priorities: United States Government agencies,

Reconstruction Finance Corporation (for resale to small businesses), state and local governments, and non-profit institutions. In Alabama, for example, on February 20, 1947 the Birmingham *Age-Herald* contained a large advertisement describing the sale of thousands of feet of water pipe, electrical equipment, and a telephone communications system which were no longer needed at the deactivated Aliceville PW Camp. Subsequently, the camp lands there were also sold, some to private citizens and others to the City of Aliceville. The Camp Opelika property was in the 1950's converted to industrial development and, of course, the lands once used for holding prisoners at Camp Rucker and Camp McClellan were soon diverted to other military uses by the United States Forces.

Today, less than twenty-five years after the closing of the prisoner of war camps in Alabama, precious little remains to suggest that they ever existed. At Aliceville, for example, where an estimated five thousand men and women—prisoners, administrative officers, enlisted men, guards, nurses, and other personnel—spent the better part of three war-weary years, nothing is left but several crumbling old wooden houses now errily empty or in use as a chicken hatchery, a rusting, leaning water-tower, the potholed and weed-grown paved streets running crazily to nowhere, and the fairly-well-preserved Post Engineers Headquarters building which houses the offices of a commercial firm. Everywhere weeds have grown head high and plum thickets and briar patches abound. Even the recollections of the local citizens are somewhat hazy and fading—the older generation forgetting the details but remembering the whole as a sort of nightmarish dream, the younger largely unaware of and/or oblivious to the history that was so short a while ago quickly made and quickly unmade at their very doorstep. Now and then, it is said in Aliceville, a German who was a prisoner there has returned to see where he once was incarcerated—but he, too, goes on, sadly keeping his bitter memories to himself.

Luckily, however, Aliceville PW Camp will doubtless be remembered better and longer than almost any other camp in the United States. For there in 1944 two German prisoners, Unteroffiziers Hermann Kalbe and Hans Fanselow, both accomplished artists, were given permission to draw fifty pen-and-ink sketches of the commanding officers, panoramas of the camp, close-ups of the buildings, the interiors of the barracks, the chapel, the hospital and many other structures, all beautifully and skillfully completed. This rare book, plus the accounts which appeared in local newspapers—and generously cited in this essay—make up the bulk of extant data on the Aliceville prison.

As for the other prisoner of war camps in Alabama (as well as those in other states) only the scantiest records seem to have been preserved. Nothing apparently remains in the office of the Chief of Military History, Department of the Army, except a short list of the camps by locations and types of work performed by the prisoners (quoted above). A similar list is on file in the Federal Records Center, General Services Administration, Kansas City, Missouri. The Office of the Provost Marshal General has categorically declared that "all records of individual prisoner of war camps during the WWII period have been destroyed. In addition, all WWII records of the OPMG have long since been retired." The Library of Congress, as has been stated, contains a few scattered issues of prisoner of war newspapers published in the camps throughout the United States, including those in Alabama, nothing more. The Alabama State Department of Archives and History has no material whatsoever on the several prison establishments within the state, although its collection of state newspapers is an invaluable aid to local historical research.

THE FACE IN THE WINDOW!

Birmingham [Alabama] *News Monthly Magazine*, August 8, 1954.

After a long and relentless manhunt which ended on a stormy day in March, 1878, Henry Wells, a young Negro, was captured by Sheriff J. P. Gates of Pickens County, Alabama, and imprisoned. Shortly after, he was indicted on four charges—carrying concealed weapons, assult with intent to kill, burglary, and arson.

Eighteen months before, the $20,000 Pickens County Courthouse in Carrollton had been burned to the ground in a midnight fire which destroyed all Circuit Court and Probate records and the official files of the sheriff's office. "The burning was unquestionably the work of an incendiary," the weekly *West Alabamian* reported, Nov. 22, 1876. "It took fire in several places at about the same time."

And Henry Wells, it was charged, was doubtless the fire-bug. Anyway, his unsavory reputation was already established and some citizens, outraged by wanton destruction of public property, were quick to act. They stormed the jail, demanding that Henry Wells be handed over to them for justice. No one doubted the Alabama mob's intentions. Quick-thinking Sheriff Gates slipped the prisoner out of a rear door, however, and before his plot was discovered, he had sneaked Wells across the blustering, rainswept street and locked him up high in the garret of the new courthouse on Carrollton's Public Square.

As soon as the mob realized what had happened, it turned as one man to the new seat of justice, chanting "We want Wells—we want Wells." And the accused, looking down in sweaty horror at the sea of white faces upturned, cried out his innocence. At that precise instant—just as Henry Wells looked down in terror upon his irate fellow-citizens—a sharp, brilliant flash of lightning struck the garret, played for a split second around the window frame, and ran sharply down the walls to its grounding. The crowd recoiled, shading its eyes. Wells was knocked back, unharmed, against the inner wall. And forever left to tell the story of the lightning flash was Wells' face, indelibly, mysteriously photographed on the window pane.

To this day, in spite of weathering and scrubing, Henry Wells' likeness, "photographed by lightning," looks down from the garret window oldtimers claim, in answer to his shouted vow: "I am innocent—my face will always haunt you." Throughout three-quarters of a century the window pane has been replaced many times, but each time the face weirdly reappears to leer at the inhabitants. Indeed, the town of Carrollton has made use of the phenomenon by printing a publicity pamphlet which details the events of "The Face in the Window."

And in the years there have grown up at least a dozen variants of the story, each differing in minor details of crime, time, and names, but each religiously holding to the salient fact that God's lightning lens etched Henry Wells' picture on the window pane. However that may be, it is as right as rain that the face may be clearly, easily seen today by all who look, and best from the very spot where on that stormy night the angry mob gathered in the courtyard.

If you have begun to scoff—hold on for a moment. The phenomenon of photography by lightning is not too impossible or unreal—or IS it?

In 1887 Augusta Evans Wilson, the distinguished Alabama novelist, used lightning photography in the 28th chapter of her best-selling novel, "At the Mercy of Tiberius," to solve the murder of Gen. Darrington by a house thief. As the two men struggled, a "vivid flash of lightning . . . photographed both men, and the interior of the room on the wide glass panel of the door. Forms, faces, features, even the pattern of the cloth coat, are printed plainly there, for the whole world to study." But a New York book reviewer, obviously a very prosaic fellow, poked fun at Mrs. Wilson's "convenient results," saying that she had doubtless been "stirred" by recent discoveries in photography and that she had failed to explain "Who, or what, developed the negative and manipulated the collodion."

Mrs. Wilson was none too pleased with the sneers of the "wise and infallible literary autocrats." In a personal letter to her friend, Sir Norfleet Harris, United States consul at Leeds, England, she stated that before she wrote "At the Mercy of Tiberius" she "carefully investigated electrical phenomena" and collected "four or five well authenticated instances of faces photographed on window panes by flashes of lightning." Several persons, she added, had since written to her "narrating similar experiences with electrical photography." It is difficult to believe that one of America's most popular last-century novelists was not telling her distinguished friend the truth, for this letter in her own handwriting, italics and all, is on file in the University of Alabama Library.

At Chunnennuggee Ridge, near Union Springs, Ala., a similar phenomenon is said to have occurred in the home of Col. Richard H. Powell. Since Augusta Evans Wilson was related to the Powell family and a frequent visitor in their home, it is altogether possible that this incident was one of the "four or five well authenticated instances" known to the novelist. Again the facts in the case were proved by the picture on glass, a glass which has since experienced an interesting history.

Col. Powell, so the Chunnennuggee story goes, was entering the back porch of his home during a thunder storm. A quick but severe bolt of lightning flashed, instantly engraving his profile on the glass door panel. Neither the house nor the man was harmed—yet the face of the Colonel was plainly visible for years afterwards, etched in the glass. Not long ago a member of the family, fascinated by the fantastic photograph, removed the glass and shipped it to his Texas home. Later, he donated the weird relic to the Alabama Department of Archives and History, but in shipping the glass was broken to smithereens. Thus vanished all proof of the Chunnennuggee legend.

Other instances of mysterious photography by lightning are told in Alabama and at least one, a variant of the Henry Wells tale, has been heard in nearby Chickasaw County, Mississippi. Each follows generally the Carrollton model. As recent as Jan. 17, 1949, the press carried a strange story of the weird appearance on a Tuscaloosa window-pane of the face of a woman who had been dead 35 years. The image was seen by such crowds as to justify police intervention. However, Officer W. C. Tompkins unimaginatively recorded the incident as "merely the shadow caused by a door screen when a porch light was turned on." No mention of lightning was made in the official reports.

Apparently, the miracle of lightning photography is confined to the Deep South. According to American folklorists, who make studies of such phenomena, and to their authoritative, many-volumed *Motif-Index of American Legends and Myths*, the image on glass tale or any similar motif has not been found—except in Alabama. However, one variant, never before printed, was told this writer by Richard E. Banta of Crawfordsville, Ind., author of "The Ohio" in "The Rivers of America Series." The Indiana version concerns lightning striking a group of boys in a shady swimming hole and photographing the images of tree leaves on their naked bodies. No glass windows or doors are involved.

Was the unique story of Henry Wells the first of a series of strange Alabama tales of photography by lightning? Or was the incident pure hokum? Old legal records on file in the Pickens County Courthouse

[224]

answer for us—but not too conclusively. The "Trial Docket of State Cases" and the "Circuit Court Minutes" of the county for 1878 both substantiate Wells' arrest, imprisonment and the charge of arson. The truth as recorded, however, is that the case of "The State vs. Henry Wells" never reached an Alabama court—for the Defendant Henry Wells actually died in jail before his trial! How? The records do not say.

Indeed, the terse and official conclusion leaves many questions unanswered. Did lightning strike Wells? Was his image electrically photographed on the glass pane? If it wasn't, then who can explain the ghostly image which still looks out of the Carrollton Courthouse window?

SIMMS' *MICHAEL BONHAM:*
A "FORGOTTEN" DRAMA OF
THE TEXAS REVOLUTION

The Southwestern Historical Quarterly, University of Texas, Austin, January, 1943.

One of the least known, but in several respects one of the most intriguing literary efforts to grow out of the siege of San Antonio, the Alamo, and Texas' fight for independence, is William Gilmore Simms' drama, *Michael Bonham, or The Fall of Béxar.* Only four copies of the play, which appeared in paperback form in 1852 under the imprint of Macfarlane & Fergusson of Richmond, have been located, though as a serial it doubtless had some contemporary following in the columns of the *Southern Literary Messenger.*

Simms was a prolific author and a dominating figure in Southern American literature throughout a large part of the last century. During the forty-five years between 1825 and 1870 he published at least eighty volumes of fiction, poetry, drama, geography, biography, and miscellanies. In addition, he contributed to many periodicals, was active as a lecturer, served as literary advisor to a group of younger writers which included Henry Timrod and Paul Hamilton Hayne, and as a magazine editor had a remarkable career.

Only three or four of Simms' works, however, were in the field of drama, and only one of his plays was ever produced. This was *Michael Bonham,* presented at the Charleston Theatre on the nights of March 26, 27, 28, 1855, with a cast which included Joseph E. Eagle as Bonham, Frank Rea as Crockett, John Sloan as Sparrow, Mrs. John Sloan as Donna Olivia, and Kate Saxon as Donna Maria. The play was generously received as "melodramatic in character," original "both in the plot and characters" and "effective situations." Commenting editorially on the first performance, the *Charleston Mercury* stated:

> We do not even remember ever having seen a play received with
> more marked signs of favor. . . . It abounds in scenes of pathos and passion

arranged to give the highest stage effect, and we feel confident in the prediction that it will increase in popularity with its repetition, and greatly add to the reputation of its author, Mr. Simms.

The *Charleston Courier,* which had the day before published a long synopsis of the play and an appeal for "a generous and intelligent auditory," declared that

> The new drama of *Michael Bonham*—the production of our versatile and gifted Simms—was produced last evening to a large audience, whose interested attention throughout, no less than their frequent demonstrations of applause, testified their gratification at this offering from the pen of one who has ministered to Southern readers in all the moods of authorship.

The *Charleston Evening News* devoted an entire editorial column to the first performance of *Michael Bonham,* saying that Simms had admirably "blended two of the passions, love and revenge, with the action of the play," but added that the author had suffered by "too great *nearness* to the period in which he writes." The critic continued,

> The dialogue is spiritual and natural. This is a characteristic of Mr. Simms in all his works of fiction and invention, in which dialogue is introduced. The colloquy interchanged by his characters is almost invariably dramatic. In *Michael Bonham* his verse has an ease of movement and mellifluous flow, harmony of numbers being another of Simms' peculiarities. The poetry of passion pervades several of the passages, in which the animation of dialogue enters. On the whole this drama will prove an acquisition to the stage, in the class to which it belongs, being capable of scenic effect, having rapidity of movement, a well constructed plot, not dividing the interest by unnecessary complications, and possessing scenes and situations that form striking dramatic pictures.

The major fault found by the *News'* critic was in the rôle of Sparrow, the "comic relief." A punster in general modelled after Falstaff, he is included only "to produce diversity.... [His] language is the unmitigated expression of grossness without *piquancy* to give it flavor. He is an excrescence which ought to undergo the process of excision." The *Courier* had earlier (March 26) commented on Sparrow as "a huge feeder and wit... a dramatic distillation of Capt. Porgy, a great favorite with all who have enjoyed his acquaintance through the introduction of the novelist of the Carolina revolution."

In spite of these tributes, by few, if any, standards could *Michael Bonham* be judged a first-rate drama. Simms himself in an introductory comment admitted that "the tale ... was originally prepared with a view to performance. Subsequently, however, I have persuaded myself that it would be read better as a story." William Peterfield Trent remarks that "when read in the closet the play seems to be the work of precocious youth of eighteen rather than of a practical writer and constant student and spectator of the drama." When read today it is slow and dull. Its chief appeal is the interesting way in which the author altered historical facts, and particularly, in the liberties he took with the prototype of his chief personage.

The plot of the play is as follows: Michael Bonham, second in command of the Texan army, disguised as a Mexican cavalier, and Davy Crockett, disguised as a mule driver, gain entrance into the walls of Béxar. Bonham, under the name of Don Amador, asks Don Esteban de Monteneros, the Mexican Governor, for his daughter, Donna Olivia. Don Esteban, however, has made plans for Donna Olivia to marry Don Pedro de Zavalo, but believes Don Amador a wise choice for his niece, Donna Maria de Pacheco. The Governor plans a masked ball to work out the stratagem. Before the ball, however, Donna Maria discovers that Don Amador and the mule driver are Texans and threatens to reveal their identities unless Don Amador promises to marry her. Bonham begs for an hour in which to make his decision. Meanwhile, Donna Olivia has also penetrated the disguises. She tells Bonham that she still loves him and will marry him. The battle for Béxar begins; Bonham kills Don Pedro. The Texans rout the enemy and capture the palace and the Governor, who gives his daughter to Bonham. Donna Maria, seeing that she has been outwitted, asks Bonham and Donna Olivia to forgive her. But as Donna Olivia embraces her, Donna Maria quickly attempts to stab her. When they try to disarm Donna Maria, she knifes herself and dies, saying that she loved Bonham to the end.

There was of course no "Michael" Bonham. The only Bonham associated with the Texas Revolution was the adventuresome James Butler Bonham, of Edgefield, South Carolina, who died in the Alamo. He had come to Texas at the request of William Barret Travis, another Carolinian, his schoolmate and boyhood friend. In 1855, when Simms' play was produced, James had been dead nineteen years.

But very much alive was the well-known Milledge Luke Bonham—brother of James—who had served in the South Carolina legislature from 1840 to 1844, had been lieutenant-colonel in the 12th Infantry, U. S. Army, under Captain Winfield Scott Hancock in the Mexican War, and had been cited for conspicuous service by General Franklin Pierce. For one year after the war he had filled the post of military governor of one of the conquered Mexican provinces; and, upon his return to Carolina in 1848, he had been elected solicitor of the southern district of South Carolina, which position he held until 1857. There can be no question, therefore, of the fact that Milledge Luke Bonham was an important figure in the South in the 1850's. James had fought the Mexicans in 1836, Milledge in 1848; the former was dead, the latter alive—and, doubtless, the story of Milledge's heroic services in the Mexican War was fresher in the minds of most

[227]

Carolinians than that of his brother James' sacrifices in the Alamo. Under the aegis of "poetic license"—Simms states that he took "some liberties" with the historical facts . . . "but the history will suffer little from my freedoms, while, I believe, the story gains by them"—the author, it appears, tempted readers, perhaps unconsciously, to associate with his play the name of Milledge, one of the state's most affluent citizens, as well as (if not rather than) James, the dead hero of the Alamo.

To accuse Simms of purposely attempting to misguide even by insinuation would be quite unfair; nor would available evidence substantiate such a charge. In the drama Michael is a companion-in-arms of Ben Milam and Davy Crockett, but in real life James was companion-in-arms of Davy Crockett but not of Ben Milam, for Milam fell at the siege of Béxar a month or two before James got to the Alamo. Whereas James entered the Alamo never to return, Michael comes through the siege unharmed to win the Mexican governor's daughter's hand in matrimony. To be sure, the name "Michael" is more suggestive of Milledge than of James—but this evidence is not strong enough, even though the author acknowledges in his foreword that he took "some liberties."

William Peterfield Trent, Simms' only biographer, was completely taken in by the confusion and believed without question, when he did his work for the *American Men of Letters* series in 1892, that the playwright's hero was Milledge—not James. He states that "the hero of the play was then [1855] living in Carolina" and that "General [*sic*] Milledge L. Bonham, the hero, was a well-known man." In another place he refers to Milledge as a "crusader" who "more recently . . . had served with distinction in the Mexican War, and it was probably this fact which suggested to Simms the propriety of writing his drama." And later he adds "how the original of the romantic hero could have been flattered at finding himself carried through a series of duels and cut-throat adventures is hard to conceive."

No evidence has been found to support the theory that Charlestonians who saw the play were misled, as was Simms' biographer. There could have been doubt in the minds of some people as to which Bonham the prototype of the hero really was, but this is unlikely—especially if they remembered their history and did not allow Milledge's valor of more recent date to supplant that of James. None of the Charleston papers (*Courier, Mercury,* or *Evening News*) mentions either Milledge or James in their notices. The theatrical critic of the *Courier* in a review based on a reading of the play, indicated that he knew which man was being portrayed, but he failed to mention James by name:

> Of the hero, *Bonham,* who gives name to the piece, we need say little. He is too well known as one, and a most conspicuous one . . .

an associate of *Travis* and *Bowie* and *Crockett,* and the small but hardy band of crusaders who first planted near the "Great River" of the American Spaniards, the lone star flag. . . .

The press had reported James' death in 1836, two decades before, and the supposition is that his gallant end in the Alamo was known to all. However, Milledge's name had been currently before the public, and, when one recalls that to last-century Carolinians Texas was extremely far away and her history vague, one may rightly expect and condone some confusion. To those who were clear about James' search for reinforcements and his subsequent heroic dash back into the Alamo, the drama itself must have held fuller significance. For example, Travis, who does not appear in the play, is mentioned in the last act as follows:

> *Davis:* 'Tis Travis. He takes command. Bonham is to leave us; to take dispatches to Sam Houston. . . . They say that Santa Anna is marching down upon us with twenty thousand men.
> *Crockett:* We must stand a siege then?

Here again, however, the author succeeded in juggling the facts and it is possible that the allusion to James' chivalric search for aid for the besieged Texans might have passed unnoticed. Furthermore, James actually took no part in the seige of Béxar from December 5 to 9, 1835, as Simms would have it in the play. On those days the Texas revolutionists were wresting the city from General Cos and his Mexican forces. He did not arrive until a month or two after the Texans had captured the Alamo, January or February, 1836 at which time he joined his friend Travis and the garrison in the Alamo. Santa Anna did not capture the fort and massacre all the defenders until March 6. In other words, the action of Simms' play, so far as Bonham is concerned, should not have begun until three months after its end.

It is not known whether Milledge Bonham ever saw the play presented; most probably he did not. There can be no doubt, however, of his having been pleased with the idea: Major M. C. M. Hammond, a friend of Simms, wrote him, "Saw Bonham (M.L.) yesterday. His vanity is flattered. He was gratified at your success, of which I told him." In all fairness it must be conceded that Milledge's vanity was flattered because of his family pride, not, as Trent believed, because of any belief that the public was seeing in Michael the hero of the Mexican War. Especially so, when he had lent James the money to go to Texas and, in 1838, had visited Texas at the expense of $500 of James' estate "to ascertain all he could of his brother's last days, and settle up his estate." Milledge was too famous in his own right to need to bask in reflected glory.

When the play was presented in the Charleston Theatre, Simms was, as Trent records, "so nervously interested in the success" that he could not be persuaded to attend the performances. He did, how-ever, keep account of the attendances and hoped that he would make "some much-needed money." In a letter to Hammond he declared himself "slightly chagrined at the fact that the audience did not call for the author." Hammond replied that he had never heard of an author's being called in Charleston, but that the audience had paid him "the very highest compliment known to them, and quite unusual, too, that of encoring *scenes!* A song might do. But scenes! it is surely a *rara avis.*"

Unhappily for Simms, *Michael Bonham* was not a success and, after the three performances in Charleston, was forgotten. Its principal claims for attention now lie in its rarity, in the erroneous interpretation Trent gave it in what for almost fifty years has been the only biography of the author, in the confusion which could possibly have arisen con-cerning the prototype of the chief character, in the fact that it was the only one of Simms' dramas ever produced, and in its appeal as an "unknown" item of Texas history.

TWO FAMOUS THEATRES OF THE
OLD SOUTH

South Atlantic Quarterly, Duke University,
Durham, North Carolina, July, 1937.

Readers of Charleston's *City Gazette and Daily Advertiser*, July 27, 1792, were doubtless enthusiastic over the possible outcome of Harry Grant's announcement that "The subscribers to the Theatre are requested to meet at William's Coffee-House, *This Day*, at one o'clock, on business of importance." For nearly sixty years Charleston had been foremost among Southern cities in theatricals; now the drama, which "had lain dormant" for some time because of the lack of a playhouse, was once again to be revived. A second meeting was called four days later, and on August 1 "Thomas Beekman, Treasurer," gave notice that "one-fourth part" of all subscriptions had to be paid by August 6.

The immediacy with which the necessary funds were raised attests to Charleston's interest in dramatics, for in less than a fortnight the *Gazette* stated in a conspicuous article that on the tenth of August the ground had been surveyed for the new structure, and the "corner-stone of the foundation is to be laid the 20 inst."

This was not Charleston's first theatre—the first having been the old Dock-Street Theatre, opened February 12, 1736, and later appropri-ated to other uses—but since the closing (1787) of Godwin's Harmony Hall, the city had been without regular theatrical performances for almost six years.

The time was propitious, therefore, for Thomas Wade West and John Bignall, producers and managers well-known in American stage annals, to attempt a revival of the art in the Carolina seaport. Canvassing the town for subscriptions, these promoters, with the help of a local committee composed of Timothy Ford, Samuel Beekman, Edward Penman, and John Mitchell, which stood in security for the loans, secured "monies to the amount of two thousand eight hundred pounds." Upwards of fifty prominent citizens contributed, each of whom was given "a little metallic check" for use as a pass into the theatre. Of this sum, 350 pounds was used as first payment (the total purchase price being 500 pounds) to Henry Middleton for a lot of land 60' x 150' on the triangular corner of Broad and Middleton [now New] streets, bordering Savage's Green. The balance was applied towards the erection of the building.

West, who had had wide experience in English theatres, was selected to supervise the construction. He was assisted by Anthony Toomer, and Messrs. Hoban, Hook & Nevison, architects and decorators, who contracted to have the work completed by January 10, 1793.

The dimensions of the theatre, as advertised in the *Gazette* of August 14, 1792, were 125' x 56' x 37', "with an handsome pediment, stone ornaments, a large flight of stone steps, and a courtyard palisaded." The interior consisted of a 56' circular-front stage illuminated by "three rows of patent lamps," a pit, and "three tiers of boxes, decorated with thirty-nine columns; to each column a glass chandelier, with five lights." Each box was equipped with "a window and a Venetian blind," and, whereas the upper tiers were paneled, the lower was elegantly "balustraded." All mouldings were painted silver against a background of French white. The pit entrance was on the southeast, opening into Middleton Street, and the front or box entrance faced north on Broad. All other features were modeled in general after those of the London Opera House. The seating capacity was twelve hundred. In short, Charleston's new theatre was a combination of "elegance and novelty," and there were those whose enthusiasm led them to say that such "beauty and convenience" rendered it "the first theatre on the continent."

From the gala opening night of February 11, 1793, when West & Bignall's Company of Comedians staged O'Keefe's *The Highland Reel* and Inchbald's *The Adventures of a Shawl*, until the final closing, May 8, 1833, when Laurent Duresse's Troupe presented M. M. Noah's *Marion, or The Carolina Swamp Fox*, this playhouse remained Charleston's chief center of amusement. Managed successively by West & Bignall, Alexander Placide, Joseph G. Holman, Charles Gilfert, Joe Cowell, John B. Irving, John Jay Adams, Thomas Faulkner, Frederick Brown, and Vincent DeCamp, this theatre attracted many

[231]

leading performers to the city. Among the stars who appeared there from time to time were Thomas Apthorpe Cooper, Edmund Kean, Clara Fisher, Edwin Forrest, James Hackett, J. W. Wallack, Josephine Clifton, Mrs. Charles Gilfert [née Holman], and others of note.

In 1833, however, the proprietors (the building changed hands several times in the forty years) offered the establishment for sale. Advertisements were run in New York, Philadelphia, and Boston papers to no avail. When, therefore, the newly organized Medical College of the State of South Carolina (1832) set about to acquire a building for classroom use, the owners of the theatre were glad to deal with them. On August 6, 1833, Benjamin F. Pepoon, President, and R. Witherspoon, Secretary and Treasurer, of The Proprietors of the Charleston Theatre, transferred the building with two small adjoining lots to the college for $12,000.

The interior of the edifice was immediately remodeled to fit the needs of a medical school, but no changes were made in the exterior. Thus ended the career of one of Charleston's most famous playhouses. Tyrone Power, Irish comedian who visited Charleston in 1834, wrote humorously that the building originally erected for a theatre has been "changed into a school of anatomy; so *cutting up* is still the order of the day; only the practice is no longer confined to the poets, but extended to the subjects generally."

From 1833 to 1837 theatrical production in Charleston was at an extremely low ebb. Since there was no regular theatre, a temporary stage was erected in the "Old Circus, at the Corner of Queen and Friend [now Legaré] Streets," and that "barn," as Power called it, served as playhouse. Nevertheless, Power, Cooper, Hackett, Judah, and others, performed in this make-shift building during the five years that W. Hardy and Hart managed it.

Early in 1835 Robert Witherspoon, James Rose, Henry Gourdin, Richard W. Cogdell, and William A. Carson, local citizens, raised $12,500 with which to purchase a lot 99' x 253', fronting on the west side of Meeting Street, between Market Street and Horlbeck Alley. Shortly thereafter, Witherspoon, "Chairman of the Board of Trustees," and George W. Logan, "Secretary and Treasurer," of "The Charleston New Theatre Company," began the solicitation of subscribers. By March 15, 1837, Herr Reichardt of Prussia, architect, and Messrs. Curtis, Fogartie & Sutton, builders, had the work "going on with despatch, to be completed by November next." And towards the end of the year the state granted the proprietors an act of incorporation with a capital of $60,000, with the privilege of increasing the amount to $100,000, if desired.

As contracted, the building, which was 121' x 73', "comprehended in two stories on a high basement," was completed in November. In Grecian style the upper story showed "a portico of four Ionic columns *tetrastules,* supporting an entablature and pediment," and a porch "protected by a large abutment at either end." Three front doors, approached by a flight of stairs, opened into a vestibule, on one side of which was the ticket office, "and on the other a withdrawing room for ladies, handsomely carpeted and fitted up with mirrors and lamps." A corridor led from the vestibule to the boxes which formed "a sort of segment of about two-thirds of a circle, receding as they approach the stage, something in the shape of a horseshoe." The pit contained "nicely cushioned seats," and was connected with the dress circle "like French theatres." Boxes were equipped with "sofa seats, covered with crimson moreen," against a background of "peach blossom color—perhaps of all colors the best adapted to display to the best advantage the beauty of the fairer part of the audience." Two and one-half inch pillars supported the upper tiers of boxes, "so that a view of the stage on the back seats is not obstructed."

The interior decorating, under the direction of Chizzola and Nixon, consisted of ornamental relief work around the upper boxes, appropriate dramatic designs on medallions separating the compartments, and a large dome "of commingled splendour, ornamented with arabesque and emblematic figures, richly and beautifully executed in the brightest colors, subdivided by gilt moulding." At the summit of the dome was a forty-eight lamp chandelier with strong reflectors. The house was accommodated to seat "comfortably" twelve hundred people.

On Friday, December 15, 1837, the Charleston New Theatre was opened under the guidance of William Abbott, formerly of the Haymarket, Park, and Chestnut theatres. Procedures began with the reading of a poetical address "written for the occasion by our highly distinguished fellow citizen, William Gilmore Simms." The opening bill was *The Honeymoon* and *The Waterman,* Abbott, W. H. Latham, and Miss Melton playing the principal rôles. Long before the curtain was raised, said the *Courier,* the theatre "was literally crammed in every part; many had to go away from the doors."

Without noticeable opposition this theatre, under the managements of Abbott, Latham, W. C. Forbes, H. W. Preston, A. Macallister, F. C. Adams, John Sloman, and G. F. Marchant, continued for twenty-four years, staking Charleston's greatest claim to theatrical distinction. Lucius Booth, Fanny Elssler, W. C. McCready, Lester Wallack, Edwin Forrest, Anna Cora Mowatt, Jenny Lind, John Drew, Julia Dean, Charlotte Cusman, Edwin L. Davenport, Ellen Tree, and others played on its boards—not to mention the many opera troupes which came from season to season.

Five days before Christmas, 1860, South Carolina seceded from the Union. Throngs of ladies and gentlemen crowded the fashionable promenade known as The Battery to watch the activities at Fort Sumter.

Citadel cadets fired upon "The Star of the West"; Sumter was evacuated; the city was besieged. The embarkation of troops to Virginia and other matters more weighty than burlesque, comedy, or make-believe tragedy filled the hearts of Charlestonians. Manager Marchant tried unsuccessfully to carry on the show. On November 19, 1861, word was received that Port Royal had fallen—an invasion of Carolina was on foot. Calls for volunteers filled the newssheets, soldiers were rushed, and fortifications were thrown up. And among it all Marchant quietly announced the opening of a new season November 25, with the Zouaves, French soldiers of Crimea and Algeria, in *The Troubadour Soldier* and *Une Fille Terrible*. Poorly attended, this bill continued for several days; and on November 30, the last performance in the Charleston Theatre, the Zouaves were augmented by exhibitory drills by "local battalions."

On the night of December 11, 1861, almost twenty-four years to the day and hour of its proud and auspicious opening, the theatre was burned in a devastating fire (not a result of the war) which consumed about one-third of the city. Of the Charleston Theatre the next morning nothing was left but the smoke of smoldering ruins and a "flight of steps, protected by a large abutment at either end," a picture which may now be seen in *The Photographic History of the Civil War* (III, 329), edited by Francis T. Miller (New York, 1911).

THE PLACE OF THE COLLEGE LIBRARY IN THE INSTRUCTIONAL PROGRAM

The Journal of Higher Education, Ohio State University, Columbus, Ohio, October, 1943.

About 150 persons — presidents, deans, and instructors—representing all types of colleges and universities in the South, attended the Work Conference on Higher Education sponsored by the Southern Association of Colleges and Secondary Schools held at the University of the South. Six librarians were invited to serve as consultants—three from universities, two from colleges, and one from a secondary school.

Participants were divided into the following groups: Improvement of Instruction, Improvement of the Curriculum, Personnel Problems and Services, Responsibility of the Liberal-Arts College for the Education of Teachers, General Education, An Interpretation in the Light of Present Needs and Practices, and Values of a Liberal-Arts Education. In regularly scheduled sessions, committee meetings, and private conferences administrators, faculty members, and librarians (one was assigned to each group) discussed freely and sincerely the many problems confronting higher education in the region. The proper place of the library in the instructional program was a topic of major emphasis throughout the Work Conference. Heretofore, it has been customary for librarians to discuss among themselves the importance of libraries, while teachers, meeting separately, discussed the importance of teaching. So far as the writer knows this is the first time administrators, librarians, and teachers have met together to study and to attempt to solve their common problem: how books may be most effectively used to strengthen the educational program.

The Conference agreed at the outset that the most distinguishing feature of the college library during the last twenty years is its growth. Competition, harem-scarem collecting, or the administrator who measured success by number of accessions may have accounted for this situation, although it is reasonable to suppose that monetary grants from foundations and the standards of various accrediting associations have also played their parts. Another outstanding feature, it was stated, is the employment of librarians who are technically adequate but who, somewhere along their training, have failed to acquire a love of learning for its own sake and a proper appreciation of the power of books in the education of others. In short, librarians have long been concerned with mechanics; now the time has come for them to share the responsibility of teaching with books.

No attempt was made, however, to place the entire burden upon the librarian. Other representatives were also quite ready to acknowledge their own shortcomings; in fact, the library was analyzed from the standpoints of both administration and faculty, and much attention was devoted to book collections and their functions.

Briefly, the functions of the library in the educational program were summarized as follows:

1. To strengthen instruction by making readily available an authoritative working collection of all kinds of materials, including motion pictures, maps, music (notations, records, and the like), microfilms, glass and film slides, and art pictures in addition to books, periodicals, documents, and pamphlets.
2. To meet specific curriculum reference needs and general reference needs in all areas.
3. To provide and to promote interest in noncurricular reading.
4. To meet the research needs of the faculty by interlibrary loans, microphotography, and allied services.
5. To stimulate the use of the library and develop more effective service by co-operative planning of administration, faculty, and staff.

To a great degree use of the library depends upon faculty promotion and co-operation in intergrating its services with the various educational processes of the institution. In every course the instructor should, for instance, indicate definitely the required reading, differentiate clearly between it and optional reading, and, to facilitate matters for himself, students, and staff, supply mimeographed biblio-

[235]

graphies or reading schedules. Reserved book reading should, however, in all cases be kept at a minimum by restricting it to vital materials only, and they should be properly gauged to the ability and understanding of the students. The librarian, on the other hand, should report frequently on the use made of each reserved-book title and indicate difficulties and enthusiasms expressed by the readers. Since, in the last analysis, education is largely individual instruction, whenever possible the instructor should work directly with separate students in using the library. This is especially true in the case of honors courses, seminars or term papers, and independent reading. Moreover, the instructor should make it a part of his classroom procedure to familiarize students with the library's reference resources, to teach effective library use in general, and in particular to encourage individual programs of cultural or recreational reading.

In the past, it was agreed, too much emphasis has been placed on the quantity of books in the college library and not enough on the quality. The chief concern now seems to be the wise selection of the best materials for improving instruction and for enlarging the opportunities to contribute to growth of the college community. Book collections should be built with these suggestions in mind:

1. Library funds should be allotted to each department according to its needs, and, to encourage the participation of all members, no single person should dominate selection.
2. Subject sections of the reference collection should be developed by the librarian with the assistance of departments concerned.
3. Books for general reading should be selected co-operatively by the faculty and the staff and, whenever possible, with students' aid.
4. Rare books should not be bought for the college library at the expense of materials necessary for instruction.
5. Curriculum committees should not admit new courses in fields in which library resources are inadequate.
6. In general, the small college should discourage departmental libraries, especially those in the social sciences or humanities.
7. The librarian should be responsible for the proper development of the whole collection, should make available to the faculty helpful bibliographical tools, and should systematically check holdings against authoritative lists.
8. The librarian should notify the faculty member of the arrival of books he has requested or in which he is particularly interested, publish classified mimeographed lists (at least fortnightly) of new acquisitions, and place new titles on proper display before stacking them.

As has been mentioned, the conferees agreed that the librarian has in the past been particularly concerned with the techniques of his profession—to the sometimes unhappy exclusion of an appreciation of the rôle books play in the educational program. Briefly, he has worked with the outside of books far more than he has with the inside. To be sure, he should be trained in the techniques necessary for the successful performance of his mechanical tasks; but beyond that he should be fitted by his academic background to work effectively and on a basis of mutual understanding and respect with the faculty in the promotion of educational development. This work would include, among other duties, serving on curriculum committees and others concerned especially with instruction. Toward these ends he should be encouraged to enroll in courses while in service, to take leaves of absence for study, and to read widely and consistently in both general and professional fields. Furthermore, he should be urged to participate in professional organizations and to contribute to library and other educational literature. It is apparent that the librarian should enjoy the academic or administrative status which will made him most useful to the institution; but if he would merit this esteem, he must first earn it by being more than a mere "check boy in the parcel room of culture."

It is regrettable to know that in many institutions approximately 25 per cent of the students never use the library and that an even larger number make only negligible use of it. If the keynote for college library development in the future is to be intelligent use, rather than phenomenal growth, the ultimate responsibility for conduct and character of the library depends upon the administrator.

He may ensure this function, first, by defining the kind of library program his institution needs and, second, by employing the librarian best qualified in all ways to direct that service. Third, he must assume the responsibility of seeing that the librarian is brought into vital relationship with the educational program. This he may do by many means, but surely he must consider the librarian's interest in teaching with books, his academic as well as technical qualifications, his ability to deal effectively with people, and his desire to integrate as far as possible the book collection with the instructional policies of the institution. Fourth, the administrator must insist that careful enrichment and constant use of library facilities stand second in importance to good teaching on his campus. Fifth, he must ask the complete co-operation of faculty and library staff in working together for mutual good. Never must he forget that the college library, if it is to do its job completely should always be, as W. J. McConnell has written,

> the co-ordinating center of the institution, ... a place of emanation, not simply one of impingement, ... a place from which ideas which call for action should radiate to the departments of instruction, not simply a place where ideas originating with the departments should converge.

The importance in the college program of general reading (variously called recreational, leisure-time, or extra-curricular) on the part of students, faculty, and administration has been mentioned. Judging by the frequency with which this topic was discussed at the Conference, it deserves further consideration.

[237]

Perhaps no phase of college work has a more abiding effect upon the individual, now and in the future, than learning to live with books. If as a formal student he acquires the habit of reading, of appreciating the best that has been said and thought in the world and is to be found only in good books, he has come a long way toward becoming what his college wants him to become—an educated man.

But can he do this, if between him and books there are too many bars? Hardly. For this reason the Conference declared: "Students should be given as much direct access to books as possible even though it entails some loss."

In this connection the writer belives that the most significant comment was made by Chancellor Oliver C. Carmichael of Vanderbilt University, General Chairman of the Work Conference. Said he:

> I have often wondered why an administrator will concern himself so greatly about the $400 or $500 or $600 worth of books that are lost or stolen from the college library during the year. The same man may see that amount and more poured down the sink or burned up in laboratory test tubes, and think nothing about it. He may even see much more torn to shreds on the football field. It might be a good idea to set aside a certain sum each year for the purchase of good books in inexpensive editions just to put around in places convenient for reading—on library tables, in dormitory lounging rooms, or wherever they may be easily used. To begin with the amount might be considered a financial "dead loss"; but I am convinced that the value to students of having direct, unhampered access to these choice books would be incalculable.

OF THE LIBRARIAN'S EDUCATION

The American Scholar, Washington, D.C., winter, 1943–44
(reprinted in *Of, By, and For Librarians*, Hamden, Conn.: Shoe String Press, 1960).

The modern American librarian has been called the Bookman Belligerent. His duty, he is told, is no longer passive or custodial. Rather, he is to fight hard, for upon him more than anyone else depends the destiny of Man's mind.

It is indeed heartening to think of the librarian as civilization's intellectual commando. Once, perhaps, when the prerequisite of the profession was profundity, such an appellative would not have been remarkable. Dr. Thomas Bray, for example, the first advocate of public libraries in America, wrote in *Bibliothecae Americanae* (1697) that since libraries "give Requisite Helps to Considerable Attainment in All the Parts of Necessary and Usefull Knowledge," it was impossible to believe that those in charge "should be Able to Communicate to others, what they are not themselves first become Masters of."

But the changes of time have changed the focus on librarianship, and the librarian, like the old gray mare, is not what he used to be. He is past master in classifying, cataloguing, and circulating books.

With wizardly skill he microphotographs them. He is administrator, comptroller, and statistician all in one: *si monumentum requiris, circumspice*. In fact, he is good at doing everything to or for books that an enlightened civilization could ask of him—except reading them. Like Timothy, "being so much at Paul's beck, as to be his Cloack-carrier and Book-bearer," he has been painstakingly drilled to be the hand-maiden of wisdom or, as Sir Thomas Wotton would have said, "the brusher of noblemen's clothes." Certainly, none can deny him praise so far as this lackeydom goes. But at the eternal wedding of People and Print it is regrettable to see him always as the best man and never the groom.

Recently, I was invited by several of my colleagues of the faculty to attend the Southwestern convention of the Modern Language Association. At luncheon the talk naturally turned to books. For an hour we tossed back and forth across the table choice literary witticisms, running the gamut from *Piers Plowman* to *The Moon Is Down*. I felt strangely at home in this austere company of English professors: when I was suspiciously eyed, I knew it was because I was not wearing the badge of the order.

Presently, my neighbor, a Professor of American literature in a large Oklahoma university, asked me what "field" I was in. I replied that I was in all fields or no field, depending on how you looked at it—that I was a librarian.

"A librarian?"

When I assured him, he fairly shouted to his fellows, "My God! He's a librarian—a librarian who *reads* books!"

I had all along supposed that it was a part of my business to know something about the insides as well as the outsides of the books I hand out to students and faculty. Besides, I enjoy reading. But the idea grew to nightmarish proportions as time went on. My God, thought I, borrowing the Professor's epithet, will *librarian* never cease to conjure up a graying old woman of either sex who steps mouselike about her ossuary and thinks the progression of Life lies somewhere in the 900's?

No, I answered. Not until the librarian is taught or teaches himself that the inside of a library and the outside of a book are one thing, the outside of a library and the inside of a book another. A tailor wears clothes, a doctor takes his own medicine—need he who makes shoes always go barefoot himself? On what ground does the librarian exempt himself from knowing more about his stock-in-trade than the packages they are wrapped in?

The difference between the librarian who keeps the Book and another who keeps the Word has been carefully drawn. The latter, as Archibald MacLeish has written, cannot be passive. He must represent his client, "the inherited culture entrusted to his care," as its

[239]

attorney against those who would black out or mutilate the Word, against those who would batten down our cultural hatches, against tyrants and artful liars. This he must do, not by waiting for attack, but by attacking. Defense never won a battle, not even the Battle of Books.

Ability to preserve cultural traditions, however, depends on an understanding of them—"the authority of art and learning rests on knowledge of the arts and learning." Emerson had the same idea in mind when he wrote in *Society and Solitude:* "The colleges, whilst they provide us with libraries, furnish no professors of books; and, I think, no chair is so much wanted."

The semi-mechanized librarian who by code spots one volume in a million and parcels it out to you in no time at all will doubtless never be more than learning's short-order clerk. It is to the other, the librarian who *believes* in the Word and is eager to "profess" it, that the profession must turn for advancement, even for preservation.

Lately, the librarian has been subjected to many attacks by academicians, administrators, and the public. He has been told that much of the trapping he has built up about his work is tinsel and tawdry. He has been compared to Thomas Fuller's dunce, "void of learning but full of books." Moreover, prophets of his own group have warned him that he must answer society's demand for more intelligent service and less scientific ritual or be swept off his feet. No one, to be sure, has gone so far as to call his profession "shyster," except by inference, perhaps, but commentaries on the librarian's inadequacy have not been too carefully buried between the lines.

It is significant to note that educators have in large measure recruited their librarians from the classroom rather than from the ranks of the professionally trained. Many successful college and university librarians have received their training in areas other than library economy; and it is the rule rather than the exception to find in the larger public libraries men who have been appointed because of their experience, their general knowledge of men and affairs, or their success in another profession, such as law, literature, or administration. Surely, one concludes, librarianship must be the only profession in which the rocky road to learning has such macadamized detours.

Specific examples of these transfer-pundits are not difficult to draw, as every librarian knows, from the Librarian of Congress, about whose appointment "professionals" raised such a shameful howl, down through the university, college, and public libraries, to those in the smallest school systems. Among them are to be found many of the profession's leading thinkers. According to *The Library Journal*, only 86 of the 187 active librarians in *Who's Who* have library degrees and 16 others have no degrees at all—a total of 102, or 55 per cent. Earlier, the same magazine had named 64 librarians who had distinguished themselves as authors. Not all were college graduates and "not one ever attended library school," yet eight of them became presidents of the American Library Association, "in each case after having won recognition in quite other professions."

Let us look further. The General Education Board and the Carnegie Corporation have defined their positions by offering attractive subventions to young men already prepared in the humanities or social sciences to entice them into library work. Nationally known librarians, such as Raney (Chicago), Bishop (Michigan), and Munn (Pittsburgh Carnegie) have consistently demanded serious scrutiny of the "folklore" of librarianship and begged that something be done before it is too late. They know that librarians cannot forever be content as mere elevator boys in the tower of intellect.

Does the responsibility for the librarian's inadequacy rest in improper recruiting? Too poor pay to attract the better class of men and women? Hardly. There is yet no proof that the innate intelligence of librarians is second to that of other educators. Certainly students who elect teaching careers could not be dubbed mercenary. For the *faux pas* of the librarian one must look beyond the motive which directed him into the profession. One should consider, it seems, not so much why he became a librarian as why he became the kind of librarian he did.

An enthusiastic young man or woman whose native ability is not meritless interests himself in librarianship. If he already holds a bachelor's degree, he becomes a candidate for a second—the Bachelor of Science in Library Science, representing a fifth year of college work. If he wishes to do further study, routes to higher degrees are, of course, open to him; but generally his formal training ends with the B.S. in L.S. and to his place of employment he goes to join others who are already library "scientists." But somewhere between the time the eager neophyte began his training and the day he was initiated into the brotherhood, somewhere between the concept and the reality, he who loved books and reading and sought knowledge for its own sake has been stymied. He has learned that books are but physical things and the librarian is but their checker.

The extent of the librarian's loyalty to his professional school is usually evidenced by his acknowledgment that he considers himself adequately trained to perform the duties for which he has been adequately trained. The catch comes in the realization that he is trained for one thing and expected to do others. On this basis one might insist that the good librarian is good, not because of his professional training, but in spite of it. Furthermore, the librarian knows that up to now libraries are sanctioned, rather than basic, institutions in our society: when the civic-economy knife falls, it usually falls first and hardest on him. Whether self-preservation alone brought about the

[241]

re-focusing, no one can rightly say, but he has learned that he cannot survive by continuing as jailer of the sublimated personalities on his shelves.

The precise pattern future library education may take is not entirely clear at the moment, but there is much handwriting on the wall. One thing is sure: the old regime, which made the librarian a galley slave to techniques, is doomed.

The end was first sighted some twenty years ago when the Carnegie Corporation began investigating the librarian's training. Results revealed that curricula and methods of instruction needed considerable overhauling. Moreover, the analysts frankly admitted, the better library positions would doubtless always be filled by scholars "with or without library school training." Those who rose in defense could do little more than beat the bushes, for the schools, with few exceptions, continue with much the same curricula and viewpoints. One or two have adopted more humanistic approaches, but on the whole the one-year schools (whose products are numerous and, in general, account for the poor opinion held of the average "trained" librarian) remain as they have been, with little apparent wish to be otherwise.

The attack on library schools have developed along several interdependent lines: their outmoded curricula and methods, their lack of coördination within and without departmental boundaries, and their blind obeisance to national or regional accrediting associations—to mention but three. These might be summed up as academic inferiority or—better, perhaps—as "library lag." For the schools have not yet adjusted their curricula to fit the particular needs of place and time, nor have they become convinced that curricula cannot be produced *en masse* or be vacuum-tinned. In short, they still have before them the most challenging curriculum of all, a hand-tailored article.

To rest on the belief that certain courses are inviolable is but another way of saying that what one has been doing is, *ipso facto*, the right thing. The standard curriculum is not necessarily the product of omnific educators who could do no wrong. The final test for the library school, as for all others, comes when its graduate is measured in terms of intelligent service. If he fails, the system goes down with him.

The typical library school curriculum consists of thirty hours of work in basic, required courses. These are generally uniform—classification, cataloguing, book selection, reference, bibliography, and administration. And they are mandatory for every trainee. Whether he needs them or not, as was argued in the case of Latin some years ago, they are "good discipline." Indeed, they are. And there will always be need for "disciplined" librarians. Who else could properly order books from a mail-order catalogue, cards from the Library of Congress, or match quickly the digits on a patron's "call-slip" with those on a shelved book? The pity is that while he masters these "ostiaric"

duties, he is frequently deprived of drinking from the culturally ennobling fountains of the institution and, when he is graduated, his second
bachelor's degree warrants no more scholastic recognition than his
first. What's more, it seldom commands a higher salary.

One need not necessarily agree with the author of *American Librarianship from a European Angle* that it is "downright fraud to
apply the term 'bachelor in library science' to a one-year course of
elementary and didactic instruction." To do so might easily becloud
and reduce the issue to one of terminology, and the librarian is not
so much concerned with what his preparation is called as he is about
being rightly prepared for intelligent participation in the educative
progress of society. It is enough to say that until training for librarianship is made less fraudulent and more intellectually challenging it
will tend to produce robots of the first smelting. And robot, unfortunately, comes close to being a thumbnail biography of the average
American librarian.

Even the alert librarian might insist that so-called traditional courses,
if properly "integrated," may be valuable from the standpoint of utility
as well as discipline. However, the graduates of a Southern library
school who were required to outline Bostwick's *The American Public
Library* must have found the integrating factors a bit elusive. The
students in cataloguing at a large Midwestern university doubtless
wonder why they spent the better part of a class-hour belaboring
the proper size of catalogue cards—whether $3'' \times 5''$, as commonly
called, or 7.5 cm. × 12.5 cm., as actually measured. The difference,
you will want to know, is every bit the width of ten hairs. The New
York librarian who in his "Reference Training" was asked to count
the number of words devoted to Galileo in the *Encyclopedia
Britannica* and in the *Americana* and contrast "results" cannot have
failed to gain a very private opinion of the spirit of "research" in
librarianship. Future librarians, who in their classification courses are
busy memorizing Dewey Decimal digits, ask every day, "Why not
the telephone directory?"

Now there is another side. Nearly every library school has its quota of
instructors eager to garnish their subject matter with the doodads of the
"newer" learning. Witness the recent trend toward diagrams, graphs
and formulae, tables and statistics, "research methodology," "test
scores," "coefficient of correlation," and "validity." One thinker has at
long last solved the "riddle" of alloting library book funds to [college
departments—by use of the formula $A+2B+X(C_1+2C_2+4C_3+6C_4)$.]
"As a result," he writes, "the index of the department becomes

$X = \dfrac{A+2B}{C}$ That unquestionable settles the matter for all time.

Unhappily, the reduction of librarianship to a neat mathematical
equation does not satisfy. Nor does the embellishment of it with bor-

[243]

rowed verbiage. For in the final showdown librarians as well as library patrons are human beings whose everyday problems are still solved by experience, not by scientific formulae. The rearing of children, the choice of jobs, politics, religion, matters of finance and behavior—all are still within the pale of common sense or obtainable knowledge. As Pierce Butler once said, "Effective librarianship is largely a matter of accurate psychological diagnosis." With his office the librarian assumes the responsibility for exploiting books for communal advantage to the best of his ability. His success depends on his knowledge of what books are.

Adherents to the present training program insist that a student should have had his "general education" in the undergraduate college before becoming a candidate for the library degree, and that the quantity of work required for the latter does not allow him time to study in the academic departments of the institution.

The second statement insinuates that all prospective librarians must follow the same program of work. It even suggests that an extension of the area of his selectivity might be prejudicial. Nothing could be more illogical. By a process of thoughtful merger, elimination, and cooperation with other divisions of the university, library schools could perfect a curriculum immeasurably stronger than the standard requirements. But few schools have so far exhibited such professional courage. Adherence to various accrediting regulations accounts in part for their reluctance; however, this is becoming less true as time goes on, especially in the more independent institutions. On the whole, the established curriculum remains because it is traditionally entrenched.

The reply to the first statement, namely, that a student should have acquired a "background" education before he reaches the library school, is simply—he should. But the possession of a bachelor's degree is not proof that he needs or wants no further enlightening. If time for broadening his intellectual horizon could be gained by stripping the curriculum of ritualistic minutiae, why should that not be done—especially, when many of the elementary details on which the student, already a college graduate, now wastes time could be learned in service with one-tenth the time and effort? Meanwhile, his intelligence would not be insulted by piddling at the petty tasks required of him for the library degree.

To put it bluntly, the chief stumbling block to proper education for librarianship is a closed corporation called the "teaching personnel." Looking at sausages, they dream of Picasso. Mr. Hutchins' warning, in *The Higher Learning in America*, that "professional schools which have no intellectual content in their own right" must pass out, seems not to have disturbed them. So far they have made only a few futile attempts at outlining the essentials of the profession or developing what might be called a philosophy. Problems that might

[244]

change the complexion of the whole system cry out for analysis. The nearest approach to a critique on the qualifications of a "professionally trained" librarian, as contrasted, let us say, with an "unprofessionally trained" one, is based on the simple fact that the former has for thirty scholastic hours been a remunerative guest of an institution. Indeed, it is this blundering, hit-or-miss attitude on the part of library school faculties, together with the entailing of worn-out ideas from son to son, that presents so serious a problem. To paraphrase Mr. Hutchins, they do not seem to know what to teach or how to teach it; they are unclear about their aims and objectives, and fumbling in their methods, and by looking down their noses at intellectual content they have become slide-rule technicians and have all but immunized themselves against the only kind of education that would strengthen the foundation of the profession.

Because of his superior knowledge the good librarian will assume civic and social leadership. As the administrator of the community's cultural center he will manage a complicated organization, seeking large sums of money and spending them to the best interest of his patrons and his library. He will be prepared, as a personnel director, to deal with many people under constantly varying conditions. As a scholar, he must hobnob with scholars, know their methods, speak their language, and demand their respect. As technician he will select, buy, process, and arrange for use myriad materials in many different areas of learning. As a liaison officer between the citizens of his community and the world-citizens on his shelves, he must serve the intellectual body of his patrons in much the same fashion as the doctor serves the physical, the lawyer the legal, or the minister the spiritual—indeed, one might even suggest that the librarian's responsibility to his clientele is a combination of all these. And, like the physician, the attorney, the minister, he too should have received adequate education for his role in society.

If he has not, then the school that taught him has a momentous choice to make: it must junk its ineffective methods and worn-out curriculum and substitute some subject matter worth teaching, or pull down the camouflage and declare itself a vocational institute for studying artifacts, distilling techniques, and counting square feet per janitor.

If library school professors would interest themselves in graduating *educated* instead of merely *trained* librarians, they might consider the possibilities of a "consolidated curriculum." Assuming that all knowledge is related and that the librarian's duties are manifold, they could develop composite courses by cutting across the usual departmental or divisional lines of the university to draw on the several sciences and the humanities. It will be agreed, for example, that the librarian as administrator should know the fundamentals of administration. These are similar, perhaps identical, in all types of executive

[245]

responsibility. A candidate studying for public librarianship should go beyond general principles to municipal administration; the prospective college librarian, to advanced classes in college and university administration. In each case library administration would be given proper emphasis, *in its relation to the entire organization and operation* of the municipality or of the institution. The first course could be taken in the university's School of Business, perhaps, and the second in the School of Education. Such consolidation would eliminate from the library school curriculum the present catch-all known as "Library Administration." Another example: the librarian works with people, all types of people— city or college officials, alumni or politicians, faculties or smaller coteries of scholars, and with students and other patrons by the score. Yet few, if any, library schools offer in their curricula courses in personnel, social, educational, adult, or child psychology, or in the psychology of selling, behavior, or relationships. Indeed, such courses need not be introduced. Would it not be better to coördinate this important part of education for librarianship with the work offered in other departments of the university by scholars who are devoting their lives to the study of psychology?

Other examples could be drawn of the varied possibilities of a consolidated curriculum, especially in the social sciences and humanities. In fact, a good case might be made for the efficacy of consolidation in practically every phase of the present ritual for training librarians, except, of course, the technical. And this, after a fashion, is fortunate, for the area of "techniques" is admittedly the only one that the library school has mastered. Nor does this program necessarily imply the immediate abolishment of library schools. It does imply the eventual and almost complete abolishment of them as they now exist. For intellectual content would in time supplant the vocational, and out of the metamorphosis would emerge a curriculum worthy of recognition on the only ground that any professional curriculum deserves recognition—intellectual content. Moreover, from the school would be graduated sociologist-librarians, scientist-librarians, historian-librarians, economist-librarians—scholar-librarians all of whom would take their rightful places as educators in the hierarchy of learning.

The librarian ought to be the intellectual leader of his campus or community. To him everyone should be able to turn for educational guidance. He cannot be an ordinary person and be effective. His position should, therefore, be an esteemed one. It was in this spirit that Cotton des Houssayes told the General Assembly of the Sorbonne in 1780 that "your librarian" should have "an exact and precise knowledge of all the arts and sciences . . . and that exquisite politeness which conciliates the affection of his visitors while his merit secures their esteem."

Is this too much to ask? Not if one thinks of the whole library staff as a composite librarian, intellectually superimposed, as it were, one member upon another. Each is master of techniques in kind and quantity necessary to his specific tasks. Above that, each is intellectually competent in a chosen field of learning. Upon the foundation laid in his undergraduate study, perhaps, and made solid in his library education, each continually builds as a scholar. Multiply this by five, by ten, by fifty—and the school or the college library staff, small or large, becomes the "Associate Faculty"; that of the public library, the community's teaching corps. Together they form the first line of offense in today's most serious production problem—intellectual rearmament. When this is done, there will be no question about the librarian's meriting esteem, nor will there be fear for the inherited culture of America entrusted to his care.

FATHER WAS AN AUTHOR

Esquire: The Magazine for Men,
New York City, June, 1946.

If Father were alive today, he would be called an old-fashioned druggist. He believed in spatulas, mortars and pestles, rolled nasty-tasting pills, and never sold a clock in his life.

He knew everybody in our South Carolina county and everybody knew him. Yet in his forty years as a small-town pharmacist he never ran an ad in the local weekly or flashed a slide between reels at the Palace Theatre. I suppose he didn't need to, being an author.

Considered by contemporary standards, Father was a well-to-do man. When he died, he left his family comfortably fixed, as the saying goes. Looking back upon his success, I think it was mainly the result of his fair-dealing, straight-shooting attitude toward his customers (which was not necessarily odd) and to the fact that he wrote a book (which was).

In several ways Father's book was unique. He wrote it all in longhand, sweating over it in his spare time every day between customers for about twenty years, and developed scores of characters. I like to think of him as a kind of forerunner of the recent Southern literary renaissance.

Tom Wolfe would have so much enjoyed Father's stuff. So would William Faulkner, Erskine Caldwell and, perhaps, Lillian Smith, though I doubt if Father's contemporaries—Augusta Evans Wilson, say—would have pinned medals on his breast.

If Father's book was unique, so was its title. He read a great deal in the classics, but when it came to naming his own masterpiece, he wanted no literary hand-me-down.

I recall one morning at breakfast his telling mother what he planned

[247]

to call his work. Somehow, she didn't take to the idea and tried to get him to change it. He just smiled wryly.

That night he brought home a package neatly wrapped in slick, pale blue paper and laid it on the front hall table right next to our hatrack. After the supper dishes were done, mother saw it, opened it, gasped, ran into the bedroom and slammed the door. Father, calm and quite satisfied as always, continued to rock and smoke on the piazza. In his fair-dealing, straight-shooting way he had decided to call the work *My Son-of-a-B—-Book*. To this day I've never understood why Father left the *itch* out of the title, unless it was out of regard for mother.

My Son-of-a-B—-Book was never actually published. You will search in vain for it in the Library of Congress or among Chicago's Hundred Best, though by comparison it has some merit.

To be parson pure, I should say the book was never *printed*. Yet it was published, all right. In his day everybody that mattered knew about Father's book—everybody that mattered to Father, that is. They published it widely for him.

Meanwhile, Father basked in fame. And profited by it. Like some men you must know, he had a knack, a sort of a sixth sense, for publicity. Once, for instance, when he was past fifty and curb service was slowly becoming the vogue, a courting couple puffed up in front of the pharmacy in a new brass-burdened Maxwell and honked the horn. Passing the time of day with Ed Willis, Father talked on. Presently, the driver honked again, this time a series of playful, staccato honks.

Father politely excused himself and made for the door. Had you seen him, you'd have bet he was going out to take the order. But as he reached the car, he grabbed a handful of linen duster and jerked the driver down to his level. "You young whippersnapper," said Father without raising his voice, "what the hell do you mean, blowin' a damn horn at me. I'm no foxhound. If you want a soda, come in and get it. And if it's this new 'curb service' you're after, here it is." With that, he walked back into the store to pick up the conversation with Ed while the begoggled swain picked himself up out of the gutter.

Next morning Father appeared before the Town Council to get an "anti-curb service" ordinance passed, but the Council had other ideas. They fined him five dollars and costs for disorderly conduct. For years afterwards he would laugh and call that the cheapest publicity the pharmacy ever had. "Never," he used to say in anticipation of Churchill, "did so many dollars owe so much to so few."

My Son-of-a-B—-Book, in many respects a cultural study of our community, was for Father, however, a tool of vocational rather than liberal education. It was a one-man Retail Credit Association. When a customer called for a bottle of Dr. Miles' Nervine or a quarter's worth of C. C. pills and said, "Charge it, Doc," Father would thumb the book. If the customer's name were among the characters portrayed, Father would turn the book around and point to the overdue account. Never in my memory did a single customer offer any back talk.

Social economists who have examined the *S.O.B. Book* declare it unmatched as source material on the South of yesterday. Indeed, one eminent historian has told me that the volume, if properly edited by an alert graduate student, would satisfy the requirements of his university for the Ph.D. degree. Doubtless, it would. But the time-eating, meticulous task of editing Father's work would, in my opinion, leave the doctoral candidate precious little energy with which to combat a twelve-hour weekly teaching schedule after graduation.

One sheet, by chance open before me now, will prove the enormity of the job and, simultaneously, serve to illustrate (a) Father's literary technique, (b) the exacting scholarship demanded by an interpretation of it and (c) the far-reaching sociological implications of the book as a whole:

```
Milling R. Cogswell, B.D.A.,¹ S.C.V.²
   %Chet Manwell's Place³
   Swift Creek Rd.⁴ (C.L. $16)⁵
Jan.  1. Acct. brought fwd ...................................$11.65
      5. Rx 79864 (.85),⁶ Gum Ass.
         (.25)⁷ ............................................1.10
     10. BWI ($1),⁸ Lemex (.75)⁹ ..............................1.75
     18. Baldy ($1),¹⁰ Mdse. (.50)¹¹ ..........................1.50
                         T.A.B.¹²                 $16.00
   (See footnotes below)
```

As a literary historian, I could of course throw much light on the influence of Father's private life upon his writing (or vice versa). But all this I leave to more capable scholars who will doubtless now work

---

[1] *Broken Down Aristocracy*, a social group, prevalent in the South, which strove to make the Civil War a second Hundred Years' War.

[2] *Son of a Confederate Veteran.*

[3] Manwell's Place, formerly the Cogswell Plantation, was owned by its *Ex-Overseer.*

[4] At the time of this entry, Swift Creek Road ran north from the Court House. Scholars will be interested to know that it now (1946) runs in the same direction.

[5] Cogswell's *Credit Limit* (see 12, below).

[6] Well-known pharmaceutical abbreviation which, translated literally, means, "Swallow and ask questions later."

[7] Gum Asafoetida. Rolled into a pellet and worn around one's neck, this foul-smelling drug is supposed to ward off germs. If bipeds are germs, it works.

[8] Beef, Wire & Iron, a "Spring Tonic" used throughout the South during all seasons, especially Prohibition.

[9] Lemon Extract. Theoretically a cake flavoring (ditto 8, above.)

[10] Trade name for "Dr. Alexander's Remarkable Hair Restorer" (see 8 and 9, above.)

[11] Mdse., code-word used throughout the *S.O.B.* book to charge certain items of strictly personal nature which the customer did not wish to have identified on his bill.

[12] Intense research has proved this to mean *"That's All, Brother"* (see 5, above).

to pursue their new find, like a sinking star, to the utmost bounds of human thought. As for me, I feel that in casting Father's art at their feet I have fulfilled my duty to contemporary American *belles-lettres*.

THE C.S.S. *ALABAMA* AT CAPE TOWN: CENTENNIAL CELEBRATION, 1863–1963

The Alabama Review, Alabama Historical Association,
University of Alabama and Auburn University, July, 1964.

The C.S.S. *Alabama*, built in Liverpool, England by Laird Brothers Company for the Confederate States Navy, was launched on July 28, 1862, sailed to the Azores and placed under the command of Captain Raphael Semmes. During the next twelve months the gallant cruiser criss-crossed the North Atlantic, ran within two hundred miles of New York City, circled theWest Indies, fought and sank the U.S.S. *Hatteras* in the Gulf of Mexico, plowed into the South Atlantic and eastward along the Tropic of Capricorn to Cape Town, South Africa, dropping anchor there on July 29, 1863. All together she had traveled 25,000 miles and captured and destroyed fifty-odd Yankee vessels valued at more than two million dollars.

Beside the *Alabama* as she lay at anchor in Capt Town harbor was another Confederate cruiser, only recently arrived, a small barque-rigged clipper of but one-third the tonnage, the C.S.S. *Tuscaloosa,* commanded by Captain John Low, a Scotsman from Savannah who had formerly served Semmes as a lieutenant on the *Alabama.* Actually, the *Tuscaloosa* had been in Confederate service only two months. Built in Philadelphia and named the *Conrad,* she was captured by the *Alabama* off the coast of Brazil and rechristened the *Tuscaloosa* "after that pretty little town on the Black Warrior River." Semmes declared that it was meet that "a child of the *Alabama* should be named after one of the towns of that state." She was a "very pretty vessel indeed," wrote John M. Kell, Semmes's executive officer. And Arthur Sinclair stated in his *Two Years on the Alabama* that "a more beautiful specimen of the American clipper could not have been pro-duced,—she was new, well-found, and fast, with long tapering masts and flaring bow. . . ."

Semmes ordered Low to sail the *Tuscaloosa* out "on a cruise against the commerce of the United States [and] destroy all the enemy's ships which fall into your power." The two captains, after secretly agreeing to meet in Cape Town in two months, sailed away as the crew of the *Alabama* leaped into the rigging, waved their caps, and gave three lusty cheers for the newborn fighter, the C.S.S. *Tuscaloosa.*

The arrival in Cape Town of the *Alabama* and the *Tuscaloosa* created such excitement as had seldom been seen in the South African colony.

From the moment their anchors were dropped their decks were crowded with visitors who ogled the guns and the men, leaving behind fruit, fresh vegetables and native curios as tributes. Semmes's cabin was filled hour after hour with men, women, and children who pressed forward simply to shake his hand and express sympathy for the Confederate cause. As a reporter from the Cape Town *Cape Argus* dramatically put it,

> The inhabitants, rich and poor, halt, maimed, lame and blind—not only old men and maidens, young men and children, but old women 'dragons and all deep' went off to see the *Alabama,* her Captain and her officers . . . they rushed up the ladder, up the sides of the ship, swung up by the rattlings, crawled through the port holes, over the rails, wherever there was space to crawl, or anything to get hold of, there were human beings swarming like bees about a hive. They hung in bunches, scrambled over each other, buzzing, bawling and waspy old gentlemen, lazy old drones, queen bees, honey bees and bees of every description hung together and squeezed each other with dreadfully desperate determination. There were the beauty and fashion, fashion without beauty and beauty minus fashion. When the decks were full the persevering ones mounted the sides of the ship, climbed the rigging, sat about on the gun carriages, went from aft to for'd and fa'd to below in the cabin, engine room and forecastle—everywhere.

And Lieutenant Arthur Sinclair, who was in the midst of all the excitement, wrote that,

> It is safe to say that Cape Town was almost depopulated . . . by the general turnout to visit the *Alabama.* Every imaginable form and model of boats were represented in the throng around our ship. Boatmen and longshoremen, struggling, vociferating and swearing to get first alongside. Boats of rowing-clubs, their crew in neat and appropriate uniforms, yachtmen on their craft; tugs, passenger-boats, and even dug-outs; anything that could float was brought into requisition. . . . The English, the foster-fathers of the *Alabama,* are naturally proud of their creation, and they appear to be also in sympathy with us and our cause.

The *Cape Argus* and the *South African Advertiser and Mail* followed virtually every move made by Semmes and his officers and men. The editor of the latter wrote that there was really "nothing piratical" about Semmes. "He is rather below middle stature, his face care-worn and sunburnt, the features striking. . . . He is close-shaved with the exception of a grey moustache twisted a la Napoleon, above the corners of his mouth." As for his clothes, he wore "an old grey, stained uniform, the surtout, with battered shoulder straps and faded gold trimmings buttoned close up to the throat." The *Cape Argus* reporter spent two hours interviewing Semmes, declairing that "a more genial man I never met—he was as full of humour as an egg is full of meat." His officers, the writer continued, were "as fine and gentlemanly a set of fellows as we ever saw."

By this time all of Cape Town was suffering from what was called

"Alabama Fever." Visitors by the hundreds boarded the ship, bursting with enthusiasm. Thomas Bowler, a local artist, painted the cruiser in oils. Edward Searle sketched her in black and white as she stood off Moille Point Lighthouse. She was the subject of the first diorama ever drawn in South Africa. Semmes and his officers wined and dined with Admiral Sir Baldwin Walker and Governor Sir Philip E. Wodehouse, Queen Victoria's ranking military and civilian authorities in South Africa. Officers from the *Alabama* and the *Tuscaloosa* were entertained by Captain Forsyth aboard H.M.S. *Valorous*. The one-hundred twenty-odd crewmen from the two Confederate ships, rough, tough seafaring men they were, took their comfort in Cape Town saloons and bawdy houses, enjoying their shore leaves among the "ladies from the east end," getting drunk and jailed, sightseeing, fighting, and carousing, and riding up and down the roads in stagecoaches. One man, Engineer Simeon W. Cummings, of Louisiana, borrowed a gun, went hunting, and accidentally shot himself. He was buried high on a hill overlooking Saldanha Bay in the family graveyard of a friendly farmer with all honors due his rank. His shipmates erected a marker to his memory, a stone which still stands, a weather-worn and all but obliterated memorial to the only Confederate left behind in South Africa.

On August 12 Semmes appropriately presented the City of Cape Town a flag from the *Alabama* in appreciation of its courtesies and, afterwards, invited photographers aboard to make pictures of the cruiser and her officers. The pictures were later offered for sale by the *Cape Argus* and were years later published in the United States in Francis T. Miller's *The Photographic History of the Civil War*.

But the most intriguing recollection of the *Alabama* in that faraway land is the ballad, "Here Comes the Alabama," still sung in both English and Afrikaan, which the Moslem Cape Malays made and moaned as they watched the famous cruiser sailing in and out South African waters.

Here Comes the Alabama

Here comes the *Alabama*, the *Alabama* comes o'er the sea,
Here comes the *Alabama*, the *Alabama* comes o'er the sea,
Girl, girl, the reed-bed girl, the reed-bed is made-up,
The reed-bed is made for me
On which to sleep.
Girl, girl, the reed-bed girl, the reed-bed is made-up
The reed-bed is made for me
On which to sleep.

Daar Kom die Alabama

Daar kom *Alabama*, *Alabama* kom oor die see,
Daar kom *Alabama*, *Alabama* kom oor die see,
Nooi, nooi, die riet-kooi nooi, die rietkooi is gemaak,
Die rietkooi is vir my gemaak,

Om daarop te slaap
Nooi, nooi, die riet-kooi nooi, die rietkooi is gemaak,
Die rietkooi is vir my gemaak,
Om daarop te slaap.

After ten days in harbor the *Tuscaloosa*, now freshly provisioned and repaired, sailed out of Cape Town, northward and westward along the coast to her equatorial hunting grounds between Brazil and Africa, her mission to capture and kill any and all enemy bottoms which crossed her path. A few days later British Admiralty officials secretly warned Semmes that the U.S.S. *Vanderbilt* had been sighted cruising in the South Atlantic. He quickly pointed the *Alabama's* nose northeastward in the Indian Ocean, toward the Bay of Bengal and the China Sea.

For more than a hundred years the people of Cape Town have kept alive their great admiration for the *Alabama* and the *Tuscaloosa*. The fascinating history of these two gallant ships has become a part of the history of South Africa. The Confederate flag presented the city by Captain Semmes still hangs in the South African Museum. "Here Comes the Alabama" is still the best-known and most frequently sung of all the Cape Malay folk songs. Frank and Edna Bradlow, local authors, have recently written a book about the Confederate cruisers and their sojourn in Cape Town. William Fehr, a local businessman, has personally amassed a notable collection of paintings and books relating to Confederate-South African history and lore.

On July 29, 1963 enthusiastic Capetonians celebrated the one-hundreth anniversary of the arrival of the *Alabama* and the *Tuscaloosa* with appropriate ceremonies. More than two hundred people assembled in the Union-Castle building for the showing of a documentary film, made in sound and color by the Johnston-Frater Company, depicting the principal events surrounding the *Tuscaloosa's* and *Alabama's* visits to Cape Town. Among the distinguished guests were Mayor A. H. Honikman of Cape Town, Mr. J. H. Mower, United States consul in Cape Town, Mr. Charles Manning, United States consul-general in South Africa, and members of the South African National Society.

Prior to the screening of the film, Mayor Honikman read a resolution from the Sons of the Confederate Veterans, and Consul-General Manning conveyed a message of goodwill from the people of Cape Town to the people of the State of Alabama. Tape-recorded addresses, expressing congratulations and appreciation from America, written by Dr. Wm. Stanley Hoole of the University of Alabama and Mr. Oliver J. Semmes, of Pensacola, a great-grandson of Captain Semmes, were played for the assembled guests. The Central Malay Choir of Cape Town sang "Here Comes the Alabama" in both English and Afrikaan, after which the guests attended a party given by Mr. and Mrs. R. H. Johnston and Mr. Charles Frater. The next day the cere-

[253]

monies were concluded with the planting of a tree at the grave of Lieutenant Cummings by Consul Mower.

The Cape Town centennial services were broadcast over South African television and radio and a copy of the color film, *Here Comes the Alabama,* was sent to this writer for showing at the 1964 meeting of the Alabama Historical Association. It was the American premiere of the film. Following this meeting the film was then turned over to the University of Alabama Libraries for permanent deposit and for public screening throughout the state, or elsewhere.

THE GILMANS AND *THE SOUTHERN ROSE*

The North Carolina Historical Review, Raleigh,
April, 1934.

Within two years after the establishment of the first Unitarian Church of South Carolina, the pastor, Anthony M. Forster, died, and the small congregation chose as his successor the Reverend Samuel Gilman of Gloucester, Massachusetts. This young preacher had come South early in the year (1819) for a few months probationary service, had been well liked, and had returned to Gloucester in October to marry Caroline Howard, the main subject of this paper. In November he and his bride established their home in the city where they were destined to serve for more than forty years.

When the young couple reached their charge, Gilman was only 28, but already known as an author of some merit. In 1812 he had published a *Monody on the Victims of the Sufferers by the Late Conflagration in the City of Richmond;* in 1815 he had translated Florian's *Galatea,* and had delivered at Harvard the much-talked-of Phi Beta Kappa poem, *Human Life.* Besides other contributions to contemporary journals, he had published numerous translations of Boileau's *Satires.* His wife had also made her début in literary circles by publishing at the age of sixteen a poem, "Jephtha's Rash Vow," and other effusions in local newspapers. At once Mr. and Mrs. Gilman fitted themselves into the literary, social, religious, and philanthropic institutions of Charleston. The Reverend Mr. Gilman, "not only a scholar and a thinker, but a man of the greatest purity and beauty of character, beloved and respected by all," experienced no difficulty in being recognized immediately as one of the outstanding literary figures in the aristocratic southern city.

Continued literary efforts did not interfere with his work as pastor. Among other duties, he labored as a teacher in order to remove certain encumbrances on his residence, not ceasing until anonymous friends sent him "an enclosure containing $1,000," with an earnest request that he "teach no more." In 1852 he was instrumental in erecting

[254]

a new church, and in the same year presented the congregation with a new Service Book.

Meanwhile the pastor continued his excursions into literature by writing a series of essays on "Inquiry Into Cause and Effect," and by publishing it in the Boston *Christian Examiner.* In 1828 his popular and interesting "Memoirs," in which he gave his early experiences and noted the "changes that have occurred in our taste for sacred music," came from the press; in 1822, his poem, "The History of a Ray of Light," attracted general attention. In 1825 a sermon was published in pamphlet form; and a sermon preached in Augusta, Georgia, December 27, 1827, received in part the following review in *The Christian Examiner:*

> We have often expressed our pleasure on receiving this writer's productions, and it has become a matter of course with us to expect something ingenious and striking in whatever comes from his pen. We have not been disappointed in respect to the sermon before us. . . .

At intervals the minister would make trips to Massachusetts to keep in touch with relatives, Edward Everett, other friends, and *The North American Review.* At all times he was ready to aid those who needed him. Particularly attractive was his anonymously published article in behalf of the Reformed Society of Israelites of Charleston. In 1836 his interest in a national literature was incorporated in "The Influence of One National Literature upon Another; with an Application of the Subject to the Character and Development of American Literature," an essay in which the minister alleges "that every nation, like every individual, has an intellectual and moral character, orignal and peculiar to itself," and urges that Americans should "cherish in our literature the peculiar qualities of the American character, as an indispensable groundwork for the appropriation of all other materials." He lists these qualities as "the free, the intrepid, the excursive, the inventive," and adds that—

> the traces of these . . . we also perceive in what little national literature we yet can boast of, as having made an impression on the European world. The theologian Edwards,—our state papers, so eulogized by Madame de Staël,—our recent historians,—our eagle-winged Channing, and the bird-of-paradise-plumed Irving,—our Brockden Brown,—our other few distinguished novelists,—and the *élite* of Bryant's, Percival's, and other successful American poetry,—all exhibit the possession of these common characteristics.

Doctor Gilman was a particular friend of James Gates Percival, whose poems he favorably reviewed and whom he helped in other ways. When Percival went to Charleston, he found in the pastor a "warm friend." Throughout his lifetime he and Mrs. Gilman befriended Mary Elizabeth Lee, popular nineteenth century Charleston poetess; upon her death Doctor Gilman edited her poems with a forty-one-page biographical memoir. When Edward Everett's *Orations and Speeches* was published, Doctor Gilman wrote a "Critical Essay on the Oratory of Edward Everett," and one year later, at Everett's residence, delivered a poem in celebration of their graduation forty-one years before. He contributed frequently to the publications of the Unitarian Association, and was a moving force in The New England Society of Charleston. His last utterance before the Society was couched in the form of a prayer for everlasting peace and reconciliation between the fast diverging sections. In appreciation of favors extended him by Doctor Gilman and "His Estimable Lady," S. G. Bulfinch dedicated a volume of his poems to the obliging couple.

After Doctor Gilman's death in 1858 his religious tracts were put into the hands of the public. They were well received, for the writer was considered one of the most powerful members of the Unitarian faith in America. Some idea of the respect in which he was held may be obtained from a letter written by James Louis Petigru to his sister, February 18, 1858:

> How much I was shocked by Colonel Hampton's death, and Mr. Gilman's was made known the same day.... The funeral of Mr. Gilman was like that of a great minister of state. It was the best evidence of the high estimation in which he was held, that the church, long before the hours of the service, was filled to overflowing and crowds remained outside until sundown....

Mrs. Gilman's efforts in the realm of literature during her first twelve years residence in Charleston were not so numerous as her husband's. With the exception of a few widely scattered poems, nothing came from her pen. In 1823 she gave birth to a daughter, Caroline Howard, who in later years was destined to uphold the literary standard of the family; but is was not until 1832 that Mrs. Gilman, fired no doubt by her husband's interest in the children of the church, conceived the idea of printing "the first weekly newspaper for children in the United States." This hebdomadal which she affectionately called "the first juvenile newspaper, if I mistake not, in the Union," and which was instigated for the purpose of "giving to the youthful mind a right direction," made its début on August 11, 1832, under the title, *The Rose-Bud or Youth's Gazette.*

This little periodical had as its caption, "The Rose is Fairest When 'Tis Budding New," and was printed by J. S. Burgess, 44 Queen Street, Charleston. The "Editor's Column" flatters "many an American boy and girl" by stating that they are to have "a real newspaper like father," and begs of the young folk original writings. Religious and political matters are barred, writes the editor, who adds that she has chosen her title because she wants all little children to be pure like the *Rose.* A book section recommends the better sort of child literature; children's journals appear, school problems are discussed periodically, and the doings of juvenile organizations receive due space. Soon letters from subscribers begin to adorn the inner pages, side by side with Mrs. Gilman's own poetry for youthful minds. To say the least, the paper was a great favorite. "Tastefully conducted," it soon became the "sprightliest of the ephemeral publications of Charleston," and almost immediately "its character was elevated to the standard of a highly influential newspaper."

After a run of one year the editor saw fit to make marked changes in her magazine: *The Rose-Bud or Youth's Gazette* suddenly grew into *The Southern Rose-Bud*, a title which was retained until the beginning of volume four. Beginning with the issue of August 31, 1833, it was printed in "an enlarged form with improved paper" and was "adapted in many points to mature readers, though not relinquishing the juvenile department." The prospectus of volume two contains tributes to some of the prominent men of the city who had in various ways assisted the *Rose-Bud:* gradually, the children's magazine was becoming a sheet for grown-ups.

With the appearance of volume three the readers were again greeted by alterations, though the name remained *The Southern Rose-Bud*. This time it was an eight-page paper, bi-monthly instead of weekly, and more suited to "family reading . . . and the taste of young gentlemen and ladies of maturer years." The column for younger readers was not, however, entirely discarded. Startling indeed must have been the first issue with its sections called "The Pruning Knife," "The Flower Vase," "News Items," in addition to the heterogeneous but chastened effusions of wit and sentiment. Not yet satisfied, the editor announced in June, 1835, that, beginning with volume four, there were to be many and drastic changes. The reader cannot refrain from believing, however, that beneath it all Mrs. Gilman was motivated by something deeper than mere hope of commercial gain.

The new issue, volume four, now called *The Southern Rose*, and with a new caption, "Flowers of all hue, and without the Thorn the Rose," fulfilled all of the promises of the prospectus. Under the heading, "Original Pieces," the editor was able to print longer articles; in the "Exotic" section appeared translations, such as Tromlitz's *The Hand-Organ Player*, and *The Day of Granson*. Moral and religious subjects were discussed under a division by that name, usually signed by "Apollos" (Doctor Gilman), while news of the world was tersely recorded in the "Leaf and Stem Basket." "The Bud," last entrenchment of the juvenile section, included such pieces as "The Wisher—A Fairy Tale," "Anecdotes for Young Readers," and occasionally obituary notices of youthful subscribers. The "Editor's Boudoir" gave Mrs. Gilman opportunity to offer in Platonic dialogue between "Medora" and "Lisa" voluminous criticisms of the events of the day; the entire last page was devoted to "Original Poetry."

[257]

In many ways volumes IV, V, and VI were the most successful ones of the ephemeral Charleston publication. Principally, these volumes were devoted to the results of the editor's own pen: *Recollections of a Southern Matron* and *Notes of a Northern Excursion* appeared at the same time, along with many of her poems, and the contributions of her husband. "The Pruning Knife" continued to operate, this time being a critical analysis of *The Westminister Review, The London Quarterly Review, The Edinburgh Review,* and *The Foreign Quarterly Review.* Under "The Turf-Seat Shade" readers were given critical information concerning the latest American and foreign books.

By no means did the editor exclude other writers from *The Southern Rose.* On the contrary, every number is graced with poems, translations, anecdotes, and articles by some of the better known *literati* of the nineteenth century. Harriet Martineau, Mary Elizabeth Lee, Anna Maria Wells (sister of Frances S. Osgood), Robert M. Charlton, Penina Moise, William J. Rivers, Miss H. F. Gould, Elizabeth F. Ellett, William Henry Timrod (father of Henry Timrod), and William Gilmore Simms contributed to the success of Mrs. Gilman's bi-monthly publication. In addition there were many anonymous sketches, such as "Extracts of a Journal Kept on a Tour from Charleston to New York," and "New Orleans in 1832."

Upon the beginning of volume VI, further changes were made in *The Southern Rose.* Mrs. Gilman began on May 26, 1838, another serial novel: *Love's Progress, or Ruth Raymond.* Mary E. Lee, R. M. Charlton, Mary Howitt, and many initialed contributors served to enhance the popularity of the magazine. Doctor Gilman's moral and religious effusions occupy a noticeable part of the text, and there is frequent evidence of the use of scissors and paste. But the editor must have been pleased with the volume, and with the material that was coming in, for she remarked that—

> the Sixth Volume of *The Southern Rose,* of which the next number will be the last, promises to go out, so far as Contributors are concerned, in a blaze of glory.

Is there evidence here of an understatement of brooding financial dissatisfaction? Once again, in the prospectus of volume VII, the same note is faintly apparent: the editor solicits from the many patrons—

> a continuation of their favors, and from the public at large a more extended encouragement of the work. Its reputation is of such a kind, and is so well established, as to require no particular encomiums. It is only necessary to observe that the Editor of the first six volumes will sustain the same relation to *The Rose* as hitherto, and that the circle of its Contributors is continually enlarging.

Suffice it to say that the editor foresaw the end of her publication.

Attached to the first issue of the seventh volume was a fine wood-cut of Meeting Street, showing the Hall of the South Carolina Society, and St. Michael's Church. As to contents there was little change: the roster of contributors increased alarmingly, but many pieces were rejected because they did not "afford sufficient novelty for the *Rose*." Of the issue of November 24, 1838, approximately one-half is given to a flattering discussion of "the new comet, or rather meteor, shooting athwart the literary sky of old Massachusetts, in the person of Ralph Waldo Emerson," a writer who was "attracting much public attention." Doctor Gilman continued his translations of the works of Boileau, and another New Englander, Nathaniel Hawthorne, was represented by an Apologue entitled "The Lily's Quest," written "especially for *The Southern Rose*." A few issues later Hawthorne was the subject of a lengthy and just review.

Throughout the seventh volume there seems to be an ever-increasing tendency on the part of Mrs. Gilman to copy from various news-sheets over the United States. Too much padded material is obvious. Evidence indicates that the editor of "the first juvenile newspaper" was tiring of her job. On August 17, 1839, the last issue of *The Southern Rose* contained the following dismissal, called the "Valedictory Address":

> With a thousand good wishes, and in perfectly happy humor towards her large circle of subscribers, the Editor bids them, in this number, an affectionate farewell. She ceases from her pleasant toils, not in consequence of any special discouragement,—for her Publisher is desirous of continuing the periodical, and assures her that, by very slight exertions, a generous remuneration might be obtained for the expenses and labors incident to the establishment; but, as she approached her office seven years ago through an impulse perfectly voluntary, so she retires from it now with the same unimpaired feeling of liberty. Should she continue in the career of literature, towards which the public have in various ways extended such indulgent encouragement, she would prefer some mode of publication less exacting than the rigorous punctuality of a periodical work.

The editor continues to say that she will have "nothing but delightful reminiscences" of her connection with the ephemeral magazine, and that she will continue to hold in warm gratitude those who rendered her occupation "at once her pleasure and her pride." "Reader," she asks finally and most pathetically,—

> Reader, have you ever left the door of a friend with her smile still impressed on your vision, and a freshly pluck'd blossom from her hand just fastened in your bosom? With such tokens of good will are you now dismissed by
>
> THE EDITOR OF THE ROSE.

Thus was written the finale of *The Southern Rose*, the flower which grew so rapidly and so changingly in the salubrity of the rarefied atmosphere of literary Charleston for exactly seven years.

That Caroline Gilman preferred "some mode of publication less exacting than the rigorous punctuality of a periodical work" becomes a truer statement that the mere swan song of an editor, if a survey of her publications is taken into account. She had already (in 1835, 1836, 1838) published in book form some of her better works for the *Rose*, and as soon as she laid aside the tasks of editorship, other proofs of her literary efforts were rattled through the northern presses. In 1839 there were three books: *Tales and Ballads, Ladies' Annual Register,* and *Letters of Eliza Wilkinson. Love's Progress; or Ruth Raymond* was gleaned from the *Rose* and put out in one volume in 1840; and in 1841 *The Rosebud Wreath* was issued in Charleston. In 1845 *Oracles from the Poets* was printed in Philadelphia; a second edition appeared in 1853. *Sibyl, or New Oracles from the Poets,* came out in New York, in 1849, as did a book of poems old and new, called *Verses of a Life Time* (Boston). A collection of verses dedicated to children was published in 1859 under the title, *Oracles for Youth,* and in 1860 a compilation of inscriptions was put into the hands of the public. In 1872 she collaborated with her daughter to publish *Poems and Stories by a Mother and Daughter.*

Throughout her works Mrs. Gilman was "inspired by a warm domestic affection, and pure religious feeling," and her delicate wit, unaffected pathos, and vividly drawn characters drew to her hosts of readers. Griswold says of her books that they "will long be valued for the spirit and fidelity with which she has painted rural and domestic life." He praises her "skill in character writing," her "artist-like power of grouping," and her "love of nature and good sense." She was indeed "one of the most popular writers of her day." Among the authors of South Carolina she has been graced with the title, "the most eminent woman writer," but it is as the industrious editor of *The Southern Rose* that she has been chiefly remembered. Here one finds the unassuming, tender, and quite skillful editor of a periodical that won for itself not only the name of the first juvenile publication in the country, but won for its founder the title of one of the first female editors in the United States.

After the death of her husband, Mrs. Gilman retained her residence in Charleston. Thoroughly sympathetic with the South in the Civil War, she faithfully remained in the seaport town and assisted the ladies "at work for the soldiers." Throughout her many letters written during the siege of Charleston she reveals an unfaltering trust in the ideals of her adopted land, in spite of the fact that her children held opposite views. When shells began to fall into the cellar of her Orange Street residence, however, she moved, March, 1862, to Greenville, S. C., where she had engaged a house. Shortly after her arrival in that Piedmont village, she affiliated herself with the "Greenville Ladies' Association in Aid of the Volunteers of the Confederate Army," on whose minutes her name appears as "Directress" and later as an officer.

On November 14, 1865, she returned to her Charleston home to find that her "books, private papers, and pictures" had been stolen; but, undaunted, she set out to begin "a new era in life." As late as 1882 she was living with friends at 7 Orange Street, but, before 1887, she moved to Washington to live with her daughter. As far as is known, Mrs. Gilman made no further forays into the field of literature after 1872. She died in Washington, September 15, 1888, having for three score years been a loyal contributor to, and a worthy critic of, the literature of the locality which she loved so devotedly.

To be sure the Gilmans cannot be ranked with the more gloriously hailed American authors. But those who are interested in getting a glimpse of the ante-bellum South as it really was, its gayety as well as its earnestness, its tastes and its standards, and above all its fascinating power as a subject for social and literary history, have but to turn the pages of the works of this inimitable couple. Unpretentious as they were, but "better known than àny of the ephemeral publications" of the South before 1840, *The Rose-Bud or Youth's Gazette* and the maturer and more comprehensive *The Southern Rose* offer, in their quiet and dainty manner, another chapter in that gala literary history that made Charleston the mecca for literature and culture in the Old South.

ALABAMA BUILT SUBMARINE WAS FIRST TO SINK A BATTLESHIP!

Birmingham [Alabama] *News Monthly Magazine*, December, 13, 1953.

The first submarine ever to sink a battleship in time of war was built in an Alabama shipyard and piloted by an Alabama officer!

She was the *H. L. Hunley* of the Confederate States Navy.

The *Hunley* was an invention born of necessity. In 1861, when the powerful United States Navy began blockading every Confederate harbor, cutting off the South's coal, steel, wool and other urgently-needed supplies, something had to be done—and quickly. The Confederate Congress offered handsome rewards to the inventor of any device that would destroy an enemy blockader and six months later appropriated $350,00 for the establishment of the world's first "Naval Submarine Battery Service." Chief among the experimental stations was the one at Mobile, which was strategically located near iron foundries, rolling mills, powder factories, and arsenals throughout the heavily-mineralized state of Alabama.

At first, any number of fantastic torpedoes were tried by the desperate Confederates: Ram. pronged, framed, raft, buoy, key, clockwork, and electric. But they were feeble forerunners of a real iron-clad underwater vessel the Confederates began building near New Orleans in 1861 under the supervision of Capt. Horace L. Hunley of the Confederate States Navy, and his assistants, James R. McClintock and Baxter Watson, marine engineers.

On her first test cruise on Lake Pontchartrain, in February, 1861, this fish-shaped submarine, 20-odd feet long and dragging a tube of explosives behind her, dove under a target barge and blew it to smithereens. When she surfaced, all the Confederates cheered—here, at long last, was the answer to the Federal blockade!

A few days later the mysterious craft was sent out to battle the enemy fleet below New Orleans. But she sank and never came up. All eight crew members perished, marking the first submarine disaster in history.

Undaunted, Capt. Hunley and his men decided they could build a better submarine, if they had more time and better tools and forges. In the iron shops of Parks & Lyons, on Water St. in Mobile, Ala., they found all they needed—the best equipment in the South. Hastily, they moved their machinery and began the long, hard work all over again. After a year's efforts and many heartaches, they had constructed a new and much improved vessel. She was christened the *H. L. Hunley* in honor of her inventor and builder, who had paid much of the cost of the second craft out of his own pocket.

The *Hunley* was a cigar-shaped vessel 50 feet long, six feet deep and five feet wide and was made of welded sections of heavy galvanized iron. Her motive power consisted of a handscrew propeller worked by a crew of eight or 10 men. Although the only supply of air was that locked within the vessel before she submerged, the Hunley was capable of maintaining her crew under water an hour or more. Water ballast tanks, for rising and sinking, could be filled or emptied at will. Steering was controlled by a rudder and a pair of lateral fins. Light was supplied by candles. And she could do from three to five knots under smooth water.

When submerged, the Hunley showed only the tops of her conning tower. Her firepower was provided by the torpedo she towed behind her—much like a small boy pulling a toy. Diving some 300 feet or more before reaching her target, she ran beneath it, dragging the death charge which was designed to explode on contact with the enemy's hull.

The Hunley was sent to Charleston, S. C., to attempt to break the blockade of that port. It's first three attempts were tragic failures, however.

Capt. Hunley, upon receiving the news of the three tragedies, hastened up from Mobile, bringing with him his friend, Lt. George E. Dixon of Company E, 21st Alabama Volunteers. Lt. Dixon had successfully experimented with the *Hunley* in Mobile Bay and knew more about her than any other man, save her builder.

After a fourth test failure the *Hunley* was towed dismally to dry dock and under the experienced direction of Lt. Dixon, she was repaired and made seaworthy. Then, Dixon, an unusually brave, cool-headed man, applied to Commod. John R. Tucker, commanding Confederate naval forces at Charleston, for permission to use the submarine against the U.S.S. *Housatonic*, the enemy's powerful new 1240-ton warship riding at anchor in North Channel.

Commod. Tucker consented. And at 8:30 o'clock on the night of Feb. 17, 1864, the gallant Alabamian and his volunteer crew submerged the *Hunley* and slowly began their perilous underwater run across Charleston Harbor.

Thirty minutes later Master J. K. Crosby, deck officer of the *Housatonic*, spied something coming directly toward the ship that looked "like a plank moving in the water." He hesitated. Then, suddenly, frantically he sounded the alarm. All hands dashed to quarters, the cable was slipped, the warship's engines backed, and excited sailors helplessly fired rifles at the oncoming destroyer. It all took but a few minutes—but that was too long!

Lt. Dixon had closed in, fired his boom torpedo into the *Housatonic's* starboard side just forward of her mizzenmast, ripping a huge hole below her water-line. Within four minutes the mighty man-of-war lay on the bottom of the channel. Five of the *Housatonic's* crew were killed by the explosion—the others scampered up the rigging, abandoning ship.

For the first time in history a submarine had sunk a battleship in wartime. . . .

But the *Hunley* and all her men had given their last full measure of devotion. Whether swamped by water from the explosion, struck or sucked down by the *Housatonic*, no one has ever known, but again the *Hunley* had become a coffin for her entire crew.

CHARLESTON THEATRICALS DURING THE TRAGIC DECADE, 1860–1869

Journal of Southern History, Rice Institute, Houston, Texas, November, 1945.

Students of Charleston history during and immediately following the Civil War have long painted a desolate picture of attack, siege, bombardment, blockade, death, destruction by fire, surrender, and, finally, occupation by Federal forces. These truths and others equally disconsolate no one doubts. Yet there was a brighter, cheerier side. Amid their sufferings Charlestonians remained calm, eagerly determined to catch the few remaining pleasures life held out for them. Chief among these was the drama. Indeed, a century and a quarter of theatrical and musical tradition lay behind the thinking of these Carolinians, charting their course; in spite of war and its evils the show had to go on. That it did go on will ever be a tribute to the gallant city and a fighting people. This paper is an attempt to present a record of that fight for amusement during an otherwise bleak and dreary and tragic decade.

During its last season, October-December, 1861, the twenty-four-year-old Charleston Theatre, generally recognized as one of the finest theatres in America, played but a minor role in the city's cultural activities. Too many and weighty were the tragedies of real life in these stirring days for Charlestonians to be greatly concerned with make-believe. Only a year before, on December 20, 1860, South Carolina had seceded from the Union. In January of the next year the *Star of the West* had been fired upon as she attempted to reinforce Major Robert Anderson's Federal garrison in Fort Sumter. Three months later General Pierre G. T. Beauregard had arrived to assume command of the Confederate military. In April the historic attack on Fort Sumter had begun; and in May the beleaguered seaport had been blockaded by the U.S.S. *Niagara* and twenty-four men-of-war. Meanwhile, ladies' volunteer organizations knitted, sewed, and cared for the wounded. Troops arrived daily from up-state, left daily for the battlefields of Virginia. War words filled the *Courier* and the *Mercury*: reports of conflict, casualty lists, a new Congress, a new flag. And in mid-November had come news that Port Royal, fifty miles down the seacoast, had been captured by General Thomas W. Sherman. Invasion of Charleston was imminent. There was little thought for the closed theatre on Meeting Street.

Bravely, however, G. F. Marchant decided to carry on the show. Since 1857 he had managed the Charleston, bringing to its stage such famous players as Edwin Booth, Fanny Davenport, James E. Murdock, Julia Dean, Adelina Patti, Adelaide Phillips, William E. Burton, and Edward A. Sothern. Now, as the dark clouds of war hung oppressively low over the city, Manager Marchant believed more than ever that his fellow citizens needed and wanted amusement. On October 15, 1861, therefore, he opened the Charleston for its twenty-fourth year, presenting the Savannah quartette "in aid of the sick and wounded soldiers." A week later the Thespian Family played *Troubadour Soldier, Une Fille Terrible!*, and *Soldier and Boarder* "for the benefit of the Irish Volunteers." Following them came the Zouaves, French soldiers of the Crimea, who on six consecutive nights performed *Les Deux Avengeles, Les Folies Dramatiques*, and *The Barber of Seville* to "fair-sized audiences." On November 30 a short drama, appropriately entitled *The Battalion of Forlorn Hope*, was offered, and as an added attraction the Charleston Volunteers did "fancy drills upon the stage." But these attempts were only partly successful and Marchant, his finger close on the public pulse, closed the Charleston for a brief recess.

Eleven days later, on December 11, the Charleston Theatre, made famous by the Booths, the Wallacks, Jenny Lind, Anna Cora Mowatt, William Macready, Edmund Kean, and other internationally beloved celebrities of the stage, was destroyed by fire. With the theatre went one-third of the entire city: Cameron's Foundry containing an immense store of ammunition, the Art Gallery, the famous Circular Church, Apprentice Library, Institute Hall, St. Finbar's Cathedral, and hundreds of other buildings and dwellings.

Amid such tragedy it seems incredible that Charlestonians would still have demanded theatricals. But within three months after the great fire, while much of the city was yet an ash-piled ruin, Hibernian Hall on Meeting Street was being remodeled into a playhouse. On March 20, 1862, the old building, now renamed Hibernian Theatre, was formally opened by Reeves' Musical Festival Company. Blind Tom, the Inspired Musician, came after the Reeves cast left, and in April Johnson's New Orleans Minstrels, Burlesque Opera Troupe and Brass Band. Marchant, erstwhile lessee of the Charleston, frequently volunteered his services and, besides "musical and intellectual entertainments," many attempts were made by the managers to attract crowds with showings of "War Illustrations" and "Views of Battles."

But war was reaching ever closer to the besieged city. Naval and land engagements had brought shell fire within hearing distance. In June, 1862, Confederates and Federals fought the battle of Secessionville on James Island, only ten miles away. By July of the next year Union troops had captured Morris Island and Rear Admiral John B. A. Dahlgren had demolished Fort Sumter; and in August General Quincy A. Gillmore, reinforced by 3,000 fresh troops, had begun installation of the famous "Swamp Angel," a powerful eight-inch cannon capable of hurling 200-pound shells into the heart of Charleston itself. Surrounded by such a ring of fire the city was doomed. Doggedly, however, it held on. Not until February 17, 1865, after a siege of 567 days, did the Confederates evacuate and Mayor Charles Macbeth surrender the seaport to Lieutenant Colonel Augustus G. Bennett.

Meanwhile, during the siege, the Hibernian remained open, offering miscellaneous diversion for the stricken citizens. John Sloman, beloved for his comic songs in pre-war days, presented infrequent musical concerts. As late as the fall of 1864 he and his daughters attracted small audiences—with tickets five dollars each. And there were many showings of panoramic war views, band concerts, several dress balls, and "music festivals."

With the lifting of the siege and the arrival of the Federal garrison of occupation came a renewed interest in the drama. In less than six weeks the editor of the *Courier*, writing under severe military censorship, advised Charlestonians that theatricals were returning. "With the permission of the Military" C. G. Strahan and George S. Parkes, producers from New York, were on their way to "revive drama in our midst." Arriving on March 27, Strahan and Parkes brought a cast of sixteen players, including George L. Aiken, S. T. Clare, J. L. Fendall, Charles H. Howard, Georgianna and Lotty Langley, Lizzie Holmes, Laura Desmond, James Duff, and Annie Tillie.

The managers, finding little favor with the incommodious Hibernian, secured permission from Lieutenant Colonel Bennett to use the German Artillery Hall, on Wentworth Street, one-time proud home of the Fourth Brigade of St. Philip's and St. Michael's parishes. For nearly three weeks "the enterprising managers and proprietors" were "busily engaged in repairing and refitting the Hall for theatrical purposes." Meanwhile, a pleasure-hungry population composed of white citizens under "military surveillance," freed Negroes, and Union soldiers, eagerly awaited the "grand opening." "We have not the least doubt that [the managers] will be amply rewarded for their labors by a succession of crowded house," stated the *Courier*, "for the people of Charleston desire amusement, and now they have an opportunity of gratifying their tastes."

Advertising "New Theatre! New Scenery!! New Company!!!" and offering "Front seats $1, Parquett 75c, Colored seats 50c," Strahan and Parkes raised their post-war curtain on April 12, 1865, only three days after General Lee's surrender at Appomattox. The play was *The Honeymoon*—the same comedy that twenty-eight years before, in the peaceful, prosperous days of 1837, had christened the Charleston Theatre. Said the *Courier* the next morning: "The Theatre opened last evening under favorable auspices. There was a large attendance, nearly every seat being occupied. The various characters throughout were admirably performed, and elicited much applause and frequent presents of bouquets thrown on the stage to the several actors engaged."

Night after night, from April 12 to July 10, Strahan and Parkes kept Artillery Hall Theatre open and, if the censored *Courier* may be taken literally, with great success. Frequent editorials attested to the popularity of the players and such comments as "complete and gratifying success" and "the house was well filled" were plentiful. Occasionally, the managers, "with permission of the Military," presented added attractions. On May 9 the 127th New York Volunteers Band gave a concert "for the poor of Charleston"; on May 26 L. I. Woolfe, "a celebrated Southerner just arrived," played *Don Caesar de Bazan*; and on June 17 James Walker, "celebrated jig dancer of the 54th

Massachusetts Volunteers," danced between the acts of the Monrovia Serenaders' concert.

Strahan and Parkes continually varied their offerings. Such dramatic favorites as *The Little Treasure, Retribution, Time Tries All, Still Waters Run Deep, Nora Creina, The Maid of Croissey, Robert Macaire, Somebody Else, Captain of the Watch,* and *The Rival Pages* were most popular and allegedly attracted fair patronage. But in spite of newspaper advertisements and complimentary notices, legitimate drama soon gave way to minstrels, and during the summer and fall Artillery Hall was frequently occupied by burlesques, serenaders, tamborinists, and "bone players." Indeed, it is not unlikely that the many circuses which came in rapid succession to Citadel Square did a far better business than the theatre.

Between 1866 and 1869, as Charleston slowly regained its financial footing and citizens looked to a peaceful future, Hibernian Hall was again converted into a theatre. Called variously "Charleston Theatre," "The New Canterbury Theatre," and "The Metropolitan Theatre," it served for several years as the city's only playhouse. Early in 1866 Ghioni and Susini's Grand Italian Opera Troupe presented *Il Trovatore, Martha, Ernani, The Barber of Seville,* and *Norma.* In the fall the company returned and shortly afterward came Leonard Grover's Grand Opera Company. Meanwhile, there were many other attractions: musical and panoramic exhibitions, wizards, Barnum's History Museum, acrobats, and on Citadel Green the inevitable circuses. But it was not until November, 1867, that legitimate drama reappeared at the Hibernian, now called "The Charleston Theatre." John Templeton, "of the Savannah and Vicksburg theatres," with a cast of twenty-nine players ("the best Company in the South") opened on the eighteenth with *Little Barefoot.* Presenting *The Heir at Law, Black Crook, Seven Sisters,* and other current favorites, and featuring Isabel and Alice Vane in dances, the Templeton cast fared well for three weeks. Then it left for a tour of "other Southern theatres." On February 3, 1868, the Templetons returned for a winter engagement which lasted until May 1. Again starring the Vanes, Mr. and Mrs. Howard Watkins, and Mary Gladstone, the company returned in October for a third season which lasted until November 23. The John V. Gilbert Dramatic Company came next to present *Under the Gaslight, East Lynne, Leah the Forsaken,* and *Ten Nights in a Bar Room,* November 23–27. Enthusiastically received, this cast came back in January, 1869, and remained a month. The editor of the *Courier* praised Gilbert highly for "reestablishing the drama in our midst." Late in February Templeton again renewed his lease on the Hibernian, brought Whitman's Celebrated Parisian Ballet Troupe and a "$15,000 Great Transformation Scene," and featured "the world's greatest spectacle, *The*

White Fawn." Following the *Fawn*, which ran nine consecutive nights to packed houses, Templeton presented Marie Frederici's Grand German Opera Troupe in *Martha, Diavolo, Der Freyschutz, Faust, The Magic Flute,* and *Il Trovatore*. Nightly, reported the *Courier*, the house was filled to capacity. In April Manager Templeton engaged the Grand Female Operetta Company, the English Opera Bouffe, the Grand German Opera Company, and Whitman's Ballet Troupe in rapid succession, bringing the successful season to a close in May.

In the fall of 1869 the Hibernian, this time advertised as "The Metropolitan Theatre," was leased by Collins and Morse, theatrical agents, who began their season on October 4 with *The Ticket of Leave Man*. With a large cast, including Walter Benn, Mark Read, and Kate Raymond, the new company performed regularly until early in November. At that time, according to the *Courier*, a misunderstanding developed among the cast members and the company was disbanded.

It was now apparent that Charleston was slowly regaining its position in the world of lights and shadows. With a long and excellent theatrical tradition to uphold, however, much remained to be done. Everyone realized that prestige could not be fully restored until the city had better, modern accomodations to offer the traveling stage companies. Much dissatisfaction had been expressed concerning the inadequacy of Hibernian Hall as a proper place for drama and opera. It was too small, seating only about six hundred people; it had none of the new and better stage equipment. As early as March 14, 1866, while Ghioni and Susini's Opera Troupe was nightly filling the small hall, the *Courier* had stated:

> The presence of an Opera Troupe in this community at this time is somewhat of an uncommon event. All of five years have passed since we have been favored with the theatrical or operatic entertainment of a *recherche* order. This is not because the citizens of Charleston have lost any of their old taste for the refined and beautiful in the musical art, but on account of the depleted and desolated condition into which the city has been plunged by the circumstances of war.... The troupe [now playing] possess ability and talent, but it is like hiding a candle under a bushel to place them in Hibernian Hall. What we want in this city is an Academy of Music, constructed on modern principles.... The merchants of Charleston cannot afford to allow the city to become dull, stupid and shunned on account of a lack of attention and refined amusements. By all means give us an Academy of Music!!

Such an attitude was quite understandable. For more than a hundred years Charleston had been the South's leading theatrical center. Regularly, year after year, especially after 1800, leading European and American actors had visited the city. The first Charleston Theatre, erected in 1793, had been the finest south of Philadelphia; the second Charleston, built in 1837, was unsurpassed in America. Each had had a seating capacity of 1,200. But the Hibernian, a makeshift, was in

[268]

no way comparable to its predecessors. It is not surprising that Charlestonians were reluctant to let their theatricals remain "dull, stupid and shunned."

Late in the summer of 1869 the decision was reached: a new theatre, the Charleston Opera House, was to be built on the corner of King and Market streets. Plans drawn by John A. Devereaux for John Chadwick, the owner, called for a $35,000 remodeling of the $160,000 Adger Building into a theatre similar to Booth's Theatre in New York. Seating 1,200 people, the building was to contain a dress circle, a family circle, parquette, orchestra, and gallery, all "in the shape of a horseshoe." The stage, a copy of Brougham's Fifth Avenue Theatre and designed to be "quite as large as the stages of the principal stages in the North," was to be forty-five feet deep, fifty-four feet wide, and the proscenium opening thirty by forty feet. Over all there was to be grandeur of appointment in keeping with the nation's best theatrical practices— frescoed ceiling, red plush velvet seats, and delicately hued walls. Indeed, it was designed as "one of the handsomest theatres between Baltimore and New Orleans."

Amid appropriate ceremonies Chadwick laid the first brick of the new structure on September 6. On November 29 the *Courier* proudly announced that the theatre, its name changed to the Academy of Music, had been leased by John T. Ford of Holliday Street Theatre, Baltimore, and that for the formal opening, on December 1, Thomas W. Robertson's popular comedy, *School*, "as produced at Wallack's Theatre, New York," had been selected.

The first performance was a tremendous success. A dedicatory address, written by the city's distinguished William Gilmore Simms, was spoken by Miss Lillie Eldridge, a cast-member, and programs were printed on sheets of silk cloth! *School* proved "a brilliant inauguration of the dramatic season." Among the players were Laura Alexander, Harry H. Wood, and James O'Neill, later to become world-famous as the *Count of Monte Cristo*. Complimenting the manager, the cast, the performance, the "attentive and polite ushers," and the acoustics, the next morning's *Courier* reviewed the production of *School* as follows:

> Never since the dark clouds of war passed from our beloved country have we ever witnessed so large, so enthusiastic, and so brilliant an assemblage of ladies and gentlemen, as—notwithstanding the very inclement weather—filled the new Academy of Music last evening. Every seat had an occupant; the boxes were filled, the stalls occupied, the galleries and dress circles bore their teeming crowds—men were sandwiched in the passageways and clung to the pillars to obtain standing positions; and yet, notwithstanding that, it had been repeated with many wise shakes of the head by every old fogy in town, that the building was bound to fall in, that it was not strong enough.

The tragic decade had ended; the drama had returned to Charleston.

From December 1, 1869, throughout the bitter days of Reconstruction and on until after the turn of the nineteenth century, the Academy of Music held its place as a leading theatrical center of the South. Season after season eminent actors and actresses played upon its boards—Laura Keene, Neil Warner, James H. Hackett, Edwin Forrest, Junius Brutus Booth, Lawrence Barrett, Joseph Jefferson, Fanny Davenport, Kate Putnam, Dion Boucicault, Robert Mantell, Henry Irving, Ellen Terry, John Drew, Sarah Bernhardt, and many more—presenting the finest in American dramatic and operatic entertainment. Not until 1936, after sixty-seven years of service, was the Academy finally razed to make room for a modern structure.

IT'S NOT HOW OLD YOU ARE
From 9 to 99 Men Have Dared—and Accomplished

Facts, Chicago, Illinois, October, 1943.

On December 5, 1942, President Roosevelt appointed Paul V. McNutt man power commissioner and simultaneously halted induction into the armed forces of all men over 38 years of age.

If you'd been nursing any doubt about whether you were an unwanted "old" man, unfit for military service and wondering how (with your bloated paunch) you could ever lug a 70-pound pack and a nine-pound Garand for 25 miles, the Chief made up your mind for you. You are unwanted and you couldn't carry the load!

You're through. You can now take your seat in the back of the room alongside what's left of the old "Boys in Blue" and the Confederate veterans. Brother, militarily you're as dead as a Minieball.

From now on you're society's surplus, a drag on the man-market—as unwelcome as an illegitimate child at a family reunion. All that's left for you to do is consult your undertaker.

David Farragut was appointed midshipman in the U. S. Navy at the ripe old age of nine and at 24 was a lieutenant on the *Brandywine*, assigned the task of convoying Lafayette back to France. John Paul Jones at 32 commanded the *Bonhomme Richard* that defeated the *Serapis* in one of the most desperate and sanguinary battles in all naval history. Brigadier-General Thomas J. Jackson of the Confederate Army was 37 when he won the sobriquet "Stonewall" at the Battle of Bull Run. George Washington was sent as ambassador to the French at 22.

At 27 Napoleon Bonaparte was Commander-in-Chief of the Army of Italy—he was 35 when crowned Emperor of France. Alexander the Great, at the age of 30, broke down and cried because there were no more worlds to conquer. Patrick Henry was 27 when he shouted, "Give me liberty or give me death!"

[270]

At 20 Alexander Hamilton was Washington's aide-de-camp and at 32 the Secretary of the Treasury. The Declaration of Independence was written by "Old Man" Jefferson at 33.

Still think you're not a dodo?

Ben Franklin had finished *Poor Richard's Almanac* at 26. McCormick was 23 when he invented the reaper. At 24 Newton had perfected the law of gravitation. By the time he was 33 Shakespeare had written a dozen of his most famous plays. Poe published his first book at 18 and at 25 had done much of his best work. At 25 Dickens had all but finished *Pickwick Papers* and was busy on *Oliver Twist*. Lord Byron was dead at 36, Shelley at 30, and Keats at 25.

O heck! Get your crutches and let's hobble down to the mortician's for our measurements—I'm 39 myself!

But wait. "Nothing is too late till the tired heart shall cease to palpitate." At least, so said Longfellow—at 68. James Q. Howard, for 15 years reference chief of the Congressional Library, went the poet one better by adding that man is "immature, unripe, callow, vealy, verdant, sappy, bumptious, bat-blind, and grass-green, until he reaches the age of 40 years." Maybe the old boys had something. And maybe we can make it without those crutches, after all. Let's see.

At 98 Titian painted his famous "Battle of Lepanto." Von Moltke at 88 was in full uniform as Chief of Staff of the Prussian Army, having crushed the France of Napoleon III at the youthful age of 72. Between 70 and 80 Commodore Vanderbilt added 10,000 miles to his railroad lines and $100,000,000 to his bank roll.

John Wesley was preaching a sermon daily at 88 and directing the religious movement he had founded—up to that time he had travelled 250,000 miles in an era that knew no trains, cars, planes or buses.

Palmerston was Prime Minister of England at 80, and at 83 Franklin was putting the finishing touches on his *Autobiography. Othello*, Verdi's great opera, was produced during the composer's 74th year. And *"Paradise,"* Tintoretto's "crowning achievement," 74 by 30 feet, reputedly the world's largest painting on canvas—was painted at 70. A youngster named Tennyson penned "Crossing the Bar" when he was 83; Goethe wrote *Faust* at 80; Chaucer, the *Canterbury Tales* at 60—and at a mere 80 Cato learned Greek, Plutarch was studying Latin, and Socrates began taking music lessons!

At the boyish age of 99 Charles Macklin was still treading the English stage and Joe Jefferson, when only 24 years younger, was playing Rip van Winkle. Monroe, at 65, formulated the Doctrine that has preserved the independence of the United States. Voltaire wrote *Irene* and made a five-day journey from Geneva to Paris to see it performed when he was 64.

At 63 Pasteur was active and bold enough to perform the first antirabies inoculation upon a human being. Michelangelo completed "The

Last Judgment" at 66, and between 60 and 70 both Wagner and Gounod composed their greatest music. Locke wrote *Thoughts on Education,* Darwin *The Descent of Man,* and Cervantes the second part of *Don Quixote* at 61, 62, and 68, respectively.

Boys between 50 and 60 have also managed somehow to hold their own. At 56 Columbus set out on his fourth voyage to America. Talleyrand overthrew the entire Empire of Napoleon I at 60 and Cromwell ousted Charles I and established his Protectorate of England at 55. After leading the Confederate armies, Robert E. Lee accepted the presidency of Washington College at 58.

Gutenberg invented the printing press at age 56. Logarithm tables were worked out by a 50-year-old youngster named Kepler, and Galvani enunciated the theory of animal electricity in his late 50's.

Take heart, Old Men of 40—snow on the mountain doesn't necessarily mean the fire's out in the furnace.

Harvey published his famous work on the circulation of the blood at 50—just thirty-six years before he was elected president of the College of Physicians in London! William Penn signed his treaty with the Indians when he was 56, and Washington became the first President of the United States well after he'd passed the half-century mark.

Wellington, at 46, whipped the daylights out of Napoleon at Waterloo. Priestly discovered oxygen only three years after "life begins"—the same age at which Bessemer perfected his process for manufacturing steel and Sir Christopher Wren designed St. Paul's Cathedral. Longfellow wrote a little piece called *Hiawatha* at 48, then sat around for 34 more years enjoying the praise.

At 49 Jenner began inoculating patients against smallpox. *Tom Jones,* one of the best novels of all time, was published by a chap named Henry Fielding when 41. And LaSalle the explorer was sailing down the Mississippi River—the first white man ever to see it—at the tottering age of 39.

Just how far does the gulfstream of youth flow into the arctic regions of man's life? Is old age but a fiction?

From here it looks as if Grandpa slammed the nail on the head when he opined, "It ain't how many teeth you got in your head, son—it's how they hit that counts." Bring on your infant whippersnappers under 38 and let's see who cries "Uncle"!

THE LIBRARY IN EDUCATION

Southern Association Quarterly, Atlanta, Georgia, May, 1943.

I have been asked to talk to you on "The Library in Education." I have been assigned fifteen minutes in which to do this. For some reason I am reminded of the student who selected for his term theme in English 400 the modest subject, "The Plays of William Shakespeare."

You will bear with me if I assume that each of you has already studied the report on "The Relation of the Library to Instruction" which was adopted at the Second Sewanee Work Conference on Higher Education and published recently by this Association. There you have found tersely stated and in neat summary the combined opinions of some fifty educators who spent the better part of a week discussing the college library, its functions and possibilities, and the proper role administration and faculty may play in its development. What I may say here, if it contain a groat's worth of wit, must, therefore, elaborate upon the published report or add to it. In either case I am hard pressed.

Instruction in any institution may be seen from at least three vantages: (1) the curriculum, which is the common denominator of all; (2) personalized teaching, which includes conferences, honors courses, tutorial systems, and the like; and (3) the *ex curia* interests of those students who lead themselves beyond the confines of the class-hour by independent study. In each approach books have a greater or lesser part. Indeed, since teaching is after all the main business of institutions of higher learning, it is difficult to imagine any approach which does not involve the use of the library.

Yet not too difficult. For surveys a-plenty have shown that an astonishing number of college students do not make use of the library. Recent studies covering periods of from nine weeks to nine months and involving 6,052 students on eight separate campuses reveal that 1,774 (29.3 per cent) withdrew no books from their libraries, and 3,631 (60 per cent) withdrew less than one book per month, or nine volumes in the course of an entire scholastic year. Another study, based on records kept from 70 to 110 days in thirty-five colleges, shows that the mean number of volumes borrowed per student per semester was less than six. Similar analysis in almost any other group of institutions would doubtless produce comparable results.

These are the facts in the case. Whatever we as teachers or administrators may say by way of defense can amount to little more than beating the bushes. The odd angle of it all is that up to now there has been no substantial evidence to prove that library usage has much, if any thing, to do with undergraduate scholarship. Students who consistently use the library manage to pass their courses and receive their diplomas in the spring. Students who never use the library manage to pass their courses and receive their diplomas in the spring. What difference does it make?

Outwardly, none at all. Each graduate in the convocation line, reader or non-reader, is sicklied over with the black robe of learning—an unsuspecting public makes no distinction. But passing before us, the educators, in smiling procession is, we know, one of the saddest commentaries on modern higher education in America. We know too that the blame is balanced finely upon the heads of all three accessories after the fact—the administrator, the teacher, and the librarian.

It has been repeatedly said that the most noteworthy feature of the college library during the past forty or fifty years has been its growth. Figures kept for the last quarter century in fourteen university libraries reveal that their combined holdings were increased 282 per cent, from five to fourteen million volumes, and that in the majority annual expenditures were increased by as much as 300 per cent. Now this is not altogether bad. No one can rightly deny that books, most of them at least, added to the college library bode nobody evil. In fact, money spent for these materials will perhaps in the long run bring to the campus a more abiding influence than that spent for any other purpose, unless it be for men to interpret them. We are grateful, therefore, to college administrators and to the officials of accrediting associations for seeing to it during the past twenty-five years that libraries have grown in buildings, equipment, books, and staff. Moreover, we are exceedingly thankful for the generosity of various foundations which has made this expansion possible in several institutions.

Emerson, we believe, once said that consistency is the hobgoblin of little minds. If that be true, it is but further proof that college people are of gargantuan intelligence. For nowhere in higher education will one find greater inconsistency than this: while libraries have grown a hundred times over in size, they have remained dwarfs in service. Indeed, they have up to this time, judging from the standpoints of usage and correlation with students' grades, failed to justify themselves in terms of either effort or expenditure.

This brings us back where we started, to the triumvirate—administrator, teacher, and librarian.

Now the college administrator is almost invariably a good and wise man. He is not without the common attributes of greatness which, we are thankful, include a genuinely good sense of humor. Like most men he too has his share of that quality known as pride, as distinguished from cupidity, which propels him to think in typical national fashion like, let us say, the secretary of a Chamber of Commerce. The "general," or descriptive, section of last year's college catalog presents mute evidence of his wizardry of words: if the college stands on the highest hill in the country or owns a thousand acres or has a hundred native-stone buildings, why should not these facts be made known? Likewise, if the library contains 10,000 or 100,000 volumes, why should this not be told? By all means it should. There could certainly be no virtue in his stating that "our library contains 25,000 volumes of which only 5,000 were used in 1940–41 by only 40 per cent of our student body." But he would do well to study the facts that lead up to such a condition.

The administrator's responsibility for the welfare and character of the college library is ultimate. Financial support, though vital, is not enough. With his office he also assumes the responsibility of determining the kind of library service most needed in his institution, and through the selection of his librarian and faculty, the responsibility of guaranteeing that this service be employed in as many phases of the educational program as is feasible. Furthermore, he will rightly demand of his instructors—all of them, not a chosen few—their coöperation in developing and interpreting the resources of the library. Indeed, in appraising his faculty the administrator could do no wrong in considering enthusiasm for and use of the library as important as good teaching. In the long run they are the one and the same. Doubtless, many institutions are but the lengthened shadow of one man; but not always the college library. The well-rounded college libraries of America are those in which the librarian has received over the years the thoughtful assistance, both in acquisition and use, of the entire administrative and instructional staffs.

If the administrator is the dynamo, the teacher must be the transformer in this work of generating an appreciation of good books on the college campus. Nothing is so enthusiastic as enthusiasm itself. One good instructor can do more to stimulate interest in reading than all the publicity the library could possibly produce. The talent for teaching consists largely, we are convinced, in communicable ardor. It does not derive in any event from erudition.

Enthusiasm for books, however, presupposes an appreciation of the importance of books in the learning process. On every college campus (except, of course, those of the Southern Association!) there lives and has his being the well-known Professor Legion, that remarkable man who year in and year out uses the library neither in his teaching nor for his own enjoyment. That he continually fails to avail himself of the best that has been said and thought in the world is bad enough, but it is of slight import compared with the rank injustice he perpetrates against the many who look upon him as "teacher." Add to this his colossal conceit in believing that one little head and one textbook contain all of truth and beauty that ye know and all ye need to know. What we get is the educational counterpart of the man without a country or the evangelist who never goes to church. To this teacher (or to his colleague who demonstrated his interest in the library by placing ten books on "reserve" in the "Fall of '34") we would never turn for coöperation in the development of an active library program. He would not agree that stimulation of self-education is the better part of instruction, or that the teacher is only the catalyzer in the educative process, not the final end. So far man has devised no osmotic system by which learning is made either quick or easy. The wise teacher knows that the best he can do is to furnish the stimulus and point the way. On the college campus, unless we are mistaken, the way leads to the library.

The college library is an institution within the institution. It is presided over by the librarian—an unfortunate appellative, we sometimes think, for the term bears the same connotation today as it did six centuries ago, "the keeper of books." Emerson suggested in 1870 that the proper title for the office might be "Professor of Books," and in certain places that designation has received some favor. Perhaps a more apt name would be "Dean of Instruction," though, as we say it, we know that there are very few incumbents who would merit that distinction on the basis of either training or scholarship.

If there is anything the progressive librarian does not want to do, it is to "keep" books. Even by implication he dislikes to be dubbed an ossuary. If his title were suggestive of the distribution of books, not the accumulation of them, of the use of books and not the embalming of them, it might have a deciding effect on the focus he has for years put on his profession.

The prerequisite of "professing" books is, of course, a knowledge of books. On this basis the librarian's learning should be as profound, his training as solid, and his scholarship as contributive as that of any other member of the college faculty. This is not yet the case, except on a limited number of campuses. Elsewhere, the librarian has had difficulty demanding equality with or, in some instances, the respect of, other members of the teaching corps. To some extent he is himself responsible for this condition. Sometimes it is a matter of tradition. Certainly there is no proof as yet that the librarian is innately inferior to other educators. Generally, it is because he has been trained, or trained himself, to do everything to or for books that a college community could rightly ask of him—except to read them. He has not been taught that books are good for nothing but to inspire, that no manner of marking them can ever take the place of studying them. For the past several decades the emphasis in his schooling has been on techniques and routines, and today the library stands as a monument to his mastery of mechanics. Much of this emphasis has been necessary. Certainly, as spadework it has brought the library out of chaos into organization and made it into one of the most efficient of our national institutions. But during this time the librarian was encouraged to forget that the contents of a book, not the cover, is the important part. It is no wonder he made techniques a fetish and minutiae a ritual. The wonder is that he himself did not emerge as the Frankenstein of modern higher education.

Let us hope that the librarian has passed through but the first stage in his development and at last has his house in order. With full realization that what he has done is but a means to the end, he must now knuckle down to the challenging task of making the library a real service, not an imaginary one, in the instructional program. This he will do, we believe, by actively conjoining with others in the art of interpreting books. In no other way can he ever completely justify his position on the American campus.

An attempt to appraise the library in education leads, as we have seen, to an examination of many phases of the college program and includes administrator, teacher, and librarian alike. This is as it should be, for nowhere else on the campus will we find so revealing a microcosm, so perfect a reflection of the coördinated efforts of all.

JOHN GORMAN BARR:
"FORGOTTEN" ALABAMA HUMORIST

The Alabama Review, Alabama Historical Association,
University of Alabama & Auburn University, April, 1951.

Devotees of humor of the Old Southwest have long paid homage to two Alabamians, Johnson Jones Hooper (1815–1862) and Joseph Glover Baldwin (1815–1864), both of whom are generally regarded as foremost in the field of antebellum frontier story-telling. Indeed, Hooper's *Some Adventures of Captain Simon Suggs, Late of the Tallapoosa Volunteers*, eleven editions of which appeared between 1845 and 1856, and Baldwin's *The Flush Times of Alabama and Mississippi* (1853), printed at least four times within four years, have earned places of high honor among the brilliant galaxy of American humorous writings which at last came to full fruition in the masterpieces of Mark Twain. But until now, almost a century after his tragic and untimely death, a third early Alabama humorist, John Gorman Barr, has been summarily overlooked by literary historians. A contemporary of Hooper and Baldwin, between 1855 and 1857 and under the pseudonym "Omega," Barr contributed many "rich, racy, sterling, and unsurpassed" yarns to the internationally-known *Spirit of the Times* and *Porter's Spirit of the Times*, the leading journals of their type in America. His numerous comic tales were "most highly prized for the richest humor and wit and ... received the loftiest encomiums of the best critics." And Hooper, whose name was (and is) synonymous with the choicest in native American humor of his day, described Barr's stories as among the richest ever published.

The story of Barr's life itself, like his intriguing tall tales, borders on the incredible. He lived but thirty-four years, from November 22, 1823 until May 18, 1858, yet in that brief time he was printer, scholar, editor, lawyer, college professor, soldier, district attorney, orator, politician, author, and ambassador. At twelve he was an orphan in an Indian-infested frontier village hundreds of miles from his birthplace, at nineteen he had earned two university degrees and a Phi Beta Kappa key, at twenty-four he was a captain in the United States Army in Mexico, at thirty-three he was a nominee for the national Congress, and the next year personally selected by President James Buchanan as consul of the United States at Melbourne, Australia. Shortly after, on his way to his new post and 3000 miles from home, he was buried with full consular honors in the Indian Ocean.

Barr was born at Milton, Caswell County, North Carolina, the son of Thomas and Mary Jane Gorman Barr, both of whom had shortly before immigrated to America from Scotland. In 1826, when young Barr was but three years old, his father died and his mother as best she could earned the living for her son and a younger daughter, Martha Margarette. For a few years the family resided in Raleigh, but most probably for reasons economic in 1835 Mrs. Barr and her children moved to Tuscaloosa, Alabama, where the boy immediately went to work as a printer's apprentice. The long trip westward evidently proved too strenuous for Mrs. Barr, however, for in early 1836 (or late 1835) she died, leaving John and Martha, aged twelve and ten (?), without means of support. A prominent Tuscaloosa merchant, David [Daniel?] M. Boyd, admiring the unfortunate boy's ability and determination, adopted him (and perhaps his sister) and on October 20, 1838, when Barr was less than fifteen, entered him as a special "full-course" scholarship student (from Tuscaloosa County) in the newly-established University of Alabama.

Barr's scholastic record in the University, then under the distinguished leadership of President Basil Manly, was little short of phenomenal. At the end of his freshman year, on June 24, 1839, Barr ranked at the top of his class with 346 out of a possible 350 units. In 1839 he was secretary of the Philomathic Society and on July 10, 1840 he was chosen by the faculty to deliver an address at the "Junior Exhibition" on the subject of "The Inquisition," and upon the completion of his senior year, he and a classmate, Edward B. King, were tied with scholastic averages of .99 for 1841 and 1.00 for the entire course, 1838–1841. The faculty voted to "divide honors between them; that Barr deliver the Valedictory orations; King the Latin Salutatory" at the eleventh annual commencement of the University, December 15, 1841.

Earning the Bachelor of Arts degree seems, however, to have but stimulated Barr to further formal education, for early in 1842 he qualified as a "Resident Graduate" of the University and during the year "pursued professional studies" which earned him the degree of Master of Arts in the Class of 1842. On December 13 he delivered the special "Resident Graduate Oration" entitled "Science and Nature, Handmaids of Revealed Truth," sharing honors of the occasion with the distinguished South Carolina novelist, William Gilmore Simms, who had journeyed from Charleston to address the Erosophic Literary Society, to accept an LL.D. degree, and otherwise to be honored by the University and a coterie of state officials including Governor Benjamin Fitzpatrick.

Immediately after receiving his second degree, the twenty-year-old Barr, encouraged by Professor Frederick A. P. Barnard, head of the mathematics department, accepted a tutorship at the University with the understanding that he would be nominated for the position of librarian the next year. However, when the faculty election was held on December 22, 1843, Barr was defeated by a very narrow margin and under most peculiar circumstances, a defeat, incidentally, which brought clearly into the light of day the mounting antagonism that existed between President Basil Manly and Secretary of the Faculty Barnard.

Although curiously deprived of the librarianship, Barr remained on the University staff as tutor of mathematics throughout 1844 and 1845, assuming his share of classroom work, private coaching, proctoring and otherwise attempting to maintain discipline in the rowdy frontier institution. Nor did he escape the censure of President Manly, who in the summer of 1845 twice recorded in his diary that Barr and other officers were known to have been participants in "drunken frolics" at the homes of Mr. [Harvey W. ?] Ellison and Professor Barnard. Nevertheless, Barr was apparently highly regarded by the college community, for in 1845 he was elected president of the University Alumni Society, chosen as the "next [1846] Anniversary Orator," and appointed one of five men to petition the Board of Trustees "to establish a Law Professorship at the University of Alabama."

Barr's appointment to the committee seeking a professorship of law was not without significance, for he had been reading law in the office of Harvey W. Ellis during most of his spare time since graduation. And on February 11, 1846 the following advertisement appeared for the first time in the Tuscaloosa *Independent Monitor:*

John G. Barr,
Attorney and Counsellor at Law.
Will practice in all the Courts holden in this City, and in the Courts of Pickens, Fayette, Shelby and Jefferson counties. Office No. 9, Washington Hall, under United States' Court Room.

Evidently, Barr's pursuit of the law was successful (the above notice appeared regularly until April 13, 1847), for in less than four months he was appointed "attorney of the Middle District of Alabama of the District Court of the United States." Meanwhile, he became a writer for (but most probably not editor of) the weekly Tuscaloosa *Observer*, and in the summer of 1847 was an unsuccessful candidate for the Alabama House of Representatives. During this while he had no official connection with the University of Alabama, although early in 1847 he did sign, actively circulate and present to the Governor of Alabama and the Executive Committee of the Board of Trustees a petition in behalf of Professor Frederick Thomas who, Barr and forty-odd other petitioners believed, was "being prejudiced on mere rumor" and unfairly forced by President Manly and the faculty to resign his position as an instructor of English.

By mid-1847, however, the war with Mexico was attracting great attention throughout the state. As early as the previous summer Alabama's Governor Joshua L. Martin had issued in Tuscaloosa, which was the capital of the state, a call for volunteers for the "Army of Occupation in Texas," and students of the University of Alabama had petitioned the faculty to permit them to form a military company. When they were refused, a number had joined a Tuscaloosa "Volunteer Military Company"—but they were severely reprimanded, "such a proceeding being contrary to the laws of the college." However, by July the University officials had so relinquished their authority as to allow the Tuscaloosa Riflemen, Captain McCrohan commanding, to "join in the procession on the 24th at the Junior Exhibition." The non-student citizens of Tuscaloosa were likewise stirred by events on the Mexican-Texas border. Late in August Judge S. D. J. Moore, a graduate of the United States Military Academy, Alabama's Quarter-master General Carter R. Harrison, and John G. Barr left Tuscaloosa on a recruiting expedition throughout Tuscaloosa and adjoining counties. And on November 9, 1847, according to the *Independent Monitor,*

> Capt. J. G. Barr marched into this city on Saturday morning last, with about half a company of volunteers for the war, from Bibb county. We understand that Capt. Barr has more than a full company enrolled. He left, yesterday morning, for Shelby, to bring in another squad. The Bibb volunteers are a sturdy looking set, and to us seem to exhibit an appearance of more than ordinary intelligence. They look like sensible, as well as, stout men. Capt. Barr is encamped, at present, about two miles from the city. His little camp presents a very cheerful appearance.

In less than ten days Captain Barr had completed his recruiting, and on November 19 the Warrior Guards, as the thirty-year-old company was (and now, 103 years later is) known, "struck their tents" and, after being addressed at the dock by Governor Martin and cheered by "a large assemblage of citizens," embarked on the Warrior River steamer *Arkansas* for Mobile. Just before leaving, the Guards elected their lieutenants and other officers.

On Tuesday, November 23, the company arrived in Mobile, were "comfortably quartered at the Independent Press," and two days later were mustered into the United States Army as Company A, 1st Battalion, Alabama Volunteers, Major John J. Seibels commanding. The battalion consisted of five companies from Tuscaloosa, Wilcox, Dallas,

[280]

Lowndes, Barbour, Mobile and Sumter counties, and at the time Company A included, besides Captain Barr, eleven other officers and sixty-seven "rank and file." Exactly when the troops embarked from Mobile for Mexico is not recorded, but it is known that "the battalion reached Vera Cruz too late to join General Scott's forces, but was on garrison duty in the interior, principally at Orizaba, till the peace."

As an officer Captain Barr was signally successful, according to those who knew him. Although his company was not actively engaged in battle with the Mexicans, one account states,

> ... [Barr's] great skill and tact daily exhibited in drilling his Company, did not escape the attention and admiration of officers higher in command; and he was called upon to discharge the active duties of Lieutenant-Colonel of his battalion—duties which were so often and ably performed, that he acquired the distinction of Lieutenant-Colonel himself. And when the war ended in 1848, and he was discharged from service, he bore the distinction home to Tuscaloosa.

Official records indicate also that Captain Barr was several times called upon to exercise his legal training by serving as an officer in regimental courtmartial proceedings. And a century later it was recorded in a history of the Warrior Guards that he was "not only ... a very able commander in the field, but he was summoned to assist in arranging the terms of the peace."

In early summer of 1848 the 1st Battalion sailed northward from Vera Cruz on the bark *Mopang*, arriving in Mobile June 21 or 22. "We are gratified to learn," stated the *Register and Journal*, "that in this battalion the general health of officers and men is good, and that the return home has given new vigor to the invalids." On June 28 the outfit, which altogether had served slightly more than seven months in the United States Army, was officially paid off, mustered out and the next day honored at a mammoth barbecue dinner celebration given by the City of Mobile. The soldiers of Company A, the Warrior Guards, having been officially discharged in Mobile, did not reach Tuscaloosa in a body and only a few of them accompanied their captain as he disembarked from the steamer *Russell* on July 4. The large reception which had been planned for "the patriotic volunteers" was therefore cancelled. But "our brave townsman, Captain Barr" was quite the same, although he unfortunately "appears to have forgotten his razor, when he embarked for Mexico." He admitted that "since his arrival in Mobile, he had suffered from an attack of rheumatism. Nothing, however, can subdue his native cheerfulness: and he treats the sneaking malady so lightly, that it will probably leave him soon, out of spite."

Actually, Barr's sojourn in the Army had done him in more seriously that was at first supposed, for he suffered bad health for an undetermined while before being able to resume his practice of law. It was at this juncture in his career (1848–1849) that he also accepted the "editorial management" of the *Observer*, a new Tuscaloosa newspaper to which he had earlier contributed and for which during the next few years he was to write "many masterly productions." An enthusiastic member of the Episcopal Church and of the Independent Order of Odd Fellows, he was in this last decade of his life called upon to serve in many public capacities and "by his ... occasional, brilliant, eloquent efforts upon the stump, he became, in every sense, a prominent politician." The facts that he was chosen to address the Warrior Division of the Sons of Temperance on a special occasion in 1848 and elected to serve as "Marshall at the laying of the cornerstone of the Alabama Asylum for the Insane," July 14, 1853, attest to his prominence as a public-spirited and influential citizen of Tuscaloosa. In the University of Alabama community he was also held in high regard: for instance, in July, 1857 he was appointed to write the obituary of and deliver an oration before the Erosophic and Philomatic societies for the distinguished Colonel Burwell Boykin, who had died suddenly after but four days illness. Possessed of a "remarkably sprightly and highly imaginative mind, stored with a rich fund of general miscellaneous reading and information," Barr, the lawyer-editor, was not infrequently the center of attention in legal, literary and social circles. "His conversation ... was characterized by the richest humor and most brilliant repartee, and rendered him eminently entertaining and attractive" in almost any company and in all levels of association.

Meanwhile, as a *littérateur* his reputation was being greatly enhanced: with Alexander B. Meek, William R. Smith, Frederick A. P. Barnard, G. P. Blevins and others he composed what has been described as Tuscaloosa's "Brilliant galaxy of young men." But his fame as a graceful writer and humorist had by the mid-1850's extended far beyond the borders of his county and state, bringing him "to some extent, a national literary reputation." *The Spirit of the Times* and *Porter's Spirit*, New York weeklies, were eagerly printing his many humorous stories, all of which were "highly prized for the richest humor and wit," and at least one of his more serious efforts, "Piscatory Reflections and Reminiscences," was published in *The Knickerbocker, New York Monthly Magazine*.

Barr's first contribution to the *Spirit* was a story entitled "Salted Him, or An Auctioneer Doing All the Bidding," in the issue of October 20, 1855. It was signed "Omega," and described by the editor as "from a *New* Alabama Correspondent." Actually, "Salted Him," although written expressly for the *Spirit*, had orginally appeared in the Tuscaloosa *Independent Monitor* (under the title, "Skin, Slayed and Salted") "for the benefit of the readers [in Alabama] who are well acquainted with the characters." Johnson J. Hooper, editor of the Montgomery *Mail,* called it "one of the richest stories ever published" and the *Independent Monitor's* editor boastfully declared that he had taken the liberty of using the story, trusting that to the editor of the *Spirit* it made no difference whether his paper published it *"before* or *after"* its appearance in the metropolitan weekly. In less than a month a second of Barr's yarns, "Old Charley and the President's Veto," was issued by the *Spirit,* and before the end of the year a third appeared, "Old Charley and His Impromptu Ride." As the new year got under way, the *Spirit* carried another long humorous essay entitled the "Matrimonial Club of Alabama," copied from a January issue of the Tuscaloosa *Independent Monitor.* Although unsigned, the article has all the earmarks of Barr's subject matter and style and it is reasonable to suppose that he at least had a hand in its preparation. Two more of Barr's witty pieces appeared in May, "A Hand-Around Supper in Alabama" and "A Steamboat Captain's Love Adventure," and in June, July and August one each—"How Tom Croghan Carved the Turkey," "Spiritualism Explained," and "Piscatory Reflections and Reminiscences," the last-named having been copied from the August (1856) *Knickerbocker Magazine.*

At this precise time William T. Porter, the distinguished editor of the *Spirit* and the man who had encouraged Barr to continue his efforts in the humorous vein, resigned his position and announced that at once he would begin publication of a rival "Spirit" to be entitled *Porter's Spirit of the Times.* He was succeeded as editor of the *Spirit* by Edward E. Jones who "for more than twenty-one years" had been connected with the original weekly. Both men, once colleagues but now rivals, sought eagerly the continuing services of "Omega," the fruitful Alabama editor-lawyer-humorist. Jones advertised that Barr (as well as other distinguished correspondents) would "keep on writing for the *Spirit,*" and early in 1857 continued to list "Omega" as a contributor. But never was Jones able to publish another of Barr's stories in the "old" *Spirit.* Porter, meanwhile, by virtue of his past kindnesses to Barr, was far more successful. For the very first issue of his new *Porter's Spirit,* September 6, 1856, contained a robust, delightful tale by "Omega," entitled "New York Drummer's Ride to Greensboro," accompanied by the following enthusiastic comment in which the New Yorker compared the Alabamian to the great English Dickens:

> We point with pride to the appearance and contents of the present number ... look at the contribution from "Omega," a lesson of humorous style and artistic finish, which might be consulted with advantage by the crowd of writers trying to follow in the path of Dickens ...

Barr, apparently appreciating Porter's interest in his work, obligingly wrote him a long letter, signed "Omega," which Porter printed:

[283]

Your favor of the 8th inst., came to hand yesterday morning, and I forthwith determined, with such leisure as I could command, to endeavor to comply with your flatteringly-expressed request. You perceive the time I have had, and enclosed please find the result of its occupation. The story ["New York Drummer's Ride to Greensboro"] is a *true* one, and is even yet repeated in our community,—I trust you may find it worthy your columns. Such as I could, send I unto thee ...

A week later Porter announced that his next issue would contain another "slashing paper from Omega," a prediction which was fulfilled by the appearance of "Jemmy Owen's Fifty Dollar Note; or Moind Whay Ye Say" in the issue of September 20. In February, 1857 two more of Barr's long stories were published, "John Bealle's Accident; or, How the Widow Dudu Treated Insanity" and "Relief for Ireland! or, John Brown's Bad Luck with His Pickled Beef." The first of these was enthusiastically greeted by the following editorial:

Omega in the Field once More!—We shall publish next week a superb story by this brilliant member of the "Old Guard." It will be entitled, "How the Widow Dudu Treated Insanity," and we think our readers will agree with us, that it quite equals, and if possible exceeds, the inimitable sketches previously published in our columns, under the titles of "Jemmy Owen's Fifty Dollar Note"—and "The New York Drummer's Ride to Greensboro." The story will occupy nearly three pages of our paper, but it will pay the time. So hats off in front, and look out for the Widow Dudu!

When "Widow Dudu" appeared, Porter described it as "Omega's admirable story," adding that he had also received "another contribution from the same master-hand, entitled 'Relief for Ireland ...' " These were followed in March by "A Lively Village; or, Brisk Speculation in a New Commodity," about which Porter enthusiastically commented, "*Omega Again.* Let no one who is fond of a good laugh omit to read the admirable story of Omega, on the first page."

Meanwhile, *Porter's Spirit* was prospering. In September, 1856, after the publication of but four issues, the editor announced that his circulation had jumped to "more than 30,000 copies" and that his goal was 100,000 by the end of the year. Barr's stories were of course in some small measure responsible for Porter's success, for, as has been indicated, he had contributed five original stories to the new hebdomadal between September and March. However, after March 28, 1857 nothing of "Omega's" appeared for seven months, until October 24, at which time "Misplaced Confidence; or, Bilking a Boniface" was heralded by Porter in these words:

Omega Again. Our readers will be glad to meet with their old friend, the rich, racy, sterling, and unsurpassed Omega, on the first page, once more. Though no one will omit reading him, we seize this opportunity of shaking hands with him in this way, after his long absence, and of passing him into the presence of the public with congratulations on the pleasure which we will enjoy in common, on his reappearance.

[284]

Had the genial Porter known the reason, he would not have chastised Barr, even so mildly, for his "long absence." For Barr was too much involved in Alabama politics in the summer of 1857 to find time to write "sterling and unsurpassed" essays for *Porter's Spirit*. In the early weeks of that year he announced himself a candidate for United States Congress from the Fourth Alabama District. Against him stood three opponents, two of whom were recognized as powerful: Judge Sydenham Moore, a Democrat (as was Barr), a man named Lee, and the incumbent, the well-known Judge William R. Smith, who was candidate for re-election, on the American or Know-Nothing ticket.

Like so many lawyers and editor-lawyers on the early American frontiers Barr had long had a propensity for politics. Since his defeat for the House of Representatives in 1847, he had doubtless planned at one time or another again to run for public office. A staunch Democrat, he had not failed the opportunity in the summer of 1856 to play well his role as elector from the Fourth Alabama District at the State Democratic Convention in Montgomery. And it was a widely known fact, as later developments unquestionably proved, that by his personal platform appearances and by perspicaciously casting his vote as an elector he had been "largely instrumental" in winning for President Buchanan and Vice-President Breckinridge large Alabama majorities over Millard Fillmore and A. J. Donelson. As one historian has declared, as elector "Barr canvassed with great power and effect for Buchanan and Breckinridge. His political information was sound, and his style of speaking very attractive. Crowds followed to hear him."

By April the congressional race had become an angry one. The *Independent Monitor*, a strong Smith paper, quoted the Marion (Alabama) *American* as follows:

> The Barr Fight. There has been a very rough and angry *bar-fight* going on for several weeks in this District, principally between the Greensboro' *Beacon*, the Tuscaloosa *Observer*, and the Linden *Jeffersonian* ... They are all quarreling ... over a very small matter,—which of the aspirants Moore, Barr, or Lee shall have the honor of being beaten by Billy Smith for Congress.

"Whispering campaigns" were employed by all candidates and in early July it looked as if there would be new Alabama representation in Washington. Barr drew his share of fire. Throughout May and June he was sharply attacked in the enemy press as a two-faced politician: two years before, in the 1855 race, he had voted *for* Judge Smith, but now he was running *against* him, the *Independent Monitor* complained. Quickly, Barr's supporters denied the charges: their candidate had never voted for Smith or any Know-Nothing. But the Smith voters thought otherwise, accusing Barr of even then himself being a Know-Nothing, secretly, in 1857. Moreover, they declared that Barr had always previously supported and should now support Smith because without him he (Barr) would never have got his captain's commission in the war with Mexico ten years before.

Whether Barr was actually vulnerable to these attacks or whether he ultimately saw political wisdom in concentrating all Democratic power in one candidate against Know-Nothing Smith, he suddenly announced on June 1 that he had withdrawn from the congressional race, thus throwing his support to Judge Moore. For this he was also vigorously denounced, it being claimed that he was printing and distributing political circulars through the *Observer* press. As it proved, Barr's withdrawal gave "the Democracy" a complete victory—Moore was elected by a 1400 majority over Smith who had twice defeated him previously. "The whole delegation [i.e., the state] went Democratic," and in Barr's Fourth District Buchanan scored 5252 votes against 4701 for Fillmore. In short, the Democrats—Barr's party—won all around.

The "great power and effect" with which Barr had canvassed for Buchanan and Breckinridge, to say nothing of the sagacious way he had maneuvered Judge Sydenham Moore's victory over the distinguished Judge William R. Smith and quieted the "feuds and contentions threatening the harmony of the party," did not pass unnoticed in the halls of the Democratic assemblies of Montgomery or of Washington. When the new state legislature convened in the fall of 1857, all Democratic members including Crawford M. Jackson, Speaker of the House, and James M. Calhoun, President of the Senate, signed a "flattering testimonial" in Barr's behalf, urging the President of the United States to "give him an appointment worthy of his distinguished talents and great party services."

Barr hurried to Washington to present his credentials, file the proper papers and—wait. Just as the new year came, so did his reward. On January 19, 1858 President Buchanan personally nominated him "to be consul of the United States at Melbourne, in place of I. M. Tarlton, recalled." The next day the nomination was referred to the Committee on Commerce and the day after quickly approved by the Senate. A Washington correspondent for the Montgomery *Daily Confederation* summed up the appointment thus:

> The President and Gen. [Lewis] Cass, duly appreciating the services of John G. Barr, of your State, in the cause of the Democracy, have conferred upon him one of the best Consulates in their gift, that at Melbourne, Australia, and as soon as he can complete arrangements, he will proceed there to enter on his duties.

To that quoted report the gossipy editor of the Tuscaloosa *Independent Monitor* added, "We understand that the Consulate ... is worth some four thousand dollars per annum, and we congratulate our townsman upon his good fortune."

Barr sailed from New York on the Royal Mail steamer *Emeu* in late March, and several weeks later, on May 18, 1858, between Suez and Melbourne, only three days out from his destination, he died of *coup de soleil*—a sunstroke—and was buried at sea, his body wrapped in the Stars and Stripes.

Notice of his death did not reach Alabama for three months. On August 31 the *Daily Confederation* reported that the news would be "melancholy tidings to his numerous friends.... Alabama loses a patriotic and valuable citizen—a son whose future promised to adorn a bright page in her history." Barr's friend, the noted humorist-editor, Johnson Jones Hooper, wrote:

> Omega Dead! With the deepest regret we learn of the death of our accomplished friend John G. Barr, of Tuscaloosa, on board the vessel conveying him to Melbourne, at which post he had been appointed Counsul.... We knew Mr. Barr intimately. No nobler nature ever existed. In intellect, as well as moral constitution, he was peculiarly gifted. The pages of the "Knickerbocker" and of "Porter's Spirit" amply attest his genius. Mr. Barr was about thirty-four years of age. He leaves, we believe, no relatives except a sister who resides at Tuscaloosa.

In Tuscaloosa the editor of the *Independent Monitor*, visibly disturbed, briefly reported, "Is it possible that Col. Barr is dead! He left us so recently, bouyant with health and brilliant prospects, and now so suddenly cut down! It is difficult to realize...." One week later the *Observer* printed a carefully detailed two-column obituary of Barr's life. This was copied in its entirety by the *Independent Monitor* in its following issue, and early in October given international distribution in the *Spirit of the Times*. Meanwhile, Tuscaloosans, deeply moved by the death of their young but distinguished fellow citizen, held a public memorial service in his honor. It was generally agreed, as one admirer wrote to the Centreville (Alabama) *Enquirer*, that "a man of brilliant parts" had died, a man whose "social qualities ... endeared him to all who had the good fortune to be thrown in his company."

John Gorman Barr will now be principally remembered for his humorous stories, fifteen of which he contributed to the *Spirit* and *Porter's Spirit* between October 20, 1855 and October 24, 1857. Coarse, rowdy, rough yarns they were, filled with homespun crudities and told in the salty vernacular of the frontier. Some of them were doubtless apocryphal, first heard by their recorder around the blazing log fires of Duffee's Tavern in Tuscaloosa, on a Warrior River steamboat or the University of Alabama campus or in a squatter's cabin far in the backwoods. Others Barr may have pieced together or completely fabricated. Now, at any rate, after a century these yarns—like those of many of his contemporaries—have at last drifted into that hazy literary region known as folklore. But whatever they were or are, the tall tales of the Old Southwest represent a simple, home-made literature of the people, by the people and for the people. As a contemporary critic in *Porter's Spirit* described this "American Sporting Literature," it was "fresh, crisp, vigorous, elastic, graphic . . . , full of force, readiness, actuality, and point." Moreover, he continued:

> [It] was not stewed in the closet, or fretted out at some pale pensioned laborer's desk, but sparkled from the cheerful leisure of the easy scholar—poured in from the emulous officers in barracks, or at sea—emanated from the jocund poet—and flowed from every mead, or lake, or mountain—in the land where the rifle or the rod was known.

Indeed, these yarns were America's frontier in action, a literature as indigenous as a camp-meeting-with-dinner-on-the-ground, corn-shuckings or house-warmings. They were the Old South looking at itself, laughing at itself, and talking about itself. They were and are as near as America has yet come to a literature all its own. Until lately, within the last twenty-five years, the writings of these frontier stalwarts have been pretty much overlooked, "elegantly ignored by most of our writers of American history . . . and students of American literature, who have been, for the most part, either ignorant of the field or superior to it." More recently, however, they have attracted deservedly increasing attention as a highly important element of America's literary heritage.

Few, if any, of the writers in this so-called "Big Bear School of American Humor" were professionals. Rather, they were—like Hooper and Baldwin and Barr—mostly respectable lawyers or editors, or they were doctors, surveyors, preachers, printers, planters, soldiers or actors. But they had keen eyes for the incongruous, they knew how to blend horseplay with horse-sense to make horse-laughs and in so doing they created, perhaps unconsciously, a distinctly national type of literary expression. Many of these writers are well-known: Davy Crockett, George W. Harris ("Sut Lovingood"), Augustus Baldwin Longstreet, William T. Thompson ("Major Jones"), Sol Smith, Johnson Jones Hooper, and a host of others. And all were tongue-in-cheek raconteurs for whom everything on the frontier was grist for the literary mill—gambling, horse-racing, backwoods weddings and funerals, murders, local customs, revival meetings and just plain back-country rowdyism. To them American literature owes a great debt. Without them our social history would be but dull drivel of a pseudo-chivalric past, a ruffled record of dyspeptic lords and crinolined ladies—as *un*-American as five o'clock tea. But with them is an almost inexhaustible treasury of life in the rough, reported by men with shrewd and humorous insight who were not afraid in early, hurly-burly America to look at themselves and—laugh.

John Gorman Barr's stories range in length from about 4000 to 8000 words and without exception the scenes are laid in Alabama, mostly in his own Tuscaloosa. The following yarn, "New York Drummer's

Ride to Greensboro','' (which the author described as a *"true* one, and is even yet repeated in our community") appeared in the first issue of the new *Porter's Spirit,* September 6, 1856. Porter, it will be remembered, called it "a lesson of humorous style and artistic finish, which might be consulted with advantage by the crowd of writers trying to follow in the path of Dickens." The story is used here, not necessarily because it is considered Barr's "best" by any means, but because it well represents his style, is illustrative of his type, and, being the shortest of his fifteen published stories, could well be reproduced.

New York Drummer's Ride to Greensboro

During the fast times of 1837, when the city of Tuskaloosa was a central point in the State of Alabama, and the Washington Hall Hotel a central point in the city, on a dreary winter's afternoon, a cosmopolitan arrived, worn and weak of body, in the western stage coach. He was an unmistakable type of a class of ubiquitous beings called—in the parlance of the times—New York drummers. For a score or more of weeks the coach had been his only shelter from the winter blast, and his transit had been so interrupted by mud and hill and flood as almost to preclude the recreation of sleep. Indeed, the "sweet restorer" had, with her "leaden legs and batty wings" only visited him during this period in brief and fitful slumbers, the more tantalizing in that they never satisfied the constant cravings of nature. Though he had many persons to see and much business to transact in the city, imperious engagements ahead would not admit his lying over a day or losing a stage in Tuskaloosa. He had consequently to bestir himself, with quiet activity, during the short space of time that would elapse before the departure of the Greensboro' stage, and fully equal was he to all his engagements, for if pedestrian speed is estimated by any ascertained time, he was emphatically an insider.

The coach, containing the traveller, had drawn up in front of the hotel named above, and one foot was yet upon its step, when he accosted the porter in this wise:—

"Where is Mr. H——'s store?"

"On the next corner, sir," was the prompt response.

"When does the stage leave for Greensboro'?"

"Nine o'clock to-night, sir," was the reply.

"Where is the stage office?"

"In the hotel, sir."

Though the baggage was removed from the coach with all the expedition usual in such cases, it had scarcely been done, ere our drummer, having passed to Mr. H——'s store and transacted business therein, had returned to the office of the hotel, and was engaged with the clerk after this manner:—

[289]

"Where is Mr. T——'s store?"

"Midway the next square, on this side of the street," replied the clerk.

"When does the Greensboro' stage leave?"

"Nine o'clock to-night," was responded.

"Is this the stage office?"

Being answered in the affirmative, he was off like an arrow, and might have been seen plunging along up the street in the direction of the store last enquired for. His fellow passengers had barely registered their names and called for rooms, when our enterprising man of business dashed into the hotel, having accomplished his mission, and meeting with Nat. Duffee, the proprietor of the house, hurriedly addressed him, with the slight variation, as follows:

"Where is attorney P——'s office?"

"It's in the second story over yon corner," responded Boniface, pointing with his hand diagonally across the street.

"When does the Greensboro' stage leave?"

"Nine o'clock to-night," was the answer.

"This is the stage office, is it?"

Scarcely waiting to receive the information sought by the last interrogation, he pitched out of the house and made off as if his life depended on the rapidity of his movements.

In the briefest possible time, he despatched his business with the lawyer, and returning to the hotel, and making enquiries for another store, preceded his departure for it, by earnest interrogatories to the manner and effect above stated, until their repetition, together with the impetuosity of his manner, the anxiety portrayed in his countenance and his deep solicitude touching the hour when the stage for Greensboro' left the city, had interested in his mission Tom Conning and Tom Jenkins, two youngsters, afflicted with an uncommon share of animal spirits and such notable proclivities for fun and frolic, as to have gained them the expressive soubriquet, among the "b'hoys," of the "Devil's Own."

Tom Conning and Tom Jenkins—lads just attaining the age when nascent mustacho engrosses attention—were inseparable companions, very Siamese twins in tastes and dispositions. And salient and striking beyond all other traits in their characters was a keen relish for rough sport and wild, mischievous pranks. The boldness and originality of their conceptions of practical jokes was only equalled by their energy and intrepidity in executing them. Confident in their manhood and self-reliant in all emergencies, they had acquired a dexterity in their management of game, which would have done credit to more experienced heads. Of easy and self-possessed address, good command of countenance and singularly precocious in all that pertains to mischief, this rollicking twain rarely failed when they had selected a victim,

[290]

to put him through in the most finished and artistic style. In short, to use the apt language of the old play, they were

"As prone to mischief, as able to perform it."

Conning, beckoning our drummer aside, addressed him in a manner in which was blended more of friendly interest than idle curiosity, after this style:—

"Excuse me, sir. You seem to be like myself, a stranger in these parts? Does your route take you beyond Tuskaloosa? I mean no offence by the enquiry, nor do I wish to pry into your affairs, but my own destination being Selma, and this being a rough country and dangerous times,—two men were killed in the stage between here and Selma last week and robbed,—I thought as a matter of mutual protection, in case our routes fell together, we should come to some understanding."

"No offence, I assure you, sir," quickly replied our drummer, evincing much alarm in his manner, "I had not heard that the roads hereabouts were infested with robbers; I had not heard of the murders you mention."

"Quite likely," rejoined Conning, "these things are so common about here that they excite but little attention. There was a man—the only passenger in the stage from here to Greensboro' about three weeks ago—shot through the head and then robbed and the driver knew nothing about it until he drove up to the hotel in Greensboro', when the discovery was made, yet I don't think the circumstance was mentioned in the newspapers, for fear, perhaps, that it would diminish the travel on the line."

"I appreciate your kindness," gratefully responded the drummer, becoming more restive and affrighted as the conversation proceded. "My engagements require me to be in Greensboro' to-morrow morning. I shall be glad to have your company. Doesn't Greensboro' lie between this and Selma, your point of destination."

"It does," continued Conning, in reply, "and my business is likewise of an imperious nature. It is my intention to take the stage for Greensboro' to-night and if every tree on the road was highway robber, my mind is made up to make the trip. But, a word in your ear,—there is a difficulty, aside from the assassin's pistol and bowie-knife, which may prove quite as fatal to our prospect of reaching Greensboro' by morning. I am told that just at present there is an unprecedented throng of travel on this line and so many simultaneous applications for seats, that to avoid any difficulty which might result from a discrimination on the part of the agent among applicants, he has peremptorily refused to register seats to any one, stating that he would receive passage money from each one, and would let it rest among those who had paid, to decide who shall remain over for the next stage. Now I have a project in view by which, my friend and travelling companion, Jenkins and myself, expect to overcome this obstacle and avoid the likelihood of detention. Our scheme can be more effectually carried out by additional assistance, and hence my reason for laying it before you."

"Assuredly, assuredly," eagerly exclaimed our traveller, "I will most cheerfully bear a hand in any project that will facilitate my progress to Greensboro'. Count on me. What is the scheme?"

"It is simply this," said Conning, in an exceedingly confidential and friendly manner, "you observe the empty coach across the street, now without horses,—that is the Greensboro' stage—it leaves to-night about nine o'clock—our plan is, upon rising from supper to repair to the coach, take our seats and retain them, against all contestants, until it starts. A little fighting may stand us in hand, but that's no matter—we're well armed—so we hold our seats."

"I'm in," enthusiastically responded the victim, accepting the proposition with a manifestation of earnestness, behind which some fear and apprehension was plainly visible, "I'm in and thank you, too; but I trust we may accomplish our purpose with out a fight; I am well armed however—always go thus when travelling in the South—and never desert a friend,—depend upon *me*."

"I knew," interposed Jenkins, drawing near the parties, and now taking part for the first time in the conversation, although he had been an attentive listener from its beginning, "I knew, as soon as I observed the cut of your jib, stranger, that you'd do. I was satisfied, from the cock of your eye, that you had *gizzard!* We have no time to lose. Let's slug-sup and prepare for business."

The liquor was despatched, supper bolted, stage-fare paid, pistols freshly capped, and the trio made their way speedily to the coach heretofore designated, into which Conning and the drummer entered and selecting their seats, flung themselves into them with the resolute air and bearing of men who were not to be ousted without risk and trouble; whilst Jenkins, protesting that it made him sea-sick to occupy an inside seat, mounted the box with the intention of keeping the driver company.

The night was cold, gusty and dark as an Egyptian fog could have made it. The curtains of the coach were fastened in their places, our insiders disposed themselves as comfortably in their seats as circumstances permitted, and the drummer announced his intention to pay his respects to the drowsy god, between whom and himself there had existed but little intercourse for a length of time. The last sound that fell upon the ear of the weary traveller as he sunk into the unconsciousness of sleep, was the voice of our friend Jenkins on the driver's seat bidding adieu to an excited and rather clamorous concourse of friends, who had assembled to see him off. The shouts and laughter of these leave-takers—their earnestly-expressed wishes for Jenkins' success in his present undertaking—the warm admonitions to that popular individual to "take care of himself," "keep his eye skinned," "not to get his nose knocked out of joint," remembrances to friends in Greensboro', entreaties to *fire up* once more before setting out,—all this hubbub and confusion, lasting as it did a length of while, did not impede, but rather accelerated the fatigued drummer's transit to the land of Nod. In spite of all, he was soon locked, fast and sound, in the embrace of sleep.

In this state of blissful unconsciousness, he had remained above a couple of hours, when he was aroused to a partial state of intelligence, by the friendly hand of his fellow-passenger, Tom Conning, shaking him gently by the shoulder, who addressed him, as follows:—

"My friend, I dislike to disturb your dreams; but the night is so infernally cold, I thought I would ask if you wouldn't swallow a 'slug' of Carthage blue-head, just by way of warming you up a little. We have travelled fifteen miles,—and are now changing horses at Carthage—and if you have no objection I will shout to Tom Jenkins, who has gone into the Carthage Astor House to wet his whistle, to bring us out something to drink."

"Thank you," yawned out the drummer, stretching and gaping, "thank you, I will join you in a stiffener in celebration of our good luck to-night. Carthage—fifteen miles, you say—one-fourth of the distance to Greensboro'—I should not have believed I could have slept so sound,—I've been lucky from my cradle. How many passengers have we along?"

"We are not crowded," replied Conning, "several who intended taking the stage, got drunk before the time of its departure, and so missed it. We have only three insiders besides ourselves, all of whom are now in the tavern firing up. Hello! Tom, when you've finished imbibing, bring us a couple of 'stiff tods' out here."

The latter part of this speech, yelled at the top of his voice by the speaker through the coach window, was addressed to Tom Jenkins, who had abandoned, during the changing of horses, his cold and comfortless seat outside, and gone into the hotel.

"Ay, ay," affirmatively roared Jenkins from the door of the house, "the bar-keeper is mixing it now,—keep your shirt on—I'll bring it out in a jiffy."

After the lapse of a few minutes, Jenkins appeared at the door of the coach, bearing the warming potations.

"Pretty raw time you've had outside?" half interrogatively asked the drummer.

"Why, yes," responded Jenkins; "but it was not so bad as it might have been: it threatened rain awhile back, and still the clouds are black and lowering, but I have escaped with a dry skin! How do you get along inside?"

[293]

"Tolerably comfortable, considering," replied our drummer, "I never slept sounder in my life. But when a man has lost rest as long as I have, jolted and bumped nearly to death by the *corduroy* turnpikes, it is not surprising that, on the smooth and excellent road we have been travelling to-night, that even a stage-coach should become a provocative to sleep. I fell asleep before we left Tuskaloosa—did not know when the stage left—and slept uninterruptedly until we stopped here to change horses."

"How long before we get off from Carthage, Tom?" asked the hitherto silent fellow-insider of the individual, who, having just ministered to their creature comforts, was moving with the empty tumblers away from the stage.

"Not long, I reckon," answered Jenkins, "I hear a fuss down at the stable, and suppose they are gearing up the team."

"Suppose we fix ourselves for another snooze," gapingly proposed Tom Conning to the drummer. "The road from here to Havanna, distant about ten miles, is as level as a floor, and, perchance, we may nap it as pleasantly as we did in the earlier part of the night?"

"Agreed, with all my heart!" chimed in the drummer. "I am still a week's solid sleep behind; so, here goes!"

And, true enough, his perfect stillness and regular breathing soon indicated that he was carrying the intention just expressed into happy and refreshing execution. Had he kept awake, it is barely possible that he would have been duly impressed with the extensiveness of Jenkins' popularity, as was manifested here, like it had been in Tuskaloosa, by even still more hearty and boisterous expressions of interest and friendship, and still warmer and more emphatic leave-takings from a numerous assemblage, as that estimable and universally beliked individual left the hotel, and ascended the elevated seat appropriated to the driver.

An hour had scarcely elapsed, ere our somniferous drummer was again brought to his waking senses by Tom Conning, who, shaking him, thus spoke:

"Well, my friend, you are one of the seven sleepers, sure. Here are a parcel of fellows in front of the Eagle Hotel, in the village of Havanna, where we arrived some half hour ago, who have been making all sorts of frightful and hideous noises, and kicking up the devil's delight, generally,—they are evidently on an unqualified bender,— and still you sleep as quietly with your head on your valise, as an infant on its mother's bosom. Wake up, man, and say what you'll take to moisten your clay with! The bar-room, at the Eagle Hotel, Havanna, is hard to beat. What shall it be? Cocktails? Well—cocktails be it. O, Tom, send or bring us out a brace of rousing cocktails: it's too cold to leave our snug quarters in the stage; so, let us have them here."

"This is passing strange!" exclaimed the bewildered drummer. "My sleep is wonderfully sound! How far have we travelled since leaving Carthage? Ten miles, you say? It's downright curious! I have not the slightest recollection of a single occurrence by the way. I seem to have reversed the order of nature, and sleep soundest when in motion."

At this instant, Jenkins opened the coach door, and, presenting the stimulating beverages, accosted the inriders with:

"Gents, you are a brace of the best sleepers I've met with lately. I haven't slept a wink to-night, and am as wide awake now as I ever was. Stranger, you were never in Havanna before? Judging from present signs, I reckon you think it a right lively village, with about fifty fellows, now, at the hour of two o'clock, on an uproarious *burst*; but don't set the place down as too 'small potatoes,' on account of what you now hear, for I was here about six months ago, when there were at least a hundred chaps, blowing it out much stronger than they now are, and kept it up till morning, exercising one another, first and last, in thirty-seven fights, and only five killed at daylight. It's a *stirring* village, I tell *you!*"

With this striking encomium on the village, Jenkins left the coach, and plunged into the midst of the noisy and rollicking crowd.

"Mr. Conning," said the drummer, having seemed for a few moments to be absorbed in meditation, "it occurs to me that your friend Mr. Jenkins is a very widely known, as well as very popular man; he seems to be as well acquainted and as much at home here as he was in Tuskaloosa or Carthage. I can't tell when, judging from all I have seen to-night, I've met any one who seemed to have a more extensive circle of warm, devoted and enthusiastic friends."

"You say truly," answered Conning, "Tom Jenkins is a noble-hearted, generous, high-souled fellow, who is esteemed warmly wherever he is known; few men of his age have a more numerous or more devoted circle of friends and admirers."

"How long does the stage usually stop here?" asked the now slightly nervous drummer, as he caught a sound from the hilarious crowd, which indicated that a proposition was undergoing discussion, relative to taking somebody out of the stage.

"From a half hour to an hour, depending upon whether the stage is up with or behind time," responded Conning. "We can remain here an hour or two, and still get to Greensboro' by early breakfast. I wish that crowd of noisy fellows would go to bed, for I feel sleepier than I have felt before to-night; how is it with you?"

"Why, I believe I can go to sleep at the drop of a hat," lazily rejoined our drummer, as snugly ensconcing himself once more in the cushions, he sunk into the arms of Morpheus. "No poppy, nor mandragora, nor all the drowsy syrups of the East," could have sooner sealed him in complete obliviousness.

Eight o'clock the next morning, after these occurrences, the sun was shining brightly, the breakfast bells were pealing their cheering summons, as our drowsy drummer, rousing himself from his protracted slumbers, discovered that he was the sole tenant of the stage-coach in which he had travelled so smoothly, and slept so soundly during the night. Shaking himself to reestablish circulation and relax his stiffened limbs, he essayed to look through the glass window of the coach, and was delighted to find, despite the obscurity of the glass, that he was *in town*. Nevertheless, he could not keep from wondering and speculating as to the reason he had been left sleeping by his friendly fellow passengers, and the singular conduct of the hotel keepers in Greensboro', which would permit a traveller, who had ridden in the cold all night, to remain in the stage after he had arrived in town, until the horses were taken from it, and the breakfast bells were ringing. Another feature in the case, too, sufficiently singular to command his attention, was the fact, discovered by him as he emerged from the coach, that he was just in front of an old carriage and smith shop, and what seemed to be the hotel was across the street.

A loud, cachinnatory roar saluted him, from a numerous assemblage of persons, who seemed to be gathered about the hotel corner, as, valise in hand, he bent his steps in their direction. Their vociferation and prolonged laughter, their boisterous shouts and clamorous yells brought forcibly to his mind the midnight revellers he had encountered at Carthage and Havanna, between whom and the present excited and uproarious multitude there occurred to his bewildered faculties to be only this difference: the one set did their work at night, whilst the other begun their exercises at early morning.

Passing into the hotel, the bellowing crowd pressing on his heels, he appeared for an instant to be somewhat taken aback by the striking resemblance which its interior arrangements and furniture, to say nothing of the enormous capitals, WASHINGTON HALL, painted along the whole length of the spacious bar-room, bore to the hotel in Tuskaloosa. Pondering as best he could, amid the deafening din and dire confusion by which he was surrounded, and attempting to reconcile these strange similarities, he was precipitated still further into doubt, perplexity and uncertainty, as he observed a large man move across the room, whose appearance was a *fac simile* of old Nat. Duffee, the hotel keeper whom he had left in Tuskaloosa the night before!

Sorely puzzled and staggered by the last mentioned circumstance, he made an effort to cast off the bewildering doubts that oppressed his mind, by boldly accosting the clerk, after first examining his memoranda-book, with the following enquiries:

"Where is the store-house of Messrs. Johnson & Henden?"

"I really don't know, sir," innocently and honestly answered the clerk; "I never heard of the firm before."

Another reference to the memoranda-book was followed by the question:

"Can you tell me where I will find the store of Messrs. Dickens, Webb & Co.?"

"I cannot inform you, sir. There is no such firm, I'm sure, in Tuskaloosa."

"Tuska----!" the astonished drummer began to ejaculate, but the sound died away on his lips. Moving forward to the desk on which laid the hotel register of arrivals and departures, he beheld his own name, written in his dashing, clerk-like hand!

Asking for a room as soon as his wandering intellect permitted him to do so, he retired from the presence of the half-frantic crowd; and, in the depths of his chamber, hid his mortification, and nursed his revenge. Sometime during the day, he left the city in a private conveyance, undisturbed of idlers, and without making any demonstration of his purpose, further than to acquaint the hotel keeper, in direst accents of indignation, that he intended, on his arrival home, to expose, through the public press, the whole affair, and all the parties; or, to use what is still repeated in our city as the exact language of his threat, "He intended to publish the stage agent, the hotel keeper, and every man who was concerned in the scandalous transaction."

Having waited nineteen long years for the fulfilment of his threat, and never having seen word or line exhibiting the affair, we have essayed to rescue the facto from oblivion, in the present impartial and veracious history, yclept

"NEW YORK DRUMMER'S RIDE TO GREENSBORO'!"

OMEGA.

UNCLE STIN WAS A HERO

Esquire: The Magazine for Men, New York City, November, 1946.

If only the members of my family who knew him best said so you would not believe me. You'd say, sure, every family in the South has its own Confederate hero. But with my Great Uncle Stin it was different. He was revered by everyone in our little Carolina town where he was born and where today on Shady Grove Hill he waits the final muster roll. With him of course rest his comrades of the Kershaw Grays. But of them all Uncle Stin alone has remained the symbol of their chivalry. He was, I tell you, a hero's hero.

Uncle Stin's heroism rests largely but not wholly, as you will see, upon his military career. As a young man of fifteen, he enlisted in the 8th Carolina Volunteers—the Kershaw Grays—as a drummer boy. It was along toward the end of The War and for some reason his first few weeks of service were spent in training, quite out of the sound of musketry. No one ever knew why a fighter of his caliber should have been deprived of quicker blood; anyhow, not until Chickamaugua did he receive baptism of fire. At high noon, as the Confederates, readying for a charge, crawled out of the woods beyond Snodgrass Hill, Colonel Rickey, of the famous Ole Virginny Rickeys, turned to Uncle Stin, his drummer, and shouted, "All right, boy—beat it!" Uncle Stin, true soldier that he was, obeyed. As father used to say, he beat it back across Alexander's Bridge to Ringgold and, a day or so later, footsore and weary, wound up in Atlanta. Meanwhile, of course, news of the great Confederate victory had come through on the wires and by the time Uncle Stin got home, hungry, bleeding, and fit to be killed from exhaustion, he was welcomed as a harbinger of victory, feted and fed.

No one ever doubted that his wounded leg housed a Minie ball as big as a hen egg. And Uncle Stin, always the unassuming hero, had his own good reasons, I suppose, for not telling a grateful people about the misfortunes which befell him in swimming the Savannah on his heroic journey home.

After Appomattox, Uncle Stin settled down, along with other heroes of the Lost Cause, to a well-earned life of peaceful complacency. He joined the Ku Klux and actively participated in the permanent freeing from fear of a dozen emanicipated residents of our county, rode with Hampton's Red Shirts, fought in the Carolina Liquor Riot and otherwise led the comfortable, easygoing existence of a Confederate veteran and a gentleman. Somewhere along his line of progress he acquired a gray mare which he called Reb, and a buggy, a hankering after red-eye and old peach, and a conspicuous rise in rank. These promotions crept up on him, as it were, somewhat by spells. Starting out as Captain he was for a brief time Major; but, before anyone really had time to count the stripes, he had sneaked up to a Southern Colonelcy. And there the matter stood.

Thus fortified with transportation, a handy surcease from his horrifying war experiences, and a rank not below that of all other Confederates, Uncle Stin passed his years beloved by everyone, a true gallant of the South.

Call it family pride, if you like, but even with Father, who was his closest confidante, Uncle Stin's vocation was a subject taboo. All he'd ever say was, "Son, when you get to be a hero like Uncle Stin, you don't need to work." But everyone knew that his assets were unquestionably liquid.

Naturally, there was his Confederate pension. And friends, ever mindful of the Minie ball limp in his leg, considered him a genial and mealtimely visitor. Off and on, as circumstances demanded, he would slap a mortgage on his mare, but Reb, herself a wearer of the Gray, Father said, didn't seem to mind. Enviably, therefore, did Uncle Stin tote the togs of his heroism, his life one round of Confederate Reunions with-dinner-on-the-ground, Memorial Days and unselfish collaboration with the constable.

You will recall from your history that following The War there swept over the South a revival of such intensity as to be likened, or so scholars have declared, only unto the Second Coming. This fervor, as you may rightly reckon, did not pass Uncle Stin by. He fought, bled, lived, died, it didn't matter, for Marse Robert. At the mere mention of the General's name, Uncle Stin would click his heels, come to attention, touch his campaign hat and mutter an unintelligible requiem. And, like dozens of hundreds of his Confederate compatriots who had never been nearer their leader than a calendar, he would have had you know that along the unquiet Potomac he'd often slapped Marse Robert on the back and called him Bobby.

Now I doubt if the General appreciated such adoration, but even the vital statistics were against him: by actual count eight out of ten white babies born below the Mason-Dixon during these fervent days emerged as either Robert E.'s or Roberta Edwina's. These figures of course exclude hotels, highways, steamboats, schools, colleges, and distilleries of the same name. On our public square alone there were six such establishments. One, "Blind Tiger" Malone's Robert E. Lee Saloon, stood catty-corner across the street from the Robert E. Lee Bible Class of the Balm of Gilead Church—a fact which for some reason greatly disturbed the Ladies' Auxiliary. One Sunday morning a delegation from that highly respectable body called on "Blind Tiger" to beseech him in the name of civic decency to change the title of his firm. The details of the visitation never came to light, but several Sundays later the auxiliary bought a new piano and the name of the class became the Robert E. Malone Bible Class. That, Father used to say quietly, was perhaps the highest tide of the Confederacy.

But back to Uncle Stin. If his devotion to Marse Robert was unique, it was not devouring. His passion for funerals, theatricals and school-closings was equally Kiwanian. Wherever more than three people gathered in our aristocratic little town, he was there, waving the Stars and Bars. Like some men you must know, he had a knack, a sort of Chamber of Commerce complex, one might say, for community service.

On one occasion, Father said, Uncle Stin and Reb chanced to be driving around our public square just as a crowd lined up at the ticket office of the Dixie Opera House. Out of curiosity Reb stopped and

Uncle Stin, aided by the buggy shafts, swung out and onto the end of the slowly moving queue.

It was a one-night showing by the Southern Thespian Troupe of William Gillette's *Secret Service,* "a Popular Drama of the Southern Confederacy in Four Acts." Flashing his Colonelcy in the face of an harassed doorman, Uncle Stin sidled down the gas-lit aisle and took a choice seat in the dress circle.

Promptly at eight the hand-painted view of Fort Sumter rolled creakily up, revealing the drawing room of General Varney's Richmond home during the siege. Brave Confederate women were busy knitting, rolling bandages and sewing coarse sandbags. Through the window (rear) nurses could be seen caring for the piles of Confederate wounded and through a door (right side) troops rushed madly about in utmost confusion and excitement. Church bells rang in the distance, mingling their Confederate sweetness with the booms of Yankee siege guns. Suffering and uncertainty hung oppressively low in the heaven as well as on the Varney draperies. Yet through it all everyone was obviously attempting gaiety by keeping as busy as a crow in a cornfield.

Presently onto the stage tripped Edith Varney, the General's winsome and eligible daughter, to announce that through her father's influence she had just arranged for her lover, Captain Thorne, C.S.A., to remain in the beleaguered city. Of course everyone was happy over this. Everyone, that is, except the audience and Mr. Benton Arrelsford of the Confederate Secret Service. For he alone of all the players had somehow learned that Captain Thorne, his rival, was actually Mr. Lewis Dumont of the *United States* Secret Service!

Well, everything rocked along as well as could be hoped for under the circumstances. Throughout the first two acts Uncle Stin remained merely a spectator. But as the auditors, many of whom had been his battle comrades, hissed and heckled the struggling performers, his Southern soul was pierced to the quick. By the middle of Act III he could stand it no longer. Hell-bent for action, he jumped to his feet, waved his campaign hat in circles above his head and started up and down the aisle hollering, "Hurrah for Marse Robert."

Meanwhile, Dumont the spy, tricked by the heroic Arrelsford into sending a message to his Yankee brethren over the Confederate tickers, is caught red-handed in the War Department Telegraph Office. "Drop that gun or you're a dead man!" the Southerner shouts. "I've got you where I want you at last!" At this moment guards dash in from all directions and quick-thinking Dumont, still in his Confederate Captain's uniform, of course, suddenly reverses procedures by ordering Arrelsford arrested as a traitor!

That was the last straw. Screaming, "You've got the wrong man! You've got the wrong man!" Uncle Stin dashed down the aisle to the orchestra pit. There he stopped short, turned, gave a resounding Rebel yell, sprang across the footlights, and grabbed Dumont by the throat. By now, one after another of his comrades of the Kershaw Grays, responding to the old battle cry, had followed suit. The stage was a mingled mass of fighting, scratching Confederates, one after another in wild pursuit. The orchestra struck up *Dixie*, women screamed and fainted, and stage scenery collapsed under the strain of combat. Uncle Stin, his mission accomplished, crawled offstage (right) and, weaving in and out among the excited onlookers, headed up the outer aisle. Once in the clear he made for the buggy, clucked to Reb and struck out down Swift Creek Road like a martin to his gourd.

Early next morning, Father said, Uncle Stin and the owner of the Opera House were seen chatting warmly in front of the Robert E. Lee Saloon, but so far as he knew nothing came of their mutual interest in histrionics. One thing is sure, however. Our town was somehow deprived of theatricals until the coming of *Madame Butterfly*, five years later.

As his official chronicler I could of course go at length into Uncle Stin's private life or public affairs (or vice versa). His abiding love for our local Academy, for example, or his periodic interest in sacred harp singing as led by the shapely alto of the Balm of Gilead Choir. But these, comparatively speaking, are but moments to be skipped in a long and heroic life. It was his timely passing that really drenched our town in tears.

At ten on Memorial Day folks from miles around were clustered about the Confederate Monument on Court House Square eagerly waiting to hear Master Robert E. Odum, the high school valedictorian, recite Father Ryan's *The Conquered Banner*. The Fifth Grade Sextet (mixed) had already rendered *The Bonnie Blue Flag* and eight stanzas of *Dixie*, and Mayor Robert E. Stucky had announced that after the ceremonies one and all would march to Shady Grove Hill to place flowers on the graves of the honored dead.

As Master Odum squirmed his poetic way down to "Furl that Banner! True 'tis gory, Yet 'tis wreathed around with glory..." someone screamed and the crowd turned to see Reb, her head bowed, unevenly jerking an empty buggy around the square. A squad of veterans, together with a few common citizens, ran out to stop her.

Underneath the dashboard, his heroic leg curiously caught in the spokes and Reb's taut reins about his neck, hung Uncle Stin, pallid, ghostly, his hands flapping in the dust. Several women flinched and shrank away. An old soldier who had once hobnobbed with horror stood as if staked.

[301]

Halfmast up the buggy whip Uncle Stin's Stars and Bars trembled in the Carolina breeze.

After dinner-on-the-ground Master Odum was asked to conclude *The Conquered Banner*. Then, without delay, the celebrants trailed a floral-draped hearse through the religious twilight of the afternoon to Shady Grove Hill. Ahead of them all was faithful Reb flanked by a platoon of Grays.

Everyone commented on the timing. Uncle Stin would have preferred Memorial Day, they said. But Father always believed that delay would have helped matters little, anyway. "Embalming a man like Uncle Stin," he often remarked, "would have been like robbing Peter to pay Paul."

Yes, I tell you, Uncle Stin was a hero's hero.

VIZETELLY COVERS THE CONFEDERACY
THE PREFACE

Confederate Publishing Company,
Tuscaloosa, Alabama, 1957.

My interest in the *pictorial* history of the War for Southern Independence began long before my interest in the *verbal* history of that awful and long-lingering conflict. And for good reasons.

My father was born on New Year's Day, 1860. He never knew his father, the Lieutenant-Colonel John Axella Hoole, Eighth South Carolina Volunteers, Kershaw's Brigade, McLaw's Division, Longstreet's Corps, who yielded up his life to the Yankees on the morning of September 20, 1863 on a hillside called Horseshoe Ridge near a village of no importance named Chickamauga. But my father did indeed know the pain and the suffering and the bellyaching hunger that lay in Sherman's unholy swath across the South. He saw his young mother's valiant struggle to keep her family in cornbread and yams (there was also a sister, three years older than my father, and a younger, posthumous brother), he saw her lose her little farm to a conniving money-lender (not a Yankee, as God is my witness, but a local "patriot") and he was a mere lad when he saw his father's body arrive in a wooden box, wagon-drawn from North Georgia, and amid simple ceremonies laid in our family burial plot. (The Lieutenant-Colonel's sword he cherished until his death and I have cherished since.)

My father knew Reconstruction, too, every bitter day of it. He saw his home town designated as Headquarters, Second Brigade, Military District of Eastern South Carolina, Colonel George H. Nye, U. S. A., commanding. He saw Yankee troops of the Twenty-ninth Maine Volunteers, some of them black as night, gun-butting white men off the sidewalks and terrorizing white ladies with smirks and insinuations and drooling threats. And he was a mature young man of sixteen, my father was, when the Ku Klux rode and Wade Hampton's Red Shirts put an end to Carpetbag-Scalawag rule in South Carolina.

My father, as you may fancy, had little or no schooling—few Southern lads did in that tragic era. I think he attended the local academy through possibly the high school grades, but for all practical purposes he was self-taught. Yet he was the best-read, most intelligent man I ever knew and even now, after all my years of formal schooling, I am humbled by the memory of his wit and his wisdom.

As a young boy of thirteen or fourteen my father went to work as a drugstore clerk in our little South Carolina town to help support his mother—I remember the blind old lady years later, rocking, rocking on our front porch, her pupil-less eyes gray and dull with cataracts—and his little brother, John Axella, Jr., the posthumous one. All his life he worked there, finally owning the store and another one besides and earning a gracious living for his family and giving all of us the opportunities he had never had. I say he worked there all his life—I mean until lung tuberculosis cut him down in middle age. Tuberculosis, I must add, which gained its start in malnutrition: cornbread and yams are not what you'd call a balanced diet for a growing boy. And when he died, the local weekly declared his funeral procession the longest within recollection of our town's oldest patriarch.

On his mother's knee my father heard over and over again the story of The War, as did countless thousands of boys and girls of his sad, impoverished generation. And on his knee I heard it, too, over and over again until he left me to tell it for myself.

In 1911 or '12—my father was just a short year or so this side of the end—he brought home from the drugstore a brand-new set of books, the like of which I had never in the wide world dreamt could ever be. They were big, heavy books, bound in bright blue, so heavy I could scarcely lift them one at a time, and they were filled with pictures from one end to the other. And although I knew, because father had told me, that the volumes were wrongly-named—not the Civil war, surely not civil—I cannot but say that *The Photographic History of the Civil War*, published by the old *Review of Reviews* and filled with the magic of Mathew Brady, was the most intriguing, the most captivating thing that had ever come into my eight-year-old life.

I remember as if it were yesterday how those pictures hypnotized me—the bloated Federal dead at Gettysburg, the little fourteen-year-old Confederate with a bayonet through his chest at Fort Mahone, the haunting faces of Lee's haggard, hungry men at Coxey's Landing, and Columbia, Charleston, Vicksburg and Richmond in ruins, and hundreds more. Day after day I thumbed the pages, marvelling at the wizardry of Brady's wet-plate art, its depth and detail, reading as best I could the captions and the text and alway seeing myself

[303]

in each picture—now as the drummer-boy with Beauregard, now as the dead young Rebel on Little Round Top, now as Lee on Traveller, but most often imagining myself my father's father on Horseshoe Ridge the instant that Yankee bullet plowed into his chest, spinning him in agony about and flinging his body to the crimson earth . . .

Many years and many volumes later something of the same thrill came back to me, when I opened the *Illustrated London News*, 1861 –1865, and for the first time feasted my eyes on the art of Frank Vizetelly, the only artist-correspondent who covered the Army of the Confederate States of America. True it is that the Yankees had many reporters and artists on their side—Al Waud, Thomas Nast, and Alex A. Simplot of *Harper's Weekly*, for examples, and the distinguished Henri Lovie of *Frank Leslie's Illustrated Weekly*, and many more. But the South's side of the irrepressible conflict would never have been illustrated for posterity had not Frank Vizetelly of the *Illustrated London News* divorced the North in disgust in the fall of 1862 to cast his lot with the Rebels below the Potomac. And I vowed somehow, someday to tell his story.

I like to think that Frank Vizetelly and Lieutenant-Colonel Hoole might have shaken hands that September morning on the banks of Chickamauga Creek. They were most certainly in the same battle sector. The Englishman had hastened up from Charleston to describe the battle for his paper, the Carolinian had been dispatched with Kershaw's Brigade of Longstreet's Corps from the faraway Army of Northern Virginia to bolster the weakening Army of Tennessee, which was fighting desperately to keep the Federals out of the Confederacy's back yard. The two men arrived at Ringgold on the same rail line, almost simultaneously. Both crossed over Alexander's bridge above Lee and Gordon's mill and both were with Longstreet's exultant Confederates as they fought their irrestible way up the steep slope of Horseshoe Ridge, down, and up again, pounding the Yankee lines and sweeping everything before them. For on that day Vizetelly, "neutral" British correspondent though he was, actually struck for the South and on the battlefield was commissioned an honorary captain in the Confederate Army by none other than General Longstreet, himself!

I say, I like to think the Lieutenant-Colonel and the Honorary Captain might have shaken hands that day of battle. Perhaps they did. They had much in common, they did, the fighter and the writer. I believe they would have made fast friends. But if perchance one was too busy sketching and the other too consumed with killing, then I am privileged to bring them together here, albeit ninety-four years too late.

For I alone am beholden to both.

JEREMIAH CLEMENS, NOVELIST

The Alabama Review, Alabama Historical Association,
University of Alabama and Auburn University, January, 1965.

The checkered career of Jeremiah Clemens (1814–1865), attorney, politician, soldier, planter, and deserter from the Confederate States of America, has often been told, but his career as a fiction writer has attracted little or no attention. Yet, now, as reviewed after a hundred years, his four full-length novels, published between 1856 and 1865, seem destined to be his most unique reason for recognition among the immortals of Alabama.

Clemens, a student in the first class of the University of Alabama (1831), studied law at Transylvania University and in 1834 began practice in Huntsville, his birthplace, at the age of twenty. On December 4 of the same year he married Mary L. Read, daughter of Colonel John Read, a local merchant and farmer. Shortly after, he joined the United States Army as a private to fight the Cherokee Indians. In 1837 President Martin Van Buren appointed him district judge for North Alabama, a position which he resigned upon his election to the Alabama House of Representatives in 1839. He was re-elected two years later, but before completing the term he resigned to become captain of a company of volunteers pledged to support the new Republic of Texas in its war with Mexico.

At this time (1840) the brilliant and dashing young lawyer-soldier was also one of the handsomest and most desirable of men—at least, so thought the charming fifteen-year-old Virginia Caroline Tunstall of Tuscaloosa, niece of Alabama's Secretary of State Thomas B. Tunstall, who years later revealed her intense but brief young love for Clemens in *A Belle of the Fifties:*

> Never had my eyes beheld so pleasing a masculine wonder! He was the personification of manly beauty! His head was shapely as Tasso's (in after life I often heard the comparison made), and in his eyes there burned a romantic fire that enslaved me from the moment their gaze rested upon me. At their warmth all the ardour, all the ideals upon which a romantic heart had fed rose in recognition of their realisation in him. During the evening he paid me some pretty compliments, remarking upon my hazel eyes and the gleam of gold in my hair, and he touched my curls admiringly, as if they were revered by him.
>
> My head swam! Lohengrin never dazzled Elsa more completely than did this knight of the poet's head charm the maiden that was I! We danced together frequently throughout the evening, and my hero rendered me every attention a kind man may offer to the little daughter of a valued friend. When at last we [Virginia and Uncle Thomas] stepped into the carriage and turned homeward, the whole world was changed for me.

On the way home as she excitedly told her kinsman how much

she had enjoyed the evening, he replied, "And was I not kind to provide you with such a gallant cavalier? Isn't Colonel Jere Clemens a handsome man?"

> Ah was he not! My full heart sang out his praises with an unmistakable note. My uncle listened sympathetically. Then he continued, 'Yes, he's a fine fellow! A fine fellow, Virginia, and he has a nice little wife and baby!'
> No thunderbolt ever fell more crushingly upon the unsuspecting than did these awful words from the lips of my uncle! I know not how I reached my room, but once there I wept passionately throughout the night and much of the following morning. Within my own heart I accused my erstwhile hero of the rankest perfidy; of villainy of every imaginable quality; and in this recoil of injured pride perished my first love dream, vanished the heroic wrappings of my quondam knight!

After five months of active service in the United States Army in and about Corpus Christi in 1841–1843, Clemens returned to Huntsville a hero and was soon re-elected to the House of Representatives (1844). When the Mexican War began, he was commissioned a major in the United States Thirteenth Infantry. For almost two years he served in the Thirteenth and in the Ninth Infantry, composed mostly of Massachusetts troops, both under the command of General Winfield Scott, rising in rank from major to colonel. Upon his return to Alabama in July, 1848, he was promptly elected to the United States Senate on a Democrat-Whig coalition ticket to fill the unexpired term of Senator Dixon H. Lewis, deceased. In 1853, however, when he offered himself for re-election, he was defeated—he had become too closely indentified with "Unionism" to be popular among the Democrats. And, although it was rumored that President Franklin Pierce would appoint him to a high political or diplomatic post, Clemens, now forty-two years old and one of Alabama's most widely-known citizens, returned to Huntsville, resumed the practice of law, supervised his plantations and, largely as an avocation, undertook to write fiction based for the most part on his many and varied experiences as a soldier in two wars along the Texas-Mexican border.

The first of Clemens' novels was *Bernard Lile; an Historical-Romance Embracing the Periods of the Texas Revolution and the Mexican War*, published in 1856 by J. B. Lippincott & Company of Philadelphia. Dedicated to George W. Neal, of Huntsville, the 287-page volume purported to be based on facts.

> Although a romance in name, imagination has had little to do with its preparation [the author stated in his preface]. It records events the most of which will be familiar to many who read it. Most of the characters are drawn from real life. Not a place is described I have not visited. Scarcely a scene is depicted which is not based upon an actual occurrence. It is a book of life—or life not as I wished it, or thought it ought to be, but as I have found it.

Then, philosophically, Clemens added that the romance had "no plan, for human life has none" and that in its titular role he had made "no attempt to paint [his] ideal of a perfect man...," for no such man existed. "There are none of us so free from errors that we can afford, without self-condemnation, to be uncharitable to the sins of others; and I know of no good that can be accomplished by freeing the hero of a romance from the faults incident to humanity."

Clemens' careful declaration that his book had no plan and his forewarning about the faults and errors of his chief character were apt, indeed. For few if any novels of the middle of the last century could possibly have had so little plan or so unappealing a hero as did *Bernard Lile*. It is doubtful, even, that the romance accomplished its primary motive of stirring men's patriotism, of making men proud to be citizens of the United States of America:

> Every man who writes a book, I suppose has a motive; but very few tell it in the *preface*. Perhaps I shall best escape the suspicion of like disingenuousness by keeping mine a secret; remarking only, that if the American, when he lays it down, feels in his bosom a warmer throb for his country, a higher appreciation of its excellencies, and a more devoted attachment to its institutions, he need not look further for the *motive* which induced the author to undergo the labor it has cost, or the *hope* which sustains him in submitting his production to the criticism of the press.

In its barest outline *Bernard Lile* is a confused, rambling, incoherent story of a wandering, swashbuckling gambler, drunkard and roué who deserts his sick wife and goes to Texas to fight the Mexicans (1835–1837). After suffering through the Alamo, Goliad, San Jacinto and a prairie battle or two with the Comanches, he returns home to spend his time in riotous living in Washington, New Orleans, New York, New Hampshire, Cuba, and on the Ohio and Mississippi rivers. Upon the outbreak of the Mexican War (1846) he returns to Texas, joins the United States Army, fights at Matamoros, Monterrey, Buena Vista, Vera Cruz and elsewhere until he is finally killed at Guadalupe Hidalgo near Mexico City.

Perhaps the best that can be said of *Bernard Lile* is that, with all its verbosity, sermonizing and grandiloquent digressions, it reveals the author's considerable knowledge of frontier life, of red-eye guzzling, riverboat gambling, fist fighting, murdering, panther shooting, slaughtering of Mexicans and Comanches, and of service in the United States Army in the Southwest during the early Nineteenth Century. According to Clemens, the work was designed "to show that no strength of will, no genius, no gifts of fortune, and no accomplishments are sufficient of themselves to save us from the greatest errors in our journey through the world." It does that: Bernard Lile, mysterious man without a past or a future, marches inexorably to his doom, his patriotism and his love of liberty his sole redeeming traits. However, as a novel *Bernard Lile* must have been unimpressive, even to Clemens' contemporaries. It is crudely built, virtually plotless. It moves forward slowly incident by disjointed incident, episode by episode. The characters are prosaic, stereotyped. And, alas, whatever little might have remained to excite or entertain the reader is buried beneath a florid style which all but destroys his attention. Clemens' descriptions are long, repetitious, and overbearing. Even the climaxes of his faltering narrative, such as the story of Lile's heroic offer to carry a message from the Alamo through the Mexican lines, lose their force in sentimental bombast.

> Amidst the applauding murmurs which followed Davey Crockett's harangue, Bernard Lile walked to the side of Colonel William Travis, the commanding officer.
> 'I am comparatively a stranger, Colonel,' he said, 'and it is most fit the lot should fall on me. I came here to serve Texas, and it matters little to me in what capacity the service is rendered.'
> 'Let him go, Colonel,' shouted a dozen voices at once, 'we saw him when he lifted old Ben Milam from the street, and if mortal man can get through yonder lines, he will do it.'
> So it was arranged that Bernard Lile should that night be the bearer of despatches to the President of the Convention, or to General Houston, (then supposed to be in Victoria), as circumstances might determine.
> When darkness came, Lile was ushered from the gate by Travis himself. 'God bless you!' said the hero, grasping the hand of his messenger for the last time. 'We shall meet no more. In a few days, I and the brave fellows with me will be food for the vultures. You, sir, are said to have a heart that never knew fear, and an arm that never met its equal. Use both for Texas, if you would have the blessing of a dying man. Say to our friends to take no thought about avenging our deaths. We will avenge ourselves. But tell them to learn from us that life without liberty is worthless, and if they cease to struggle while one hostile foot is left upon the soil of Texas, we will come back to curse it. Again, good-bye. In another world we may recall the memory of this hour. In this one we are parted for ever.'

Bernard Lile attracted almost no press attention upon its appearance in the fall of 1856, although its author was a former United States senator and a distinguished veteran of two wars. All of the major American literary journals, except *Godey's Lady's Book and Magazine* (New York), ignored the new novel, and that one remarked only that,

> This volume is copyrighted by Jeremiah Clemens, at one time a member of the National Legislature, and whom we presume to be the author. It appears to have been written with more vigor and care than are usually bestowed on similar works. And, while we cheerfully admit that the narrative is admirably conducted, and the characters powerfully drawn, we cannot turn from many of the latter without feelings of abhorrence.

Perhaps the Philadelphia *Daily News*, October 17, 1856, explained why *Bernard Lile* was ignored, even by the local papers, when it stated the following in its "Literary Intelligence" column:

A friend asked us why we seemed to pay more attention to what New York and Boston booksellers were doing than those of our own City. We suppose the reason to be that the booksellers of those cities have sense and enterprise enough to let us know what they are doing, whilst the trade of Philadelphia, for all practical purposes of information, are asleep.

Clemens was not to be outdone, however. Before *Bernard Lile* had reached the galleys he had begun another novel, *Mustang Gray: A Romance*, which was dedicated to Nicholas Davis of Huntsville. Although copyrighted in 1857 the 296-page volume, also issued by Lippincott, was actually dated and did not appear on American book-stalls until 1858. In his preface Clemens claimed (as he had similarly claimed in *Bernard Lile*) that his narrative was based entirely on facts. He vowed that Mustang Gray was a real man whose "name and exploits" were well-known in the Southwest.

I knew him long and well [Clemens continued]. With all his faults, he was one 'who loved me, and whom I loved long ago.' There are hundreds now living, who will attest that the portrait I have drawn is true to the original. His adventures might have been swelled to a volume of treble the present size, and yet much have been left untold. I have confined myself to such only as I considered necessary to the development of his character.

In many respects *Mustang Gray* is a sequel to *Bernard Lile*. The central character, Mabry ("Mustang") Gray, is a sort of dare-devil ne'er-do-well, a blackguard who kills Robert Taliafero over a love affair with Julia Allison, leaves for Texas, and there becomes involved in smuggling guns, liquor, and other commodities across the Mexican border. Later he joins the Army of the Texas Republic to fight the Comanches and, when the United States goes to war with Mexico, organizes a company of Rangers and serves under Zachary Taylor at Corpus Christi and elsewhere. Mustang dies at long last of fever and is buried beside Inez Montero, a beautiful Mexican girl who had years before saved his life.

In Clemens' own words the "leading object" of *Mustang Gray*, as it was of *Bernard Lile*, was to suggest that "no associations, no natural gentleness of disposition, and no pious training in early life, will suffice to prevent us from yielding to the temptations of passion." In short, the moral of both novels was that "at all times, and under all circumstances, we are weak and helpless against the evil tendency of our own inclinations, if unaided by the protecting presence of a merciful God." In both the author sought directly "to impress on the mind of the reader the *one* great truth, that the only way to escape from Hell, is to keep our eyes forever fixed on Heaven." In both

[309]

books the chief personage closes out his worthless career in a blaze of patriotic fervor. Both carry the same theme, both are replete with long asides and irrelevant descriptions, and both seem designed principally as media through which the author could flaunt his knowledge of life and love on the Texas frontier. To say that the two novels are autobiographical would be unfair to Clemens, but certainly he could not have written either without drawing heavily upon his own personal experiences. The line between fiction and fact can never be precisely drawn, of course, but in Clemens' case it seems very, very thin.

With all its heavy sermonizing, *Mustang Gray* was for a short time a fairly popular romance, especially in the South and Southwest. By comparison, it attracted far more attention than had its predecessor, *Bernard Lile,* perhaps because the often Byronic, gloomy Mustang is a kinder, more understandable and hence more likeable character than Bernard—and because their creator had no doubt profited by practice. Here and there, one might even say that Clemens wrote well, as judged by Nineteenth Century standards, as this description of Gray's almost single-handed attack on a detachment of Mexican cavalrymen suggests:

The strength and speed of Gray's horse, soon carried him far ahead of his comrades . . . [and] the Mexicans had become aware that the pursuit was conducted by a mere handful of their foes. A squad of them halted —formed a regular order, and presented their escopetas. With a yell that more resembled the cry of a hungry panther than any human sound, Gray rushed upon them. He was received by an irregular volley, so ill directed that only one ball grazed his side, while his own sabre was crimsoned to the hilt, as he broke unharmed through the shattered line. Here he was opposed by a stronger body, armed with muskets and bayonets, which he instantly perceived it would be madness to charge . . . [and] even while the horse's forefeet were in the air, the bridle was drawn hard, and the animal wheeled backwards as if on a pivot. A considerable circuit removed him from the danger of a direct fire, and in a few minutes he rejoined his comrades, who were slaughtering the fugitives he had passed in his headlong career. All that could be effected had been done. The main body were too far off to support them, and the Mexicans, though still retreating, were no longer scattered here and there, but formed in regular order, with a rear guard strong enough to protect them. A loud shout for 'Texas and liberty,' rang over the plains, and the little party galloped back to the position occupied by Col. Moore. In his precipitate flight, the enemy had abandoned his baggage, which fell into the hands of the volunteers, who marched into Gonzales without the loss of a single man, in high spirits at the result of their first encounter with the myrmidons of the oppressor.

Mustang Gray, like *Bernard Lile,* was virtually overlooked by contemporary journals. *Russell's Magazine* of Charleston alone gave the new novel generous notice, calling it a simple narrative, somewhat disjointed and heavily moral "but always told with effective earnestness and spirit."

> And truly [the reviewer continued], Mustang Gray, the hero, is somewhat more than a scapegrace. With all his brave exploits, and the admiration they naturally excite, we cannot conceal from ourselves the fact that he is very decidedly a desperado, and not a little of a blackguard. We must confess that we do not fancy the *school* of fiction to which Mr. Clemens' 'romance' belongs, but it is certainly a clever book of its kind.

Nevertheless, *Russell's* went on to devote some twenty-four hundred words to *Mustang Gray*, a long review, indeed, although most of it was composed of direct quotations describing the confused Gray-Allison-Taliafero triangle.

The Philadelphia *Daily News*, March 29, 1858, having earlier ignored *Bernard Lile*, made up for the delinquency by declaring,

> *Mustang Gray* is a very readable novel.... It is from the lively and graphic pen of the Hon. Jere Clemens, of Alabama, author of *Bernard Lile*, a work which has attained a high degree of popularity, but which, in our opinion, is far inferior to the very pleasant story under consideration. We have, it is true, read more fascinating novels than *Mustang Gray*, more highly polished productions, but none that inculcates more useful lessons, or which presents more natural and vivid pictures of domestic life. The style is lively—often brilliant, always easy. We predict that *Mustang Gray* will amuse thousands.

Tedious and overbearing as *Bernard Lile* and *Mustang Gray* may be to present-day readers, there can be no doubt that they filled a niche, however small, in the ever-expanding structure of early American fiction. The Southwest, the independence and annexation of Texas, and the Mexican War were in many respects the most colorful, crucial, and newsworthy events of their time, and books about them, even highly imaginative, rambling romances, have long stirred men's blood—from the appearance of the anonymous *L'Heroine du Texas* in 1819 to *Inez: A Tale of the Alamo* (1855) by Augusta Evans Wilson; *Remember the Alamo!* (1888) by Amelia Barr; and on down to *The Road to San Jacinto* (1936) by J. Frank Davis and *The Wine of San Lorenzo* (1945) by Herbert Gorman. That Jeremiah Clemens' contributions to this literature failed of great immediate success does not negate its over-all value. After all, as a novice in historical fiction the former senator-soldier was facing hard and experienced competition in his bid for the literary spotlight of the late 1850's. William Gilmore Simms, James Fenimore Cooper, and Herman Melville were still much in vogue, as were such lesser romancers as John Esten Cooke, Harriet Beecher Stowe, Robert Montgomery Bird, John Pendleton Kennedy, and a host of others. In his native State of Alabama alone Clemens met almost insurmountable rivalry in Caroline Lee Hentz and Augusta Jane Evans. The former's *Linda* (1850), *The Planter's Northern Bride*

[311]

(1854), *Robert Graham* (1855), and *Ernest Linwood* (1856), and the latter's *Inez* (1855) and *Beulah* (1859) completely overshadowed his efforts in contemporary recognition, sales, and readership.

Third-string though *Bernard Lile* and *Mustang Gray* may have been in the line-up of early American fiction, they are not now wholly without merit. As examples of realism they are good: they ring true historically, and they are largely based on real people and real events. They are packed with fascinating exploits and adventures and, although often pedantic, they are doubtless as readable as the majority of their contemporaries. And they deserve attention, if for no other reason than that they were among the very first of a seemingly never-ending procession of narratives, actual or imaginary, about the hard-ridin', fast-drawin', fist-fightin' Wild West which for a hundred and twenty-five years has strutted across the national scene in hardbacks, paperbacks, and pulps, in movies, radio, and television—the one truly epic subject of American history.

For his third foray into fiction Clemens chose another historical subject, the celebrated feud between two of America's most distin-guished citizens, Aaron Burr and Alexander Hamilton—a theme which had previously been used by others, such as Joseph H. Ingraham's *Burton, or The Sieges* (1838), Eliza Dupuy's *The Conspirators* (1843), and Harriet Beecher Stowe's *The Minister's Wooing* (1859), and one which was destined to be used again and again in the years to come. Entitled *The Rivals: A Tale of the Times of Aaron Burr and Alexander Hamilton*, Clemens' novel appeared in 1860 and was dedicated to Colonel John Read, father of his "dear wife who has been to me a solace and a support in every trial and every sorrow which has come upon me."

In his preface to *The Rivals* Clemens forthrightly stated that the romance had been written in great hast "midst many and pressing engagements," and that he had not even read over the last part before mailing it to Lippincott. And as for his reason for undertaking the work, he was at once candid and concise: he believed that Aaron Burr, "unsurpassed as a soldier, unrivaled as a lawyer, pure, upright, and untarnished as a statesman," had been mercilessly maligned by the public and particularly maltreated by his biographers.

> The history of the war [Clemens continued] proves conclusively that there was no better soldier, or more devoted patriot, in the long list of revolutionary heroes, than Aaron Burr; and all contemporary testimony agrees that no man ever lived of a more genial, hospitable, and kindly nature. Yet this man ... became, from the force of circumstances, the object of the bitterest calumnies that malice could invent or the blindest prejudice could believe. Persecution dogged him to the grave; and, although the life of a generation has passed away since then, justice still hesitates to approach the spot where the bones of the patriot-soldier repose.

For Hamilton, on the obvious contrary, Clemens held nothing but contempt. The more he examined the man and his writings, the more he hated his memory.

> That I have entertained strong prejudices against him from boyhood, is true [he continued]; that those prejudices may have influenced my judgment, is possible; but I tried to discard them, and look at his character in the light of reason alone. The more I studied it, the more I became convinced that the world never presented such a combination of greatness and of meanness, of daring courage and of vile malignity, of high aspirings and of low hypocrisy. Shrewd, artful, and unscrupulous, there were no means he would not employ to accomplish his ends—no tool too base to be used when its services were needful. Loose in his own morals, even to licentiousness, he criticized those of Thomas Jefferson with a severity no other antagonist ever equaled. Slander was his favorite weapon, and no one stood in his way who did not feel the venom of his tongue and pen.

In his attempt to exonerate Burr, Clemens also insisted that he had gone back to the original sources, extracting from them "enough of the truth" to enable him to form a "just estimate" of Burr's character as well as that of Hamilton. And on these "main historical facts," plus his imagination, he had built *The Rivals* in hopes that he could "contribute [his] mite toward relieving [Burr's] memory from the unjust aspersions which embittered his life."

The Rivals, a shorter book (286 pages) than either *Bernard Lile* or *Mustang Gray*, concentrates on the animosity between Burr and Hamilton against the background of the American Revolution, particularly insofar as it concerns Adelaide Clifton of New York City who is in love with Burr but whom Hamilton attempts to seduce. The episode ends as Hamilton's vicious slander drives Adelaide mad and eventually to her death. Burr next falls in love with Margaret Moncrieffe, daughter of a British major who is being held within the American lines, and again Hamilton spreads licentious gossip. Burr, meanwhile, displays great leadership in the Battle of Monmouth, but becomes ill and leaves the army—only to learn that Margaret had been forced by her parents to marry a man she does not love. After the passage of several years Burr, now a successful lawyer in New Jersey, marries Theodosia Prevost who bears him one child, a daughter, named for her mother. Hamilton, also a successful lawyer, re-emerges as Burr's arch political rival, provoking him unmercifully even after Burr becomes vice president of the United States. At last, the book ends abruptly as Burr kills Hamilton in a duel on July 11, 1804.

Clemens' prefatory explanation that he had written *The Rivals* in great haste among many distractions was scarcely necessary to an appreciation of the novel: even the most casual reader may note that it is adventitious, stumbling, and awkwardly partitioned into three virtually independent, unique episodes, crudely held together by the

[313]

hatred of the principal characters. The first episode concerns Burr versus Hamilton over Miss Clifton, the second over Miss Moncrieffe, and the third over politics. The transition from one to two and to three is graceless—and the grand finale, the challenge and duel, is dismissed in less than two short pages, suggesting that Clemens was weary of the whole business and eager to bring the burdensome task to an end. Here, in Clemens' own words, is Burr's bombastic, almost unbelievable challenge, delivered personally to Hamilton at his home:

'General Hamilton, do you know me?'

'Colonel Burr!' replied Hamilton, in surprise.

'Yes, sir; and I have called to tell you that I did not seek satisfaction from you on account of the petty slanders contained in the pamphlet of Dr. Cooper, however fully you may have authorized their publication. But a few nights ago I sat by the death-couch of James Billings, and heard him go over the whole secret history of the past. He told how Adelaide Clifton was maddened and murdered; how the reputation of Margaret Moncrieffe had withered under the baleful influence of your poisonous breath; how you had pursued me with causeless, bitter, and remorseless hate; and he placed in my hand documents to prove the truth of his story. . . . I did not wish to furnish the gossiping world with all the revolting particulars of that tale of horrors. I sought, and found another pretext. And now, sir, you will understand how useless it is to submit propositions of adjustment, and what consequences will be likely to flow to yourself from a refusal to accede to my demand. Good night, sir. I hope to meet you once more, and but once.'

He turned and walked away. Hamilton stood as if petrified. It was long before he shook off the numbing torpor that seized upon every limb; and when he re-entered his own door, the presage of coming doom weighed heavily upon him.

At the duel on Weehawken Heights Burr's pistol fires first. Hamilton falls heavily forward and Burr, unhurt, is led away to face the slings and arrows of eternal criticism. Long years afterward (wrote Clemens), when time had bowed Burr's form and dimmed his eye, he returned to the spot where Hamilton had fallen, and proclaimed:

'He wronged me,' he said, 'and I forgave him! He wronged her, and I slew him! If twenty lives had centered in his single body, it would have been a poor atonement! When I saw him fall headlong to the ground, a weight seemed lifted from my breast, and a peaceful tranquility settled there I never could have known while the same earth sustained us both. He has gone long ago to render his account at that judgment bar before which I too must soon appear. Face to face, in presence of the God who must pronounce our several dooms, I shall say that he deserved the death he received at my hands; and never, for one moment, has a thought of repentance obtruded itself upon my soul!'

The Rivals, like Bernard Lile and Mustang Gray, received almost no attention in the current press. Godey's slurringly called it "a kind of historical novel," adding that it openly condemned Davis' and Parton's biographies of Burr "as unjust and accused their authors of fearing

[314]

to meet the waves of popular opinion or prejudice in doing him justice." Afterwards, the notice contended, *The Rivals* "proceeds in its own way, by presenting the matter in a different light, in which Hamilton is treated with less leniency, and his antagonist with less severity." *The Knickerbocker Magazine* (New York) was scarcely more complimentary, although it did find the "extra-gushing" novel "interesting":

> We once heard Hon. Jere. Clemens deliver a 'repellent' speech in the crowded Senate-chamber of the United States at Washington; and we were struck at the time with his energy, the closeness of his argument, and the force of the blows which he dealt his antagonist; at the same time, his coolness and perfect self possession excited general remark and admiration. He avows the existence of the strongest prejudice in his own mind, in the very outset.... Under the garb of fiction [he] has endeavored to 'relieve' Burr's memory from the unjust suspicions which embittered his life.... With such prejudiced views as these, frankly admitted and urged in our author's preface, his work may be safely left to the conscientious and discriminating judgment of his readers. The work is certainly interesting, in parts eminently so: but its style, especially where a mild halo is attempted to be thrown over seduction, as in the account given of Burr's *liaison* with the beautiful Miss Moncrieffe, is of that species which may be described as 'extra-gushin.'

Regardless of its merit, forty years after its first publication *The Rivals* was reissued (1900) by O. Wolfe Publishing Company of Akron, Ohio in a 315-page paper-backed book as *An American Colonel: A Story of Thrilling Times During the Revolution and the Great Rivalry of Aaron Burr and Alexander Hamilton*. As such, Clemens' novel might well have been a factor in the resurgence of interest in the Burr-Hamilton controversy which at the turn of the new century produced Charles F. Pidgen's *Blennerhasset* (1901), Gertrude Atherton's *The Conqueror* (1902), and several years later, Mary Johnston's *Lewis Rand* (1908), Alfred H. Lewis' *An American Patrician* (1908), and Emerson Hough's *The Magnificent Adventure* (1916).

Between 1853, when he was defeated in his bid for reelection to the United States Senate, and 1862, when he wantonly deserted his native Alabama and the Confederacy, Clemens' political philosophy was most complex, vacillating, and all but imponderable. In the early 1850's more Whig than Democrat, he slowly became more Democrat than Whig. By 1855 his political instability was well-known and openly discussed in the press and elsewhere—nominally a Whig-Democrat, he now leaned towards the American or Know-Nothing Party. Indeed, by 1856 he was actually attacking the Democratic presidential nominee, James Buchanan, and throwing his support towards Millard Fillmore, the American candidate. During that heated campaign he stumped the state for Fillmore, repeatedly debating William Lowndes Yancey, the fire-eating Democrat and advocate of states' rights. Upon Buchanan's election Clemens retired from active politics and devoted himself to the practice of law in North Alabama, briefly to journalism, and, as has been shown, to the production of *Bernard Lile* (1856), *Mustang Gray* (1858), and *The Rivals* (1860).

By 1860, as the South moved inexorably toward independence, Clemens, the ardent American, vigorously opposed secession. He affiliated himself with the Constitutional-Unionist Party whose presidential and vice-presidential candidates were John Bell and Edward Everett, respectively. He spoke, wrote, and organized against the Southern Democrats (who were supporting John C. Breckinridge and Joseph Lane), the Northern Democrats (whose candidates were Stephen A. Douglas and Herschel V. Johnson), and the Black Republicans (Abraham Lincoln and Hannibal Hamlin).

As the campaign grew tenser and election day neared, Clemens became consumed by a single thought—"The preservation of the Union." Although a native Alabamian and a Southerner, he had served the United States in three wars and in the Senate: he could not now bring himself to support any political doctrine which he believed would inevitably lead to disunion and civil conflict. Thus, only by supporting the Constitutional-Unionist Party, he stated, could he do his part to save the "Constitution of the country, the Union of the states, and the enforcement of the laws." As he reasoned,

> If the followers of Breckinridge may secede from the Union because Lincoln is elected, so may the followers of Lincoln secede if Breckinridge is elected, and so may either, or both of them secede if Douglas, or Bell is elected....
> Go out of the Union because a Republican is elected President? Good God! Where is this to end?... How long will it be before counties, or neighborhoods follow the example?

But, again, as in 1856, Alabamians listened not to Clemens but to Yancey, the fiery Secessionist—and the Breckinridge-Bell ticket won a decisive victory, carrying thirty-eight out of the forty-five counties in the state. Six months later, however, in the national presidential election, the Republicans overwhelmed the Democrats. And as Abraham Lincoln began his move into the White House, Alabama and the other Southern states were busily charting their course for the creation of the Confederate States of America.

Clemens now faced the greatest dilemma of his political career. A strong Unionist, he nevertheless believed that Lincoln's election would lead to war between the North and the South—and he was first and foremost an Alabamian and Southerner. During the late summer and fall he wrote many letters to newspapers and made many speeches opposing disunion, ridiculing secession, and begging for a peaceful settlement of sectional differences. Realizing the importance of time, he publicly supported all attempts to confer and conciliate, but privately he doubted that anything could stop the headlong rush to secession. In November, 1860 he believed that the large majority of Alabamians were strongly in favor of withdrawing from the Union, adding, "I do not admit the *right* to secession at all. I do not admit the *right* of a majority to drag me into treason."

On December 6 Alabama's Governor Andrew B. Moore called a state-wide election to be held on the twenty-fourth for the purpose of choosing one hundred delegates to a Convention of the People of Alabama on January 7, 1861. Immediately, the opposing political forces—the Secessionists and the Co-operationists—rallied their forces. In Madison County Jeremiah Clemens and Nicholas Davis were nominated to represent the Co-operationists, and George P. Beirne and M. P. Roberts the Secessionists. At the polls on December 24 Clemens and Davis won hands down: Clemens, 1,487 votes; Davis, 1,480; Beirne, 404; and Roberts, 371. This decisive victory for the Co-operationists apparently surprised no one: North Alabama had long been recognized as a stronghold of Union or conciliation sentiment. Indeed, Clemens had openly predicted his own victory by a wide margin, although it was equally well-known that he and other Co-operationists would face vigorous opposition at the state convention only two weeks away.

As the convention began, a Committee of Thirteen was appointed, including Clemens and his old rival, Yancey, and charged with the responsibility of drafting an ordinance for consideration by the entire assembly. Four days later Yancey, the chairman, presented the committee's Majority Report, "An Ordinance to dissolve the Union between the State of Alabama and the other States under the compact styled 'The Constitution of the United States of America.'" On behalf of himself and the five other Co-operationists on the Committee of Thirteen, who had voted against the ordinance, Clemens presented a Minority Report which was promptly rejected by the Convention, 54 to 45. Then, in a vigorous speech Yancey urged the immediate and unanimous adoption of the Ordinance of Secession—"we have gone too far to recede with dignity and self-respect," he declared. And Jeremiah Clemens, putting his state and his people ahead of himself, surprisingly replied that, although he opposed the ordinance, he would vote for it. "Whatever may be my opinion of the wisdom and justice of the course pursued by the majority," he declared, "I do not choose that any man shall put himself in danger of a halter in defense of the honor and rights of my native State, without sharing that danger with him."

I give my vote, therefore [he continued], partly as an assurance that I intend in good faith to redeem the pledge which I have made again and again, in public or in private, in speeches, and through the press, that whenever the summons came to me to defend the soil of Alabama,

[317]

whether it be at midnight or at mid-day—whether I believe her right or wrong, it should be freely, promptly answered.... For the present, it is enough to say that I am a son of Alabama; her destiny is mine; her people are mine; her enemies are mine. I see plainly enough, that clouds and storms are gathering above us; but when the thunder rolls and lightning flashes, I trust that I shall neither shrink or cower—neither murmur nor complain. Acting upon the convictions of a life-time, calmly and deliberately I walk with you into revolution. Be its perils—be its privations—be its sufferings what they may, I share them with you, although as a member of this Convention I oppose your Ordinance. Side by side with yours ... my name shall stand upon the original roll, and side by side with you I brave the consequences. I vote the affirmative.

When the final vote was taken, the ordinance passed, 61 to 39. True to his word, Clemens, along with six other Cooperationists, voted in the affirmative—but his friend and fellow delegate from Madison County, Nicholas Davis, was not among them.

A week later, on January 18, the convention moved toward the naming of a man to assume charge of the military affairs of the new Republic of Alabama. Colonels J. M. Withers and Emmet Seibels of Mobile and Jeremiah Clemens of Huntsville were prominently mentioned for the high position. Although the Montgomery *Mail* eagerly supported Clemens, on January 16 calling him a "dashing, gallant fellow ... under [whom] 'the boys' would be likely to see the actual," Clemens reputedly expressed disinterest in the post and added that as a soldier his proper place would be "in the field." Nevertheless, shortly afterwards he accepted the appointment from Governor Moore as major-general of the Army of Alabama, the highest ranking military position in the short-lived republic (it was whispered that the Secessionists had guaranteed him the post for "throwing his followers to vote in favor of secession"), and promptly left for a tour of inspection of the forts encircling Mobile.

As the weeks passed Major-General Clemens ran headlong into opposition, not only from Confederate military officials, such as Adjutant-General Samuel Cooper and Colonel W. J. Hardee, but also from the newly-appointed Secretary of War Leroy Pope Walker. After the organization of the Confederate States Army, Clemens' state post rapidly diminished in importance and prestige. His political enemies—and none ever forgot for a moment that he was at heart a Union-inclined Co-operationist—blocked his chances for appointment to another office in either Alabama or the Confederacy, civil or military. Even President Jefferson Davis, suspicious, failed to aid him. And Clemens' declining health slowly rendered him unfit for active service in the military. Thus, distrusted, disillusioned, and disgusted, the sick, sensitive former senator and soldier, no doubt seeing himself as some kind of martyr, returned to Huntsville and to the open, waiting arms of the North Alabama Unionists who at once encour-

[318]

aged him outright and publicly to repudiate the Confederacy. Opportunely forgetting the noble pledge of loyalty he had so recently made on the floor of the secession convention, Clemens soon became a leader of the Tories, eager to use his prior political and military affiliations with the United States Government in whatever way possible to support it and to bring an end to the conflict between the North and the South.

In April, 1862 Huntsville (along with much of North Alabama) surrendered to Federal forces under Major-General O. M. Mitchell, and the area more than ever became a center of refuge for traitors, deserters, renegades, mossbacks, and marauding outlaws who terrorized the countryside, destroying property, raping, murdering and committing other atrocious crimes. Clemens and other Unionists made overtures to Mitchell, offering their services. Clemens personally asked permission to present the Unionist cause to high officials in Washington. Permission was refused—even President Lincoln had little or no faith in any political prestige or power that the vacillating former Senator Jeremiah Clemens might have had. And, when Clemens insisted, Secretary of War Edwin M. Stanton personally advised him to stay in Alabama because he thought he could do more for the United States in the South than he could in the North. Again denied, Clemens spent the next three years behind the Union lines, mostly in Nashville, Tennessee, from which place he and other Tories conducted newspaper and pamphlet campaigns advising their "fellow-citizens" of Alabama to surrender to the United States. Occasionally, Clemens returned to Huntsville where he entertained Yankee officers and civil officials in his home. Now and again, as the months passed, he traveled frequently to Philadelphia to work with the Union League and to write "Letters" castigating the South and urging Southerners to defect to the North.

> If the love of law, order, and tranquility still holds a place in your bosoms—[he wrote in October, 1864] if you are wearied with carnage and worn out by executions—if the sanctity of your homes is yet dear to you, and if the freedom and welfare of your children and your children's children, for generations to come, claim a serious thought, you ought to abandon at once the attitude of armed resistance to a Government which never wronged you, and a people whose hearts now bleed in sympathy with yours over the miseries which the mad ambition of your leaders has produced. Return, as you may now do without dishonor, to the protection of that banner which has been for nearly a century the symbol of freedom and the harbinger of happiness. You have exhibited on the battlefield a heroism which, in a better cause, would have won for you immortal honor. Prove to the world that you are capable of the still higher heroism of *daring to do right* in defiance of the scoffs or sneers, or threatened coercion of the guilty criminals who led you astray.

By 1864, having long before deserted the Democratic Party, Clemens publicly advocated the re-election of Republican Abraham Lincoln —"Thank God," he declared, "there is now no prospect of the Confederacy succeeding."

Meantime, as Clemens divided his time among Huntsville, Nashville, and Philadelphia, he returned his attention to writing. Four years had passed since the publication of *The Rivals* and he had not been able to produce its promised sequel, a volume which would have carried the Aaron Burr story to its logical conclusion, Burr's death. Too many had been the distractions since 1860 and, besides, Clemens declared, his interest in the subject had been supplanted by attention to "events of a more exciting character," the "Titantic contest" at the very heart of which he had found himself located for more than three years.

The subject which now consumed the sick, sad, bitter man was, of course, the Confederate War, and particularly that part of it in North Alabama seen through the eyes of a Southern Unionist. Entitled *Tobias Wilson: A Tale of the Great Rebellion*, the 328-page novel was completed in his West Philadelphia home in January, 1865 and dedicated to his wife whose love was "as pure and trustful as ever glowed in the bosom of a daughter of Earth."

> In what I have written [Clemens stated in his preface], and in what I shall write hereafter, for this book is only the first of a series, my object is to give a true and faithful picture of life during the first years of the rebellion, at least in parts of the Southern States. *Omnia vidi magna pars fui*, if not literally true as to every incident, is true as to the greater part.
>
> It is impossible for any one who has not witnessed them to appreciate the wrongs, indignities, and outrages to which the Southern Union men have been subjected. Their property taken or destroyed, their persons constantly threatened with incarceration, if not assassination, and their sons dragged to the slaughter-pen; these were common occurrences, whose frequent recurrence deprived them of half their horror. The sending of our wives into exile, without the means of subsistence, and dependent for bread upon the charity of the people of the North, or of such chance refugees who had escaped under happier auspices,—this, too, in time ceased to be a subject of complaint. But there were a thousand acts of brutality which cannot be described without giving offense to the ears of decency. From a faithful picture of such things the eyes of a modest woman would turn away with unutterable loathing. From the present series all of these are omitted, and only such matter is introduced as may be read without a blush, unless it be a blush of indignation rather than of shame.

Repeating himself, Clemens emphasized the fact that all the characters in *Tobias Wilson* were "real." Nothing was depicted, he stoutly maintained, that had not actually occurred. "In this volume, everything has been sacrificed to the painting of a correct portrait. If my readers look for other adjuncts to keep alive their interest in the tale, they will be apt to reap disappointment."

[320]

Tobias Wilson, also a product of the Lippincott firm, was the last and is unquestionably the best of Clemens' four novels. Experience had been a good teacher, indeed. The book has a respectable plot which moves quickly, enthusiastically, and smoothly along, and the characters in most instances are truly well-drawn. The subject doubtless lent the author great sincerity, for no writer of his time could have suffered more deeply than did Jeremiah Clemens, sometime distinguished statesman and soldier who now, suddenly, found himself the target of political acrimony, hated and jeered at as the epitome of treachery and cowardice, and openly described as a traitor to his State of Alabama and to the Confederate States of America. Into *Tobias Wilson*, one may truly say, Clemens poured his very lifeblood.

Tobias Wilson is obviously one of the first, if not the very first, in a long parade of Confederate War novels which reaches from 1865 to 1965 and will no doubt continue for many decades yet to come. The book is particularly unique in that it was written *before* the fighting ended, not long afterward, as were the more popular narratives. *Tobias Wilson* appeared two years before John W. DeForest's better-known *Miss Ravenel's Conversion from Secession to Loyalty* (which is also told from the Union viewpoint), and one year before John Esten Cooke's *Surrey of Eagles Nest*, the first of the genre to be generally accepted by the reading public, both North and South. But it was not until the hurts of the conflict had somewhat healed that stories about it began to become a clearly identifiable segment of American historical fiction, not until the turn of the new century, in fact, with the appearance of such masterpieces as Winston Churchill's *The Crisis* (1901), Ellen Glasgow's *The Battle-Ground* (1902), Upton Sinclair's *Manassas* (1904), George W. Cable's *Kincaid's Battery* (1908) and Mary Johnston's *The Long Roll* (1911) and *Cease Firing* (1912). And however much *Tobias Wilson* may pale by comparison with these and other Confederate War narratives, its author cannot be denied his position as a forerunner in the field, one who was far ahead in recognizing the tremendous literary potential of a realistic portrayal of the fractricidal conflict between North and South.

Tobias Wilson is the story of a family of Union sympathizers—called Tories or Loyalists, depending on one's viewpoint—of North Alabama who refused to cast their lot with the Confederacy and of the countless harassments to which the members are subjected by their former friends and neighbors during 1861–1865. Into this, the main stream of the narrative, flow such troublesome tributaries as murder, arson, thievery, ambush, intrigue, treachery, and revenge. Everywhere, throughout the novel, the author contrasts the innocence, goodness, and purity of the Tories with countless acts of lawlessness and the evils of Confederate soldiers and civilians. So much so, in fact, that in the end Tobias Wilson and his bosom friend and brother-in-law,

[321]

Tom Rogers, the chief characters and "pacifists" at heart, are driven to join the Union forces on the northern bank of the Tennessee River—allegedly to protect North Alabama from the ravages of Confederate marauders.

Three lesser climaxes of *Tobias Wilson* come as Tom Rogers one by one seeks out and kills Jim Biles, Josh Wilkins, and Parson Williams, in revenge for their murder of Robert Johnson, Tobias' grandfather. The description of Rogers' shooting of Williams demonstrates by its tone and structure the nature of the author's accomplishments:

'How are you this morning, Parson Williams?'

The individual thus addressed started as if an adder had stung him. A deadly pallor spread over his face, and the basket dropped from his nerveless hand. Recovering himself by a great effort, and observing who it was that stood before him, he answered surlily:

'Is that you, Thomas Rogers? and what are you doing here? . . . I heard that you were in league with your country's enemies, and this wandering about all night, nobody knows where, or on what errand, looks mighty like it.'

'Ah, parson!' replied Rogers, with a bitter sneer, 'I was afraid you had heard something of the sort about me, or rather about my father, and I have come to relieve your mind upon the subject. But first tell me who killed Robert Johnson in cold blood, when he was peacefully at work in his own field, without dreaming of harm to a human being?'

Parson Williams was poorly prepared to meet this searching query. Resolute as he was, he trembled in every limb. He tried to answer firmly, but his voice would not be controlled, and his pitiless enemy marked its tremulous tones with a degree of satisfaction little less than that with which the savage hails the shriek of his victim at the stake.

'What do I know of Robert Johnson, and what is he to you that you should come here at this hour to ask me about him? What fool's notion have you got in your head now?'

'A spirit whispered to me in my sleep,' responded Rogers, 'that Captain Wilkins, James Biles, and Parson Williams killed an old man, who was very dear to me, because he would not turn traitor to his country, and the same spirit warned me that the blood-hounds were on my father's track. Josh Wilkins died—and owned nothing. Jim Biles died—and confessed all before he went. It is your turn now!' Then changing his tone to one expressive of scorn and hate combined, he continued:

'Fool! Did you suppose such a deed of blood could be allowed to go unavenged? From the hour that Tobias Wilson and I met you at the foot of the mountain, I have been upon your track. Your last hour has come.'

Parson Williams, as before stated, was no coward. The immediate presence of physical danger acted as a restorative, and he sprang for his gun with an agility no one would have expected him to exhibit. But at no period of his life could he have been accounted a match, under equal circumstances, for the quick eye and steady hand that were now opposed to him. He was still several steps distant from his weapon when a puff of light-blue smoke was belched forth from the muzzle of Rogers' rifle, a sharp report followed, the frightened swine scattered through the woods, and the Baptist minister fell forward on his face a lifeless corpse.

[322]

Tobias Wilson ends all too abruptly, suggesting that the adventures of Tom and Tobe had by no means ceased. In fact, Clemens had in his introduction prepared his readers for more by stating that "this book is only the first of a series." The writing of another book or two in the same vein might have proved more successful—at least, it would have given the author further opportunity to perfect his style of presentation, to describe (as he did so well) North Alabama towns and countryside, as well as military events, and, perhaps, to improve upon such fictional innovations as Negro dialect. He might also have learned, although it is doubtful, to have presented his narratives with less prejudice and hate and bitterness toward those who had once been his loyal friends and supporters.

Suffice it to say that no American novel has ever been published at such an inopportune moment in history as was *Tobias Wilson* in the spring of 1865. It appeared for sale on almost precisely the same day that General Lee surrendered to General Grant at Appomattox. Two days later, at high noon, the United States flag was run up over Fort Sumter. And that very night, at ten o'clock, President Lincoln was assassinated in Washington. Small wonder that *Tobias Wilson* met with little or no notice in the daily press or in the current literary journals.

Meanwhile, as the war neared its end, Clemens, believing that he would be "very popular with the loyal people of the State," made efforts to persuade the United States authorities to appoint him "military governor of Alabama." Failing to do so—and now publicly described as the "arch traitor" to the Confederacy—he began his tedious journey from Philadelphia back to Huntsville. There is no extant account of his reception in his old home town—but one may imagine. Clemens, only fifty-one years old, but nearly blind, dying of tuberculosis, and broken in spirit, was carried to his bed. In less than a month, on the morning of May 21, 1865, at half after seven, he passed away, his wife and only child holding his swollen hands, as the slight quiver of a smile faded from his emaciated face.

Notice of his death was flashed to Philadelphia. The *Daily News* dismissed the fact in two lines; the *Morning Pennsylvanian* did not mention it. The *Age* recorded his career briefly, adding that he was "well-remembered" (for his opposition to the secession movement) but that he "had taken no part in public affairs for the past two years." The *Inquirer*, more generous, published a lengthy obituary which ended with these words:

> Mr. Clemens was a member of the Convention in Alabama which voted the State out of the Union, but protested against its action. He subsequently gave way to the popular tide setting so strongly against him, and for a time accepted office under the bogus Confederacy. In 1864, however, he had returned to his former allegiance, and in a letter

[323]

addressed to his fellow citizens, warmly advocated the re-election of Mr. Lincoln and defended his policy. He lived long enough to see the triumph of the principles he seemed to have really at heart, although he permitted himself for a long time to act contrary to their dictates. Mr. Clemens had also appealed to the public as a writer, and in 1853 published *Bernard Lile,* which was followed in 1857 by *Mustang Gray.*

In the fall of 1864, during a brief residence in Philadelphia, Mr. Clemens wrote a series of articles for the Philadelphia *Inquirer,* under the title *Facts and Reflections for the Consideration of the People.* In these he evidenced his loyalty to the Union, and exposed in a scathing manner the utter fallacy of the doctrine of Secession, and the wicked conduct of the leaders of the Rebellion and their abettors of the North.

In Alabama, newspapers either completely ignored Clemens' death or noticed it but tersely, as did the Montgomery *Daily Mail,* May 31, when it reported that "the Ex- U. S. Senator from Alabama" had died of lung congestion at his residence in Huntsville.

Jeremiah Clemens was unquestionably a man of genuine ability, versatile, and highly intelligent. In his own bizarre way he was a genius: at twenty a lawyer, at twenty-three a district judge, at twenty-five a state representative, at thirty-three a colonel in the United States Army, at thirty-four a United States senator, at forty a successful novelist, and at forty-seven a major-general in the Army of the Republic of Alabama. But he was also erratic, undependable, vacillating and there is some reason to believe that his brilliant but ill-starred career was too often tarnished by his intemperance. Yet, there is proof in plenty that few men of his day could match wit or wisdom with him. Perhaps, after all, it was Clemens' gigantic and all-consuming ambition, like that of Julius Caesar, which eventually engulfed him.

> Clemens was the dash of the mountain stream, rather than the buoying and staying power of the deep lake [wrote B. F. Riley]. A rapid thinker and a man of brilliant action, he was more the subject of impulse than of calm and judicial poise. This neutralizing element alone prevented [him] from being a great leader. That he had qualities of leadership no one denied, but he lacked the poise that made his position a stable one.

As a novelist Clemens is for the sophisticated modern reader more monotonous than moving, more prolix than precise, but in the opinion of his contemporaries he was an epitome of romantic adventure, half fact, half fiction, but always highly emotional and exciting. His diction was rosy and rolling, his thought radiant. His hair-raising exploits, recounted against a back drop of pure history and personal experience, satisfied his readers during an era when men's actual deeds—not their threats, white papers, protocols, hot lines, and verbal encounters in air-conditioned security councils—were the determinants of the course of empire. His particular place in history of American fiction is small, indeed, but it was well-earned and it is secure. He deserves to be remembered.

NON-SMOKERS HAVE SOME
RIGHTS ... TOO!

Birmingham [Alabama] *News Monthly Magazine*, July 10, 1955.

Recently, I attended a business conference along with some eight or 10 men and two women. The chairman, meaning to put everyone at his ease, opened the discussion by saying, "Now, we want everybody to feel at home. Be free to smoke, if you wish."

And smoke everybody did—everybody, that is, except one of the women and me. We happen to be non-smokers, members of the Disregarded Third of the American adult population, those who for one reason or another are not wedded to the weed.

For several hours the conference dragged on. Ash trays overflowed with cigar and cigaret butts. The smoke-laden air, stale and stinking, permeated every nook and cranny of the room. Everyone's clothes reeked with tobacco odor. Even the draperies and furniture smelled to high heaven. And at long, smelly last, when the meeting ended, my non-smoking friend and I were all but sick at our stomachs, our smarting eyes were bloodshot, and we left the group thoroughly indignant because our rights as free, tax-paying, non-smoking American citizens of the State of Alabama had been so flagrantly violated!

Surely, in no other phase of our national life is so little consideration given to the well-being of others as in the use of tobacco.

After all, non-smokers have rights, too!

Smoking has become so routine for so many people nowadays that little or nothing is done to protect the privileges of abstainers. Hostesses at home and officials in public places, including trains, buses, and planes, are so eager to please the majority that they have lost all consideration of the rights of the minority. It is assumed that everybody wants to smoke, that smokers have the inalienable right to befoul the air whenever and wherever they please.

Well, I disagree. And I demand fair treatment for the host of non-smokers. Don't forget, we still number one-third of the adult population, or about 35 million adults. Our side, though outnumbered, is jolly well fed up with being stenched and skunked. We demand that something be done about it!

Now, mind you, our quarrel is not with smoking as such. The smoker has every right to smoke, if he wishes. But has he the right, moral or legal, to impose his unwanted habit upon us, making his enjoyment of tobacco spoil our enjoyment of living? Sure, we're willing to be reasonable. We would pass no laws to ban smoking. All we ask is that the smoker observe certain basic decencies respecting his fellowman. You'd expect no less from a housebroken dog—would you? And by any code of ethics our request is as right as rain!

Unless you are the one-in-three who does not indulge in the filthy

[325]

weed, you may be unaware of the callous disregard which smokers constantly exhibit for everyone else.

When a non-smoker boards a train, for example, he puts himself at the mercy of a battalion of smokers who have long ago signed a non-aggression pact with the conductor and the portor. Prominently-displayed "No Smoking" placards are altogether ignored, and the fixed, see-nothing, say-nothing stare on the trainman's face indicates his lack of concern with the whole smokey situation.

Coaches on most trains fairly reek with eye-stinging smoke and on Pullmans I personally have often lain awake nights, unable to sleep because of cigar or cigaret fumes emerging from a nearby berth. Once I even mustered up courage enough to complain to the porter about the matter. His reply was something of a classic. He suggested that I might like to step back into the men's lounge until the atmosphere cleared. No one was smoking back there, he added.

On buses the story is much the same. "No Smoking" signs mean little or nothing. I have long ago learned that I must get a front seat —where the air is usually less acrid—or suffer dire consequences. If I am compelled to sit in the rear, I know I'll breathe old, stale, used, tobacco-y air until my journey's end, and wind up with a headache for hours afterwards. And I have seen more than one bus driver himself smoking while in transit, completely unmindful of that large placard above his head.

Consider, now, the matter of smoking in one's own castle, so-called. Time was when a visitor had the courtesy to ask his host's permission to smoke in his home or office. It may have been perfunctory politeness, to be true, but at least it was decent. And the host appreciated the gesture. Those days have gone forever. Now, nobody asks. They just light up and like as not flick ashes on the floor.

In my own living room I've experienced nausea, giddiness, smarting, watery eyes, a drippy nose and hour-long headaches purely because I had not the discourtesy to ask my visitors not to smoke. Why shouldn't they have thought to ask me? After all, it's my house. How can smokers be so inconsiderate—or so stupid—as to think that, because they like tobacco fumes, everybody does?

Once I sat in my home, discussing an important matter with a caller—a woman, incidentally. She lit one cigaret after another, chain fashion. As the smoke staled and thickened, my eyes grew runny red. I sniffed, sneezed, snorted. All the while I noticed my guest was slowly backing her chair away from me, putting greater distance between us.

"I hope you'll forgive me," she finally remarked, lighting another cigaret, "but I don't want to catch your cold."

Perhaps I should feel about smoking as my roommate and I did about chewing tobacco, back when we were noble, clowning college boys. On our door we posted this sign:

WELCOME!
If You Spit on Floor at Home,
Please Do So Here.
WE WANT YOU TO FEEL
AT HOME!

Well, I'm not that noble now. If an onion-eater blows his breath in my face, I label him a low-life ingrate, a boar, and an ill-bred commoner. Why in heaven's name should I greet with open arms the tobacco-smoker who putrefies the very air I breathe and sends me reeling with nausea? Unfortunately, a smoker cannot smell a fellow-smoker's breath—but the helpless non-smoker, whose taste and smell buds have not been atrophied by nicotine, can detect the repulsive odor of a smoker's breath at 10 feet!

Actually, a non-smoker's sense of smell is so keen that he can detect smoke, especially cigar smoke, in a room a week after it was left there. I know, alas, because I have done it.

Smokers don't wish to be the inconsiderate, thoughtless lot they are, I'm sure. Theirs is an error of judgment—nothing else. They assume that, because they enjoy tobacco fumes, everybody does. It's a hugely false assumption and it wreaks a vast discomfort on millions of innocent non-smokers who are powerless to challenge it, except in the arena of fair play.

That's where my 35 million fellow-sufferers and I make our appeal.

Americans are noted for good sportsmanship, for their recognition of the other fellow's opinions. It's the American way, we say—give a guy a break!

Well, the harassed non-smokers of America beg a break.

THE PRESIDENT'S NATIONAL ADVISORY COMMISSION ON LIBRARIES: A SUMMARY REPORT

Association of Research Libraries, *Minutes of the 72nd Meeting* [Kansas City, Missouri], Washington, D.C., 1968.

My appearance on this program is based primarily on the fact that I served as consultant to the Subcommittee on Public Hearings of the President's National Advisory Commission on Libraries from August, 1967, to February, 1968.

As you know, this Commission was composed of twenty distinguished citizens, including Douglas M. Knight, President of Duke University, as Chairman, and Verner W. Clapp, Herman H. Fussler, and Emerson Greenaway from the library world. Melville J. Ruggles, now Program Officer of the Council on Library Resources, was the first executive director of the Commission.

President Johnson directed the Commission, "... to appraise the role and adequacy of our libraries, now and in the future, as sources for scholarly research, as centers for the distribution of knowledge, and as links in our nation's rapidly evolving communications networks." The President also asked the Commission, "... to evaluate policies programs, and practices of public agencies and private organizations... and to recommend actions which might be taken by public and private groups to ensure an effective, efficient library system for the nation."

While the Washington office contracted for studies on numerous phases of librarianship in America (such as school libraries in the United States, extra-library information services, library statistics, public library trends, the economics of librarianship, etc.), the Subcommittee on Public Hearings, chaired by Mrs. Merlin M. Moore of Arkansas and former Congressman, Carl Elliott, co-author of the National Defense Education Act and a longtime friend of American librarians, conducted a series of hearings which began in St. Louis, Missouri, on April 12 and ended in Tucson, Arizona on October 27. Between these dates hearings were held in Tampa , Florida; Great Falls, Montana; Portland, Oregon; Anchorage and Nome, Alaska; Bismarck, North Dakota; Lubbock, Texas; Wilkes Barre, Pennsylvania; Baton Rouge, Louisiana; and Pikeville, Kentucky.

All together in these eleven public hearings, 319 respondents, representing every walk of life, accounted for 3,638 transcript pages of testimony, or nearly one million words. Of these 319 witnesses, forty-six (14 per cent) represented twenty-eight institutions of higher learning, including universities, senior colleges, and junior or community colleges.

Needless to say, no facet of the library profession went unnoticed. A content analysis of the hearings reveals that twenty-nine different topics were frequently and widely discussed: five under "Objectives for Overcoming Current Inadequacies"; five under "Recommendations for Achieving Objectives"; seven under the broad heading of "Problems"; and twelve under "Means of Attacking Problems."

As far as university libraries are particularly concerned, the remarks of the forty-six respondents generally followed a wearisome and often repetitious pattern, centered about these major points:

   1) A good library is the heart of a good university;
   2) The rapid growth of graduate study and faculty research places an increasingly heavy burden on the university library;
   3) The university library must modernize or perish, and modernization includes state, regional, and national cooperation;

4) Computerization, including information retrieval, will largely determine the welfare of the library of the future;

5) Cooperative acquisitions programs, regional resource storage centers, and centralized cataloging are absolute necessities of the future; and,

6) The shortage of librarians is crucial, suggesting the need for more and more federal support for a) scholarships, b) material resources, c) physical plants, and d) more library schools with improved, updated curriculums and teachers who are eager and willing to innovate rather than imitate.

The Commission is now putting the finishing touches on its final *Report* which will be submitted to the President within a month. In addition, the Commission is also preparing a supplementary volume based on the materials gathered during the last two years. The latter, which will be published in the fall, will contain a chapter on libraries and the university by Dr. Knight, who is also general editor of the volume.

I have not seen the manuscript of the *Report*, but my familiarity with the public hearings, plus my knowledge of the personal opinions of some of the Commission members, lead me to believe that in it the university library, as such, will receive light treatment. Rather, focus will be centered on research libraries in general, including university libraries. Specifically, the central idea in the *Report* is that all research libraries, large and small, somehow fall short of fulfilling their complete mission and thus need help of all kinds—more space, more personnel, more equipment (to effect automation), more materials, and more money from both public and private sources. If they do not get this help, the library as a sanctioned social institution in our society will eventually be doomed.

In summary, throughout the nation the Subcommittee on Public Hearings found the following major viewpoints more frequently expressed:

1) The need for greater strengthening of America's public libraries in order to make them centers of learning in fact, instead of in name;

2) The need for a permanent national commission on libraries to look after the welfare and progress of all types of libraries;

3) The conversion of the Library of Congress into a truly national library of the United States;

4) The full acceptance of the power and prestige of the U. S. Office of Education in the development of national library services;

5) The undergirding of state library agencies in order that they may properly function as the focal point for coordination of all public library activity both upward to the federal level and downward to the urban and rural levels in each state in the Union; and,

6) The need for more and better educated professional librarians, broadly discussed under the general and over-riding topic of "Manpower Shortage."

One final conclusion should be mentioned. The role of all libraries in the nation (school, college, university, public, and special) must inevitably change with the changing times—or perish. And this change, among other things, suggests considerable soul-searching on the part of librarians, a soul-searching that will eventually lead to perceptive reappraisals of our profession and in all probability significant re-directions of our day-by-day efforts.

RURAL LITERATURE IN AMERICA SURVEYED IN DEFINITIVE STUDY

A review of Ima Honaker Herron, *The Small Town in American Literature,*
Duke University Press (Durham, 1939),
From The Dallas *Morning News*, May 21, 1939.

When Dr. Ima Honaker Herron entered the field, no previous study had been made of the small town and its influence on American litera-ture. Now that she has passed over the ground no subsequent study need be begun. That is how completely Dr. Herron has harvested her subject. At once accurate and interesting, readable and definite, *The Small Town in American Literature* is a tribute to the ability of its maker as well as a brilliant contribution to the best that American scholarship has placed at the foot of our monument to national literary independence.

There have of course been earlier studies which touched upon the small-town influence in our literature—off-hand we think of Hazard's *The Frontier in American Literature*, Parrington's *Main Currents in American Thought*, Turner's *The Rise of the New West*— but none of these was a concentrated effort to show conclusively that village life in America, particularly during the last century, was a decisive force in the moulding of our literary consciousness. Many of our better-known fiction characters are products of the towns: Huck Finn and Tom Sawyer, David Harum and Lulu Bett, Penrod and Sam, Silas Lapham, Carol Kennicott, and George Willard, to mention but a few. Many American authors were born and reared in small towns: Mark Twain from Hannibal, Hawthorne and Prescott from Salem, Thoreau from Concord, Whittier from Haverhill, Masters from Garnett (Kansas), Sandburg from Galesville, Millay from Rockland, Gale from Portage, Anderson from Camden, Ohio, Suckow from Hawarden, and Faulkner from Oxford. The combined force, therefore, of American small-towners writing about American small-towners for an audience com-posed mostly of small-town people (the majority of our population lives in rural or semi-rural communities), makes a study of this nature an extremely important literary document as well as a valuable insight into current economic and sociological problems. Furthermore, since

[330]

Dr. Julia Patton so exhaustively analyzed the English village and its relation to English letters twenty years ago, the time was ripe for a study of American towns.

Dr. Herron has approached her subject from several angles, each in itself vital to any careful interpretation of the village spirit in American literature. First, she assumes, in the words of Woodrow Wilson, that "the history of a nation is only the history of its villages written large." Second, she contends that village literary records furnish historians with a "rich store of materials." From Chaucer's time to now literature has developed constantly and consistently with small-town life. The English village theme which so characterized both English and American literary production in the Eighteenth and early Nineteenth Centuries was the basis for much of our best early writing.

Third, it was "but in accordance with human custom" that local historians should have emphasized the "minutiae of community activity"; and it was also but natural that the earlier American prototype of the English village should have succumbed to the typically American product, the small town. Fourth, "the very richness and widespread use of such literary materials so significantly delineative of an important phase of American life justify . . . a history of the various trends in the portrayal of the small town in our literature." Fifth, Dr. Herron sees the literary evolution of the American small town through these three phases: (1) "that of slavish imitation of the English village tradition," (2) "that of the changing village pattern produced by the widely extended westward movements," and (3) "that marked by the growth of standardization, or the development of the urban spirit."

Dr. Herron meticulously differentiates between the village and the small town, asserting that the first name "both in actual and literary usage, is something of an outmoded term," and that "small town" is a more modern appellative. After reading her analysis, we feel that Dr. Herron is herself never completely satisfied with her distinction. Population alone (as Dr. Herron testifies) cannot be accepted as criterion, for Lewis' *Main Street* is a town of approximately 5,000; Zenith is a "city" of 100,000, and Mrs. Stowe's Holyoke contains "only a few hundred souls"—yet all are towns in the common denominator of their citizenship. Communities in the Middle West and Southwest may possess all of the earmarks of towns or villages, while Eastern places of the same size, because of their proximity to the metropolises, are "so urban-minded that they are merely extensions of the city." In general the author is forced to rely upon United States census reports and accepted opinion that a small town is a community with a population ranging from 2,500 to 5,000.

Historically, Southern towns were outgrowths of colonization experiments. A spirit of individualism, marked by a lack of organization and cohesion, characterized such places as Jamestown and Port Royal;

only a few communities (Charleston, Annapolis, Williamsburg) became really important in the South during the colonial period. The New England settlements, on the contrary, concentrated around compact little communities where local registries were established and town meetings were frequently held. As early as 1630 plans were set up for village communities in Massachusetts and Connecticut; Boston, Salem, Charlestown, Portsmouth, New Haven and other places were thus systematically organized. Colonization in the Middle Colonies and beyond the seaboard was marked by expansion along navigable rivers, and by diversified interests and the lack of religious restrictions and an isolation typical of, for example, the Southern plantation.

Today the small town—that is, the literary small town—after having passed through the many stages of evolutionary development, remains very much an enigma. What of its future, the author asks? Will smoke-belching factories dirty the prettiest streams and alien-tongued workers alter the customs of old-time villagers? Will radio, rapid transportation, the enormous circulations of magazines, movies and telephones bring about a leveling of small towns—and is that leveling wanted? As Dr. Herron has stated, that is a problem for the future. But the fact will remain that the definite impress which small town civilization has left upon our native literature is a noteworthy one, deserving of consideration by everyone interested in the American way of life.

The central portion of *The Small Town in American Literature* is devoted to a chronological interpretation of the effects of small town life on American writers. The early New England village is studied largely in the light of the past, with Hawthorne as its mentor; later through the eyes of Sarah Orne Jewett, the Beechers, and Mary Wilkins Freeman. For her westward trends Dr. Herron has relied upon James Fenimore Cooper; for the middle border upon such realists as Hamlin Garland and Edward Eggleston; for the Mississippi town upon Mark Twain; the Western town upon Emerson Hough, Bret Harte, and Owen Wister; the Southern town upon Augustus Baldwin Longstreet, J. G. Baldwin, William Gilmore Simms, John Esten Cooke, and Ellen Glasgow; and the modern town upon a galaxy of writers ranging from Zona Gale and Edgar Lee Masters to Sherwood Anderson, Thomas Wolfe, Sinclair Lewis, and Floyd Dell.

In the last section Dr. Herron glances backward "at the patterns determining the literary history of the American small town." The town in literature has been, at least since the early Eighteenth Century, at the mercy of the ever-moving frontier. Books about New England towns were not common until the mid-Nineteenth Century—years after the village as such had ceased to exist. Meanwhile, such delineators of frontier village life have always been "captivated" by "social themes and backgrounds." To Hamlin Garland the frontier

[332]

town was realistic; to Masters it was fit subject for satire; to Tarkington it was romantic or sentimental; to Zona Gale it was both Victorian and subject to caricature. In the South, where development was greatly retarded by "a plantation system and the dominance of landed aristocracy," a small town literature until quite recently has been negligible.

It would be useless to attempt more than a brief summary of the many and varying analyses which Dr. Herron has brought together in this work. So completely does she cover the subject that one feels, after having read her book, that there is scarcely anything left for future scholars in the field to say. Her every statement is fully documented, and she goes so far at times as to disarm any would-be objectors to her theories by laying bare the basic principles of their counter arguments. One is amazed by the tremendous amount of research Dr. Herron has done in gathering the basic materials for her study. No more exhaustive book has come to our attention; it is by no means difficult to understand why the author spent upwards of twelve years in the preparation of her manuscript. If we have any fault to find with *The Small Town in American Literature*, it is that Dr. Herron has too carefully, too guardèdly presented her materials. But those who find serious fault with the book will do so largely on a basis of prejudice in viewpoints. We believe the volume a brilliant success, and think that it will at once establish the author as an authority on town life and its influence on native literature.

THE MAN WHO HATED LINCOLN

From *Argosy Magazine*, August, 1956. Reprinted, with revisions, in *Birmingham News Monthly Magazine*, April 14, 1957.

Abraham Lincoln had millions of friends, but nobody ever hated him like John Wilkes Booth of Maryland and Joseph Pinkney Parker of Alabama.

Booth's hatred of Abe Lincoln is patent. Every schoolboy can describe how the villainous assassin sneaked into Ford's Theater on the night of April 14, 1865 and fired the shot that sent the Great Emancipator into eternity—and martyrdom.

Few people know about Pink Parker, however, He was the man who hated Abe Lincoln so long and so hard that he celebrated the anniversary of the president's death regularly for 56 years and erected a monument in his front yard to honor the "hero" who murdered him.

Parker, the son of a well-to-do Coffee County, Alabama planter, joined the Confederate Army in 1861 and served throughout the war with General Lee in Northern Virginia.

After the South's defeat, he returned to his native state to find his

[333]

ancestral home burned to the ground, his slaves gone, his livestock stolen, his fertile land in weeds, and his family inheritance eaten up by debts.

War-weary and now bitterly enraged, Parker was consumed by a violent hatred for the United States, for the North, for all Yankees living or dead, and especially for the one man who somehow personified everything he so very fiercely despised—Abraham Lincoln.

When Parker's last remaining bit of property was confiscated for taxes, he—a former Spring Hill Academy student—was forced to earn a living as a "track walker" on the railroad and a country school teacher who worked for "board and keep." Finally, reduced almost to poverty, he moved to the town of Troy, Alabama and hired out as a policeman.

Meantime, his hatred for Abraham Lincoln continued to be the one sad, mad obsession of his life. He refused to take the Federal oath of allegiance, openly boasting that he was the "bitterest Rebel in the South."

The mere mention of Lincoln's name brought forth from his lips impassioned flights of vilest profanity. Even his shocked and mortified friends avoided him. The Baptist Church, of which he had long been a devout member, removed him from its rolls.

But still Parker's evergrowing hatred for the martyred president was like an angry thorn piercing his heart.

Regularly each year, on April 15, Parker celebrated Booth's murder of Lincoln by dressing up in his Sunday suit, pinning a homemade paper badge on his lapel, and parading around the town square. The badge bore the date and the numbered anniversary of the "Death of Old Abe Lincoln."

On the 41st anniversary, in 1906, Parker bought a fine granite monument, properly inscribed to suit his loathing, and proudly presented it to the town of Troy to be placed on the public square. The inscription, which misspelled Booth's middle name, read as follows:

Erected by
PINK PARKER
in honor of
JOHN WILKS
BOOTH
for killing old
ABE LINCOLN

When Troy officials declined the offer, Parker erected the stone in his own front yard on West Madison Street—and there it stayed for fifteen years, an object of great curiosity to tourists.

Parker was as proud as could be of his accomplishment. One anniversary he gleefully had his photograph taken to exhibit his hateful lapel badge. When his friends teased him about the difficulty he'd have getting along with Yankees when he ascended into Heaven, Parker

[334]

would say that he didn't believe there'd be enough of them up there to bother him!

Parker slowly went blind, as the years passed, and his health failed. But the thorn in his heart grew stronger.

When Troy began to gain much unfavorable notoriety because of the Booth monument, Parker steadfastly refused to remove it. Once a delegation of Northern people called upon Parker to request the monument's destruction. But he declined, claiming that he had a right to memorialize anybody he pleased on his own premises.

In June, 1921, the Women's League of Republican Voters in Alabama petitioned citizens throughout America, regardless of party affiliations, to come to its aid in destroying the monument forever. News stories about the matter appeared locally and in such papers as the *Brooklyn Eagle,* the *Washington Post,* the *St. Louis Post-Dispatch,* and *Grit.*

Letters poured in from all over the country, but the league's plan finally fizzled and, when Parker was taken to Georgia to be cared for by relatives, small boys pulled the marker down as a Halloween prank.

Six months later Parker died, and his 82-year-old body was returned to Troy for burial in the family plot in Oakwood Cemetery. His sons hauled the old monument to the stonecutter, who shaved off the inscription to John Wilkes Booth and neatly recarved the marker as a headstone for Parker's own grave!

Not long afterwards, the monument began to lean, pushed over by a thorn tree that grew directly out of the grave. Since then, or so the story goes, as often as the stone is righted the tree grows back to force it aside again.

Folks in Troy doubt if there'll ever be an end to this struggle, for the thorn tree, some say, is a strong one, the one that took root many years ago in Pink Parker's heart.

NEGRO WOMAN'S NOVEL OF HER RACE WIDELY PRAISED

Review of Zora Neale Hurston, *Their Eyes Were Watching God,*
From Waco (Texas) *Tribune-Herald,* November 7, 1937.

When another white man adds another novel to an already bent-backed list of novels about Negro life in the South, it's just fiction added to fiction. But when a *black* woman writes a novel about her own people, a frank, unbiased discussion of Negro life as she knows it—that's news. In *Their Eyes Were Watching God,* a title which fails miserably to do justice to a jam-up good story, Zora Neale Hurston reaches new heights as a novelist and gives fact upon fact to show her own keen insight into national racial problems and characteristics.

Their Eyes Were Watching God is a simple story, so simple that one is likely to pass lightly over the deeper rumblings of racial frustration. The chief character, Janie, long-haired mulatto built more for love than for work, cruises through three separate affairs of the heart before many pages have passed. From the first one she escapes to dash-away-from-it-all with silk-shirted Joe Starks, red necktie, plug hat, striped socks and all. Joe, if nothing else, is the big boy of Main Street, a gogetter. Soon Eatonville, an all-Negro town in Florida, is at his feet; he becomes ward boss, autocrat, plutocrat, mayor, and chief lady-killer. Janie, modest and unassuming and faithful after a fashion, watches gleefully her man's success only to find ultimately he grows weary of her. When he does not love her any more, she parts company with him, goes off with Tea Cake, a worthless skin gambler who makes life paradoxically miserable and happy. The remainder of *Their Eyes Were Watching God* is a faithful account of life on a sandy Florida plantation where a sort of trumped up tornado brings the book to a conclusion only fairly credible.

Zora Neale Hurston, Floridian graduate of Columbia University, holder of two Guggenheim fellowships, and member of the Book-of-the-Month roll of honor, writes in *Their Eyes Were Watching God* her third book. *Mules and Men,* her second, was received last year by eminent critics the country over as one of the outstanding racial books of the decade. No fairer, truer portayal of Negro life has yet come forth. Her use of folk tales, voodoo, and vernacular of Negro life in the South won editorial comment from reviewers in every section. Perhaps the only fault to be found with her *Their Eyes Were Watching God* lies in its awkward technicalities. Occasional warped expressions give clumsiness to her dialogue, and sometimes her scenes are forced; the hurricane scene at the end, for example. All in all, however, *Their Eyes Were Watching God* is as fine a Negro story, and as fair and unassuming, as has been on the bookstalls for years.

More than a year ago Zora Hurston, in a letter addressed to this reviewer (who had commented on *Mules and Men* for a Southern weekly), stated: "My next book is to be a novel about a woman who from childhood was hungry for life and the earth.... At 40 she got her chance at mud, lush and fecund with a buck Negro called Tea Cake. He took her down into the Everglades where people worked and sweated and loved and died violently..., but since I narrate mostly in dialogue, I can give you no feeling in these few lines of the life of this brown woman. But this is the barest statement of the story." The result, modified in the year, is *Their Eyes Were Watching God.*

Outstanding in Hurston's volume is dialogue. No writer in the South handles Negro dialogue so well as she, and no writer builds up such irresistible images in words. Almost every level of Negro society finds

[336]

its way into Hurston's racy dialogue-narrative. Her beauty of phraseology would do credit to the most polished writer. And her humor is of first rank. Indeed, taken all in all, this book is an almost perfect story of blacks in the South, written by one who is close enough to know her people and yet far away enough to be able to see the glory.

SOUTHERN RESEARCH MATERIALS

A Review of Robert B. Downs, Editor, *Resources of Southern Libraries*, (Chicago: American Library Association, 1938). From *The Library Journal*, January 1, 1939.

This reviewer's best loved undergraduate teacher frequently told his students that the next best thing to knowing the answer to a problem is to know where to find it. We grant the unoriginality of the thought, for both Samuel Johnson and Alexander Pope, to name but two, had said the same oft-quoted thing many years before, and with a sight more finesse, but the idea stuck. And all the while we were reading Robert B. Downs's *Resources of Southern Libraries* we were reminded of the aphorism; surely, if ever a book were written to tell people where to find materials, this is it.

Every reader of this journal is doubtless already familiar with the motives which prompted the General Education Board to subsidize this study and the methods followed in gathering the data. Suffice it to say that Downs was ably assisted in each of the thirteen Southern states covered by the survey by a committee of independently operating searchers, too numerous to list here, familiar with conditions in their respective areas. The findings of each committee were forwarded to Downs who tabulated and edited them for this report.

As the editor states, "so far as can be determined from available information, the present work is the first attempt to study all classes of library research materials distributed over a large region." This compilation would doubtless not have been begun, he suggests, had it not been for the inability of the American Library Association Committee on Resources of Southern Libraries to function without further data on research materials available in Southern states. "The Committee found itself working in the dark for lack of information about library holdings. No intelligent division of collecting interests, development of union catalogs, or other cooperative enterprise could go forward without a more adequate basis of fact on which to build. A systematic survey of book holdings in every type of institution containing materials of potential value for study and research was the logical outcome." If the A.L.A. Committee should for any reason fail to function further in coordinating and increasing facilities for study in the South, it will have performed nobly in getting Robert B. Downs, et al., to produce *Resources of Southern Libraries.*

This volume is not a check-list of research materials. That task, though not an impossible one, would have been too bulky for a volume or perhaps even a set. Rather, the book is a summary-survey of the kinds and numbers of materials held by approximately 400 principal public, college, university, historical society, state, and special libraries throughout an area covering 863,250 square miles. The aim was, "to prepare highly condensed descriptions of entire collections of material according to form or subject." Downs has wisely divided his work into twelve sections; (1) Reference books, bibliography, and related materials, (2) government publications, (3) manuscripts, (4) newspapers, (5) general periodicals and society publications, (6) language and literature, (7) philosophy and religion, (8) fine arts, (9) history, (10) social sciences, (11) sciences, and (12) technology. Each section is in turn divided into numerous sub-sections as, for example, science, which includes (a) general science, (b) geology, (c) geography, (d) mathematics, (c) astronomy, (f) chemistry, (g) physics, (h) biology, (I) botany, (j) zoology, (k) psychology, (l) medicine, and (m) allied medical sciences, including bacteriology and public health, pharmacy and materia medica, dentistry, and nursing. Specific titles are mentioned only occasionally and then only for illustrative purposes; but an interested researcher will have no difficulty in locating key collections in his chosen field in the South once he has consulted Downs's "guide-book."

We feel that *Resources of Southern Libraries* would have been a more useful tool had the editor added a summary chapter or appendix, showing graphically, perhaps, the results of at least a part of his findings. An appendix, let us say, not unlike the "Report of Committee on Resources of Southern Libraries," prepared as a preliminary study by Downs and the Committee on Resources of Southern Libraries, and printed as pages 103–129 of Tommie Dora Barker's *Libraries of the South* (A.L.A., 1936). Certainly the two work hand in hand, and it would have facilitated matters had some coordination been effected.

The importance of such a book as *Resources of Southern Libraries* is recognized only when one considers its potential value. As the editor states, the survey will "(1) provide a basis for interlibrary loans; (2) assist scholars and advanced students to find the best collections in their fields; (3) give a basis for planning, as in agreements to divide acquisition activities; (4) aid national and regional union catalogs; (5) locate and describe little-known collections of value for research; (6) discover particular weaknesses in libraries in the southern area; and (1) stimulate the development of research collections."

Resources of Southern Libraries serves still another purpose: it shows that a long lethargic South is waking up to an understanding of its library deficiencies and is trying to do something about them. The two books mentioned in this paper are evidences of such progress. We hope there will be more.

It was a gigantic undertaking; it is now a monumental accomplishment reflecting credit upon its makers. It is the kind of library analysis so badly needed in the South. And we feel that Editor Downs's book will be the criterion for those which may come after it.

ACKNOWLEDGMENTS

The author is grateful for permission to reprint the following essays, articles, and reviews:

The Alabama Review, Alabama Historical Association, University of Alabama and Auburn University, for "John Gorman Barr: Forgotten Alabama Humorist," April, 1951, "Alabama and W. Gilmore Simms," April, July, 1963, "The C.S.S. *Alabama* at Cape Town: Centennial Celebration, 1863–1963," July, 1964, "Jeremiah Clemens, Novelist," January, 1965, "Willis Brewer as a Novelist," July, 1965, "*Alabama:* Drama of Reconciliation," April, 1966 and "Alabama's World War II Prisoner of War Camps," April, 1967; *The American Scholar*, Washington, D.C., for "Of the Librarian's Education," Winter, 1943–1944 (reprinted in *Of, By, and For Librarians*, Hamden, Conneticut: Shoe String Press, © 1960); *Argosy Magazine*, New York City, for "The Man Who Hated Lincoln," August, 1956; *Birmingham (Alabama) News Monthly Magazine*, for "Were White Men Here in 1232?" October 11, 1953, "Alabama-Built Submarine Was First to Sink a Battleship," December 13, 1953, "The Face in the Window," August 8, 1954, "Non-Smokers Have Rights ... Too!" July 10, 1955, "The Day Tecumseh Spoke," February 2, 1969, "Elyton and the Connecticut Yankee," January 4, 1970, and "The Madame Was A Lady," May 3, 1970;

Childhood Education, Washington, D.C., for "My Daughter's Father," November, 1943; Confederate Publishing Company, Tuscaloosa, Alabama, for "The Preface" from *Vizetelly Covers the Confederacy*, 1957, "The Preface" from *Lawley Covers the Confederacy*, 1964, and "The Prologue" and "Chronology of the Regiment" from *Alabama Tories: The First Alabama Cavalry, U.S.A., 1862–1865*, 1960;

Dallas [Texas] *Morning News* for review-article "Rural Literature in America Surveyed in Definitive Study," May 21, 1939;

Waco [Texas] *Tribune-Herald,* for review-articles, "Negro Women's Novel of Her Race Widely Praised," November 7, 1937 and "On the Book Reviewer," December 25, 1938.

PUBLISHER'S NOTE

For the convenience of the general reader, the footnotes have been stripped from almost all the articles herein published. Scholars who may wish to consult Dean Hoole's sources are referred to the learned publications that first published the articles in question.